# Understanding **Linguistic Fieldwork**

*Understanding Linguistic Fieldwork* offers a diverse and practical introduction to research methods used in field linguistics. Designed to teach students how to collect quality linguistic data in an ethical and responsible manner, the key features include:

- A focus on fieldwork in countries and continents that have undergone colonial expansion, including Australia, the United States of America, Canada, South America and Africa;
- A description of specialist methods used to conduct research on phonological, grammatical and lexical description, but also including methods for research on gesture and sign, language acquisition, language contact and the verbal arts;
- Examples of resources that have resulted from collaborations with language communities and which both advance linguistic understanding and support language revitalisation work;
- Annotated guidance on sources for further reading.

This book is essential reading for students studying modules relating to linguistic fieldwork or those looking to embark upon field research.

**Felicity Meakins** is a Research Fellow at the University of Queensland. She specialises in the documentation of Australian languages in the Victoria River District in northern Australia and the effect of English on Indigenous languages.

**Jennifer Green** is a Research Fellow at the University of Melbourne. Her main research interests are descriptive linguistics, lexicography, multimodality in narrative practices and sign language.

**Myfany Turpin** is a Research Fellow at the University of Sydney. Her research is in descriptive linguistics, poetry, song, ethnobiology and language revitalization.

**Understanding Language series**

*Series Editors:*

**Bernard Comrie**, University of California, Santa Barbara, USA
**Greville Corbett**, University of Surrey, UK

The Understanding Language series provides approachable, yet authoritative, introductions to major topics in linguistics. Ideal for students with little or no prior knowledge of linguistics, each book carefully explains the basics, emphasising understanding of the essential notions rather than arguing for a particular theoretical position.

Other titles in the series:

*Understanding Phonetics*
Patricia Ashby

*Understanding Morphology, Second Edition*
Martin Haspelmath and Andrea D. Sims

*Understanding Language Testing*
Dan Douglas

*Understanding Second Language Acquisition*
Lourdes Ortega

*Understanding Pragmatics*
Gunter Senft

*Understanding Child Language Acquisition*
Caroline Rowland

*Understanding Semantics, Second Edition*
Sebastian Löbner

*Understanding Syntax, Fourth Edition*
Maggie Tallerman

*Study Skills for Linguistics*
Jeanette Sakel

*Understanding Language Change*
Kate Burridge and Alexander Bergs

*Understanding Phonology, Fourth Edition*
Carlos Gussenhoven and Haike Jacobs

*Understanding Linguistic Fieldwork*
Felicity Meakins, Jennifer Green and Myfany Turpin

For more information on any of these titles, or to order, go to
www.routledge.com/series/ULAN

# Understanding Linguistic Fieldwork

Felicity Meakins
Jennifer Green
Myfany Turpin

LONDON AND NEW YORK

First edition published 2018
by Routledge
2 Park Square, Milton Park, Abingdon, Oxon, OX14 4RN

and by Routledge
711 Third Avenue, New York, NY 10017

*Routledge is an imprint of the Taylor & Francis Group, an informa business*

© 2018 Felicity Meakins, Jennifer Green, Myfany Turpin

The right of Felicity Meakins, Jennifer Green and Myfany Turpin to be identified as authors of this work has been asserted by them in accordance with sections 77 and 78 of the Copyright, Designs and Patents Act 1988.

All rights reserved. No part of this book may be reprinted or reproduced or utilised in any form or by any electronic, mechanical, or other means, now known or hereafter invented, including photocopying and recording, or in any information storage or retrieval system, without permission in writing from the publishers.

*Trademark notice*: Product or corporate names may be trademarks or registered trademarks, and are used only for identification and explanation without intent to infringe.

*British Library Cataloguing-in-Publication Data*
A catalogue record for this book is available from the British Library

*Library of Congress Cataloging-in-Publication Data*
Names: Meakins, Felicity, author. | Turpin, Myfany, 1972– author. |
Green, Jennifer, 1954– author.
Title: Understanding linguistic fieldwork / Felicity Meakins,
Myfany Turpin, Jennifer Green.
Description: First edition. | Milton Park, Abingdon, Oxon : New York, NY :
Routledge, [2018] | Series: Understanding language series; 1 |
Includes bibliographical references and index.
Identifiers: LCCN 2017046542 | ISBN 9780415786126 (hardback : alk. paper) |
ISBN 9780415786133 (pbk. : alk. paper) | ISBN 9780203701294 (ebook : alk. paper)
Subjects: LCSH: Linguistics–Fieldwork. | Linguistic Anthropology.
Classification: LCC P128.F53 M424 2018 | DDC 410.72–dc23
LC record available at https://lccn.loc.gov/2017046542

ISBN: 978-0-415-78612-6 (hbk)
ISBN: 978-0-415-78613-3 (pbk)
ISBN: 978-0-203-70129-4 (ebk)

Typeset in Minion Pro and Times New Roman
by Out of House Publishing

Cover image: Bush potato or desert yam (*Ipomoea costata*). Photo: Jennifer Green

# Contents

| | | |
|---|---|---|
| List of figures | | xii |
| List of tables | | xv |
| Acknowledgements | | xvi |
| Linguistic abbreviations | | xviii |

| **1** | **Introduction** | **1** |
|---|---|---|
| 1.1 | Overview | 2 |
| 1.2 | Definitions | 3 |
| | 1.2.1 What makes a good field linguist? | 3 |
| | 1.2.2 'Insider' and 'outsider' linguists | 4 |
| | 1.2.3 What is meant by 'fieldwork'? | 6 |
| | 1.2.4 Linguistic description versus language documentation | 8 |
| | 1.2.5 Language vitality | 10 |
| | 1.2.6 Who is a speaker? | 11 |
| 1.3 | Your project | 12 |
| 1.4 | Workflow from go to woe | 16 |
| 1.5 | About us (first person plural exclusive) | 21 |
| 1.6 | Summary | 22 |
| 1.7 | Further reading | 22 |
| References | | 22 |

| **2** | **Planning for fieldwork** | **25** |
|---|---|---|
| 2.1 | Introduction | 25 |
| 2.2 | Identifying a speech community | 25 |
| 2.3 | Research on the field location | 27 |
| 2.4 | Ways of working in the field | 28 |
| | 2.4.1 Who is the fieldworker responsible to? | 29 |
| | 2.4.2 Who controls the research? | 30 |
| | 2.4.3 Ownership, access and uses of research materials | 31 |
| | 2.4.4 Intellectual property, copyright and licensing | 32 |
| | 2.4.5 Balancing rights in the field | 33 |
| 2.5 | Formal ethics applications and procedures | 34 |
| | 2.5.1 Project information sheet | 35 |
| | 2.5.2 Participant consent form | 37 |

**vi** *Contents*

| | | |
|---|---|---|
| 2.6 | Authorship and acknowledgements | 38 |
| | 2.6.1 Referring to your examples in publications | 40 |
| 2.7 | Planning ahead for the field | 41 |
| | 2.7.1 Visas, vaccinations and vehicles | 41 |
| | 2.7.2 Timing of field trips | 42 |
| | 2.7.3 Organising remuneration for research participants | 42 |
| | 2.7.4 Gathering resources | 43 |
| | 2.7.5 Keeping in touch | 44 |
| 2.8 | Summary | 44 |
| 2.9 | Further reading | 45 |
| References | | 45 |

**3 Equipment and recording** — **48**

| | | |
|---|---|---|
| 3.1 | Introduction | 48 |
| 3.2 | Recording equipment | 48 |
| | 3.2.1 Audio recording equipment | 50 |
| | 3.2.2 Microphones | 51 |
| | 3.2.3 Windshields | 53 |
| | 3.2.4 Microphone cables | 54 |
| | 3.2.5 Video recording equipment | 55 |
| | 3.2.6 Still photography | 57 |
| | 3.2.7 Backups, batteries, memory cards and storage | 57 |
| | 3.2.8 User-friendly choices | 58 |
| | 3.2.9 Looking after equipment | 58 |
| | 3.2.10 Other useful gear | 59 |
| | 3.2.11 Trying things out | 60 |
| | 3.2.12 Before you head off | 60 |
| 3.3 | During fieldwork | 61 |
| | 3.3.1 Safety first | 61 |
| | 3.3.2 Making good audio recordings | 61 |
| | 3.3.3 Making good video recordings | 65 |
| | 3.3.4 Keeping good notebooks | 68 |
| 3.4 | The first fieldwork session | 69 |
| 3.5 | At the end of the day | 71 |
| 3.6 | Summary | 71 |
| 3.7 | Further reading | 71 |
| References | | 72 |

**4 Data management, annotation and archiving** — **73**

| | | |
|---|---|---|
| 4.1 | Introduction | 73 |
| 4.2 | First steps in data management | 73 |
| | 4.2.1 File naming | 73 |
| | 4.2.2 What is metadata and why is it important? | 75 |
| | 4.2.3 Categories of metadata | 76 |
| | 4.2.4 Where to keep your metadata | 77 |

_Contents_ vii

| | | |
|---|---|---|
| 4.3 | Transcription and annotation | 79 |
| | 4.3.1 Time-aligning transcriptions and annotations | 79 |
| | 4.3.2 Software tools | 80 |
| | 4.3.3 Segmentation | 82 |
| | 4.3.4 Transcription techniques | 83 |
| 4.4 | Archiving | 83 |
| | 4.4.1 Exploring archives | 85 |
| | 4.4.2 Depositing in archives – when, where, what and how? | 88 |
| | 4.4.3 Landing pages and access platforms | 88 |
| | 4.4.4 Challenges for archives and their users | 89 |
| | 4.4.5 Scholarly recognition and transparency | 90 |
| | 4.4.6 The open access question | 91 |
| 4.5 | Summary | 92 |
| 4.6 | Further reading | 92 |
| | References | 93 |

| | | |
|---|---|---|
| **5** | **Phonetics and phonology** | **96** |
| 5.1 | Introduction | 96 |
| 5.2 | Recording data | 98 |
| 5.3 | Phonetic transcription | 99 |
| 5.4 | Phonological analysis | 100 |
| | 5.4.1 Minimal pairs and near minimal pairs | 101 |
| | 5.4.2 Identifying allophones | 102 |
| 5.5 | Native speaker intuitions on phonology | 105 |
| 5.6 | Phonemic transcription | 106 |
| 5.7 | Identifying tone | 107 |
| 5.8 | Stress, phonotactics and prosody | 108 |
| 5.9 | Experimental design | 109 |
| 5.10 | Instrumental phonetic fieldwork | 112 |
| 5.11 | Orthography | 114 |
| | 5.11.1 Phonological considerations | 115 |
| | 5.11.2 Grapheme or literacy considerations | 115 |
| | 5.11.3 Socio-political considerations | 116 |
| 5.12 | Summary | 118 |
| 5.13 | Further reading | 118 |
| | References | 119 |

| | | |
|---|---|---|
| **6** | **Morpho-syntax** | **121** |
| 6.1 | The value of formal elicitation for grammatical description | 122 |
| 6.2 | What language to perform elicitation in? | 123 |
| 6.3 | What equipment to use? | 124 |
| 6.4 | Establishing parts of speech | 124 |
| 6.5 | Getting started with clause-level elicitation | 126 |

viii    *Contents*

| | | |
|---|---|---|
| 6.6 | Suggestions for successful elicitation | 127 |
| | 6.6.1 General tips | 127 |
| | 6.6.2 Back translation | 128 |
| | 6.6.3 A culturally embedded grammar | 129 |
| | 6.6.4 Mindful elicitation | 129 |
| 6.7 | Areas of grammar to focus on | 130 |
| | 6.7.1 Grammatical relations | 131 |
| | 6.7.2 Verb distinctions | 133 |
| | 6.7.3 Possession | 137 |
| | 6.7.4 Pronoun distinctions | 138 |
| | 6.7.5 Spatial relations | 140 |
| | 6.7.6 Number | 142 |
| | 6.7.7 Information structure categories | 142 |
| | 6.7.8 Noun classes and gender | 142 |
| | 6.7.9 Evidentiality | 144 |
| | 6.7.10 Derivation vs inflection | 145 |
| | 6.7.11 Clitics vs affixes | 146 |
| 6.8 | Finding a home for your grammatical description | 147 |
| 6.9 | Summary | 149 |
| 6.10 | Further reading | 149 |
| | References | 150 |

**7 Semantic fieldwork and lexicography**      **153**

| | | |
|---|---|---|
| 7.1 | Introduction | 153 |
| 7.2 | Eliciting vocabulary | 154 |
| | 7.2.1 Semantic domains | 154 |
| | 7.2.2 Taxonomies and other classification systems | 157 |
| 7.3 | Elicitation using non-linguistic stimuli | 160 |
| 7.4 | Special registers | 162 |
| 7.5 | Lexicography | 164 |
| | 7.5.1 Types of dictionaries | 164 |
| | 7.5.2 Starting small | 167 |
| 7.6 | What's in a dictionary | 168 |
| | 7.6.1 Headwords | 168 |
| | 7.6.2 Writing definitions | 170 |
| | 7.6.3 Putting encyclopaedic and cultural knowledge in definitions | 171 |
| | 7.6.4 Folk definitions | 171 |
| | 7.6.5 Illustrative examples | 172 |
| | 7.6.6 Finders and reversals | 173 |
| | 7.6.7 Front matter and end matter | 174 |
| | 7.6.8 What words to put in and what to leave out? | 174 |
| 7.7 | Tools for making and displaying dictionaries | 175 |
| | 7.7.1 Tools for making dictionaries | 175 |
| | 7.7.2 Digital dictionary interfaces | 177 |

*Contents*  ix

| | | |
|---|---|---|
| 7.8 | Summary | 180 |
| 7.9 | Further reading | 180 |
| References | | 181 |

# 8 Sign and gesture — 185

| | | |
|---|---|---|
| 8.1 | Introduction | 185 |
| 8.2 | Different types of sign languages | 186 |
| 8.3 | Gesture | 187 |
| 8.4 | Some reasons to study sign and gesture | 189 |
| 8.5 | Some considerations when working on sign languages | 191 |
| | 8.5.1 Working in teams | 191 |
| | 8.5.2 Speech effects on sign language | 192 |
| | 8.5.3 Number of participants | 192 |
| | 8.5.4 Informed consent | 192 |
| | 8.5.5 Anonymity | 192 |
| | 8.5.6 Metadata for sign languages and gesture | 193 |
| 8.6 | Research methods for documenting gesture and sign | 193 |
| | 8.6.1 Elicitation and other methods | 194 |
| | 8.6.2 Quizzes and decoding tests | 196 |
| | 8.6.3 Filming gesture and sign | 197 |
| 8.7 | Annotating sign languages and gesture | 199 |
| | 8.7.1 What to annotate first | 199 |
| | 8.7.2 Building a corpus of sign | 203 |
| | 8.7.3 Representing gesture and sign in publications | 204 |
| | 8.7.4 Sign language dictionaries | 209 |
| 8.8 | Summary | 211 |
| 8.9 | Further reading | 211 |
| References | | 212 |

# 9 Child language acquisition — 216

| | | |
|---|---|---|
| 9.1 | Introduction | 216 |
| 9.2 | Why document child language acquisition? | 216 |
| 9.3 | Special considerations for acquisition work | 219 |
| | 9.3.1 Funding | 219 |
| | 9.3.2 Choosing a field site | 220 |
| | 9.3.3 Existing documentation | 221 |
| | 9.3.4 Ethical considerations | 222 |
| | 9.3.5 Gender of researcher | 223 |
| | 9.3.6 Health considerations | 223 |
| | 9.3.7 Recruitment of project team | 224 |
| 9.4 | Methods in acquisition research | 225 |
| | 9.4.1 Creating a longitudinal corpus | 225 |
| | 9.4.1.1 How many children? | 226 |
| | 9.4.1.2 What age to start recording at? | 227 |

x Contents

| | | | |
|---|---|---|---|
| | 9.4.1.3 | How to record children? | 227 |
| | 9.4.1.4 | Where to record children? | 229 |
| | 9.4.1.5 | Frequency and regularity of recordings? | 229 |
| | 9.4.1.6 | Who does the transcription? | 230 |
| 9.4.2 | Cross-sectional experimental studies | | 230 |
| | 9.4.2.1 | How many children to test? | 231 |
| | 9.4.2.2 | Methods for exploring perception or comprehension | 231 |
| | 9.4.2.3 | Methods for eliciting speech | 233 |

9.5 Summary 234
9.6 Further reading 234
References 235

# 10 Contact languages 238

10.1 Introduction 238
  10.1.1 What are contact languages? 238
  10.1.2 Why document a contact language? 239
10.2 Types of contact languages 240
  10.2.1 Pidgin and creole languages 240
  10.2.2 Normative code-switching 242
  10.2.3 Mixed languages 243
  10.2.4 Language shift varieties 244
10.3 Special considerations 245
  10.3.1 How much to document? 246
  10.3.2 Existing documentation of source languages 246
  10.3.3 Linguistic variation 246
  10.3.4 Language pride 248
  10.3.5 Gender of researchers 248
  10.3.6 Speaking a contact language as an 'outsider' linguist 249
  10.3.7 Naming a contact language 250
10.4 Methods for documenting contact languages 250
  10.4.1 Problems with formal elicitation methods 250
  10.4.2 Corpus development 251
  10.4.3 Peer elicitation 253
  10.4.4 (Semi-)experimental methods 254
    10.4.4.1 Director-matcher tasks 254
    10.4.4.2 Card games 255
    10.4.4.3 Picture-prompt books 255
  10.4.5 Experimental methods 256
    10.4.5.1 Getting enough participants 256
    10.4.5.2 Assessing language proficiency in bilingual situations 257
10.5 Summary 258
10.6 Further reading 258
References 258

# 11 Verbal art 261

| | |
|---|---|
| 11.1 Introduction | 261 |
| 11.2 Why document song and other verbal arts? | 262 |
| 11.3 Preparing for fieldwork on verbal art | 263 |
| 11.4 Methods for documentation | 265 |
| 11.5 Recording performances | 266 |
| 11.6 Playing back recordings | 267 |
| 11.7 Transcribing verbal art | 268 |
| 11.7.1 Texts and variation | 270 |
| 11.7.2 Notation systems and software | 271 |
| 11.8 Form in verbal art | 272 |
| 11.9 Translating verbal art | 273 |
| 11.10 Managing recordings | 274 |
| 11.11 Copies for the community | 276 |
| 11.12 Publishing verbal art | 277 |
| 11.12.1 Copyright and authorship | 279 |
| 11.13 Archiving and access | 279 |
| 11.14 Performances and intercultural exchanges | 281 |
| 11.15 Summary | 282 |
| 11.16 Further reading | 282 |
| References | 283 |

# 12 A final word 285

| | |
|---|---|
| Reference | 287 |

# Appendices 289

| | |
|---|---|
| Appendix 1: Map of major languages referred to in this book | 290 |
| Appendix 2: Answers to exercises | 291 |
| Appendix 3: Glossary | 315 |
| Appendix 4: Acronyms | 320 |

# Index 321

# Figures

| | |
|---|---|
| 1.1 Field methods workflow used for the Gurindji history project | 17 |
| 1.2 Recording stories near Ngangi | 18 |
| 1.3 A CLAN excerpt of Ronnie Wavehill's story transcribed in Gurindji and translated into English | 19 |
| 1.4 Excerpt from *Bilinarra, Gurindji and Malngin Plants and Animals* | 20 |
| 2.1 An example of a participation statement developed by Caroline Jones for a project on Kriol | 36 |
| 3.1 Horace Watson recording Mrs Fanny Cochrane Smith. Sandy Bay, 10 October, 1903 | 49 |
| 3.2 View of an audio waveform in Audacity that shows a well-recorded segment of speech contrasted with a segment where the levels were set way too high and there is extreme clipping | 63 |
| 3.3 Recording Kaytetye sand stories. Carol Thompson, Myfany Turpin and Tommy Thompson | 67 |
| 4.1 Metadata attached to a recording made on a cassette tape | 78 |
| 4.2 A simplified view of the structure of a relational database for keeping track of metadata | 78 |
| 4.3 Representation of a screenshot from an ELAN annotation file with a video clip and an audio file imported | 81 |
| 4.4 Bush potatoes as an illustration of a "hub and spokes" model of archives | 87 |
| 5.1 Drawing on native speaker intuitions about tone in Tai Phake | 108 |
| 5.2 An example of one of the 35 Kaytetye target words and corresponding images (here 'in the scrub' [ɐ'ʈɳeŋ]) in a carrier phrase 'Say X!', pre-recorded by a native speaker. | 111 |
| 5.3 Limbardo Payaguaje, a Shiwiar speaker, demonstrates the use of the earbuds. The updated methodology positions just one earbud *under* (rather than *in*) the nose and one next to the mouth. Limbardo was keen to demonstrate the original positioning which he found humorous | 114 |
| 6.1 Groupings of A (transitive subject), S (intransitive subject) and O (object) in an accusative system (non-dotted line) and ergative (dotted line) system | 131 |
| 6.2 Silverstein's hierarchy and ergative/accusative splits | 133 |

*List of figures* xiii

6.3 Some Aktionsart categories 134
6.4 A simplified aspectual schema 135
6.5 Front cover of *Lakota Grammar Handbook* 148
7.1 AIATSIS list of semantic domains for Australian languages 155
7.2 A page from the *Central Anmatyerr Picture Dictionary* that illustrates some person terms 166
7.3 A guide to the parts of a dictionary entry in the *Central & Eastern Anmatyerr to English Dictionary* 169
7.4 Definitions for some of the words derived from *daa'* 'horn' or 'antler' in Koyukon 170
7.5 The dictionary definition of the word 'SMI' in Kalam 171
7.6 Part of the finder list entry for 'uncle' in the *Central & Eastern Anmatyerr to English Dictionary* 174
7.7 Example of the MDF codes used in an entry from the Gurindji to English Dictionary 176
7.8 An example from the Iquito dictionary in FLEx, showing the headword information (citation forms, related forms, morphological type) and the beginning of the next section on meanings where reversal fields are located 178
7.9 An entry from the dictionary of Archi 179
8.1 Documenting alternate sign languages in Central Australia with Anmatyerr women Clarrie Kemarr and Eileen Perrwerl, and linguist Gail Woods. The blue curtain is hung inside the tent 'studio' 198
8.2 Phases of an action that accompanies speech. Ngaatjatjarra linguist Lizzie Marrkilyi Ellis works with her mother Tjawina Porter, Alice Springs, Northern Territory, Australia, 2012 200
8.3 An ELAN template that allows for annotation of the phases of an action, and for morphological glossing of the co-occurring speech 200
8.4 A screenshot from ELAN, showing the controlled vocabulary option which enables you to set the values for an annotation 201
8.5 Representation of a screenshot from an ELAN annotation file, showing sign ID glosses in Dutch 202
8.6 The Anmatyerr sign MOTHER 204
8.7 Pompey Raymond demonstrates the sign for *lukarrarra* (*Portulaca filifolia*), Elliott, Northern Territory, 2017 206
8.8 A schematic representation of graphic units drawn on the ground: (a) the first sequence; (b) the second sequence 207
8.9 The Anmatyerr sign HUSBAND/WIFE 208
8.10 The Iltyem-iltyem sign language project workflow 210
9.1 A 'picture-choice' task used with Warlpiri children 232
9.2 A scene from 'The Guitar Story' 234

| | | |
|---|---|---|
| 10.1 | Cassandra Algy Nimarra and Felicity Meakins record director-matcher tasks with Jamieisha Barry Nangala, Regina Crowson Nangari and Quitayah Frith Namija | 254 |
| 11.1 | A text illustrating the difference between sung and spoken song texts | 269 |
| 11.2 | A transcription of a line of song in modern western music notation of rhythm alone, and the same material represented by a metrical grid | 271 |
| 11.3 | File hierarchy of the archival recording JS01_153.wav transcribed and segmented into sequential song items (JS01_153-01.mp3 etc.). The original audio file is JS01_153.wav and the transcription of this audio is in various formats – .eaf, .trs, .pfsx and .txt | 275 |
| Map 1 | Map of locations of major languages referred to in this book | 290 |

# Tables

| | |
|---|---|
| 1.1 Fishman's Graded Intergenerational Disruption Scale (GIDS) | 10 |
| 4.1 Examples of file naming | 74 |
| 4.2 Some metadata types and categories | 76 |
| 5.1 Ten Kaytetye words from an elicitation session, 20151029MT | 103 |
| 5.2 Elicited words assembled by vowel sounds (underlining marks the relevant vowel) | 103 |
| 5.3 Chart of local environments of vowel sounds | 103 |
| 5.4 Comparing different Kaytetye speakers' pronunciations of the same words – superscript 'h' represents aspiration and the small circle devoicing | 107 |
| 5.5 Gap in the attested consonant clusters in a hypothetical language: is /ɾk/ non-permissible or an accidental gap? | 110 |
| 6.1 Tips for determining some common word classes | 125 |
| 6.2 Verb conjugations in Bilinarra, which has five major classes of verbs and a number of irregular verbs | 136 |
| 6.3 Bilinarra pronouns assumed to be a singular – dual – plural system | 140 |
| 6.4 Bilinarra pronouns as a minimal-UA-augmented system with the crucial pronoun highlighted | 140 |
| 6.5 Evidentiality and tense marking in Tariana | 145 |
| 7.1 An example of a semantically based elicitation list | 156 |
| 7.2 Literal names for the constellation *Ursa Major* in Alaskan languages | 159 |
| 7.3 A comparison of some words in Ordinary Awiakay and Mountain Awiakay | 164 |

# Acknowledgements

Our heartfelt gratitude is first and foremost to all of the speakers of endangered minority languages who have mentored, trained and hosted us during our extensive times in the field. Although there are too many to mention in person we extend particular thanks to Cassandra Algy, Topsy Dodd, Lizzie Marrkilyi Ellis, Clarrie Long Kemarr, April Campbell Pengart, Veronica Dobson Perrurle (AM), Hilda Price Pwerl, Eileen Campbell Pwerrerl, Alison Ross, Tommy Thompson, Margaret Kemarre Turner (OAM), Violet Wadrill, and Biddy Wavehill. We would not have written this book without the lessons they have taught us. We are also immensely grateful to those who provided personal reflections on their own experiences as fieldworkers, or those who gave us access to field materials: Grev Corbett, Nicholas Evans, Murray Garde, Diana Guillemin, Al Harvey, Stephen Levinson, Miriam Meyerhoff, Lev Michael, Marianne Mithun, Jane Simpson and Jesse Stewart. We are also enormously grateful to the many linguists and others who read and commented on drafts of the chapters in this book. Thomas Allen gave us direction on the legal content of Chapter 2, and Lesley Woods kindly gave us access to her thesis on ethics in linguistic research with Indigenous communities. Nick Thieberger, Margaret Carew and Ben Foley provided feedback on Chapters 3 & 4, and Katie Jepson gave advice about audio recording settings in Chapter 3. Thanks to Michael Proctor, Andrew Nevin, Tom Ennever, and Isabel O'Keeffe for suggestions for Chapter 5 on phonology. Rachel Nordlinger provided valuable input and ideas on Chapter 6 on grammatical elicitation. David Osgarby, Ivan Kapitonov, David Nash, Nay San and Mary Laughren provided helpful language-specific advice on aspects of Chapter 7. We thank David Wilkins, Gabrielle Hodge, Connie de Vos, Lizzie Marrkilyi Ellis, Inge Kral, Onno Crasborn, Han Sloetjes, Lauren Reed and Lauren Gawne for their feedback and assistance on Chapter 8, and Evan Kidd, Sabine Stoll, Carmel O'Shannessy and Bill Forshaw for commenting on Chapter 9 on child language acquisition. Evangelia Adamou provided feedback on Chapter 10 on contact languages. We thank Linda Barwick and Stephen Morey for commenting on Chapter 11, Brenda Thornley for the map that appears in this publication, and Maxine Addinsall for many of the original figures. Other photos and illustrations have been reproduced with the permission of the Tasmanian Museum and Art Gallery, IAD Press, Onno Crasborn, Carmel O'Shannessy, Caroline Jones and Jenny Taylor. Thanks also to Mignon Turpin for assistance with copyediting and Vivien Dunn for producing the index. We also thank the series editors, Bernard Comrie and Grev Corbett, for their thorough and thoughtful feedback on the penultimate version of the manuscript. The time to write this textbook would not have been possible without our various

Australian Research Council fellowships: ARC Discovery Early Career Researcher Award (DECRA) 'Out of the mouths of babes: The role of Indigenous children in language change' (CI Meakins, DE140100854, 2014–2017); ARC DECRA, 'Visible talk: Using Australian Indigenous sign languages' (CI Green, DE160100873, 2016–2019); and an ARC Future Fellowship 'A typology of Aboriginal song: social and ecological significances for Australia' (CI Turpin, FT140100783, 2014–2018). We also thank the ARC Centre of Excellence for the Dynamics of Language (Project ID: CE140100041).

# Linguistic abbreviations

| | |
|---|---|
| ABS | absolutive |
| ACC | accusative |
| ALL | allative |
| ANTIPASS | antipassive |
| ATEL | atelic |
| AUG | augmented |
| CAT | catalyst |
| COMP | complementiser |
| CONT | continuous |
| CONTR | contrast |
| DAT | dative |
| DER | derivational |
| DIR | directional |
| DUB | dubitative |
| DUR | durative |
| EMPH | emphatic |
| ERG | ergative |
| EXC | exclusive |
| F | feminine |
| FEM | feminine |
| FOC | focus |
| FUT | future |
| IMP | imperative |
| IMPF | imperfect |
| INC | inclusive |
| INFL | inflectional |
| INST | instrumental |
| LOC | locative |
| M | masculine |
| MASC | masculine |
| MID | middle voice |
| MIN | minimal |
| N | neuter |
| NEUT | neuter |
| NOM | nominative |
| O | object |

| | |
|---|---|
| OBL | oblique |
| ONLY | restrictive |
| PAUC | paucal |
| PL | plural |
| PROG | progressive |
| PROP | proprietive |
| PRS | present |
| PST | past |
| RED | reduplication |
| REL | relativiser |
| S | subject |
| SEQ | sequential |
| SG | singular |
| SMSG | same patrimoiety, same generation moiety |
| SUBJ | subject |
| TEL | telic |
| TOP | topic |
| TR | transitive |
| UA | unit augmented |
| V | vegetable |
| VEG | vegetable |
| 1 | first person |
| 2 | second person |
| 3 | third person |
| - | morpheme break |
| = | clitic break |

# 1

# Introduction

---

**A potato by any other name ....**

> Without the name, any flower is still more or less a stranger to you.
> The name betrays its family, its relationship to other flowers,
> and gives the mind something tangible to grasp.
> – John Burroughs (1894), American naturalist and essayist

On the front cover of this textbook is a picture of an *anaty* which is the Alyawarr (Pama-Nyungan, Australia) name of a type of bush potato or yam (*Ipomoea costata*). This name and its associations are also found in the related Arandic languages Kaytetye and Anmatyerr. The *anaty* plant grows to a metre high, with green leafy tendrils that creep across the red desert sand, and large edible tubers that are found underneath its surface. In certain seasons the plants are prolific and women head to favourite destinations to dig them up. The pink trumpet-like flowers are called *nalal*, young tubers are known as *akwerrk* 'young, newly grown' and the main yam is called *amikw* 'mother'.

But what has a bush potato got to do with a textbook on linguistic fieldwork? The various names of the plant reveal how important it is to Alyawarr people. Other vocabulary coalesces around the plant: for example a bird called **anaty**elepwerray (*Melanodryas cucullata*) originated as an *anaty* in the creation period or 'Dreamtime' (Green, 1992, p. 42). In neighbouring Kaytetye **anaty**aylewene 'potato-singer' refers to a lizard (*Lialis burtonis*) that makes a whistling sound said to encourage the plant to proliferate; and also to a beetle whose shrill sound has the same effect (Turpin & Ross, 2012, pp. 110, 442). The *anaty* plant features in songs and verbal arts practices, and is also found in the sign languages of the region. In-depth documentation of this small network of semantic and cultural signification helps us understand a little of the Alyawarr worldview and how ethnobiological knowledge and language inter-relate. It demonstrates the value of a multi-faceted approach to language documentation that draws on expertise from different domains.

## 2 Introduction

# 1.1 OVERVIEW

In a world where increasing numbers of languages are losing speakers (§1.2.5), the place of fieldwork in the discipline of linguistics and its relevance for speech communities is gaining importance. The term 'fieldwork' has been used to describe linguistic research in many different contexts (§1.2.3), but the focus of this textbook is on the methods, ethical practices and procedures for researching under-described languages in endangered language settings. We pay particular attention to fieldwork in countries and continents which have undergone European or other expansion (e.g. Australia and the Pacific, the United States, Canada, South America, Africa) and the roles and responsibilities of linguists in engaging with communities in these settings (cf. Austin & Sallabank, 2011).

If we are to understand more about the rich diversity of the world's remaining languages, then fieldwork is essential. Taking stock of the inventory of linguistic structures across the world's languages and their parameters of use is basic to an understanding of the human language faculty. Capturing this diversity means undertaking research in remote areas of the world and getting training in how to work in an ethical and responsible manner (Chapter 2) and in how to collect and curate quality linguistic data (Chapters 3–4). This data is important to all of the standard subfields of linguistics, e.g. phonology, morpho-syntax and semantics (Chapters 5–7), and also to other areas of linguistics, for example typology and historical linguistics. Some of these sub-disciplines require particular methods and ethical considerations. As such, we devote chapters to discussion of gesture and sign (Chapter 8), language acquisition (Chapter 9), language contact (Chapter 10), and poetry and song (Chapter 11). In doing so, we take a broad view of language, including not only speech, but also multimodal forms of communication, and the performative and visual dimensions of language. Many of the discussions and scenarios presented in this book also include other disciplines that involve the collection of primary linguistic data of under-described languages such as ethnobiology and anthropology.

Not all of the things you will learn in this book can be practised in your field methods class where the language, the speaker and ethics processes have all been organised by your lecturer. You will also probably work with only one speaker in class, which tends to give consistent data, whereas in the field you will work with multiple speakers. As a result, you are likely to encounter inter-speaker variation and other complexities of language-in-use. Finding the systematicity in this seemingly 'messy' data can be challenging (but fun!). Another difference is that in a field methods class the speaker is usually the outsider, whereas in the actual field you will be the outsider unless you are an 'insider' linguist (§1.2.2). Finally, previous documentation of the language is usually out of bounds for field methods students as you are expected to work things out from scratch. In the field you should be on top of all that has been written on the language before you go there (§2.7.4 & §6.6.1).

*Introduction* 3

## 1.2 DEFINITIONS

Before we launch into the details of field methods, it is important to think about what we mean by 'field linguist' and 'fieldwork'. Another distinction – between 'linguistic description' and 'language documentation' – has also become very important in recent decades to the way that fieldwork is conceptualised and planned. How you undertake fieldwork may vary depending on how endangered the language you plan to work on is and the varying skills of the language team.

### 1.2.1 What makes a good field linguist?

How do you know if you've 'got what it takes' to be a field linguist? Linguistic training and the ability to undertake analysis is obviously important, but is there a personality type that makes a good field linguist? The most common stereotype around is that of the adventurous and outgoing "dirty-feet linguist" (Crowley, 2007, p. 12) but in fact field linguists come in all different personality types and dispositions. Marianne Mithun, who has collaborated with First Nations people in North America for decades, describes her own beginnings as a field linguist and reflects on what she believes constitutes a good linguist. She talks about the happy accident of how she came to work with the Mohawk. It turned out that their astute and energetic approach to language learning matched Mithun's own nature.

---

**Ingredients for collaborating with the community – Marianne Mithun**

What makes for successful collaboration between linguists and communities? For the linguist, some things are obvious: Training: the more you know about languages in general, the faster you'll spot categories and patterns in a new language and the less speaker patience you'll waste; Attentiveness: most people volunteer information they think will interest their audience; Respect: the longer you work, the more you discover how much speakers know; But perhaps the most powerful factors are happy accidents.

Some time ago, members of a Mohawk community in Quebec noticed that children were no longer speaking the language. They soon realised that being a good speaker did not automatically make one an effective teacher. Being very enterprising, they approached the provincial powers that be and demanded university training in Mohawk linguistics. The result was a series of intensive summer courses for speakers of all languages indigenous to Quebec, held in an idyllic, remote mountain area. Though I was just a graduate student and had never heard Mohawk, I was invited to work with the Mohawk group because of my experience with a related language.

Mohawks are generally some of the sharpest, liveliest, kindest people one could ever hope to meet. Our days and nights were filled with rollicking conversation and laughter, people talking all at once but always in collaboration. At one point I noticed a ring of faces around the doorway at the back of our room, each registering wide-eyed wonder. They belonged to members of a colleague's group who, drawn by the noise, had been observing in silence. As my colleague later explained, in their culture people normally do not talk unless they have something to say. This friend, who is naturally taciturn, conducted class by simply starting to write on the blackboard. Participants would drift in, watch for a while, then eventually try it themselves. Sometimes when I would pass by their room I would think at first that everyone had left, only to discover that the room was full of people working. My friend explained that this is a traditional way of learning: children watch how things are done, then gradually imitate what they have observed. The two of us are extremely grateful that we each landed with the group we did. Now many years later, I still feel extraordinarily fortunate to have these amazing Mohawks and their language in my life. And it started with a happy accident.

What makes a good field linguist is someone who has an interest in understanding other languages and cultures and enjoys working with people. The qualities of patience, humility, humour and the ability to think laterally also help to make a good fieldworker. A good ear, a knack for seeing patterns and a respect for data – even obsession – without losing sight of the big picture, are other abilities that also serve the field linguist well.

## 1.2.2 'Insider' and 'outsider' linguists

Some of the Mohawk students Mithun worked with went on to become linguists themselves which leads us to an important distinction which we use throughout this book – between 'insider' and 'outsider' linguists (cf. Crowley, 2007, p. 56; Evans, 2011, p. 222). 'Insider' linguists belong to the speech community where the fieldwork is based and they study their own language. They may be a native speaker of the language or perhaps their language is only still spoken by older members of the community. 'Insider' linguists typically have a lot of personal investment in their project as their own family and history is embedded in the speech community. As an insider, their influence in the community is often very different from that of an outsider. They may be focused on the position of the language in the community and, more broadly, the status of the language in the region, particularly where their community is a minority or marginalised group. 'Insider' linguists who live in the speech community may also have other roles such as teachers or interpreters.

'Insider' linguists have a clear advantage over 'outsider' linguists. They often speak the language they are researching and have a pre-existing relationship with its speakers. They also have a good understanding of the research context and identify potential ethical dilemmas quickly. There are some pitfalls, however. As James Crippen (2009), a Tlingit linguist from British Columbia points out, because 'home' and the 'field' are one and the same, there can be many demands made on 'insider' linguists:

> (W)hile at home, 'real life' may interfere with research; consultant patience ... may be lower; restricted data may not be publishable ... [the insider linguist] may become a political proxy for non-linguistic issues, may be blamed for language policy failures, and may be expected to be a language teacher and not a researcher ... The expert role the [insider] linguist assumes may also alienate them from their peer group.

'Outsider' linguists are external to the speech community and are often members of the dominant group in the very country that may be responsible for the marginalisation of the speech community. All 'outsider' linguists need to be mindful of the impact of their research projects in communities, understand fully their responsibility to the community, communicate openly with the leaders in those communities, and negotiate projects with speakers (§2.4). While many 'outsider' linguists may have a political or ideological investment in their project, and may be motivated by notions of 'saving' languages and supporting speakers of endangered languages, it is also important to be sensitive to the notion that "the line between empowerment and imperialism is very thin" (Kusters, 2012, p. 42).

A final category of field linguist is the 'insider-outsider' linguist. These are people who are from a marginalised group themselves, but not from the speech community which is the focus of their research. Sometimes they come from another minority language group in the same country and can identify with many local issues of disempowerment. For example, Annelies Kusters is a deaf linguist who has conducted research on sign languages in Ghana.

> As a deaf person, I understand certain deaf-related experiences from the inside out, for example, being primarily visually oriented and experiencing barriers ... There were other obvious limitations in my understanding: I am deaf, but I am not Adamorobee, not Ghanaian and not black. I am deaf, but I did not grow up with sign language and I experienced oralism. I am deaf and I can read; I am educated, while they are not. I am deaf and I married a deaf person without any problem, a right that they cannot enjoy. In short: I am an insider in terms of being 'biologically deaf' and certain socio-cultural experiences that come with it but I am an outsider in many other domains.
>
> (Kusters, 2012, pp. 39, 40)

For both the 'outsider' and 'insider-outsider' linguist, a sensitivity to the pain of language loss may be required. People who have lost their language due to the coloniser society (which you may be from) may feel upset that an outsider has the ability to learn their ancestral language, has access to funds and is paid to work on their ancestral language with their elders. Giving thought to ways of ensuring that community members have key roles in the field project and building opportunities for language learning and training into the project can help alleviate some of these concerns.

### 1.2.3 What is meant by 'fieldwork'?

Linguistic fieldwork has been defined in different ways. For some people it has a very broad meaning. For example Sakel & Everett (2012, p. 5) define fieldwork as "the activity of a researcher systematically analysing parts of a language, usually other than one's native language and usually in a community of speakers of that language". Their definition includes city-based projects such as William Labov's classic sociolinguistic work on varieties of American English, and controlled psycholinguistic or phonetic experimental work requiring university laboratories. Under this broad definition, it is hard to see how any linguistic research based on primary data collection would not be considered fieldwork, other than perhaps self-applied grammaticality judgement tests on your own language. For others, the definition is very narrow and only includes the study of an unfamiliar language in the society in which it is spoken, with the researcher spending time outside their own culture.

> A more pure-minded fieldworker might also want to argue in any case that fieldwork at home in the comfort of your living room involves insufficient levels of self-deprivation. There is a part of me which says that for your grammar to be truly worthy, you must have suffered at least one bout of malaria – or some other impressive-sounding tropical ailment – in its writing, or you should have had at least one toenail ripped off by your hiking boots, or you should have developed a nasty boil on an unmentionable part of your body.
>
> (Crowley, 2007, p. 16)

Although partly in jest, Crowley's definition does explicitly reject 'urban fieldwork' as fieldwork. Hyman (2001) has a similar perspective on what constitutes 'the field'. Urban fieldwork is a more recent phenomenon where languages of diaspora groups (often refugees or economic migrants) are studied in Western settings, often in so-called 'super diverse' cities such London or Auckland. Urban fieldwork often refers to research in the city or town where you, as a linguist, live. This type of fieldwork works well for linguists who are unable to leave home for extended periods due to a lack of research funds, caring or family commitments, or heavy teaching loads. It also may not be possible to travel to a remote field site due to political unrest and other circumstances. Urban fieldwork is also a great opportunity to build diverse networks in your own city. It can also be a chance for a linguist to make connections with a diaspora group in a pilot study with a view to conducting fieldwork in the original speech community if funding becomes available.

We are mostly concerned with methods for documenting fragile languages in contexts of language endangerment and shift (§1.2.5). For the most part, this means fieldwork is often undertaken in remote locations, but this does not exclude research in urban contexts. For example, some lesser-studied languages, particularly in India, South America and Africa, have been spoken in large urban centres for a long time, by speakers who are embedded in well-developed social networks and cultural practices. In other cities, under-described languages are spoken by newer speech communities, for example

*Introduction* 7

refugee groups, in recently transformed cultural contexts. Finally, many language contact projects have these cultural and linguistic contexts as their object of study (Chapter 10).

---

### Exercise 1  Discuss why you think the following are or aren't examples of fieldwork?

- You speak an undescribed, endangered language. You are writing a grammar of your language and you decide which sentences are grammatical and ungrammatical yourself.
- You are working with a refugee group in the city where you live, documenting their language.
- You and some other students are in a field methods class at your university working with a speaker of a small language spoken elsewhere in your country.
- You work on your own language in the field which you call home.
- You live in Kuala Lumpur and record yourself outside pronouncing words to figure out the vowel space of your English variety and are infected with malaria in the process.
- You are a phonetician and accompany another linguist to the field and spend a week making enough recordings for your thesis.
- You hear that speakers of an endangered language from western China are visiting the anthropology department and you conduct a number of psycholinguistic tasks in the lab while they are there.

---

In this book we discuss the most challenging types of fieldwork situations, and give strategies that may help in a whole range of fieldwork contexts. Some will be of value more generally, and some may not apply in urban settings or for the 'insider' linguist. Whether work is carried out in remote areas or urban contexts, by an 'insider' or 'outsider', the field linguist enters into a partnership with the speech community; and data is created and analysed in the context of, and as a result of, these partnerships.

In this textbook we provide steps in how to develop an audio-visual corpus through the collection of a range of linguistic data including texts (narrative, procedural, conversation etc.) and elicitation. From this corpus, the field linguist seeks to elucidate the lexical and constructional resources within a language, their formal properties and expressive scope. We also consider linguistic fieldwork to be research that is embedded within its cultural and social context. Indeed Hill (2006, p. 113) suggests that "linguists need to be ethnographers, because they venture into communities that may have very different forms of language use from those of the communities in which they were socialised as human beings or trained as scholars".

8  *Introduction*

---

**Exercise 2  Being conscience of your presence**

It is well known in ethnography that your presence changes the way people behave. This is called the **observer's paradox**. Imagine you work in a community where only the oldest people speak the language under study and most of the community has shifted to the regionally dominant language which you also speak. How might people change the way they speak in your presence. How can you minimise the influence of your presence?

---

This definition of fieldwork comes with particular contexts that require specific methodologies. For example, endangered languages often have small numbers of speakers, and so the quantitative methods standard to phonetics (§5.9), language acquisition (and psycholinguistics) (§9.4.2) and contact linguistics (§10.4) often require some adjustment and compromises. For example, sociolinguistic experimental tasks such as matched-guise tests require anonymity to work properly. Matched-guise tests involve participants listening to recordings of speakers reading a passage of text and making judgements about speaker attributes (e.g. class, generosity, intelligence) based on their speech. In small communities where everyone knows each other these methods are compromised. Participants in small communities tend to rate the speaker based on what they know about the person rather than on their speech. Similarly, grammaticality judgements of semantically weird sentences such as "colourless green ideas sleep furiously" may be problematic in communities whose theories of language are highly culturally embedded (§6.6.1). Finally, all remote communities in endangered language contexts involve members of what ethics committees often refer to as 'vulnerable populations'. In these situations very specific thought about how well participants understand the project and their options for archiving and future use of recordings is required in order to obtain truly informed consent (§2.5). This is even more the case if your work involves deaf communities (§8.5.4) or children (§9.3.4), or languages held in low regard by the speech community such as creole languages (§10.3.4).

### **1.2.4** Linguistic description versus language documentation

The type of fieldwork advocated for in this book takes a holistic view of language and culture. This view builds on the work of some of the earliest anthropological linguists, for example Franz Boas and some of his students, such as Edward Sapir, who worked in North America in the early twentieth century (e.g. Boas, 1917, 1991). This pioneering work established what is now known as the Boasian trilogy, a collection that includes a grammar, a dictionary and texts, forming the descriptive canon of a language. In particular, the text collection offered a culturally rich and more community-orientated approach to the lexical and grammatical descriptions.

> (T)exts offer access to questions of grammar, style, history, and culture; furthermore, they provide crucial insights into indigenous perspectives or 'fundamental ethnic ideas' ... The text-based Boasian framework prioritizes the study of language on its own terms and within its wider cultural context, and in so doing gestures to a more collaborative relationship among community outsiders and insiders in producing research.
>
> (Epps, Webster, & Woodbury, 2017, p. 42)

A related endeavour is language documentation, following the seminal article by Nikolaus Himmelmann (1998, p. 9), a field linguist who has devoted decades to studying Austronesian languages in South-East Asia. Himmelmann describes the enterprise of language documentation as making a "record of the linguistic practices and traditions of a speech community". Pawley (2015, p. 135) reiterates this perspective, suggesting that, "(w)hereas in the descriptive paradigm primary data are appended to the analysis, in documentary work analysis is appended to the primary data". Phonology (Chapter 5), morpho-syntax (Chapter 6) and developing dictionaries (Chapter 7) remain central aims of fieldwork, but their basis in a text collection has now been transformed into a 'corpus' which may include many different discourse types and genres:

- narratives (with/without audience; oral history, sacred texts)
- elicitation (words, sentences, sound contrasts)
- commentary (recounting news, a story, film, game)
- definitions or explanations
- dialogue/conversation (greetings, meal-time discussion, socialising)
- procedurals ('how to make ...').

Other important genres are different registers, such as song (Chapter 11) or child-directed speech (Chapter 9); and modalities other than speech, such as gesture and sign (Chapter 8). In this respect, Hill (2006, p. 113) suggests that "documentary linguistics takes up a vision of the integration of the study of language structure, language use, and the culture of language" which was advocated by the early anthropological linguists such as Boas.

The corpus has become a more technologically advanced beast since the days of Boas and his field notebooks. The ideal corpus is now an archived audio-visual record of language practices in which recordings are transcribed, translated and annotated using various types of software (§4.3). It aims to be "a record of the language and culture of a human community that will outlast the individual memories of those creating it" (Boerger et al., 2017, p. 1). Even the grammar and dictionary have been transformed by the ability to embed media and hyperlink lexical entries or sections of a grammar (Nordhoff, 2012). The corpus (and now the grammar and dictionary, no longer textually static) form a powerful basis for revitalisation in language communities. In addition, the corpus and its offspring have made linguistic data accessible to other researchers, allowing theoretical claims to be verified. Falsifiability of theoretical claims through access to primary data, one of the tenets of science, is a welcome advance in linguistics.

## 1.2.5 Language vitality

> Documentary linguistics arose in the context of heightened concern over 'language endangerment,' that is, shifts, often radical, in the ecology of speaking, including the fall into disuse of ancestral lexico-grammatical codes among the only people who knew them. This concern developed among activist community members themselves as well as outside linguists.
>
> (Epps, Webster & Woodbury, 2017, p. 57)

Theories of language, which have diversity at their core, have been one of the drivers behind the push to document as many of the world's languages as is possible. Colonisation, globalisation, climate change and technological change have had, and continue to have devastating effects on many areas of diversity. Of the 7,099 languages listed in Ethnologue,[1] an online resource of endangered languages produced by SIL International, 457 are identified as no longer spoken (see also Lewis & Simons, 2009). The heaviest areas of language loss have occurred in areas such as North and South America, Africa, and the Pacific, including Australia, Papua New Guinea and Melanesia.

Language vitality is often measured by Fishman's (1991, pp. 87–109) eight-stage Graded Intergenerational Disruption Scale (GIDS) which has been adopted by UNESCO[2] and since expanded by Ethnologue (see Table 1.1).[3]

GIDS measures both active knowledge of languages, as well as comprehension, along a number of axes including generation (are there child learners?), numbers of speakers, language practices and literacy (is the language used in the school curriculum?) and official recognition by regional governments. These factors are discussed in more detail in the UNESCO *Language Vitality and Endangerment* (2003) report. A good overview of the various instruments for measuring language

Table 1.1

Fishman's Graded Intergenerational Disruption Scale (GIDS)

| | |
|---|---|
| Stage 1 | Some use of the language in higher education, occupational, national governmental and media efforts |
| Stage 2 | The language is used in regional governmental services and mass media |
| Stage 3 | The language is used in work environments (outside of the core speech community) involving interaction between native and non-native speakers of the language |
| Stage 4 | The language is used in primary education that meets the requirements of compulsory education laws |
| Stage 5 | There is literacy in language in home, school and community life, but without taking on extra-communal reinforcement of such literacy |
| Stage 6 | Intergenerational oral transmission takes place and is reinforced in the community and some institutions in the community e.g. church |
| Stage 7 | Users of the language are a socially integrated and ethnolinguistically active population but they are beyond child-bearing age |
| Stage 8 | Most remaining users of the language are socially isolated old folk and knowledge of the language is reliant on older sources |

endangerment and vitality is given by Obiero (2010) and more extended discussions can be found in Tsunoda (2005).

The field methods you use need to take into account these different kinds of language ecologies. You may be working in a monolingual context and 'monolingual field methods' will be necessary (§6.2). Alternatively, you may find yourself in a bilingual context, often a situation of language shift in the case of endangered languages. In these cases, the target language is often used by a minority group or an older generation. In this scenario, you will probably find yourself working 'through' the *lingua franca* of the community, often a contact language such as a creole. Some caution is necessary when conducting fieldwork in these contexts because delineating the linguistic entity to describe is trickier than in contexts where there is a clear difference between the target language and the *lingua franca*. But comparisons with earlier descriptive work and a good working knowledge of the contact language can help sort out where specific language structures originate.

One important point to bear in mind is that the language vitality conversation has been largely dominated by those who work on endangered heritage languages. Yet in the place of endangered languages there is often a dynamic array of contact varieties of English, Spanish and French, creole languages and other contact varieties of the heritage languages (Chapter 10). This diversity and these radically changed language ecologies all need attention and documentation. Focusing on heritage languages at the expense of new languages can be disempowering to the younger emergent language leaders.

### 1.2.6 Who is a speaker?

Situations of language endangerment result in members of a speech community with differing degrees of knowledge of the language. Some people are native speakers of a language, i.e. they learnt it as a first language and use it on an everyday basis. Obviously for language documentation purposes, native speakers are the best group to work with, but it is not always the case that a language has native speakers. This does not mean that valuable research cannot be undertaken. Other community members may be 'semi-speakers', i.e. they may have learnt the language at birth, but then due to language shift may not use the language regularly. Other people, called 'rememberers', have a passive knowledge of the language, but may not speak the language. They may have heard their parents speaking the language yet did not learn to speak it fluently themselves. 'Semi-speakers' and 'rememberers' can contribute a great deal to a research project even where native speakers are present. They are often bilingual in the dominant regional language, which may be your own language, and they can act as interpreters and translators. If legacy recordings of the language exist, these community members may be able to help translate texts and segment words and phrases that they know or understand. If you can translate texts or identify words in the recording, it is just another step to transcribing the language and ultimately analysing it.

Note that community members who are keen to participate in documentation work may have different interests in the language. Some may be better at reflecting on sounds or grammar, while others are better at semantics. Some enjoy the repetitive work of working out grammatical paradigms and other speakers are great orators who may be the source of wonderful texts. Other speakers may be reticent to actively participate themselves, but provide an attentive audience for active speakers during recording sessions. Where possible, it is a good idea to work with teams of people to draw on their different interests and abilities. It also helps iron out what features are the result of inter-speaker variation, what categories are shared in a speech community and what parts of the language might be undergoing language change, which is common in language endangerment situations (Chapter 10). You may be lucky and find a speaker who can distinguish intuitions about their own speech from that of other people in their speech community (e.g. "older people pronounce it X, while younger people pronounce it Y"; or "my father uses it to mean X, but my brother uses it to mean Y"). It is important to document which speakers have provided the intuitions on which your analysis is based. Make sure to include the language background of speakers who provide intuitions, for example which other languages they speak (§4.2.3). Tsunoda (2005, pp. 117–134) provides a detailed discussion of different speaker types and Morey (2010, p. 93) has a detailed discussion about differences between native speaker intuitions.

---

### Exercise 3  Who is a speaker?

You work in a Stage 8 community where children are no longer learning the language and it is only spoken by older generations. What types of speakers will you encounter in terms of their spoken, comprehension and literacy skills in the heritage language and the regionally dominant language? How do you put together a language team to document the language?

---

## 1.3 YOUR PROJECT

All fieldwork begins with formulating a research project. Because fieldwork requires a high level of investment (time, money, emotion), you should not undertake it without careful thought to your research questions. Before embarking on fieldwork, you need to negotiate and refine the ways that your research aligns with, and hopefully extends and interrogates the theoretical frameworks most relevant to your task. Long ago, in a letter to a friend in 1861, Charles Darwin commented on this relationship between theory and practice.[4]

> About 30 years ago there was much talk that Geologists ought only to observe and not theorise; and I well remember someone saying that at this rate a man might as well go into a gravel-pit & count the pebbles & describe their colours. How odd it is that every one should not see that all observation must be for or against some view, if it is to be of any service!

Without a theoretical framework, as Darwin implies, there would be no basis for the inclusion or exclusion of anything. Theorising, data gathering and interpretation go hand-in-hand. Terry Crowley (2007, p. 13), who pioneered fieldwork in Melanesia, also cautions that "no descriptive linguist can carry out linguistic analysis of a

*Introduction* 13

previously undescribed language in a theoretical vacuum". In this sense, fieldwork should be seen as a responsive and iterative process which allows time for your own evolving analyses and interpretations to bear fruit. This may require repeat trips to further develop and test your ideas. Your fieldwork design should also be flexible and envisage more than a single theory-driven purpose. Good workflow practices and planning can maximise the potential for the results of your work and be useful beyond the immediate time frame of your research project (Chapters 3–4).

As well as your own research interests, you should also be open to the linguistic aspirations of the community, which may involve assisting with literacy training, the development of school resources, or submissions about language issues to policy makers. Your ability to undertake this work may be restricted by time (PhDs usually have three to four year limits) or academic requirements (different universities may assess work outputs differently), but it should always be included as a long-term aim of your 'practice' as a field linguist (see Chapter 2). Attempts to adopt a scientifically dispassionate stance are usually met with disinterest from the community. Most clinically, learning the language of study as best you can and spending time in the company of members of the speech community ensures the best possible data, an observation which Franz Boas, the pioneer of descriptive linguistics, made in 1911:

> A general review of our ethnographic literature shows clearly how much better is the information obtained by observers who have command of the language, and who are on terms of intimate friendship with the natives, than that obtained through the medium of interpreters.
>
> (Boas, 1991 [1911], p. 57)

Anyone who is engaged in fieldwork should also consider the ways that the needs of endangered speech communities may be recognised, articulated and supported. As Evans (2008, p. 345) points out, "anticipating the needs of language maintenance and revival programs might point to certain types of data-gathering what would otherwise be overlooked". Below Evans describes his own first encounters with a Nen-speaking community in Papua New Guinea who had been anticipating the arrival of a missionary linguist. As Evans notes, the Bible translation work proved invaluable for many aspects of his grammatical descriptive work, showing how community work and linguistic research are inextricably connected.

---

### Mission unexpected – Nicholas Evans

In September 2008 I arrived in the village of Bimadeben in the Morehead District of southern Papua New Guinea, to begin linguistic fieldwork in Papua New Guinea on the Nen language. A chain of events had led me there. After decades of working in Indigenous Australia, and wondering whether languages just north of the Torres Strait might mirror, in their linguistic structures, some of the tantalising similarities to Australian languages that certain anthropologists had observed, I had asked my Papuanist friend Ger Reesink if he could suggest a good site. He passed the query on to a couple from his own Dutch village – Marco and Alma Boevé. The Morehead District was virtual *terra incognita* from a linguistic point of view, and the draft grammar of

Arammba, which the Boevés had written while working as missionaries in the region, piqued my interest. They suggested that Bimadeben would be an ideal site, having worked with some people from there during an AusAID-sponsored workshop to develop orthographies for local languages. "People are well-organised and keen to do something about their language", they suggested. Marco sent word to his friends in the Arammba-speaking village of Kiriwa, telling them to pass on the news of my impending arrival through the bush telegraph.

I arrived towards evening, having spent the day walking from the next village, Dimsisi, which had an airstrip. On the Boevés' advice I was laden with cargo of bush-knives, spadeheads, nails and ladies' underwear as gifts. Halfway between the two villages some young men on bikes met me and helped me carry the gear. People welcomed me informally but said that there would be a more formal meeting the next day in the community building.

I understood little of what was said at that meeting, in animated Nen. But people translated for me: Aramang, the village leader, expressed his thanks that at long last the village's prayers to send a missionary to translate the Bible into their language had been met.

This had not been my plan. As a linguist interested in what the world's diverse languages have to teach us I had come to learn about and document the language and culture. I had no missionary intent. But I also thought I detected a strong sense of expectation, and was accustomed, from my work in Aboriginal communities, to the idea that giving back to a community involves listening to what they want you to help with, even if it's not what you expect. So, as a compromise, I said something like, "I am sorry. I am not a missionary and that was not my purpose in coming here. But I do know about language, and about translating, so if this is something important to you, I'll be happy to work with you on this every Sunday". The other days, I would work according to my usual range of linguistic methods. On Saturdays I would just hang out, talk, go to gardens, walk to neighbouring hamlets, or any one of a number of things that helps learn the language more naturalistically.

This turned into a workable, fascinating and abiding arrangement. Most Sundays – not all, since sometimes people are all out in their gardens, or have other things to do – a group of ten or so people gather and spend an intense afternoon translating a few lines – ten or twelve lines in an afternoon would be usual. People in the village often have little more than grade six education, and don't read much, but they are used to reading the Bible and, perhaps more importantly, to studying it, which brings a strong focus on interpretation and the exact expression of meaning. Usually we go round in a circle, each reading from our own personal source – various English versions, the Tok Pisin Bible, the (Hiri) Motu Bible, and a rough photocopied translation in Nambo, the neighbouring language. Then we try and nut out the unclear passages. Many people speak excellent English – I regularly receive text message enquiries from Jimmy Nebni saying "Please explain what the following

English words mean: levirate, exogamous, reprehensible", which gives an idea where the outer limits of his vocabulary lie. But they're perplexed by words like 'firmament' – which after some discussion we translated as *apazéǧ* 'roof', or expressions like 'darkness was over the surface of the deep firmament' (NIV). Once refracted through the Tok Pisin *Tudak i karamapim bikpela wara* it was recondensed to elegant Nen as *Qébtiwäm aragab gumbsge yañmwe* [darkness sea deep it.covered.it.long.ago].

People's concern with accurate rendition and the inherent difficulties of the Bible throw up many questions of interest to me as a linguist. For example, Nen bristles with past tense distinctions – seven or more, depending how you count them – reaching right back. So I was interested to see what tense would be used for that first week of creation – the preterite, it turns out, which is the *we* in *yañmwe*. Or I had been stumped on how to translate free-selection indefinite pronouns like 'anyone' or 'whoever'. Even people with good English hadn't got what I was asking about during my standard language work. When the Translation Committee, rather to my surprise, bumped John's Second Epistle, the shortest book in the Bible (and not a book I'd ever read), to the top of the list a solution was found. It contains the lines **whoever** *abides in the teaching has both the Father and the Son. Do not receive into the house or welcome* **anyone** *who comes to you and does not bring this teaching.* In translating these, I finally worked out how such free-selection indefinites were formed – by preposing the word *yma* to any relevant word (suitably inflected) so that this passage was rendered using the expression *yma äräm* 'any person'.

No less interesting was people's keenness to indigenise every word – in line with the reigning purist ideology that everything should be expressible in Nen, and different from English or any other language around. 'Amen', 'exodus' and 'epistle' all got Nen neologisms (respectively *ypales* 'true', *branǧsmne yls zi buk* 'book of the story of going and leaving', and *bñe* 'carved pattern, writing'). Even the numbering of biblical passages has been indigenised, writing the verse numbers in the base-six Nen system, but written with Devanagari numerals to avoid ambiguities with English. These decisions gave further evidence of the vigour and creativity with which Nen speakers cultivate the distinctness of their own language, even as they adopt the cosmologically-homogenising religion and texts of Christianity.

Perhaps the most moving thing for me about this unexpected extra job has been watching people become literate, combining their existing memorised knowledge of the Bible in English, Tok Pisin or Motu with a driving wish to be able to read a text in the language closest to their hearts. It has made me realise how much more quickly people can become literate when they are motivated by deep personal conviction of the importance of the words they are reading, especially if – perhaps paradoxically – they know from another quarter what the words mean, as if reading while their memory supplies the subtitles.

16  *Introduction*

> I am sometimes plagued by doubts about whether I should have taken on this role. Isn't it hypocritical, given my own rather sceptical take on religion? Certainly there are many times – like when people consult the Bible (the English one!) for medical advice, treating it as the source of all knowledge – when I think my efforts would be better spent on producing information booklets on basic health or many other topics. But all such materials are in any case part of a complex dialogue that will work better once levels of literacy and mutual trust and understanding have gradually been established. And following the wishes of the community in this case – so far from what I had imagined – has led down such interesting paths that I wouldn't undo the pledge I made that day.

Keep in mind that a descriptive grammar of a language written for an academic audience may be adapted for users who want to maintain or revitalise their traditional languages (Chapters 5–6). Embedded in the grammar may be cultural information that provides new insights into local knowledge systems. All of this work may contribute to the compilation of dictionaries and other language resources that are of immense value to speech communities (Chapter 7). The trick is to keep an eye open to all of these purposes and be responsive and open to new ideas, without becoming like the pebble-counters that Darwin railed against.

Taking a short-term view of your work versus the notion of a long-term vision can present some ethical paradoxes. Some argue that language documentation and description should transcend time, and that the results should also be reusable across different scholarly communities and for different purposes (Bird & Simons, 2003, p. 558). Others point out that some research agreements may stipulate that research data can only be used for a particular purpose outlined in consent protocols. Enabling future users of materials requires a good deal of thought, and is particularly important in the case of severely endangered languages. It may be that down the track your recordings form a unique and irreplaceable record that is of great value both to language and linguistic communities alike (Chapter 2).

## 1.4 WORKFLOW FROM GO TO WOE

We now 'unpack' a real example from our own fieldwork to show all of the aspects of documentation workflow process. The example comes from the Gurindji community in northern Australia who, for three decades, have been documenting their language with 'outsider' linguists, including missionaries, academics and linguists from a regional Indigenous-run language centre. This workflow comes from a recent project which documents the early colonial history of the region through the Gurindji language. The project brought together archival recordings, and made new recordings to contribute to growing the Gurindji corpus. We now put

**Figure 1.1**
Field methods workflow used for the Gurindji history project

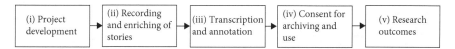

an imaginary GPS tracker on an excerpt of language and follow it from the corpus to various outputs to give you a sense of the different paths your documentation work can take. This particular example comes from extensive experience in one particular field site and might not be a place to begin but it gives you a sense of the directions your research can ultimately take. Figure 1.1 outlines the workflow and information about each step is detailed below and illustrated.

(i) The first stage was the **development of the project** with the Gurindji community. Over three decades, many Gurindji narratives (Dreamtime or creation period, historical accounts and everyday stories) have been recorded. Many speakers have since passed away and much of the knowledge is increasingly fragile. Bringing together legacy recordings and making new ones is important to the community. Meetings between linguists and the Gurindji community ascertained that narratives associated with the Dreamtime were not appropriate for dissemination beyond the community, but the historical accounts had broader interest to the Australian community. The meetings took place at Karungkarni Art and Culture Aboriginal Corporation which represents the language and culture interests of Gurindji people. With the assistance of this organisation, funding was sought from a non-academic government agency to enrich the historical narratives with information about sites and artistic responses to the stories. A year later, after successfully obtaining funding, further meetings were held with stakeholders including elders, rangers from the Central Land Council Murnkurrumurnkurru ranger group and artists from Karungkarni. Elders decided which stories to include and which places to visit to add visual documentation to the stories and to pass on these stories to the younger generations, including the ranger group who include in their work the documentation of cultural and historical knowledge about their land, as well as practical tasks such as weed and feral animal control.

(ii) We then begin the process of **recording and enriching the stories** (see Figure 1.2). The primary 'object' of the documentation process is the audio(-visual) recording (§3.3.3). In this case, Gurindji speaker Ronnie Wavehill tells of the massacre of Gurindji people by colonists in the early twentieth century near the site where it occurred. Other elders act as 'witnesses' for the story, confirming or finessing detail. Also present are local rangers, photographers documenting the sites, visual artists who later paint responses to stories relating to their country, totems, family and histories; and linguists who are interested in documenting the words and grammar of Gurindji.

18  Introduction

**Figure 1.2**
Recording stories near Ngangi (Photo: Brenda L. Croft 2014)

Ngumpit kartipa-ma walilik na walilik-ma kartipa-ma. Najing, turlwak-kulu-rni, kuyangka-ma-lu turlwak-ma kurru nyanya. Kurlarnimpa kula kajuparik nyila-ma kurlarnimpa ngarlaka-ma nganayirla-ma Ngangi-ma, Ngangi na ngarlaka Number Seventeen-ta kaarnimpa kuya, kankulupal ngarlaka Ngangi nyawa Yiparrartu nyamu nyawa kurlarnimpal yani. Yiparrartu na — Dreaming karrinya kutitijkarra.

The whitefellas came and surrounded the Gurindji. There was no hope; they were only going to shoot. The Gurindji started hearing shots. South of there, at a considerable distance, is a hill called Ngangi. It lies on the southern side down from Number 17 Bore and on top of Ngangi is an Emu Dreaming; it's where the emu spirit stood and stopped.

(iii) Next the **transcription and annotation of the story** takes place. Ronnie Wavehill's story is media-linked in the software CLAN, transcribed in Gurindji, and translated into English (Figure 1.3). Note how the speakers' names are reduced to initials. These initials reflect the participant's real first name and surname. It is an example of partial anonymity where the speaker is identifiable within the community but not to outside researchers §4.4.5. For more discussion about transcription software including CLAN, see §4.3.2. Annotations include morphological glossing, useful for grammatical analysis (§6.7) and dictionary compilation (§7.6). Additional annotation might include gesture (§8.7). Attention is also given to file naming to help keep track of all media and annotation 'objects' associated with the recording session. They are given unique identifiers, stored in the same folder and the metadata is clearly recorded (§4.2.2).

#### Figure 1.3
A CLAN excerpt of Ronnie Wavehill's story transcribed in Gurindji and translated into English (Illustration: Maxine Addinsall)

| 1 | @Begin | |
|---|---|---|
| 2 | @Languages: | gu |
| 3 | @Participants: | RWH Ronnie Wavehill Speaker, ECH Erika Charola Investigator |
| 4 | @ID: | gu\|\|RWH\|73;00.00\|male\|\|\|\|Speaker\|\|\| |
| 5 | @Media: | EC98_a027, audio |
| 6 | @Date: | 30-MAY-1998 |
| 7 | *RWH: | Ngumpit kartipa-ma walilik na walilik-ma kartipa-ma. * |
| 8 | %eng: | The kartiya came and surrounded the ngumpin. |
| 9 | *RWH: | Najing, turlwak-kulu-rni, kuyangka-ma-lu turlwak-ma kurru nyanya. * |
| 10 | %eng: | There was no hope; they were only going to shoot. The ngumpin |
| 11 | | started hearing shots. |
| 12 | *RWH: | Kurlarnimpa kula kajuparik nyila-ma kurlarnimpa ngarlaka-ma |
| 13 | | nganayirla-ma Ngangi-ma, Ngangi na ngarlaka Number Seventeen-ta |
| 14 | | kaarnimpa kuya, kankulupal ngarlaka Ngangi nyawa Yiparrartu nyamu |
| 15 | | nyawa kurlarnimpa yani. Yiparrartu na — Dreaming karrinya |
| 16 | | kutitijkarra. * |
| 17 | %eng: | South of there, at a considerable distance, is a hill called Ngangi. |
| 18 | | It lies on the southern side down from Number 17 Bore and on top of |
| 19 | | Ngangi is the Emu Dreaming; it's where the emu stood and stopped. |
| 20 | | |

- (iv) Afterwards **consent for archiving and use of story** was discussed. The story was played back to a small group which included Ronnie Wavehill, other custodians of knowledge and interested younger people. Details were discussed and anything deemed not suitable for broader dissemination was noted. Consent was given by Ronnie Wavehill orally, as well as on a signed form. All consent was witnessed by the group. The transcribed CLAN file of Ronnie's story and accompanying media were then archived according to the conditions set by the Gurindji community during the consent process. Read more about consent processes in §2.5 and archiving in §4.4.
- (v) The documentation event had a number of **research outcomes**:
  - Ronnie Wavehill's (2016) story was published in a bilingual collection of Gurindji historical narratives for the Gurindji community and broader Australian public called *Yijarni: True Stories from Gurindji Country*.

- In a subsequent art camp on Gurindji country, artists painted responses to the historical stories. The canvases were reproduced in *Yijarni* and formed a part of an exhibition *Still in My Mind: Gurindji Location, Experience and Visuality*[5] which travelled through Australian galleries.
- The massacre site itself was fenced by the ranger group to prevent further destruction by roaming cattle.
- Excerpts from the recording are also used as example sentences for dictionary entries, for example *kurlarnimpa* 'up on the south side' (Meakins et al., 2013, p. 182). This excerpt is discussed in the context of dictionary compilation in §7.6.1.
- Ethnobiological information in the story, such as the journey of Yiparrartu, the spirit emu, contributes to the documentation of this aspect of the lexicon (see Figure 1.4). For this aspect of the project, extra expertise is called upon and a biologist joined the documentation team to help map between Western and Gurindji ontologies of the natural world. The use of scientific knowledge is discussed further in §7.2.2.
- Other linguistic aspects of the recording are pursued further with Gurindji speakers, for example paradigms of cardinal terms are filled out through elicitation (§6.7.5) and the cardinal orientation of gestures is explored using methods developed for visual language modalities

**Figure 1.4**
Excerpt from *Bilinarra, Gurindji and Malngin Plants and Animals*
Source: Hector et al., 2012, p. 95

There is a **Yiparrartu** Dreaming track running through Bilinarra and Gurindji country. **Yiparrartu** came with his family from the north from **Mantijka** in Bilinarra country. They came to **Wirrirrirtkarrawirri** (on the northside of **Marlukalarni**). His wife and chicks decided to camp there. The chicks were lame because their mother wouldn't let them stop and rest. Eventually they went east. In the meantime the male emu left them and went to **Yurnturtu**

where he urinated and created a spring. Then he went to **Jampawurru** or **Langa** (Mud Spring or Red Lily) with **Pangarra** (Corella) following him overhead and created another spring by urinating. He went east across the river to **Kilkil** and deposited some red, yellow and brown ochre on the ridge (next to the Lajamanu road). Then he went south to near **Palkinykarni** then east through **Parlakurna** (No. 29 bore on Wave Hill station) and continued east to **Kunawa** (Cattle Creek station).

Emu
**Yibarrardu**, (Bil), **Yiparrartu** (Gur Mal)
**Wanyayarung** (Mal), **Yunturrman** (Mal)
**Karnanganyja** (Gur), **Kalyupurr** (Gur)

(§8.4). Language contact phenomena such as code-switches into Kriol, for example the clausal negator *najing* in the excerpt above, are explored through the development of the Gurindji corpus (§10.2.2).

Ronnie Wavehill's story is just one of thousands told across the world every day in languages that have not been systematically documented. The extent of the world's linguistic diversity is truly breath-taking and there is no shortage of potential projects, research questions and speech communities who are asking for linguistic expertise. Of course it is impossible to cover the range of fieldwork projects underway, but in this textbook we give you samples of projects from across the globe.

## 1.5 ABOUT US (FIRST PERSON PLURAL EXCLUSIVE)

Finally, a word about the authors of this textbook. We bring together a combined experience of many decades of fieldwork on Indigenous languages in Australia. Our pathways to long-term linguistic work have been diverse: Green became interested in the Alyawarr and Anmatyerr languages while working on art and craft programs in a remote Indigenous community called Utopia in Central Australia in the mid-1970s. Turpin became fascinated by Australian languages while studying music at Melbourne University in the early 1990s, and went on to work with Kaytetye people and other groups in Central Australia. Meakins took a more traditional route, cutting her teeth on formal linguistic theory at the University of Queensland in the mid-1990s before working with Ngarinyman, Bilinarra and Gurindji people in northern Australia on school programs. We have all worked in Indigenous-run language and arts centres, facilitating language support programs and producing bilingual language resources such as dictionaries, text collections and posters. We have always tried to bring a community-orientated and collaborative approach to research as a part of our practice as linguists. Our collective linguistic interests span many aspects of language: phonology, semantics, morpho-syntax, sign and gesture, multimodality and verbal arts, as well as language acquisition and contact languages. Although some of the examples used in this textbook are from our own fieldwork in Australia (as these are the ones we know best), we have attempted to reach out to colleagues from all corners of the world and to represent as best we can the diversity of the world's languages. First-hand accounts by field linguists (in boxes in the text) and case-studies (in shaded boxes) add to the breadth of the languages covered. Our approach is inter-disciplinary, drawing on themes and techniques from anthropology and musicology as well as more standard linguistic methods. The widespread use of audio-visual recording, and the increasing value attached to understanding how language is used in naturalistic everyday contexts also draws linguistic and anthropological approaches closer together (Duranti, 1997, p. 98). We also encourage research that is collaborative, reflexive and grounded in the twin expectations of both language communities and research academies.

## 1.6 SUMMARY

Knowing how to get started with fieldwork can be difficult. This textbook walks you through the process. We begin with the preliminaries of fieldwork in Chapter 2 (identifying a field site, preparation, procedures, ethics) and proceed to chapters that discuss recording equipment and how to use it (Chapter 3) and then workflows through the processes involved in archiving your work (Chapter 4). We then look at fieldwork on different aspects of language. As well as the classics of grammar writing (Chapters 5–6) and semantic description and dictionary compilation (Chapter 7), we take a broader approach to the descriptive object. We discuss methodologies for conducting field research on anthropological and socio-cultural aspects of language, sign language and gesture (Chapter 8), child language (Chapter 9), contact languages, such as creoles (Chapter 10), and verbal art (Chapter 11). These chapters cover the methodologies, ethics and procedures specific to these topics.

## 1.7 FURTHER READING

For a good overview of different views on what constitutes fieldwork, read Sakel & Everett (2012, pp. 2–8). For a detailed history of linguistic fieldwork, see Chelliah & de Reuse (2011). Read Evans (2011) for a beautifully written and wide-ranging account of linguistic diversity and why we should care about endangered languages. For more on endangered languages, see Austin & Sallabank (2011) and Sallabank (2013). For accounts of fieldwork, read Crowley (2007), Dixon (1983), Sarvasy & Forker (2018) and Everett (2008).

## NOTES

1  www.ethnologue.com Accessed 31 July 2017.
2  www.unesco.org/fileadmin/MULTIMEDIA/HQ/CI/CI/pdf/unesco_language_vitaly_ and_endangerment_methodological_guideline.pdf Accessed 31 August 2017.
3  www.ethnologue.com/about/language-status Accessed 31 August 2017.
4  Darwin's letters can be found at www.darwinproject.ac.uk Accessed 13 January 2018. We thank William McGregor for drawing our attention to this quote.
5  www.artdesign.unsw.edu.au/unsw-galleries/still-my-mind-gurindji-location-experience-and-visuality Accessed 31 August 2017.

## REFERENCES

Austin, P., & Sallabank, J. (2011). *The Cambridge handbook of endangered languages*. Cambridge: Cambridge University Press.

Bird, S., & Simons, G. (2003). Seven dimensions of portability for language documentation and description. *Language*, 79(3), 557–582.

Boas, F. (1917). Introduction. *International Journal of American Linguistics*, 1(1), 1–8.

Boas, F. (1991) [1911]. Introduction. In F. Boas (Ed.), *Handbook of American Indian Languages* (pp. 1–79). Lincoln, NE: University of Nebraska Press.

Boerger, B., Moeller, S., Self, S., & Reiman, W. (2017). *Language and culture documentation manual*. Victoria, BC: Leanpub.

Burroughs, J. (1894). *Riverby*. Boston, MA: Houghton Mifflin.

Chelliah, S., & de Reuse, W. (2011). *Handbook of descriptive linguistic fieldwork*. Heidelberg: Springer.

Crippen, J. (2009). "Studying grandmother's tongue": Heritage language and linguistics. Presented at the The 1st International Conference on Language Documentation and Conservation, Manoa: University of Hawai'i.

Crowley, T. (2007). *Field linguistics: A beginners guide*. Oxford: Oxford University Press.

Dixon, R. M. W. (1983). *Searching for Aboriginal languages: Memoirs of a field worker*. Brisbane: University of Queensland Press.

Duranti, A. (1997). *Linguistic anthropology*. Cambridge: Cambridge University Press.

Epps, P., Webster, A., & Woodbury, A. (2017). A holistic humanities of speaking: Franz Boas and the continuing centrality of texts. *International Journal of American Linguistics*, 83(1), 41–78.

Evans, N. (2008). Review of essentials of language documentation. *Language Documentation & Conservation*, 2(2), 340–350.

Evans, N. (2011). *Dying words: Endangered languages and what they have to tell us*. Malden, MA: John Wiley & Sons.

Everett, D. (2008). *Don't sleep, there are snakes: Life and language in the Amazonian jungle*. New York, NY: Pantheon Books.

Fishman, J. (1991). *Reversing language shift: Theoretical and empirical foundations of assistance to threatened languages*. Clevedon: Multilingual Matters.

Green, J. (1992). *Alyawarr to English dictionary*. Alice Springs: IAD Press.

Hector, I. K., Kalabidi, G. J., Banjo, S., Dodd, T., Wavehill, R., Danbayarri, D., Wadrill, V., Puntiyarri, B., Malyik, I., Wavehill, B., Morris, H., Campbell, L., Meakins, F., & Wightman, G. (2012). *Bilinarra, Gurindji and Malngin plants and animals*. Darwin: Northern Territory Department of Land Resource Management.

Hill, J. (2006). The ethnography of language and language documentation. In J. Gippert, N. Himmelman, & U. Mosel (Eds.), *Essentials of language documentation* (pp. 113–128). Berlin: Mouton de Gruyter.

Himmelmann, N. (1998). Documentary and descriptive linguistics. *Linguistics*, 36, 161–195.

Hyman, L. (2001). Fieldwork as a state of mind. In P. Newman & M. Ratlif (Eds.), *Linguistic fieldwork* (pp. 15–33). Cambridge: Cambridge University Press.

Kusters, A. (2012). Being a deaf white anthropologist in Adamorobe: Some ethical and methodological issues. In U. Zeshan & C. de Vos. (Eds.), *Sign languages in village communities: Anthropological and linguistic insights* (pp. 27–52). Berlin: Mouton de Gruyter.

Lewis, P., & Simons, G. (2009). Assessing endangerment: Expanding Fishman's GIDS. *Revue Roumaine de Linguistique*, 1–30.

Meakins, F., McConvell, P., Charola, E., McNair, N., McNair, H., & Campbell, L. (2013). *Gurindji to English dictionary*. Batchelor, Australia: Batchelor Press.

Morey, S. (2010). *Turung: A variety of Singpho language spoken in Assam*. Canberra: Pacific Linguistics.

Nordhoff, S. (2012). *Electronic grammaticography*. Honolulu, HI: University of Hawai'i Press.

Obiero, O. (2010). From assessing language endangerment or vitality to creating and evaluating language revitalization programmes. *Nordic Journal of African Studies*, 19(4), 201–226.

Pawley, A. (2015). Review of the Oxford Handbook of Linguistic Fieldwork. *Language Documentation & Conservation, 9*, 134–139.

Sakel, J., & Everett, D. (2012). *Linguistic fieldwork: A student guide.* Cambridge: Cambridge University Press.

Sallabank, J. (2013). *Attitudes to endangered languages: Identities and policies.* Cambridge: Cambridge University Press.

Sarvasy, H. & Forker, D. (2018). *Word Hunters: Field linguists on fieldwork.* Amsterdam: John Benjamins.

Tsunoda, T. (2005). *Language endangerment and language revitalization.* Berlin: Mouton de Gruyter.

Turpin, M. & Ross, A. (2012). *Kaytetye to English dictionary.* Alice Springs: IAD Press.

UNESCO. (2003). Language vitality and endangerment. Presented at the International Expert Meeting on UNESCO Programme Safeguarding of Endangered Languages.

Wavehill, R. (2016). Early massacres. In E. Charola & F. Meakins (Eds.), *Yijarni: True stories from Gurindji country* (pp. 32–53). Canberra: Aboriginal Studies Press.

# 2

# Planning for fieldwork

## 2.1 INTRODUCTION

In this chapter we first look at how you might go about choosing a community to work with. We then discuss your responsibilities as a fieldworker to the language consultants and their community; and to the institutions with whom you are affiliated. We discuss how to manage day-to-day concerns such as how to pay people, living in the field, transport and safety, both for yourself and the people you work with. Thinking about these issues is an essential part of planning for fieldwork. How well these aspects of fieldwork are understood and managed can make all the difference between whether fieldwork is an enjoyable and successful experience or a difficult one.

## 2.2 IDENTIFYING A SPEECH COMMUNITY

There are a number of well-worn paths to the field. If you are an 'insider' linguist (§1.2.2) one option is to work with your own language. If you are an 'outsider' linguist you might respond to a community's request for a linguist or consider working on a language spoken by a community where you have pre-existing contacts. Another option is to choose a place you have always wanted to go. Through your own travels and experience, you may have a place or language in mind which you might pitch to a potential supervisor/advisor. In this case, it is worth investigating whether there is an organisation in the region that supports language activities, such as a language, culture or arts centre, a museum, an Indigenous council, or health and education organisations. Volunteering or working for these organisations is a good opportunity to get to know a speech community and their concerns and interests, and, of course, the language itself. Another path is to join an existing project at a university either as a research assistant, an intern or a PhD student. It is ideal to apprentice yourself to a more experienced fieldworker who can lead you through the process of ethics, funding applications, consent, travel and methods.

The degree of endangerment of the language is another factor to consider. Given that there are many languages on the brink of disappearing and only a small number of fieldworkers, there are good reasons to prioritise highly endangered languages over those with lots of speakers. Some people might want to work on a language that is undocumented, and so the degree of previous documentation might be a factor in the decision. In contrast, you may want to focus

*Planning for fieldwork*

in detail on a particular area of grammar or semantics, in which case it is a good idea to work on a language that already has some documentation. Get in contact with linguists who have worked on the language previously to discuss their views on where there are known gaps and what to work on to avoid doubling up by collecting the same data (for example see Nicholas Evans' approach to starting work on Papuan languages in §1.3). Some linguists have ended up working on a language more or less by chance, as Stephen Levinson describes.

---

### Travelling to Rossel Island – Stephen Levinson

People often ask me how I chose my current field site. Well, in a way I didn't, it chose me. In 1995 I was equipped for walking up into the mountains from Popondetta in south-eastern Papua New Guinea where the Dagan languages are still under-described. But in the provincial capital there was a mission boat heading for fabled Rossel Island, where I had also thought of going but had been told that transport was too difficult. An SIL missionary had published some notes on the language that made it look intriguing, and it was famous as a totally impenetrable tongue to the multilingual inhabitants of other islands. I went in search of the bishop whose boat it was, and found him in the hold with a giant spanner. "Hop on", he said, "you'll be safe with them, the most dependable of the islanders". It was a slow cruise of six days through turquoise waters with a load of Rossel people of all ages. They set about teaching me in obvious delight, with gales of laughter at my mistakes. I was fully adopted before we even got there … It was clear that these people thought it high time someone came to study their customs and their language. Arriving at Rossel Island, the rugged mountains with swirling mists look quite forbidding, and the encircling reefs have held mariners at bay for centuries. The Catholic mission put their then considerable resources at my disposal, and I toured the island on their launch. Social life was vibrant, with large ceremonies somewhere nearly every week, constant village gatherings, local courts, marriage feasts, wild pig hunts, and canoe pulling adventures where dugout hulls are hauled down from the mountains, fishing expeditions out on the reefs in canoes – endless diversions. A rich language tapestry everywhere: All night long song-fests, funeral laments, scurrilous poetry, eloquent oratory. I was welcome everywhere. I became a life-long Rossel fan. Just as well, because it was never as easy again: the mission retrenched, and ever since transport to Rossel has become harder and harder to arrange, and mostly the trip is through high winds and dangerous seas. But the folks remain just as winning if you can only get there.

---

It goes without saying that it is not a good idea to go to a place where linguists are not welcome. As Rice (2012, p. 414) notes, "(s)ome communities are pleased to have researchers, and embrace their presence. In other communities, there is much

*Planning for fieldwork*  27

suspicion of researchers, their goals, and their values". Fortunately, there are many under-described languages with speakers who are happy to have a linguist come to work with them. For obvious reasons, it is also a bad idea to go into war zones or areas of civil unrest and areas where there are scarce resources that you would be taking up.

---

### Keeping out of trouble – Birgit Hellwig

On one of my last field trips to Nigeria, I unexpectedly found myself confronted with civil unrest. Violence broke out the very day I was travelling by local transport to my field site. As we got closer to the site, we encountered more and more worrying signs – until finally, we met a car coming towards us whose driver stopped us and told us about violence and killings in the towns ahead. All Nigerians in my bush taxi argued against continuing our journey: we turned back, and learned later that religiously motivated violence had led to a large-scale massacre in the town just adjacent to my field site. The army moved in relatively quickly and managed to stop further major outbreaks of violence, but the situation remained highly volatile, and all my Nigerian friends and colleagues strongly advised against me going to this area again. I heeded their advice, and instead worked with speakers who happened to live in a town well outside the affected area. I did not return to my field site until the next year when the situation had calmed down.

(Research Centre for Linguistic Typology, 2009, p. 13)

---

### Exercise 1  Your motivations for undertaking fieldwork

Discuss whether you see yourself doing linguistic fieldwork. What would your motivations for undertaking fieldwork be (e.g. do you speak an under-described language, do you have a burning theoretical question)? What sort of field linguist would you be? What skills do you already have and which skills would you want to develop further?

---

## 2.3 RESEARCH ON THE FIELD LOCATION

Once you have decided on where you are going to do fieldwork start reading about the area – the people, their language, culture and history, as well as the geography of the region. Talk to other people who have worked in the area and ask for tips on who to contact and the availability of power, housing, food, transport etc. Think beyond linguists, as other researchers, teachers, health professionals and government workers may have important local knowledge too. Start organising all the research that has been done on the region and prepare a broad range of tasks or questions that you plan to address in your own fieldwork. Create a bibliography and a summary of the sociolinguistic context. The Ethnologue website is a good place to start, although note that the information there may not be up to date.[1] A useful set of areas of enquiry, outlined by Van der Veen & Medjo Mvé (2010), are summarised here:

- Name(s) of the language and people who speak it. Distinguish between exonyms (names attributed by others) and endonyms (self-attributed names).
- Classification of the language: phylum, group, subgroup etc.
- The estimated number of speakers, any variation in fluency and whether there is multilingualism and, if so, with which languages.
- Attitudes towards their own, and neighbouring or dominant languages, as well as the coloniser or dominant society.
- The estimated vitality of the language. See, for example, the UNESCO criteria (§1.2.5).[2]
- Location of speakers (towns, villages, distances between localities, accessibility of localities); and their mobility.
- Extent of internal diversification (dialects, sociolects).
- Known linguistic features, e.g. sound inventories, tone, noun classes. If nothing is known, note those of neighbouring or closely related languages.
- Social and economic organisation.
- Information about socio-cultural constraints and taboos, special speech registers, singing and signing practices, and their possible impact on language use, vocabulary etc.
- Professional activities on language and language use (e.g. interpreting, schooling, Bible translations, literacy).
- Access to Western education systems.
- History of the group (often oral traditions), e.g. migration stories, origin(s) of the group.

## 2.4 WAYS OF WORKING IN THE FIELD

Concern for social relationships and the impact of the research and the researcher on the speech community should be a primary consideration in linguistic fieldwork (Ahlers & Wertheim, 2009; Kroskrity, 2015, p. 154). Working in Indigenous and minority communities requires particular sensitivity to issues of power and control, especially if you are part of a majority culture or a more powerful sector of society. Minority groups often have a history of outsiders who presume to know what is best for them. It is important to be sensitive to these issues and have a collaborative approach to research (Rice, 2010, p. 29). There are two overarching basic principles of ethical research: *respect* for a person's autonomy and rights to make decisions about research participation, and *beneficence*, or how research should maximise benefits and minimise harm (Singleton, Martin, & Morgan, 2015, p. 12). Put another way, "ethical behavior can be said to be based in a number of 'r' words – respect, relationships, reciprocity, and responsibility" (Rice, 2012, p. 427).

Linguistic fieldwork often depends upon a continuing relationship with speakers, and the depth of the insights into particular features of a language improves over time. The expectations of collaborators and the language community thus help shape the results of the work. If you are not from the community, it is important to try to understand the norms and lifestyles of the community, for example norms of politeness and friendship. Be prepared to be flexible as there may be changing needs over the course of your engagement with the speech community. You should consider whether it would be fruitful collaborating with other organisations. Look at it from a language speaker's point of view: if the school or church and you are all developing an orthography, it is better to do it together once rather than several times (§5.11)!

### 2.4.1 Who is the fieldworker responsible to?

It is important to consider the different obligations you have to the language community, and to local organisations as well as responsibilities you have to your own academic institution. As a field linguist, you have a responsibility to a number of people and organisations:

- language speakers and research participants
- the broader language community
- local organisations who have endorsed or approved your research and may use or benefit from the research now or in years to come (e.g. land and tribal councils, schools, health organisations, arts centres, language centres, regional universities)
- your own academic institution
- the funding body
- students and colleagues
- yourself (see §2.7.5).

After a time, you may find that speakers within the community introduce or refer to you as "our linguist". This is a good indication that the community has an idea of your obligations and responsibilities to the community! Sometimes what the community wants you to do and what you would like to do conflict. For example, the community may see it as your responsibility to work in the school, or, as we have seen in Nicholas Evans' story in §1.3, translate the Bible. You may be asked to seek funding on behalf of the community for some other activity that you did not intend to do. Unless these activities will seriously jeopardise you or your research, it is a good idea to give these tasks a go in the spirit of reciprocity. You never know what unintended insights these may bring.

You may have the opportunity to help facilitate or connect people to linguistic training options that exist in the region. It can be immensely beneficial to the project (and the speakers) to participate in training for language work – learning how to

Planning for fieldwork

record, document, transcribe and translate (Seyfeddinipur, 2012; Wilkins, 1992). For example, the National Breath of Life Archival Institute for Indigenous Languages in the United States runs two-week workshops for community researchers, providing training in revitalisation techniques and archive access;[3] the Endangered Languages Documentation Program (ELDP) runs in-country training programs in many African countries;[4] and the Documenting and Revitalising Indigenous Languages (DRIL) program in Australia runs certified training courses for language communities.[5] Opportunities for language speakers to take courses, attend conferences, perform their verbal arts and visit archives are of immense value to everyone and may enrich the research project.

### 2.4.2 Who controls the research?

Participation in linguistic research is voluntary, and up to the individual. But there are also systems of decision making above the level of the individual that may impact on your research. For example, if you want to conduct research in a school, in many countries you will need permission from the school or from a regional or national Education Department. Some places have Research Councils, and national governments may require evidence of support from these even before they consider visa applications. Many villages and communities have institutions and local officials that control activities within their jurisdiction, although they may or may not be formally recognised as having this power. Such influence can be based on political, geographic, religious or ethnic considerations. Some people call these 'gatekeeper' organisations, and the term can even be applied, somewhat negatively, to individuals who are seen to have disproportionate control over research in a region.

It is important to seek official approval or at least endorsement from these organisations for a number of reasons. First, it is possible that outsiders who have visited the community in the past may have had a negative impact, perhaps unwittingly. These organisations can help to ensure that your research does not go down the same path by alerting you to any cultural restrictions or local expectations. Second, the results of your research are more likely to be known beyond the language speakers with whom you work and thus have greater impact if local organisations are kept informed about your research. Third, their approval can be used to alleviate any concerns about community consent, which people with varying connections to the language community may have. In some cases, you will need consent from each organisation within the hierarchical structure of the state. These should all be obtained so that you can conduct your research with confidence and authority. In many countries, failing to follow such procedures can lead to problems, including a ban on research, despite the support of the local community.

In particular, you should consider also the rights of Indigenous minorities to control research involving them and any use of their languages, including recording and documentation. Communities and language speakers may want to be involved in making decisions about aspects of the project, such as who should participate, how the project should be organised and proceed, and how funds are spent. Such a participatory model of linguistic research highlights the value of providing

*Planning for fieldwork* 31

training and prioritising information sharing amongst members of the community (Benedicto et al., 2007; Czaykowska-Higgins, 2009). Community members are the experts about speakers (e.g. their background, skills and shortcomings) and what is important to the community. They are also the experts on ways of working that people enjoy and don't enjoy, and can advise about when is a good time to work and when isn't. Such insider knowledge is crucial to the success of a project and must be recognised and valued alongside linguistic training. In some projects, it may be important to involve young people even if they are not proficient speakers of heritage languages (§1.2.6).

---

### Controlling fieldwork on Malo Island, Vanuatu – Miriam Meyerhoff

I had been doing fieldwork for my PhD in Vanuatu on Malo Island for five months and was starting to feel like things were under control. In fact, they were, but what I didn't realise was whose control.

I was trained to do sociolinguistic fieldwork in the urban 'jungle' of Philadelphia. There, I was trained to converse and listen, and encouraged to pursue the topics that my interlocutor most warmed to in the quest for the vernacular. As in Philadelphia, my strategy in Vanuatu was to find times to hang out with people, and get their agreement to record a conversation. This was working fine. Someone had given me a lovely woven pandanus bag that was the perfect size for my tape-recorder and I felt like I was part of the local scenery, collecting quite a few recordings.

One afternoon when I was hanging out with my friend and her husband resting in the kitchen, her husband's *angkel*, a chief from further south, stopped by to chat. I had hardly been paying attention to them when he turned to me and challenged me about what I was doing on the island. I explained as best I could in my still clunky Bislama, going over the consent process, the use of the materials when I got back to the US. Satisfied that he knew enough to account for what was going on in his community further south, he exchanged some more gossip and shortly after, left.

In a panic, I turned to my friend and asked her whether I should be meeting with other local chiefs to clear my work. "No need", was her message. She had gone round to the community and church elders in the immediate village months before and done all the explaining for me. Everything *was* under control, but not mine.

---

## 2.4.3 Ownership, access and uses of research materials

Language documentation which involves recordings of stories and knowledge and expressions of culture may be of great importance to people. This knowledge may be embedded at many levels – in a word, a sentence, a sign, a story, a song or a multimodal interaction. In many cultures, language is considered no less a part of culture than is dance, song and art. Where language is specifically connected to particular geographical places (as is frequently the case) it often forms an important aspect of a speaker's cultural heritage and identity. This contrasts with international languages such as English. While the social value of linguistic research on minority and endangered languages is often framed in terms of 'saving' languages for humanity as a whole by recording them and writing them down, it is also crucial that consideration is given as to *how* the results of research will be accessible to community members (Wilkins, 1992, p. 173).

A community may have very definite views about how their language should and should not be used. In some cases, Indigenous languages and their words have been used commercially or by governments without a community's consent. This appropriation may have led to speakers deciding *not* to write their language down or share it with outsiders. A community may not want anyone using their language and the knowledge it encodes for commercial reasons without their permission, yet in making recordings and writing down a language you may inadvertently make this knowledge accessible to commercial interests.

### 2.4.4 Intellectual property, copyright and licensing

**Intellectual Property Rights** is a blanket term that refers to a collection of rights that includes copyright, patents, plant breeder's rights and trademarks. In general terms this bundle of rights is designed to protect original expressions and promote the rights of creators of original works. Copyright protects the expression of ideas, including artistic and literary works, and is born the moment the idea is reduced to a material form, for example, by being written down or recorded. As Newman (2012, p. 443) says, "[c]opyright protects the expression of facts and ideas, not facts and ideas in and of themselves". Although the duration of copyright varies from country to country, in some places, for example in Australia, it may last for the life of the creator, plus 70 years. After copyright expires the material enters the public domain. There is no internationally consistent copyright law, and details vary from country to country (Newman, 2012, p. 435). As a linguist working in the field, you may be engaged in creating language resources, dictionaries, translations, bilingual books, corpora and of course primary recordings of language in many forms. Although the relevant intellectual property laws are notoriously complicated, it pays to have some understanding of where you and the people you work with stand. As Newman (2012, p. 430) points out, if the linguist does not pay attention to some of these concerns, it can lead to frictions and complications down the track. When it comes to song, there are additional laws that protect the performers and creators of such works (see Chapter 11).

Legally, who *owns* language is a very contentious matter. Language *per se* is not protected by law in most countries. This may be at odds with the views of some language communities, where ownership of language may be regarded as being properly vested in a community or language group. In many countries, the legal owner of a document or recording of a language is simply the person who pressed the record button or wrote it down, i.e. often the linguist. Countries

Planning for fieldwork

vary as to what other aspects of culture are protected by law. For example aspects of cultures that are orally transmitted and performance-based may not be protected by copyright laws, even though these are perhaps some of the most valued aspects of language from the community point of view (Janke, 2009). Most legal systems fail to recognise rights in communally held knowledge or cultural expressions that are part of shared traditions. Knowledge of medicines, herbal cures and other products can be protected under various patent acts. However, this may not be the case if they are based on traditional knowledge handed down over many generations. Even though 'language' does not get a specific mention, some countries are signatories to various international declarations, such as the Declaration on the Rights of Indigenous People (United Nations, 2007). Article 31 states:

> Indigenous peoples have the right to maintain, control, protect and develop their cultural heritage, traditional knowledge and traditional cultural expressions, as well as the manifestations of their sciences, technologies and cultures, including human and genetic resources, seeds, medicines, knowledge of the properties of fauna and flora, oral traditions, literatures, designs, sports and traditional games and visual and performing arts. They also have the right to maintain, control, protect and develop their intellectual property over such cultural heritage, traditional knowledge, and traditional cultural expressions.[6]

To address the fact that copyright laws do not always align with Indigenous peoples' expectations, a range of licensing frameworks have been developed, including **Creative Commons**, **Traditional Knowledge Licences**, and software licences such as MIT, Apache and GPL. Creative Commons (CC) licences are written to conform to international legal treaties, are intended to be effective worldwide, and are legal tools for licensing content. A resource can be released under one of six main CC licences, allowing it to be copied, modified and/or redistributed, for commercial or non-commercial use, according to a creator's needs.[7]

Traditional Knowledge (TK) licences and labels can be used separately or in combination with CC licences to add conditions of use and information about how material should be respectfully and ethically used, reproduced or copied according to community expectations and obligations. Under such licences material may be labelled as open to all users, as restricted to women or men, as requiring attribution, or as being for either community or commercial use. Although these licences are not legally binding, they are informative and useful for developing rights awareness for a resource's users.[8]

### 2.4.5 Balancing rights in the field

Balancing moral, commercial and legal rights is complicated and not for the lay person. As Newman (2012, p. 453) points out, "(l)inguistic fieldworkers are not trained to know copyright law any more than copyright lawyers are trained to do phonetic transcription". There are, however, some useful strategies to consider when designing your fieldwork, and awareness of these issues places you in a good position to complete the formal ethics applications that most institutions require before you can commence fieldwork. Some of these involve being respectful and observant of particular community requirements about access; moderation of content and the handling of secret or sacred materials; documenting informed consent; and understanding moral rights, including the right of attribution. Custodians of knowledge may want to set boundaries about access to particular types of content for particular groups of people. Apart from issues that may be part of the standard processes of informed consent, such as documenting instructions for archiving, another way to assert a community's language rights in publications and research materials is to include specific wording. For example:

> (T)he language and information contained in this book includes the traditional knowledge and cultural expression of the X people. The information is published for the purposes of knowledge preservation, education and language maintenance.

Some publications state specifically what uses are not permitted. For example *Walmajarri Plants & Animals* (Doonday et al., 2013) expands on this:

> This information should not be used commercially in any way including in tourism, food technology including bush tucker applications, medicines, pharmaceutical products, health and beauty products, storytelling or as trade marks [sic], patents and designs, without observing the Aboriginal cultural protocols of prior informed consent, attribution to traditional Aboriginal communities, cultural integrity and the sharing of benefits.

While such statements may be unnecessary in academic journal articles, if writing a dictionary, a grammar or book with broad appeal, it can be a good idea to assert the moral rights of the community in relation to use of their language.

## 2.5 FORMAL ETHICS APPLICATIONS AND PROCEDURES

As your research involves people, most universities require you to submit an application to a human ethics committee before you can start your research. This is often a statutory requirement that must conform to national standards, and it may be a pre-condition set by the funding body. An ethics application usually includes a number of documents that you will use in the field, including a project information sheet and a consent form. Some researchers include examples of these documents in their theses. Start your ethics application early, as some universities can take many months to give final approval.

Ethics applications require you to demonstrate an understanding of the ethical issues of working with people in your disciplinary area. For a field linguist, this means respecting the rights of the language speakers ('research participants') and demonstrating that your research is of benefit to them or to society at large, or, at the very least, won't harm anybody. As Woods (2017, p. 88) notes, you should try to "find ways in [your] own work practices, that take into account that control of language and cultural knowledge is a high priority for Indigenous people and must be factored into any ethics applications and agreements processes". For example, you might explain that the community values their language yet it is endangered and that your research will provide resources and opportunities to participate in efforts to maintain the language. Bear in mind that most human ethics applications have medical research in mind and are designed primarily to minimise any physical risk to research participants and to ensure that they have given informed consent.

You may need to explain why the identity of the research participants needs to be maintained (not identifying names may be seen as disrespectful), rather than anonymised (which is the norm for many areas of research). Furthermore, in endangered language communities, which are often small and close-knit, anonymity may be impossible within the community (Singleton, Martin & Morgan, 2015, p. 11). Although audio recordings are personal records, adding film to the documentation mix adds another dimension (§8.5.5). You may need to identify any potential risks (e.g. infringement of cultural and intellectual copyright) and how you plan to mitigate these. When working with vulnerable groups such as children (§9.3.4) and minority groups, you will need to show how you plan to ensure language speakers have chosen to be research participants, rather than been coerced. If you are going to provide financial compensation to participants, you will need to state how much you will pay people and justify the rate (e.g. by citing rates used by other local researchers or organisations).

You will also need to demonstrate that participants have the option to withdraw from the research project, decide on the future of their recordings, including whether to archive or not, and determine access conditions and even destroy any recordings should they wish.

### 2.5.1 Project information sheet

A project information sheet or 'plain language statement' is for the research participant to keep. It usually includes:

- a project description in layperson's terms
- the tasks the participant will be asked to do (participate in elicitation sessions, tell a story, assist with transcription and translation)
- the recording methods that will be used (audio or video)
- the intended uses of the research data (thesis, journal articles, book, multimedia film etc.)
- the benefits of participating, and dangers (if any)
- details of remuneration for participating in research activities
- a statement of the participant's right to say no and withdraw from the project if they want
- the researcher's plan for safe-guarding research materials in the short term
- archiving options, and access conditions

- contact details for the researcher and their university's ethics committee
- who to contact if there is a complaint (for example a supervisor/advisor or an ombudsman at the researcher's university).

When formulating these statements, avoid technical language and jargon, and use common words, active voice and short sentences. Put yourself in the shoes of the interpreter who may have to translate your document! Ask your supervisor/advisor or recently graduated students for examples. There should be no need to reinvent the wheel! Although the information should not be too detailed, be prepared to explain the types of linguistic data you hope to collect (how many people, how long for, what topics), what it will be used for (e.g. PhD, publications in book, journal, audio, film or web formats) and what will happen to it (where will it be kept, who will access it and how?). Remember that some people will not know what a PhD or journal article is, so you may need to think hard about how to translate these concepts. Bringing an example to show may be a good idea.

Figure 2.1 shows a participant information sheet for a project involving Australian Indigenous people. This 'card' is translated for the research participant into north Australian Kriol by a local interpreter. Note that information about short-term and long-term benefits to the community is clearly spelt out.

Figure 2.1
An example of a participation statement developed by Caroline Jones for a project on Kriol (N.B. identifying information has been deleted)

**You are invited to take part in a research study. Our study is about how children learn to talk, and what helps children.**

You can make a choice. You don't have to agree to take part.

You would join a group conversation, and fun activities like retelling a story. We're interested in normal everyday talk, what you think.

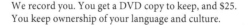

We record you. You get a DVD copy to keep, and $25.
You keep ownership of your language and culture.

 30–60 mins  You can pull out whenever you want. We won't ask why. If you get upset we will help. Remember we have to report serious criminal activity.

Long-term benefits: community, school, XXXXXXXX we're learning info to help families and teachers. No benefit for your family right now.

You can choose who sees your video and where we store it. We will write about the study, but we will check drafts with you and the community first.

If you're worried or you have questions, tell us or XXXXXXXX (your advocate). If you want to complain, phone XXXXXXXX, email XXXXXXXX or post the card in the stamped envelope.

### 2.5.2 Participant consent form

Once speakers have understood what the research project is about, anyone who wants to participate in the project will need to formally consent to being involved. A consent form usually consists of a statement that provides evidence that those who participate in the research have fully understood what the research is about. It is never permissible to make recordings without the speaker's consent. Whereas the project information document is more general in nature, individual consent forms are the place where people can set down their own views about their involvement, how they want to be acknowledged, and what they want to happen to their recordings in the future.

You will need some way to document consent, usually in written form on a consent form or by an audio or video recorded agreement, a process discussed by Rice (2012, p. 417). Ensuring that communication with research participants is optimal and that there is mutual understanding is a fundamental principle, and it is important either to use an interpreter or to translate these documents into the *lingua franca* of the community if people are literate in the language. If the language speakers have low levels of literacy, you may use a series of pictures or even a video that communicates essential aspects of the project. If working on a sign language, project information and consent documents must be translated into the deaf individual's native sign language (Singleton Martin & Morgan, 2015, p. 9). If you are working with children, consent must be given by a parent or caregiver (§9.3.4). If open access internet dissemination of project materials is envisaged, then it is important to discuss this in advance, as protection of people's identities is impossible to guarantee.

In some contexts, it may not be appropriate for each person to consent individually. As Kusters (2012, p. 31) notes, the use of individual consent forms "has little meaning or relevance in communities where it is often the leaders who make decisions". Thus it might be more appropriate to have a community leader sign a general consent form and ask each speaker to record an audio statement about their choice or willingness to be a research participant. Another option is to discuss consent with groups of participants, going through the consent forms slowly and using interpreters. It is also a good idea to review aspects of consent for the project over time, as some community attitudes may change (Rice, 2012, pp. 417–418).

Consent forms may also include instructions for archiving and future uses of recordings and they should include the relevant archives for the region where you are working (Chapter 4). However, discussing archiving can be problematic if the speakers do not know what an archive is. One option is to create a small film about archives, demonstrating how they are used, how access instructions are enforced and how materials are looked after. A consent form may also lay out various options for access. This may be restricted to known researchers, with other future researchers being required to contact the community to seek permission for access. People may also specify their views about access on a family, regional or community level. It is important to document any restrictions on who can*not* hear or obtain a copy of research materials and what they can*not* be used for. While we are unable to predict the future intended uses of recordings, we can get an idea of a speaker's intentions if we document broadly what research materials can*not* be used for. Being as specific as possible is important because, as Woods (2017, p. 87) cautions, "(a)greements that include clauses about wide ranging non-specific, ongoing secondary uses of language data is problematic [because] it denies Indigenous people the right to claim their knowledge as their own and to protect it in any way whatsoever [and] the use of such clauses shortcuts the need for ongoing consultation with the Indigenous community".

Similarly, when working with archival recordings, you may need to consult the speaker (or their next of kin if they have passed away) and get their permission to publish or reuse the recordings. Another issue that is often specified in consent forms is the speaker's right to ask the researcher to delete parts of the recordings that may contain sensitive or unusable content. If such a request is made it is important that the researcher keeps a record of the reasons why a particular recording, or part of a recording, has been deleted.

Depending on the nature of the recordings, it may be a good idea to get consent to publish the recording. For example, if it is a story that could be published in a book or be made publicly available online, you should document the speaker's or the broader community's views about this.

## 2.6 AUTHORSHIP AND ACKNOWLEDGEMENTS

> Fieldwork ... requires the cooperation of several players to succeed. The tendency, none-theless, has been to attribute all success to only one person – the lead researcher, and failure to acknowledge the 'other' invisible players.
>
> (Wasamba, 2015, p. 129)

Language speakers may invest large amounts of time and energy in teaching you and may wish to be acknowledged for their contribution. Speakers and participants in a project have the right to be acknowledged for work they do on a project. For example, if someone has undertaken consultation which ensures that the community understands the project, finds and arranges speakers to work with you, or arranges a performance to be recorded, this contribution should be acknowledged. Below are some examples of how to acknowledge different contributions that people and organisations have played in your research. Acknowledgements may go in the front matter of a book (e.g. grammar) or as a footnote on the first or last page of a journal article or a paper in an edited volume (depending on the publisher's style):

- The X language material in this study was produced by X in 2017, who lived in Z; where they are recognised as a cultural leader.
- I thank the community of X for enabling me to conduct research on language Y and am grateful to Z who welcomed me into their home and taught me with patience and encouragement.
- This research has been endorsed/approved by X organisation, which represents Indigenous interests in the region where X language is spoken.
- I thank my colleagues and collaborators in the field X, X, X etc.

Including a photo of the speaker in publications or on project websites can also be a good way of acknowledging the role and importance of local language experts to your project. In years to come, descendants may well appreciate a photo of their ancestor included in the archival deposit. Make sure the speaker consents to such uses of their photo and that you document this. Speakers should also be acknowledged in the example sentences in published work (§2.6.1).

Another issue to consider is whether collaborators should be co-authors in publications. What counts as a co-author varies in different linguistic sub-disciplines. In phonetics, psycholinguistics and computational linguistics, for example, it is common to have a long list of co-authors which often includes collaborators who have contributed significantly to the study, such as by organising research participants, or conducting experimental tasks. This approach follows the model of authorship in the sciences; however, in the humanities this is less common, although the situation is changing.

> [T]he very idea of plural authorship challenges a deep Western identification of any text's order with the intention of a single author … Nonetheless, there are signs of movement in this domain, and we may anticipate a gradual increase in experiments with multiple authorship. Anthropologists will increasingly have to share their texts, and sometimes their title pages, with those indigenous collaborators for whom the term 'informants' is no longer adequate, if it ever was.
>
> (Clifford, 1983, p. 140)

Woods (2017. p. 87) also advocates a model of authorship which acknowledges significant contributions from members of a speech community, noting that "co-authoring with Indigenous co-researchers is beginning to be considered as a practical way of managing copyright … [and] is already a practice in the hard sciences but is not yet seen as an option in the Arts and Humanities".

If there are speakers who have contributed written definitions to dictionaries this is a good basis for co-authorship (note that the maker(s) of dictionaries are more often referred to as 'compilers' rather than 'authors'). Even where speakers contribute oral definitions which are transcribed by linguists, prominent acknowledgement may be appropriate, for example by listing all of the major players on the front cover and separating roles into 'Contributor', 'Compiler' etc. A language speaker who has played a significant role in translating, transcribing, checking and providing language material that is crucial to a publication may also be a co-author.

Other rules of thumb apply to different publication types. In the case of volumes of collected texts, one model might be to name speakers as authors. Another model might be to name narrators of individual stories in the book as authors and the linguist(s) as the editor(s) of the volume. In the case of grammars, attributing authorship to speakers makes less sense, as a grammar is an analysis of a language rather than simply formatted data. In this respect, it 'belongs' to the linguist. Even so proper acknowledgement of speakers' contributions is crucial. Where a language only has a small number of speakers remaining or if you have worked with a small number of recognised language experts, you might consider including the speaker in the title of the grammar. For example, instead of "Grammar of X, a language

## 40    *Planning for fieldwork*

of Vanuatu", a possibility might be "Grammar of X, language of [speaker X] and [speaker X] from Vanuatu". As a general rule of thumb, even if language speakers are attributed authorship, it is a good idea to be specific about the roles of each of the co-authors in the front matter of the publication.

### 2.6.1 Referring to your examples in publications

Linguists are increasingly required to demonstrate the context in which their example sentences, words and meanings have been collected, and there is an expectation that sources of data be transparent and cited in academic publications. Otherwise it is often impossible to verify linguistic claims and enable meaningful peer review. No matter which way these debates go, establishing good work practices will save time in the long run and make your outputs more accountable. Consider the reference to the following example sentence which has been used to support the existence of a particular grammatical construction in the Australian language Bilinarra (Meakins & Nordlinger, 2014, p. 219):

(1)   Gula=rna=nggu              nyundu=ma   gayi      ba-rru
      NEG=1MIN.S>2MIN.O   2MIN=TOP    chase    hit-POT
      I can't chase you. (Bilinarra: AN: Narrative: RN1990-002b: 09:45 min)

The information included in the reference ensures that the example sentence links back to the corpus and is 'discoverable'. It also acknowledges the 'creators' (speakers, other linguists). The bracketed information is as follows:

- Bilinarra      language
- AN            speaker's initials
- Narrative     genre type
- RN             recordist's initials
- 1990           year (or date) of recording
- -002           sequentially numbered recording of that year or date
- 09:45 min    time into the recording where the example sentence begins

In a published work, you might also include a footnote after the first example sentence outlining the abbreviations in the sentence reference, for example:

> All examples will be referenced with the following information: Language (Bilinarra), speaker (initials), genre and recording. The Bilinarra speakers were: AN etc. The genres are procedural, description, narrative and conversation. The name of the recording includes the linguist's initials. The linguists were: RN etc. The recording label also includes the year the recording was made and the start time of the utterance in a recording, for example 09:45 min.

This information might also occur in the introduction of a grammar (Chapter 6). If you are making a dictionary database this information can be documented in the source information (Chapter 7). Alternatively, you may include it in the metadata for each recording and the source field simply refers to this.

## Planning for fieldwork 41

---

> **Exercise 2  How should your work be credited?**
>
> - You are a younger speaker of a language who has teamed up with your linguist to write dictionary definitions based on recordings you have both made with older speakers. The linguist names you as a co-author but the local council says that community elders are the 'holders' of the language and therefore should be the authors. What should you do?
> - You enjoy organising people but are less interested in actual linguistic analysis. You have assisted your linguist in arranging for 50 people to participate in a study on morpho-syntactic variation. You have interpreted the information sheets, arranged for consent forms to be signed and conducted the tasks. You haven't participated in the analysis or write-up. Should you be an author or acknowledged in a footnote?

---

## 2.7 PLANNING AHEAD FOR THE FIELD

Start preparing for your field trip well in advance. The more planning you do, the more likely it is that the fieldwork will run smoothly. Fieldwork may take unexpected turns, as seen, for example, in Stephen Levinson's story about planned work in Papua New Guinea described in §2.2. Although you cannot decide in advance exactly how your fieldwork will run you can plan for contingencies. Thus, greater planning gives you greater flexibility in the field, as you can have a number of tasks and aims at your fingertips that you can work with if circumstances suddenly alter.

### 2.7.1 Visas, vaccinations and vehicles

If your fieldwork entails overseas travel, talk to the university's international office about where you are going and the length of time you will be away. Make sure that you allow plenty of time to apply for the correct visa, given that you will be doing research (you are not a tourist). This may be a long and frustrating process and can take up to a year to organise, and even then may be denied. You may need a back-up plan, e.g. to work in another country. In §2.4.2 we discussed some of the layers of officialdom that you may need to navigate. Be aware that official permits can be revoked if the authorities in a country feel that the researcher is not adhering to the terms of their research agreement, whether or not the local community agrees.

Ensure that your passport is up-to-date and valid for re-entry to your home country on your return. If you are not a permanent resident of the country where you live make sure you have all the necessary documents to facilitate your re-entry after fieldwork. Ensure that you have comprehensive travel insurance and ask about any other administrative matters that need to be put in place.

## Planning for fieldwork

If you will be driving in the field make sure your licence and vehicle registration is up to date. Depending on where you are going, you may need to do a 4WD course. Consider whether you are better off hiring a car or encouraging your university to buy one. For long-term or repeated field trips buying a vehicle may be a more economic option than hiring a vehicle. In some countries it is difficult to hire a 4WD vehicle, or even an ordinary car, if you are under 25 years of age. If you are using local transport, study the options and consult the latest travel guides and websites.

You should consider whether you need vaccinations or other medications specific to the field site. Find out if there are any illnesses endemic to the area where you are going and where the nearest hospital is (see also §9.3.6). Even if you are not going overseas it may be a good idea to get a flu shot or rabies shot, depending on what health services are available at the field site. Before travelling your university may require you to do a formal risk assessment for your fieldwork. Don't leave this until the last minute, as you may need to purchase additional safety equipment or undertake first aid or other training. Note that first aid kits do not usually include paracetamol and other medications.

Assemble your research materials, field guides and recording equipment (which we discuss in the next chapter), and pack and weigh them. If you are flying, you may need to purchase extra luggage. Pay particular attention to any customs restrictions, either on your journey to the field or on the way back home.

### 2.7.2 Timing of field trips

In determining when you should do fieldwork consider the weather. For example, humidity and rain are not good for recording and equipment; and seasons when it is likely to flood or snow can lead to transport problems. Consider also people's availability. There may be times when people are engaged in particular activities, such as ceremonies or seasonal economic activities that mean they have little time to work with linguists. Find out whether holidays are a good time to work with people or whether they travel at this time or have personal commitments. Plan the length of your stay, and calculate how much it will cost to go to the field site and live there. If it is expensive, you may only be able to afford one longer field trip rather than several shorter ones. Beware of linguist-fatigue (your own but also the community's), and if you are working in a place where there are a lot of linguists make every attempt to coordinate with them.

### 2.7.3 Organising remuneration for research participants

It may be appropriate to offer financial compensation for research participants' time and the rates and cultural protocols about this will vary widely (Rice, 2012, p. 417). Compensation must balance respect for participant's time without introducing any element of coercion (Singleton, Martin & Morgan, 2015). Researchers can also 'give back' by making donations to relevant community organisations. Find out what is common practice amongst linguists or other social science colleagues who work in the region where you plan to go.

If you are planning to compensate speakers, consider the practicalities of this. If it is with food or other resources, how will you obtain them (see §1.3 for Evans' story about travelling to the field laden with knives and ladies' underwear)? Is money more appropriate and will it take the form of cash, cheques or a bank transfer? If cash is involved, investigate the logistics of changing money in the country where you are going. In some areas, people may not have bank accounts or access to the internet. Find out what is going to be practical in the field site and discuss it with your institution's administration section to ensure that the method you propose is acceptable to the university and that you have all the necessary paperwork. If you are paying people cash, you will need some way to document their receipt of payment. Note that in some cultures it is very offensive to ask for a signature so you may need to have oral documentation of the receipt of payment or gifts. You will also need to think in advance about how much cash you will need. Is your project a grammar, working with few people for long lengths of time; or is your project experimental, working with lots of people for short periods? These types of considerations will determine how much cash you might need and what kinds of denominations you need to organise. Your institution may also require you to fill in specific forms as regulated by your country's taxation system (if working in your own country). Also think about whether you will be paying participants after each session, at the end of the week or at the end of the field trip.

### 2.7.4 Gathering resources

Make copies of essential travel documents such as passports and visas. Collect maps of the fieldwork area to take with you. Naturalist field guides of flora and fauna are very useful to have in the field to elicit and check scientific identifications. You may need specific equipment for particular tasks. For example, if you plan to collect insects or other biological samples, you will need ethyl alcohol (95 per cent) and small vials. Because ethyl alcohol is regarded as a dangerous good, you will need to declare this and follow the country's requirements for travelling with scientific research specimens.

Pack enough copies of ethics forms and participant information sheets. It is also a good idea to have a print copy of all elicitation materials, as eliciting from a digital file on a screen (on a computer or tablet) can detract from creating a rapport with speakers. Furthermore, if you are working outdoors during the day, it can be difficult to read a computer screen. If access to power is uncertain then it is also not a good idea to depend on your computer. For the same reasons, written legacy materials should also be printed. If you plan to do monolingual fieldwork (§6.2), or if you are learning the *lingua franca*, pack enough prompts and hard copies of language learning materials. Do some research and see if there are any language or cross-cultural training courses in or near the field site.

### 2.7.5 Keeping in touch

During fieldwork it is likely that you will be isolated from your established social networks, so it is important to have mechanisms in place to keep in contact with home and to look after yourself. Find out ways that you can keep in touch with supervisors/advisors, peer support groups, family and friends. Notify your supervisor/advisor that you may only have limited email access (if this is the case). When in the field it is important to establish local support networks who know where you are and what you are up to (e.g. when you are travelling between towns), and may provide assistance if anything goes wrong. These may include community leaders, police, missionary organisations, school staff and other academic colleagues.

No doubt you will form new friendships in the field and these can have a profound effect on how you experience fieldwork. These may involve special relationships with cultural mentors, or people who take a particular interest and role in your research and act as guides or go-betweens for you and the community. Some people who do fieldwork form long-lasting bonds with people while in the field or become very close to the consultants with whom they work. Although some fieldwork manuals suggest that it is 'unprofessional' to get involved with people while on fieldwork, it is important to be able to acknowledge a wide spectrum of relationships that are formed in the field and take care of yourself and others within them. This may also involve coming to terms with grief, as elderly people you work with pass on. For a detailed discussion of personal issues in the field see Newman (2009).

## 2.8 SUMMARY

Fieldwork can be a unique, exciting and formative experience, and even though there may be logistic hurdles where things don't go entirely to plan, many seasoned fieldworkers regard their time in the field as a highlight in their training and experience as linguists. The personal and academic rewards of fieldwork – discovering new, exciting things about a language, having intercultural experiences that no travel agent could ever imagine, forming new friendships, learning new skills and discovering talents you thought you did not have – are many.

Although this book makes many suggestions for methods in the field, it is important that you maintain a critical and open mind, as some tried and tested methods that work in one situation will turn out to be a failure in others. It is OK to abandon, or adapt and innovate. Also keep in mind that, no matter what academic goals motivate the research, the rights of the host community and the personal ethics, integrity and sanity of the fieldworker must always take priority. In the next chapters we turn to techniques for recording, analysis and management of data.

## 2.9 FURTHER READING

For discussions about choosing a field site and ethics see Chapters 10 and 11 in Bowern (2015) and Chapter 1 in Newman & Ratliff (2001). For discussions of ethics and rights and responsibilities in linguistic fieldwork see Austin (2010), Rice (2006, 2012) and Wilkins (1992). Newman (2007, 2012) gives a detailed overview of copyright and legal issues in relation to linguistic fieldwork. For a discussion of ethics and research practice in sign language research see Crasborn (2010) and Singleton, Martin, & Morgan (2015). For a good 'how to' resource, see the frequently asked questions section on the Research Network for Linguistic Diversity (RNLD) website.[9] Join the mailing list! For a very extensive checklist of things to take to the field, see James Fox's list.[10]

## NOTES

1   www.ethnologue.com/ Accessed 27 August 2017.
2   www.unesco.org/new/en/culture/themes/endangered-languages/language-vitality/ Accessed 27 August 2017.
3   http://nationalbreathoflife.org Accessed 1 August 2017.
4   www.eldp.net/en/what+we+do/ Accessed 1 August 2017.
5   www.rnld.org/DRIL Accessed 1 August 2017.
6   www.un.org/esa/socdev/unpfii/documents/DRIPS_en.pdf. Others include The Convention for the Safeguarding of the Intangible Cultural Heritage (UNESCO, 2003) and the Berne Convention for the Protection of Literary and Artistic Works (1886/1979). For information about Indigenous Cultural and Intellectual Property rights in Australia, refer to www.aitb.com.au/information-sheets/entry/indigenous-cultural-and-intellectual-property-icip Accessed 1 August 2017.
7   http://creativecommons.org/licenses/ Accessed 1 August 2017.
8   www.localcontexts.org Accessed 1 August 2017.
9   www.rnld.org/FAQs Accessed 17 August 2017.
10   http://web.stanford.edu/~popolvuh/field-checklist.htm Accessed 17 August 2017.

## REFERENCES

Ahlers, J. C., & Wertheim, S. A. (2009). Introduction: Reflecting on language and culture fieldwork in the early 21st century. *Language and Communication*, 29(3), 193–198.

Austin, P. K. (2010). Communities, ethics and rights in language documentation. In P. K. Austin (Ed.), *Language documentation and description* (Vol. 7, pp. 34–54). London: SOAS University of London.

Benedicto, E., Antolín, D., Dolores, M., Feliciano, M. C., Fendly, G., Gómez, T., Baudilio, M., & Salomón, E. (2007). A model of participatory action research: The Mayangna linguists team of Nicaragua. In *Proceedings of the XI FEL Conference on 'Working Together for Endangered Languages-Research Challenges and Social Impacts'* (pp. 29–35).

Bowern, C. (2015). *Linguistic fieldwork: A practical guide*. Basingstoke (England): Palgrave Macmillan.

Clifford, J. (1983). On ethnographic authority. *Representations*, 2(1), 118–146.

Crasborn, O. (2010). What does "informed consent" mean in the internet age? Publishing sign language corpora as open content. *Sign Language Studies*, 10(2), 276–290.

Czaykowska-Higgins, E. (2009). Research models, community engagement, and linguistic fieldwork: Reflections on working within Canadian indigenous communities. *Language Documentation & Conservation*, 3(1), 15–50.

Doonday, B., Samuels, C., Clancy, E. (M.), Milner, J., Chungulla, R., Whisputt, M., Yoomarie, S., Lulu, V., Johns, A., Brown, S., Vernes, T., Richards, E., & Wightman, G. (2013). *Walmajarri plants and animals: Aboriginal biocultural knowledge from the Paruku Indigenous Protected Area, Southern Kimberley, Australia*. Darwin: NT Department of Land Resource Management.

Janke, T. (2009). *Beyond guarding ground: A vision for a National Indigenous Cultural Authority*. Rosebery, N.S.W.: Terri Janke and Co.

Kroskrity, P. V. (2015). Designing a dictionary for an endangered language community: Lexicographical deliberations, language ideological clarifications. *Language Documentation & Conservation*, 9, 140–157.

Kusters, A. (2012). Being a deaf white anthropologist in Adamorobe: Some ethical and methodological issues. In U. Zeshan & C. de Vos (Eds.) *Sign languages in village communities: Anthropological and linguistic insights* (pp. 27–52). Berlin: De Gruyter Mouton.

Meakins, F., & Nordlinger, R. (2014). *A grammar of Bilinarra: An Australian Aboriginal language of the Northern Territory*. Berlin: Mouton de Gruyter.

Newman, P. (2007). Copyright essentials for linguists. *Language Documentation & Conservation*, 1(1), 28–43.

Newman, P. (2009). Fieldwork and field methods in linguistics. *Language Documentation & Conservation*, 3(1), 113–125.

Newman, P. (2012). Copyright and other legal concerns. In N. Thieberger (Ed.), *The Oxford handbook of linguistic fieldwork* (pp. 430–556). Oxford: Oxford University Press.

Newman, P., & Ratliff, M. (Eds.). (2001). *Linguistic fieldwork*. Cambridge: Cambridge University Press.

Research Centre for Linguistic Typology. (2009). *Fieldwork manual: Fieldwork and your wellbeing*. Latrobe University.

Rice, K. (2006). Ethical issues in linguistic fieldwork: An overview. *Journal of Academic Ethics*, 4(1–4), 123–155.

Rice, K. (2010). The linguist's responsibilities to the community of speakers: Community-based research. In L. Grenoble (Ed.), *Language documentation* (pp. 25–36). Amsterdam: Benjamins.

Rice, K. (2012). Ethical issues in linguistic fieldwork. In N. Thieberger (Ed.), *The Oxford handbook of linguistic fieldwork* (pp. 407–429). Oxford: Oxford University Press.

Seyfeddinipur, M. (2012). Reasons for documenting gestures and suggestions for how to go about it. In N. Thieberger (Ed.), *The Oxford handbook of linguistic fieldwork* (pp. 147–165). Oxford: Oxford University Press.

Singleton, J. L., Martin, A. J., & Morgan, G. (2015). Ethics, Deaf-friendly research, and good practice when studying sign languages. In E. Orfanidou, B. Woll, & G. Morgan (Eds.), *Research methods in sign language studies: A practical guide* (pp. 7–20). London: Wiley Blackwell.

Van der Veen, L., & Medjo Mvé, P. (2010). Theory and practice of data collection for phonological analysis. www.ddl.ish-lyon.cnrs.fr/fulltext/Van%20Der%20Veen/2_Steps_phonological_analysis.pdf

Wasamba, P. (2015). *Contemporary oral literature fieldwork: A researcher's guide.* Nairobi: University of Nairobi Press.

Wilkins, D. (1992). Linguistic research under aboriginal control: A personal account of fieldwork in central Australia. *Australian Journal of Linguistics, 12*(1), 171–200.

Woods, L. (2017). *Ethics in linguistic research and working with Indigenous communities: Redefining collaborative linguistic research, Indigenous and non-Indigenous perspectives* (Master of Applied Linguistics). Monash University, Melbourne.

# 3

---

# Equipment and recording

## 3.1 INTRODUCTION

In Chapter 2 we have already covered some essential aspects of pre-fieldwork planning, such as obtaining ethics approval from academic institutions, designing consent processes for research participants and a more general discussion of the roles and responsibilities of fieldworkers and their relationships to the people they work with. In this chapter we discuss technical tasks that must be completed prior to going to the field, such as choosing recording equipment and learning how to use it (§3.2). We then identify things to consider when using audio-visual recording equipment in a field situation (§3.3). It is important to treat each field session as a unique opportunity. Data collection can rarely be redone in the same circumstances and with the same language experts (Perniss, 2015, p. 57). More detailed discussions of these topics are suggested in the readings at the end of the chapter.

Before we start, we look briefly at an example that poignantly illustrates the fragility of the world's languages, and, in this instance, the technologies used to record them. Fanny Cochrane Smith (1834–1905) was said to be the last surviving fluent speaker of an Indigenous language of Tasmania, Australia. Towards the end of her life, anthropologist Horace Watson recorded her songs and speech on wax cylinders (Figure 3.1). These are the only recordings ever made of a Tasmanian language, and amongst the first sound recordings ever made in Australia (Jacques, 2004). In 2017, the recordings were added to the UNESCO Australian Memory of the World Register, thus recognising their unique value to the heritage of Australia and the world. Sadly, not all of the wax cylinder recordings survived. While the sound of Fanny's voice is preserved for posterity, the wax cylinder recording of her translation of the songs was reduced to "1000 pieces in a box".[1] There was no written transcript of this recording, and the technological solutions that nowadays can be applied to the preservation of such recordings arrived too late. Who knows – maybe one day someone will work out a way to put the pieces back together.

## 3.2 RECORDING EQUIPMENT

It goes without saying that technologies are changing all the time. Without a time machine or a linguists' version of the Tardis that would enable time-travel to distant futures, it is not possible to future-proof every aspect of data collected in

**Figure 3.1**
Horace Watson recording Mrs Fanny Cochrane Smith. Sandy Bay, 10 October, 1903. Photographer: Howard & Rollings, Hobart. Collection: Tasmanian Museum and Art Gallery Q7709

fieldwork. Options for recording many aspects of language have changed dramatically since Fanny Cochrane Smith committed her voice to a wax cylinder. Whereas sound was once recorded on wax cylinders, reel-to-reel tape or analogue tapes, nowadays most items are **born-digital**. Even so, it is important to approach technological innovations with a healthy degree of scepticism. For example, whereas some clay tablets have survived for many thousands of years, the life expectancy of an analogue cassette tape is several decades at the very best. Along with the affordances of technological advances come new practical and technical issues as well as ethical ones. Because technologies are changing so rapidly, in the following sections we limit our discussion to general principles, with little information that recommends particular brands of devices or equipment. It is a good idea to ask around, see what your colleagues or supervisor/advisors do, and refer to online discussions or websites where reviews of technical equipment are posted.

Before making decisions about what kinds of equipment are suitable for your task, try to find out about the kinds of recording locations you will have access to in the field. Is it likely that recordings will be made outdoors or are there community facilities that can be turned into a temporary makeshift recording studio? Will you have access to electricity, or do you need to take lots of batteries or a portable solar

## 50 *Equipment and recording*

panel? Identify the type of recording that will best suit your research needs, and the needs of the community. Your modes of transport for the field trip will also determine what is practical in terms of the size and weight of your equipment collection. If you have access to a 4WD vehicle that is semi-permanently stationed near the field site then your choices will be very different from those you will make if you are travelling, at least part of the way, on bicycle or on foot. Budgets also limit choices. While in general terms you get what you pay for, careful attention to recording techniques enables you to make very good recordings with equipment on the less expensive end of the range.

### 3.2.1 Audio recording equipment

Nowadays audio-visual recordings are born-digital, and the only encounter you are likely to have with old analogue recordings is in the process of digitally 'capturing' analogue data from legacy recordings before the equipment for doing so becomes obsolete. That said, such old recordings may form an important part of the resources that you draw on in developing new research.

When selecting solid state/digital audio recorders, it is important to look out for the following features:

- The recording device must be capable of recording 24 bit, 96 kHz stereo in uncompressed WAV format (24 bit, 48 kHz is also OK, but falling out of favour. Also note that 32 bit/48kHz is recommended for music). MP3 is a compressed format, which discards lots of the audio data and won't capture detail in the sound that may be critical for interpreting the recording. It is less suitable for phonetic analysis, and unlikely to be suitable for depositing in archives. The **bit depth** refers to the number of bits of information in each sample, and the **sample rate**, measured in kilohertz (kHz), refers to the number of samples of audio that are carried per second. In general, higher is better. The trade off in increasing the quality of the signal is that it increases file size. Record at the highest quality your devices can achieve, and buy more hard drives for storage. Or record in mono rather than stereo if you are really running out of space in the field.
- Some digital recorders can record multiple tracks separately, enabling you to isolate the input from different speakers or musical instruments. This is particularly useful for recording conversation and musical performances.
- Sound output: it is important to be able to plug in headphones to monitor the recording.
- Sound input: it must be possible to plug in an external microphone, and to control the recording level.
- Some microphones require power to operate. Some can be powered by internal batteries while others require phantom power which comes from

the recording device. If your microphones do require phantom power, check that the recording device can supply the right level of power, as microphones may require 12V, 24V or 48V. Note that if you are running the recording device on batteries and at the same time supplying phantom power to a microphone, you will go through batteries very quickly!

- Compatibility: the recorder should have the input socket type and sensitivity/level settings to match your microphone choice.

The other thing to consider is the power source for your audio recorder. If you are working in an area with poor access to electricity, rechargeable lead-acid or lithium-ion batteries can be used to power audio recorders. Although there may be an initial cost to modify the power input on the recorder, a charged battery can last 4–7 days (depending on number of hours per day spent recording). Lead-acid batteries are robust, easy to get hold of, relatively cheap, and have a life span of 10–12 years. It is a good idea to take a back-up audio recorder. As a general principle, two of everything is often advised (depending on your mode of transport).

- When using a digital recorder, ensure that you practise with the particular model before the recording session, as some model variations of the same brand recorder have different ways of changing between play/pause/record modes!
- Check the type of memory card that your recorder uses. There are a lot of different standards (SD, CompactFlash, Memory Stick, and MMC to name a few), and even within a 'family' of standards, some devices can't use some of the variations. For example, SD cards come in SD/SDHC/SDXC types. An SD device will not be able to use an SDHC card!
- Some recorders are limited to using memory cards with certain storage capacities. Each device is different, so read the device specifications to find out.
- Work out the storage limits of the cards and find out how that compares to recording time. For example, four hours of 24bit/96kHz/stereo recording will use up approximately 8GB of storage.

### 3.2.2 Microphones

Several microphone types are regularly used in language documentation (for a detailed discussion of the pros and cons of different types see Boyd & Hardy, 2012; Margetts & Margetts, 2012, pp. 24–32). No single microphone will be suitable for all recording situations, so you should have a small range available to suit the variety of situations you expect to encounter. A stereo vocal microphone is good for recording singing and oratory; a head-mounted microphone for phonetic recordings, and a wireless lapel microphone for recording events where people might move around a lot (see §9.4.1.3 on language acquisition studies).

## Equipment and recording

There are a number of reasons why using an external microphone, as opposed to one that is built into the camera or audio recording device, is vital to making good quality audio recordings. Internal microphones pick up machine noise from the recorder itself (even in solid state recorders). This background signal created by the machine is referred to as the 'noise floor' (Margetts & Margetts, 2012, p. 21). Monitoring the recording device is also easier and less intrusive if you are using an external microphone. With a built-in microphone you need to place the recording device as close as possible to the person you are recording. If you need to fine-tune the recording levels and touch the machine while recording is underway this noise will be picked up by an internal microphone.

Microphones can be classified into two main groups: 'dynamic' and 'condenser'. Dynamic microphones are generally more robust and typically don't require power to operate. Condenser microphones generally have better fidelity and require power. Professional condenser microphones minimise noise and distortion and are accurate and sensitive, preserving the full range of frequencies. Both of these types may have different directional characteristics (the spatial range or the area around the microphone where they pick up the most sound). A multi-pattern microphone enables you to switch between different directional patterns:

- Cardioid: basic directional microphone, more sensitive to sound at the front of the microphone than the back.
- Super and hyper-cardioid: even more directional than cardioid and useful for reducing background noise.
- Omni-directional: records sound equally well in all directions around the microphone.
- Figure-8 or cross-over: records sound equally in front and behind.

Microphones are either mono (one track) or stereo (two tracks). Stereo is good for recording conversation and musical events as it captures the depth-of-field of the recording. Depth-of-field can also be captured by using two mono microphones plugged in to the left and right channels of the recording device.

Different styles of microphones are appropriate for different tasks:

- Lapel or Lavalier microphones are clipped to clothing. They are good for quiet speakers, less daunting for nervous people, and work well when there is background noise (machinery, vehicles, groups of people) or where you are trying to target only one speaker.
- Radio lapel microphones are good for use with a video camera where the receiver is mounted on the camera and is the main sound input. They ensure an appropriate sound level even where the camera is set well back from the speaker. A single video camera can usually accommodate two radio mics if they are XLR (one in the L channel, one in the R channel) although mounting two receivers may be difficult (see §9.4.1.3 for an example using zip ties). If you are using multiple microphones, you need a receiver that

accommodates many inputs. This can be very complex to set up, but is good for recording conversational data.

- Head-mounted microphones work well when there is background noise and where you are targeting only one speaker. They are particularly good for phonetic studies as the distance between the speaker and the microphone remains consistent throughout and comparable across different recordings (see §5.10).
- Shotgun microphones are mounted on a video camera, and they are ideal for capturing interactions of large groups of people, as well as soundscapes e.g. birds, and general outdoor ambience. It is possible to place two shotgun microphones in a crossed pattern to create audio depth of field.

---

**Exercise 1  What microphone for what purpose?**

The location for recording a two-person conversation is going to be a tin shed. This is less than ideal as the sound bounces off the tin, making it difficult to hear. The tin can also interfere with radio microphones. What microphones and sound absorption methods could you use? Where would be the ideal place for the language speakers to sit and microphones to be placed?

---

### 3.2.3 Windshields

No matter how good your microphone is, it is important to include a windshield in your kit. Shock mounted or suspension windshields are designed to protect your microphone from wind noise (the sound made by the wind buffeting the microphone) and from the shock and vibration caused by handling the recording device. Other windshields come in many shapes and sizes, and may be known colloquially as 'fluffies', or 'dead cats' because some of them are made from artificial fur. For effective wind protection there should be an inner foam layer and an exterior layer of fluff, and many windshields integrate these two layers. It is important to make sure the windshield is designed to fit your microphone – use a short fitted windshield for a short shotgun (i.e. a 'stubby'), and a small 'minifur' or 'dead kitten' one for a lapel microphone. When filming with a microphone and a windshield that is mounted on the camera make sure the furry bits of the windshield don't intrude into the camera shot. At times it is hard to see this happening in full sunlight conditions and with a small camera monitor, but a furry-framed film can be a very disappointing outcome. One way to combat this is to use hairspray or gel to control the fluff. Sprinkling pepper on a 'fluffy' is a good way to keep dogs from running off with your microphone if it is positioned on the ground.

## Equipment and recording

> ### The rodents ate my windshield! – Murray Garde
>
> Anyone who has ever worked in rural villages in island Melanesia will be familiar with the scourge of rats. A visiting researcher with his or her backpack full of food supplies and interesting equipment is a magnet for the local rat population. In the villages of south Pentecost in Vanuatu I have always had to wage a battle against the very persistent and intelligent rat enemy. In the early days of my fieldwork I used to place any potential rat-attracting supplies into a bag and then suspend this from the roof with fishing line. Any other kind of string or rope is just a rat highway. At times the rats would learn to leap from the walls of my bamboo hut to land on the suspended bags of food in the middle of the room, which I thought was very impressive. Even if I chased them off every half an hour through the night they would keep up the nocturnal acrobatics as soon as I dropped off to sleep again. My village hosts would solve the problem by supplying me with a rat-proof box or bucket and lid in order to keep the beasts out. Never zip up all your rat-attracting packets of food into your backpack. This only causes the rats to gnaw a hole through your expensive pack in order to get to the goodies.
>
> It's not only food that can attract rats. I once lost my Zoom recorder windshield made from soft black sponge to a rat that must have thought it great soft nesting material. I searched all morning for it just before a recording session until I realised it had been taken away to rat land never to be seen again.

### 3.2.4 Microphone cables

Choosing the right cables for your microphone and recording device setup is critical (although in many cases, cables are factory standard and come with the device). Using the right cables protects your equipment, ensures the microphones get the power they need to pick up a signal and prevents unwanted noise from entering the system. Cables are classified according to their connectors and the way they are wired. Common audio connectors include XLR, audio jack (aka mini-jack, 3.5 mm jack, ¼ inch jack) and TS/TRS/TRRS (T = tip, R = ring, S = shield; referring to the configuration of the 'male' end of the connector). The main wiring consideration for an audio cable is whether it is balanced or unbalanced.

- Balanced cables are protected against electrical interference from mobile phones or radio frequencies. Electrical interference in an unbalanced cable can add significant noise to an audio signal. XLR cables are balanced. Most audio jack (3.5 mm/mini-jack) cables are unbalanced. As a general rule, if you use unbalanced cables to connect a microphone to a camera, the greater the length of the cable, the greater the chance of audio interference or crackle. On the other hand, balanced cables can generally be run to over 200 metres without a reduction in quality.

Equipment and recording | 55

- An XLR cable can deliver phantom power from a recording device to a microphone, whereas a mini-jack cable can't supply power. So check if your microphones need to be powered. If they do, can they be battery-powered or do they need power from the recording device? Does the recording device have XLR inputs and provide phantom power?
- XLR cables are more robust than mini-jack cables and are less likely to break. If you need a mini-jack cable try to buy a coiled one that has a 90 degree angle at the plug-in end. This helps prevent the fine wires in the lead from breaking when it is plugged in and the recorder is being moved around.

To work out which cables to use for a session, begin by working out the ideal microphone/s for your situation. What power do they need? If they don't need power or can take batteries, then you can use an audio jack cable. If the microphones do require power from the device you are limited to using an XLR cable. This then restricts your audio recording device to a unit with XLR inputs for the cable. Also be aware of the placement of cables – people may trip over them and the look of a cable snaking its way across the video shot may be annoying for film purists. They can be disguised by covering them over, with sand or with a strategically placed blanket. Lapel microphone cables can be worn under shirts.

---

**Tip – Clutch your cords!**

If you are working in a team it is advisable to label your cords, cables and connectors prominently. It can be very annoying if they get mixed up and you arrive home without a crucial bit.

---

### 3.2.5 Video recording equipment

Video recorders are increasingly regarded as a standard part of the language documentation tool kit and the case for including bodily movement in studies of human communication, discussed in Chapter 8, has been well-argued by others (Seyfeddinipur, 2012). Even if your research is speech-focused and you do not anticipate an interest in visual aspects of communication such as gesture or sign (discussed in more detail in §8.6.3), the speech community may later value video recordings of late relatives or of children now grown up. It is also impossible to anticipate when non-spoken aspects of communication may become crucial to your analysis. That said, using video dramatically increases the amount of data generated, and with this come extra issues about ethics and confidentiality (§2.5), and data storage and archiving (§4.4). The additional expense of the equipment is also a consideration.

If you are planning to use video, consider how many cameras you need. There are many communicative interactions where at least two data viewpoints are

*Equipment and recording*

advantageous. For example in the BSL (British Sign Language) documentation project, four cameras were used to film sign (Schembri, 2010, p. 131). Although having more than one camera may be beyond your budget, and coordinating a multi-shoot event may seem a daunting prospect, it is worth considering the possibilities. You can always recruit others to help! If you do use more than one camera, to make editing simpler make sure that they have similar recording capacities and you use the same frame rates (see §3.3.3).

All of that said, remember that it is certainly possible to use a high-end expensive camera badly, and a lower range one well. There are three main criteria for choosing a video camera:

- There should be an output format of either AVI or AVCHD, which can be edited using professional software such as Adobe Premiere or Final Cut Pro, rather than consumer-grade editing software. Note that AVI and AVCHD are both compressed formats. This is why FCP and Premiere can use them – otherwise there would be too much data in the video stream for the software to cope! Some cameras can record both uncompressed and AVCHD, but they're not generally in the budget range of a field linguist.
- Your camera must have inputs for an external microphone(s) or radio mic receiver (see §3.2.2). It should be possible to control the recording level of the external microphone(s). Linear PCM input is recommended. This is an uncompressed audio data format and closest to the original analogue signal. Make sure your microphone outputs and camera inputs are compatible (i.e. either both mini-jack or XLR) and, if they are not, that you have adaptors. Some cameras have two or more microphone inputs, which makes it very easy to record two people on separate tracks, or to record close-up sound with one and general over-all sound with the other.
- There must be a headphone socket for monitoring sound levels. Headphones should be 'monitoring headphones' which are specifically designed for the range of the human voice.

---

**Tip – PAL is not always your pal!**

If you work predominantly in a particular country, use a camera that has that country's format to save converting to another format for local playback. NTSC is the standard used in North America, parts of South America and Japan, PAL is the format used in the UK, Australia and most of western continental Europe, and SECAM is used in France and Russia.

---

Although hand-held film recording has its place, there are good reasons to purchase a quality **tripod** for your camera(s). Apart from dramatically improving the quality of the film by avoiding the jitters, if your camera is fixed to a tripod this frees up your hands to step away from the event, be less intrusive, and concentrate on other things. Another factor is that holding a camera steady for long periods of time is very tiring.

If you don't have a tripod, a sandbag or a bucket can be a good substitute, or try sitting cross-legged with your elbows on your knees as a make-shift tripod. Small desktop or mini tripods are also very useful for mounting lapel microphones if placing them on a person's body is not an option (§3.2.2). If you anticipate that you'll be panning and tilting (moving the camera sideways and pointing it up or down) while the camera is on the tripod, ensure the tripod has a 'fluid head'. This is a lubricated system that makes for smooth horizontal and vertical motion of the camera. As a note of caution – unless you look after your tripods, the fluid heads can quickly get clogged up with sand and grit!

A **lens hood** to protect the camera lens and to prevent light from hitting the lens from the sides and creating flare is also a good idea. Pictures taken with a lens hood tend to have richer colours and deeper saturation. Don't forget to think about batteries. Many cameras come with a standard size battery that will record for a couple of hours. Most brands provide another larger battery that will fit in the camera, so buy two and develop good battery charging habits. Before a recording session the in-camera battery should be fully charged, and there should be another charged battery ready in the camera case.

### 3.2.6 Still photography

Although language documentation tends to focus on the recording of speech and action, still photos are invaluable as a record of the people, places and processes involved. Such photos can add value to community publications and help illustrate methodology sections in academic publications. For some particular purposes, such as the documentation of linguistic knowledge of plants and animals, a photo may be a very important resource that helps with the identification of species (see §7.2.2). Lastly, photos of people are highly valued, and the linguist may be called upon to supply photos for community purposes such as funerals and coming of age ceremonies.

The principles that apply to making a good video recording (§3.3.3) apply equally to taking a good photo, regardless of the sophistication of your equipment. The same applies to the importance of keeping good metadata about photographs, and curating your collections so that you can find that snap when you need it (§4.2.4).

### 3.2.7 Backups, batteries, memory cards and storage

As mentioned before, think about what you need to back up your data when in the field, and have some strategies in place to deal with equipment malfunction. The general principle about backups – having multiple backups and not having them all in the one physical location – applies as much to the field as anywhere else. This means bringing a range of external hard drives. Nowadays some are marketed as being 'rugged', i.e. able to resist water, dust and being dropped, and while it is best not to put these claims to the test, research the options and read the reviews. Some drives can get their power from the computer; others require a power supply of their own. RAID (Redundant Array of Independent Disks) are drives that combine multiple physical disks into a single unit, and dynamically mirror data across each of the disks, the idea being that if one partition fails the others will take over. That said, it is a well-known

## Equipment and recording

fact that hard drives fail, and this, along with human error, loss, theft and software corruption are all reasons to back up data regularly and meticulously. If you have multiple backups you will feel vindicated if someone sends you a message like, "lucky we did that backup the other day – the other hard drive seems to have crashed!"

When thinking about how much space you might need to back up data, do the maths. The amount of storage you will require depends on the camera you use and the recording settings. For example, a video camera that records at a bitrate of 15Mbps (megabit/second) would require under 7GB for one hour of footage. Bear in mind that the storage space required to edit the footage will be greater – an hour of ProRes 422 25fps material edited in Final Cut Pro will require up to 50GB just for the media, with additional space needed for previews and edit rendering.

Some memory cards are not suitable for the high data rates required for high quality video recording. Check the speed rating of your cards, and their compatibility with your camera. For an SD-type camera, use SDHC or SDXC cards. Consumer-quality video cameras may not be compatible with high-speed cards. Be sure to take spare memory cards in case your camera or audio recorder fills up mid-shoot. Some cameras have two slots that allow for a smooth transition between cards when one card fills up. Check the recording time of your camera batteries and make sure you have a spare, and the battery charger.

Check that you have power adaptors and chargers for all your electronic equipment, and the appropriate country-specific power plugs. Charge everything before you head to the field. You may want to start recording as soon as you arrive! Take extra audio plugs/adaptors and male/female joiners – XLR to audio-jack, RCA to audio-jack, audio extension cables, headphone jack adaptors, microphone and headphone splitters (to allow the use of multiple mics/headphones on a single channel). Always turn equipment off before changing batteries. The electronic circuits in cameras and recorders can be damaged by the sudden power surges of switching batteries while turned on. Repairs can be very expensive, not to mention the inconvenience of doing fieldwork without a recording device! Consider bringing spare drives or USB sticks to leave copies of the recordings behind for the community to use.

### 3.2.8 User-friendly choices

With all these technical specifications about equipment in mind it is also important to consider the kinds of equipment that may already be in use by the speech community, and the capacity of project team members to collaborate in the tasks of audio-visual documentation (Margetts & Margetts, 2012, p. 19). This may mean keying into local schools, councils or media centres (if they exist), and considering your research as part of an overall plan to build local participation and training.

### 3.2.9 Looking after equipment

Find out what you need to protect your equipment. A range of small zip-lock bags are good for storing hard drives, cables and batteries. Keep things with leads in separate bags so that they do not become tangled and damaged. Some audio-visual gear can be packed into robust carry cases known as pelican cases (a medium-sized one with

*Equipment and recording*  59

room for two video cameras, an extra microphone and other bits and pieces weighs around six kilograms). Inside these cases dedicated foam nests can be fashioned to protect the equipment. Other strategies to protect equipment include waterproof bags for rain, river crossings or boat trips. It is very important to keep gear clean, and in some field sites, dust can be a hazard to cameras as well as to other equipment. Buy a puffer brush and a can of compressed air to clean your camera lens.

Extreme high or low temperatures can affect equipment adversely, and working in a humid environment requires extra care. Moving from cool, air-conditioned environments such as a vehicle, to a warm, moist outdoor environment can cause condensation to form inside the camera or on the lenses and this may affect the clarity of the image, or even prevent the camera from operating. If this happens repeatedly, it can lead to mould growing in the camera. To prevent condensation from forming, wrap the camera in something like a dry towel or keep it in a cloth camera bag before moving from a cool environment to warm. This prevents the warm, moist air from coming into contact with the camera. Keep the camera covered until it has had a chance to warm to a temperature above the 'Dew Point', the temperature below which condensation will form. Silica gel crystals, or even roasted uncooked rice, can be added to airtight containers to keep equipment dry and protect it from humidity. Plugs can also be purchased to protect your computer ports from ants and other unwanted intruders.

---

**Solar panels in the field**

The weakest part of our planning turned out to be the most critical of all. The flexible solar panel we had purchased, which we had assumed to be the most robust of all equipment, turned out to simply melt in the Papua New Guinean midday sun. It failed in the first week of use, leaving us with no power for the first month. With an almost entirely digital set up, this was just about the worst thing that could have happened ... with a multimeter, tin foil from a chocolate wrapper and some gaffer-tape, I was able to chain enough of these batteries together to produce enough voltage to run or charge other equipment.

(Honeyman, 2006, p. 20)

---

### 3.2.10 Other useful gear

It is difficult to imagine all the bits and pieces that might come in useful in different field contexts, and, as seen from the example above, odd things come in handy in unforeseen circumstances. It is a good idea to make a checklist of all your equipment. Some suggestions of bits and pieces to include are as follows:

- Fold up camping chairs or stools, gaffer tape and cable-ties (think heist!), extension leads, surge-protected power-boards, a head lamp and waterproof ground sheets.
- USB hubs are handy for charging multiple electronic devices simultaneously.

## 60 *Equipment and recording*

- A GPS device to get an accurate location for your metadata.
- An SD card reader.
- A set of portable speakers to listen back to recordings in a group setting can come in handy (see Feld's story, §3.3.2). Make sure you have a charging solution for these. Bluetooth speakers are problematic in places where people have mobile phones because they constantly roam and cut out trying to connect to other devices.
- A minimal tool kit that includes small Philips-head and flathead screwdrivers and a shifting spanner may be useful for on the spot repairs to equipment or to remove tightly screwed on bolts on microphone stands.

### 3.2.11 Trying things out

Once you have your equipment together, it is a good idea to do some trial runs, right through from setting up the gear and making an actual recording to getting the media files off the recording device. Experiment with different settings and compare their effects. Make sure everything plugs in, and check to see if you need additional adaptors to make your bits and pieces fit together. Check that cables are not frayed or damaged. Practice is key, so that once you are in the field, you can comfortably operate the camera and focus your attention on what language consultants are doing. Take time to study the user manuals for the audio-visual recording devices. You don't want to be leafing through these in the middle of a recording session. Always take a copy of any manuals for equipment that you plan to use, in case you run into technical problems.

### 3.2.12 Before you head off

Make sure you pack first aid kits and telecommunication devices, for example satellite phones, epirbs (Emergency Position Indicating Radio Beacons) or spot tracking devices. Set these devices up and test them before you go. Make sure that emergency phone numbers are accessible. For example, you could attach a laminated list of emergency numbers (local police station, clinic, closest community etc.) to your sat phone. Make sure your family and supervisor/advisor have your itinerary and you have a way of contacting one another in the field in case you need to inform them of any changes to your travel plans. Check the weather – in some field sites it is important to look into the conditions of roads before you drive on them.

When working out what clothes you will need to take, climatic conditions and cultural factors may be considerations. In hot climates wear a hat, and always go for loose fitting, all enveloping garments, rather than short and skimpy ones. Make sure you are aware of which parts of your body need to be covered – it may not always be what you expect. In some communities, for example, it is not considered appropriate for a woman to wear trousers, so long skirts are the general rule.

The weight of all this gear may be a consideration, either because of the mode of travel, or simply because of the health and safety issues involved in lugging heavy gear. Also be aware that many airlines nowadays prohibit passengers from carrying batteries in checked-in luggage, so your journey will be less stressful if you think of this ahead rather than having to deconstruct all of your carefully packed luggage and locate the batteries at the airport check-in counter.

## 3.3 DURING FIELDWORK

### 3.3.1 Safety first

The safety, security, comfort and welfare of yourself (§2.7) and of fieldwork participants is paramount. This is especially important if you are working with senior people, as is often the case in work on extremely endangered languages. Maximise the consultant's comfort. Be culturally sensitive and respectful. For instance, some might feel uncomfortable if you adjust recording equipment, such as lapel microphones, which are attached to the body. Pay particular attention to any safety issues associated with the equipment. This includes, most importantly, safety for all the participants in the research. For example, although the transmitter packs of wireless microphones emit a fraction of the power of a standard cell phone, it may be advisable to think about the placement of these if working with someone who has a pacemaker or similar device. Try to keep the consultant's awareness of the recording equipment and procedure low so that they can relax as much as possible and speak naturally. Ask people if they are more comfortable sitting on a chair, standing, or sitting on the ground. If possible, try to have refreshments close at hand. Take breaks. Be relaxed and attentive to what people are saying. Ensure any microphone stand is stable and won't topple over onto anyone; you may need to put something heavy on its base.

### 3.3.2 Making good audio recordings

The physical conditions where field research takes place vary immensely. Thus, field set-ups for recording language need to be developed in a flexible fashion as a response to the challenges presented by recording film and audio in different environments where heat, cold and wind may impact on the comfort of all participants and on the quality of the recordings. Be observant! Don't be afraid to innovate! What may be possible and practical in some communities where small, endangered languages are spoken contrasts with some research paradigms where recordings are made in experimental situations, usually inside, with the participant sitting on a chair.

If you anticipate recording outdoors, it is important to consider the sound effects of wind (rustling leaves etc.), and other environmental factors, such as the sound of rain (e.g. on tin roofs), birds chirping, dogs barking, flies and other insects buzzing, the noise of passing vehicles and so on. Some of these sounds might be welcome aspects of the acoustic records of your work, but others are definitely not. Think about aspects of the environmental surround that may cause interference with the signal. Recording close to a tin roof may induce some interference if you are using a wireless set-up. If you are working inside sounds from air conditioners, clocks, urns and fridges can also be detrimental to a recording, and you may be so accustomed to these sounds that you hardly notice them (until you listen to your recordings later). It is often harder than you think to find a quiet place where human voices can be recorded with clarity. It is also a fact that the more naturalistic the field session, the less likely it is that your recordings will be 'studio quality'. For much linguistic work this does not really matter. That said, there are certain steps that can be taken to ensure the best quality audio in the circumstances, such as thoughtful selection and placement of microphones (§3.2.2).

---

### Andrew Dowding connects with his grandfather through song

I observed elders listening to these recordings many times. The intimacy of their encounters with the songs varied greatly, but on the occasions that I watched their reactions I was always struck by the evocative power that the songs seemed to have for them. My own experiences were similar. Many times I would be listening attentively to the words of the song, but also to the very fine detail captured by the microphone, such as the murmur of a child in the company of the singer, the accidental rattle of an object near the performer, the barking of a dog, the sound of a performer shuffling uncomfortably while being interviewed. All these small details of the recordings gave colour and a vividness to the image of my grandfather that was conjured in my mind. Subtle noises on the recordings – not just the songs – created a sense of context in my imagination. They filled in details around the song and the stories. The context would then be mulled over with my own family: we would ask 'Who is that kid in the background?' or 'He must be sitting on the veranda'. There is power in this process. These legacy recordings became more than just the audio files of songs; they promoted social relatedness and connectedness across time. In my case, the recordings gave a feeling of connectedness to an elder I never met; a relatedness conjured internally to support the intergenerational transfer of knowledge from my grandfather to me.

(Treloyn & Dowding 2017, p. 63)

---

### Tip – Unwanted sound effects!

If people are seated on the ground or on a 'ground-sheet' think about unwanted sound effects! Even a slight change of position on such a surface can sound very loud. Crackle-proof ground sheets, e.g. ones made from canvas, are advised.

---

When recording sound, the aim is to maximise the amplitude of the speech signal, while at the same time avoiding clipping or signal distortion. As shown in Figure 3.2, clipping occurs when the amplitude of the signal exceeds the maximum range, and it introduces high frequency components. This is particularly problematic if you're

Figure 3.2
View of an audio waveform in Audacity that shows a well-recorded segment of speech contrasted with a segment where the levels were set way too high and there is extreme clipping (Illustration: Maxine Addinsall)

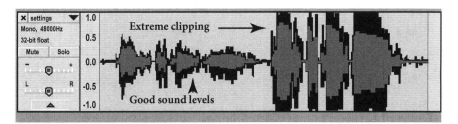

interested in any kind of spectral analysis of speech. If a single person is being recorded, the microphone should be close to their mouth, but not too close. If you are recording groups of people, thought needs to go into the placement of the recording devices. In some contexts, for example when recording songs that are owned collectively, individuals may not want their own voice on the recording to stand out against the voices of others. If using a lapel microphone, they should be clipped to the upper chest, and the lead should preferably go under clothing (if appropriate) so that the leads don't get in the way. Don't put microphones in people's pockets, as the abrasive sound of the microphone rubbing on fabric if the person moves will be picked up on the recording. If the speaker is wearing a hat this can be the ideal place acoustically to put a microphone (but may look weird on film so this needs to be weighed up for future playback in the community). Note, however, that if you are recording co-speech sign or gesture, the articulation of body-anchored signs or gestures may inadvertently impact on the microphone if it is attached to particular parts of the body.

If there is a lot of background noise, such as generators or rain, directional or lapel microphones are the best choice. You may think the background noise is not very loud at the time, but it will sound louder when it is played back. Once you are recording, minimise any movement of the microphone or stand; not only will this sound very loud on the recording, but the recording may also sound as if the speaker has moved, especially if it is a stereo microphone. If a car or a motorbike drives past right in the middle of a good story, ask the consultant if they mind re-doing the recording – it's a lot easier than trying to fix it later.

It is important to wear headphones so that you can monitor the quality of the sound you are recording, at least at the beginning (this practice can be difficult to maintain in elicitation sessions where you are talking a lot yourself). When recording outdoors, wind conditions can vary and so you may need to change from a 'fluffy' to the suspension windshield. In field situations where exposure to the sun can be a problem, sports headphones or earphones might be compatible with wearing a hat and are less cumbersome and obtrusive. In musical events, which have a large dynamic range, you should use monitoring headphones throughout, as you may need to alter levels and move microphones. If you are participating in the performance, it is a good idea to get someone else to monitor the recording.

Don't forget to record important aspects of the context of the recording session. If the session involves multiple conversations, or even if the session is a more traditional question and answer routine, make sure the audio signal from all participants is recorded with clarity, and, if necessary, adjust the placement of the microphone(s) accordingly. For instance, if somebody asks questions and the recording does not pick these up, recordings of answers such as "Yes. No. Yes" without further context may be next to useless. It is a good idea to record a few minutes of ordinary conversation before you start the session proper, as this will enable you to adjust the sound input to appropriate levels. Some people speak louder than others, and be aware that their voice may get even louder as the session continues and they relax! Record the linguist/elicitor at the beginning of the recording, giving some general facts about the session, the date and time of day, the participants, and the location of the recording. Also record a few minutes of the ambient environment with the same microphones that you'll be using for the main session. If there is general background hum or noise, this 'noise-bed' can make it a lot easier to clean up the audio later.

---

### Feld in the field

When musicologist Stephen Feld commenced fieldwork in Papua New Guinea he saw the need to be able to play recordings back to people straight away.

> At that time, 1973, I bought one of the first stereo Nagra recorders imported to the United States ... In order to demystify the whole thing I ran a lead out of the Nagra into a small cassette recorder so that everything I was recording on reel-to-reel generated a simultaneous cassette copy. I would later sit down with the reference cassette and a bunch of headphones and play the recordings back to people. It was important to play back over headphones rather than over loud-speakers because I didn't want the sound to dissipate into the world. I wanted people to listen to the recording as I had been listening when I originally recorded it. So we would sit down around the cassette recorder with one, two, three, four, five people wearing headphones and they would spontaneously start talking about the recordings as they listened. I soon realised this was the beginning of a whole methodological programme for recording and feedback and more recording. I came to call this method 'dialogic editing' and was inspired by Rouch's similar experimental methods in film feedback. Recording wasn't just about gathering things but it was the invitation to a conversation about what was going on in the world as recorded, about what we were listening to, how we knew and questioned the world by listening to it, how we edited and arranged its meanings like a composition. This became a method through which I could really engage people, so that's how it became the foundation of a dialogic recording process and the basis of all the research I did in New Guinea across the lines of language, music, song, and rainforest ecology.
>
> (Feld, 2013)

### 3.3.3 Making good video recordings

Although the capacities of 'prosumer' or semi-professional cameras are developing at an exponential rate, at the end of the day a poor camera set-up will result in disappointing outcomes, and even a high-end expensive camera can be used badly. While many use their camera successfully on automatic settings, using the manual settings provides much better control over the recorded image. If you switch to manual mode, make sure you understand the basic principles of photography and the ways that different parameters such as **focus**, **exposure**, **aperture** and **shutter speed** interact. Practise first, and be aware of the implications of choosing different settings before you get to the field. For example, a fast shutter-speed will capture sharper high-speed actions (fast motion or gesturing), but will require more light for the image to be well-exposed than a slow shutter-speed does. Video frame rates, or frames per second (fps) refer to the number of individual consecutive images that are captured by the camera each second. For good capturing of movement a higher frame rate is better. The typical options are 25, 30, 50, and 60fps. Higher frame rates capture more data, and play back motion more smoothly than lower frame rates do. They also result in correspondingly larger video files. If you have the choice, progressive mode results in crisper, clearer images, than the alternative, which is called the interlaced mode.

Observe the light in the recording situation and consider ways to get the best results in the circumstances. Learning how to set the **white balance** for your camera will greatly improve the exposure of the shot by giving the camera a reference point for what 'white' is in the particular condition. A sheet of white paper or fabric which fills the camera frame is used for this calibration process. Once the camera registers the parameters of white, it will adjust accordingly for the other colours. This can be done automatically and most cameras have a range of preset modes.

When filming outside the results will be better if there is even light – preferably full but low sunlight with no intrusion of dappled shade, the shadows of narrators and interlocutors, or of the recording rig. Early morning or late afternoon light is preferable to avoid shadows cast over people's faces by hat brims (even beanies) or eyebrows during the midday sun. Whatever your film location, you will get better results if light sources are behind the camera, and you shoot "with the light" (Margetts & Margetts, 2012, p. 39) rather than with the light behind the subject. Backlighting can lead to under-exposure of people's faces (unless you are very skilful at adjusting manual settings). For example if you are filming inside do not seat people in front of a window. Consider a dark-coloured panel of shade cloth to hang behind people if they are sitting in the shade; this can greatly improve visual quality by darkening and evening out the background. In some situations your recording may be improved by strategic use of a reflector, so that the light bounces off the reflector and adds illumination to people's faces (see Figure 3.3). These come in standard fold-up varieties, but it is also possible to improvise by using anything large and white or shiny.

Check the horizon line and make the camera level – some tripods have a spirit level which helps with this, but note that a tripod resting on sand or soft ground may get out of kilter very easily. Take time to frame your camera shot and make sure it accomplishes the aims of your research project. The importance of ensuring that the camera angle established is wide enough to capture all of the action is akin to the need to get the settings right when making audio recordings. If the camera is too close to the 'subject' this can lead to the loss of valuable data. If you are studying signs or gestures that employ a large signing or 'gesture space', it is frustrating if some of the details of how the signs or gestures formed are off-camera. Keep in mind that dynamic human interaction is by its very nature unpredictable. It is better to take a wide view that will encompass all of the 'action' than to zoom in and out, focusing on details but then probably missing subsequent relevant ones. Zooming and panning is an art that is usually poorly executed by amateurs (most field linguists!) and should be avoided. The use of film in language documentation is very different from making a movie, and it is best not to imagine that your framing problems will be solved by some magical process in post-production. Using several cameras that take different views is one way to achieve both a close-up and a distant perspective. This may be of particular importance if you are recording songs or performances with lots of people involved. When in doubt take a wide view!

Consider how the people you are filming look, and, if possible, seek local advice about any community-specific considerations. For example, are there ways of sitting that would be seen to be culturally inappropriate? In Arabic cultures, revealing the soles of your feet, or the bottom of your shoes, is regarded as being disrespectful. In other communities women will only sit with their legs to the side, or only sit cross-legged if their groin is well covered by billowing skirts. Is the clothing worn by the consultants 'presentable', or more to the point, will people be happy about how they look when they review the films later? You don't want to spend many hours filming only for the participants to decide in retrospect that they wished they had different T-shirts on or didn't have their petticoat showing! Particular patterns in clothing, for example fine stripes, are to be avoided (if possible), as they can lead to unwanted film effects. In some filming situations, the dazzling effect called the 'moiré effect' stems from interference between fine detail in the scene, and the sensors in the camera. When filming sign language, the colour and pattern of the clothing can also make a difference as to how easy it is to see the fine details of the articulation of the hands (see Chapter 8).

---

### Filming sand stories in Central Australia

Sand stories are a traditional narrative form in which skilled storytellers incorporate speech, song, sign, gesture and drawing (Green, 2014). To understand how the visual aspects of these stories work together, a filmed sand story performance needs to capture the use of the gestural space around the narrator, as well as the use of the ground in front of them. To achieve this sand stories were filmed with two cameras, thus capturing two viewpoints simultaneously. One camera, attached to a lighting stand, pointed vertically down and filmed the sand story space on the ground from above. The height of the boom was sufficient for the camera to capture the breadth of this space. This simple device is stable, yet it can be moved easily to adjust for movements of shadows and minor relocations of the storytelling space. The other camera, attached to a tripod and placed at a distance, captured a front view of the narrator, including the gestural extent of their arms (plus any augmentation provided by storywires or sticks). Audio is recorded using a separate audio recorder (see Figure 3.3).

Figure 3.3
Recording Kaytetye sand stories. Carol Thompson, Myfany Turpin and Tommy Thompson (Photo: Jennifer Green). Gear (i) 2 HD digital Panasonic video recorders, (ii) Fostex FR2 digital audio recorder, (iii) Rode NT4 microphone in a Rode Blimp windshield on the microphone stand, (iv) Sennheiser wireless microphone pack, (v) two tripods, (vi) lighting stand, (vii) reflector, (viii) two sets of headphones, (ix) pelican case for the video gear
Source: Green & Turpin, 2013

> ### Exercise 2  Light in your recording
>
> This recording took place in early morning light. What direction is the narrator facing? What is the benefit of early morning light for this type of recording?

We recommend recording audio on a separate device to the video camera. If the video recorder has an audio input, it is useful to send the output of the audio recorder directly into this with an XLR cable. If this is not possible, it is very important to synchronise all recording devices by making both a distinctive audio signal, like a loud clap, and a visual one. The old film clapper-board made a sharp 'clap' noise that can be easily identified on the audio track, and the visible action of closing the clapperboard could be identified on the video. Make sure that claps don't frighten children or dogs or interfere with claps that may be an important part of some musical performances. Although some video editing software will automatically synchronise separate files together, it is best not to rely on this method.

It is simpler in the long run if single sessions are recorded in one 'take'. Multiple small clips make for curatorial nightmares! If you are using two or more recording devices, it is even more important to make sure they are all turned on, or off, at the same time. The less fiddling with the gear, the more likely it is that people will relax. As is the case with audio-only recordings, it is good practice to audio or video record identification of the time, place, participants and other general information about a session before you start the recording proper (see metadata §4.2.4). If for some reason the recording needs to be stopped, make sure that the team who are operating the recording equipment all turn their equipment off at the same time, and that the identity of the subsequent 'take' is well documented. When you are ready to start recording again, ensure that everyone turns the equipment back on!

> ### Exercise 3  Peak clipping in video
>
> What do you think the visual equivalent of clipping an audio signal is? How would you set up a camera to avoid this?

### 3.3.4  Keeping good notebooks

Systematic note-keeping is an important part of both linguistic and anthropological field methods. Information recorded on the spot in notebooks can be very valuable even if some notebooks include off-the-record information that is not destined for posterity. Before digital recording techniques became ubiquitous and affordable, the notebook may have been the primary record of fieldwork. Today it is still important not to neglect the benefits of notebooks and let technological developments become a substitute for more traditional methods (Duranti, 1997, pp. 115–116). Keeping daily notebooks helps you to keep track of people, places and dates, field recordings, the tasks you have completed and what is still left to do, and all manner of other information that will eventually become part of your metadata (§4.2). Notebooks are also a good place for sketch maps and diagrams, either made by yourself or others in the research team.

Hardcover stitch-bound notebooks made of acid-free archival quality paper are best. Some prefer to use smaller format A5 size notebooks that are easier to carry in backpacks or handbags than are some larger A4 size ones. It is a good idea to use waterproof pens, and to write on one side of the page to avoid ink bleeding through and making the reverse page illegible. Some linguists only use the right side of the page for fieldwork sessions and keep the left page for later comments. Cross-references should be made in the notebooks to all field recordings. Notebooks can be sorted by date or by topic, depending on the diversity of your fieldwork locations and types of recordings. Make a note of all abbreviations and symbols that you use (Bowern, 2015, p. 52). Using a diary to keep track of the different tasks in each fieldwork session, and to note emerging hypotheses and to plan future work may be a good idea. Other linguists use the pages at the back of their field notebooks for this sort of information.

If you are using notebooks extensively or checking printed drafts of dictionaries or other resources, it is not a bad idea to use different coloured pens for subsequent checking sessions. The different colours can help you sort out when you made a correction to a previous annotation. For example, if you check something three times, it might be unclear which annotation was the final correction. But if you used red for corrections in the second session and green in the third session, you know to take notice of the green corrections. Coloured pens can also be useful for coding different kinds of information, for example which speaker told you what in a single recording session, which pronunciation of a word came from whom and so on. Of course you need to archive the code for your colour scheme, and hope that the colours don't fade over time!

## 3.4 THE FIRST FIELDWORK SESSION

If you are new to the language and the speech community, your first fieldwork session should involve eliciting words within a simple semantic domain, as we outline in Chapter 7. In this section we discuss the process of recording and conducting the first fieldwork session. It is a good idea to try to record one speaker in a quiet location. Other people may want to be present, but multi-party conversational interactions are too complicated to manage and transcribe, at least as a first step. Keep this first session very simple and well-planned. For this first session it is a good idea not to demand too much concentration from the speaker (and yourself) and at the same time reinforce the fact that they are the experts in their own language. Use this first session to establish a good rapport with the speaker and put a meticulous recording and management routine in place.

# Equipment and recording

Before you begin have a brief conversation with the speaker to help you both relax and feel comfortable together. The sorts of things that constitute such 'small talk' in cultures differ. If you are not sure what this is, you can always begin by saying how happy you are to be starting this work and how you are looking forward to working on the language. Following this you will need to discuss the project in general terms. Official documentation of consent might be done later after you have recorded the session and participants have a clearer idea of what they are consenting to (§2.5).

You will need to set up and test your equipment. Explain to the speaker what you would like to do in this session and run through one or two questions so that you both know what to expect. Write down basic metadata (date, time, place, speaker, topic) (§4.2.4). Do a dry run and check your equipment again. Make sure your recording device is in view so that you can see if the audio levels are right, if the batteries are getting low, or if the card is nearly full. Being able to focus on your elicitation while monitoring your equipment is a necessary skill that will develop the more you do it. When you are both ready, turn on the recording device and record some simple metadata, including the name of your field notebook and page number. Begin the elicitation. At a suitable point, after a few minutes of work, stop the session and play it back for the speaker to hear (you won't need to do this in all subsequent sessions). Continue the session.

It is important to avoid being proscriptive about what the consultant should and shouldn't say. Crowley (2007, p. 96) suggests that one of the golden rules of elicitation is to never tell the speaker that they have misunderstood. Even though you may want to hear only the target word with two repetitions; such requests may make people feel bored and unwilling to work with you in the future. If the speaker offers the word in an example sentence, even better. Don't worry if you can't understand what people are saying straight away. Rather focus your attention on writing down what you think the target word is as accurately as you can. In the initial stages of fieldwork it is good to learn a handful of useful expressions that will help you to work with people in their language, such as "Can you say that again please?" or "Could you talk a bit slower".

Once you think you have heard a target word accurately and written it down, it is time to check your pronunciation with the speaker. Take careful note of their response. You want to avoid a situation where the speaker is giving you positive feedback simply because they perceive that you are trying hard and they don't want to hurt your feelings, or because your pronunciation is close (§6.6.1). Hesitation, facial expressions or tone of voice will often tell you more than their words about how well you have pronounced the word. Always write down what they say, even if you know it's not the answer to the question you asked. Try asking your question a different way and if that doesn't work move on and come back to it another time.

At the end of the session thank the speaker and everybody who has participated. Play the whole session back to the speaker. The speaker may make some corrections or additional comments and will now be in a good position to discuss archive and access conditions; and you should now document consent (§2.5.2) and complete any other speaker-related metadata. If there is some local way of leave-taking or expressing completion, it may be a good idea to conclude each fieldwork session in this way. This first session may be no longer than 1–2 hours, including chatting, playing back recordings and paperwork.

## 3.5 AT THE END OF THE DAY

It is important to transfer your recordings from the device to a computer as soon as you have made them. It is easy to delete a file on your recording device thinking that it has been transferred already, or transferred successfully, only to find out that something went wrong. The safest approach is to have a routine at the end of each day that involves (a) transferring the recordings onto a computer, (b) checking the transferred files, (c) adding basic metadata and (d) backing all of this up on an external drive. Checking the day's recordings and adding metadata helps prepare you for the next recording session – perhaps you forgot to ask an important question, or maybe a dog barked, or an aeroplane flew overhead at a crucial point in the recording.

At the end of each day it is good practice to wind up cables, charge batteries, and check and clean the gear. If you have opted for low-tech solutions and approaches to language documentation, you will have rather less to do! In the next chapter we discuss processes for working further with data, right through to archiving the results of your efforts.

## 3.6 SUMMARY

This chapter has outlined procedures for effectively using audio, video, photography and notebooks in the field. We discussed requirements for selecting recording equipment, including the ideal specifications for microphones, cameras and audio recorders for use in particular field conditions. The chapter emphasised the importance of practising how to use your equipment before setting out. We ran through ways to conduct your first recording session in the field, and methods to make these first sessions as enjoyable and successful as possible. We concluded with the end of the recording session when the day's recordings and field notes are transferred, checked and backed up.

## 3.7 FURTHER READING

A comprehensive discussion of audio visual recording techniques is given in Margetts & Margetts (2012). See also Enfield (2013), Perniss (2015), and Seyfeddinipur (2012) on methods for documenting sign and gesture. Duranti (1997) gives a detailed discussion of methods in linguistic anthropology. For further descriptions of issues that may come up in the first fieldwork session see Bowern (2015, Chapter 3).

## NOTE

1   www.abc.net.au/radionational/programs/drive/fanny-cochrane-smith-and-horace-watson/8256806 Accessed 1 August 2017.

## REFERENCES

Bowern, C. (2015). *Linguistic fieldwork: A practical guide*. Basingstoke (England): Palgrave Macmillan.

Boyd, D. A., & Hardy, C. (2012). Understanding microphones. In D. A. Boyd, S. Cohen, B. Rakerd, & D. Rehberger (Eds.), *Oral history in the digital age*. Institute of Library and Museum Services. http://ohda.matrix.msu.edu/2012/06/understanding-microphones/. Accessed 29 August 2017.

Crowley, T. (2007). *Field linguistics: A beginner's guide*. Oxford: Oxford University Press.

Duranti, A. (1997). *Linguistic anthropology*. Cambridge: Cambridge University Press.

Enfield, N. J. (2013). Doing fieldwork on the body, language, and communication. In I. C. Müller, E. Fricke, A. Cienki, & D. McNeill (Eds.), *Body-language-communication* (pp. 974–981). Berlin: Mouton De Gruyter.

Feld, S. (2013). On field recording: Steven Feld interviewed by Angus Carlyle. In C. Lane & A. Carlyle (Eds.), *In the field: The art of field recording* (pp. 201–212). London: Uniform Books.

Green, J. (2014). *Drawn from the ground: Sound, sign and inscription in Central Australian sand stories*. Cambridge: Cambridge University Press.

Green, J., & Turpin, M. (2013). If you go down to the soak today: Symbolism and structure in an Arandic children's story. *Anthropological Linguistics*, 55(4), 358–394.

Honeyman, T. (2006). Powerless in the field: A cautionary tale of digital dependencies. In L. Barwick & N. Thieberger (Eds.), *Sustainable data from digital fieldwork* (pp. 17–22). Sydney: Sydney University Press.

Jacques, J. (2004). Passing the torch: Commemorating the songs of Fanny Cochrane Smith. In D. Crowdy (Ed.), *Popular music: Commemoration, commodification and communication* (pp. 11–20). Proceedings of the 2004 IASPM Australia New Zealand Conference, held in conjunction with the Symposium of the International Musicological Society, 11–16 July, 2004, Melbourne.

Margetts, A., & Margetts, A. (2012). Audio and video recording techniques for linguistic research. In N. Thieberger (Ed.), *The Oxford handbook of linguistic fieldwork* (pp. 13–53). Oxford: Oxford University Press.

Perniss, P. (2015). Collecting and analyzing sign language data: Video requirements and use of annotation software. In E. Orfanidou, B. Woll, & G. Morgan (Eds.), *Research methods in sign language studies: A practical guide* (pp. 55–73). London: Wiley-Blackwell.

Schembri, A. (2010). Documenting sign languages. *Language Documentation and Description*, 7, 105–143.

Seyfeddinipur, M. (2012). Reasons for documenting gestures and suggestions for how to go about it. In N. Thieberger (Ed.), *The Oxford handbook of linguistic fieldwork* (pp. 147–165). Oxford: Oxford University Press.

Treloyn, S., & Dowding, A. (2017). Thabi returns: The use of digital resources to recirculate and revitalize Thabi songs in the West Pilbara. In J. Wafer & M. Turpin (Eds.), *Revitalizing song* (pp. 56–67). Canberra: Pacific Linguistics.

# 4

# Data management, annotation and archiving

## 4.1 INTRODUCTION

Now that you have made some recordings and the data has been transferred from the recording devices and backed up, the next step is to learn how to manage all of this material. This chapter leads you through aspects of data management, and ways to transcribe and annotate the recordings. It is a good idea to begin to deal with the important aspects of data management as soon as is practical, or else matters can quickly get out of hand. The first aspect of this is deciding on systematic ways to name the files you create (§4.2.1). Associated with this is the process of recording and storing metadata relating to the recordings (§4.2.3). We then move on to discuss the different ways that linguistic data can be transcribed and annotated (§4.3), thus setting the foundation for various types of analysis. Finally, we discuss some issues involved in archiving linguistic data, maximising the chances that your data will be useful in both the immediate and the far-distant futures (§4.4). Whether or not some of these tasks can be undertaken in the field or not will depend on many factors – the length of time you are able to spend there, internet access and so on, but establishing good practices early on saves a lot of time in the long run. Also keep in mind that fieldwork can be viewed as an iterative process, with refinements of tasks building up over time.

## 4.2 FIRST STEPS IN DATA MANAGEMENT

### 4.2.1 File naming

One of the most important principles of data management is the notion of the **unique identifier**. In simple terms, this means that any object, such as a recording, a photo or a scan of a sketch in a notebook, needs a consistent and unique **file name**. The core part of the file name should remain the same across related file types, including media files, annotation files and metadata files. Only the file name extensions need vary (for example, .mov, .wmv, .wav, .mp4, .eaf, .imdi, .cha etc.). This name is thus a way to link multiple objects (media and annotation files) to a single recording session or to identify a bundle of media items that need to stay together.

It is important to settle on a consistent system for your file names early in your research, and then stick to the system. This is a big ask, especially if there are many collaborators on a project, but inconsistent and untidy practices lead to more work in the long term. There is almost nothing more frustrating than trying to weave your way through a labyrinth of random file names in an attempt to sort out which objects are identical, which are different, and which are related in some way.

You do not need to include lots of information in a file name. Dates, names of participants, languages and other information are best recorded as metadata (see §4.2.2). The important thing is that the file names are partly memorable (i.e. not too long), consistent and sequential. Also bear in mind that various archives will have different requirements as to the formats and constraints in file naming conventions, and this may extend to the number of letters and other components a name is allowed to have (§4.2.3). Table 4.1 shows a few file naming strategies – the first is an example of a 3-part name (JD2008) + (052) + (A). The second style is useful if you are working on multiple languages, while the third set is a more 'semantic' naming system, where the file name is prefixed by the type of session (i.e. sign language) and the date of the recording is part of the file name. In the long run the **persistent** part of the equation means that, once given, the name should stick. The **unique** part envisages that no-one in the world with the initial JD will make an audio recording numbered '052_A', and that on 7 November 2016 nobody else will use the same convention for naming a sign language recording (and archive them in the same place!). Also keep an eye out for software that can assist by batch-naming files, thus preventing errors and saving time.

Table 4.1

Examples of file naming

| Example file names | Components |
| --- | --- |
| JD2008_052_A.wav | JD=linguist initials; 2008=year of recording; 052=recording session; _A=sub-session (e.g. when you turned recorder off to have a tea break, or to change microphone between speakers); .wav=file type |
| MUD2008_052_A.wav | MUD=abbreviation of language (and see above) |
| JD2008_MUD052_A.wav | |
| Sign20161107_01.mov<br>Sign20161107_01.wav<br>Sign20161107_01.eaf<br>Sign20161107_01edit.mp4 | Sign=type of recording; 20161107=date of recording; _ 01=the first session recorded on that day; .mov=file extension for film; .wav= file extension for audio; .eaf= file extension for ELAN annotation file; edit=indicates a derived file or compilation made from the primary data, and .mp4 a file extension for film |

## Tip – File naming

- Do not use '.' in the file name. Most computer systems will mistake this for the beginning of a file extension. Instead use '-' or '_' to separate information in file names. In addition '-' and '_' have different statuses in some archiving systems so be consistent in how these are used.
- Even if you envisage never having more than 99 recording sessions, it is a good idea to use three digits just in case, e.g. 099, not 99. It is probably too hopeful to use 0099!
- When noting the date of a recording, use the format YYYYMMDD (if YYMMDD or MMDDYY is used this may result in some ambiguity e.g. 071206 might be 6 December 2007, 7 December 2006, or, in the American style, 12 July 2006).
- Define all 'shorthand terms' e.g. speaker initials and abbreviated versions of place names in the associated metadata.

If part of your workflow is to export segments or derived files for a website or some other purpose then it becomes even more important to be consistent in the naming of these new files so that you can trace them back to the original recording (see §4.2.1). You may choose to have the original file name as part of the segmented file name; however, it is important to keep the details of the steps taken to make derived files and the system you have chosen to name them as part of the metadata for the collection of recordings. For an example of the workflow employed to derive sign language clips for a sign language website, see §8.7.4, and for an example of how to make clips of songs for community distribution, see §11.10.

## 4.2.2 What is metadata and why is it important?

Metadata is data about data. Metadata essentially answers the **who, what, why, where, when** and **how** questions about a fieldwork session. It refers to any information about a recording, and this applies equally to still photographs, audio and video recordings, as well as written records kept in notebooks. Metadata can be used in various ways as a means to help classify, identify and locate objects. Without metadata there is a great risk that field recordings will become disconnected from details of the context in which they were made and make it virtually impossible for people to find them in the future. Even in the short term, managing sets of files that have little or no metadata becomes a difficult task. Without metadata there is little chance that your data will 'transcend time'. Think back to that precious recording of Fanny Cochrane Smith discussed in §3.1. Although some of the pieces are missing, we still know her name, where the recording was made, and what equipment was used. Adding and curating metadata may seem daunting at first, but if it is done regularly and systematically it becomes easier.

Best practice recommends that metadata be recorded as a basic part of the process of collection, *in situ*, and not afterwards. Even as you get caught up in the

76 Data management, annotation and archiving

ebb and flow of everyday events in the fieldwork situation, it is important to be disciplined about taking note of various aspects of data collection, either during or immediately after a recording session. Although you may *think* you will remember everything, in all likelihood this will not be the case. Additionally, the process of checking transferred files and creating metadata points to gaps and errors in recordings that can be remedied while you are still in the field.

### 4.2.3 Categories of metadata

There are many metadata standards. One example is the Open Languages Archive Community (OLAC),[1] an international partnership of institutions and individuals who work towards consensus on best practice for the digital archiving of language resources (Bird & Simons, 2003). The ISLE Meta Data Initiative (IMDI)[2] is another schema that has been endorsed and adopted by some documentary linguists, particularly those who worked through the DoBeS program (Documentation of Endangered Languages program funded by the Volkswagen Foundation).

Looking at the array of metadata that it is possible to record, and trying to work out what is most important for your project, can be an overwhelming prospect. We suggest you start with a simple set of categories, such as those in Table 4.2. For other examples see Bowern (2015, p. 234; IRCA, 2015).[3]

Some metadata may be automatically written or embedded into a file by a recording device, such as a camera, and this can include information about exposure, focal length, the dimensions of an image, whether or not a flash fired, the make of the camera and the time that an image was captured. Many audio recorders use the Broadcast Wav Format (BWF), which holds the minimum information considered necessary for broadcast applications, including an embedded time stamp. Many recording devices also allow the GPS location of the recording event to be automatically recorded. Metadata for video will include some categories that apply to still photos, but in addition will indicate the duration of the recording.

Table 4.2
Some metadata types and categories

| Metadata types | Some categories |
|---|---|
| Recording as a whole | Language; Session number; Content summary; Recorded by; Speaker(s); Others present; Date; Time; Place; Location, direction; Prompts, tasks and context |
| Participant metadata | Name(s), gender, date and place of birth, ethnic affiliation or clan; languages spoken or understood; languages spoken by family; residential history; profession, education or social position; skills: storyteller, interpreter, recognised cultural elder |
| Cultural rights | Cultural use; Archiving instructions; Community copies returned; Restriction start/end date |
| Technical metadata | File name; Folder/location; Transcription/annotation file; Recording Equipment; Media type: Audio/Video; Format, Encoding format; Physical format |
| Administrative metadata | Recorded/created by; Recorded/created when; Annotated by; Processing complete; Archived (Y/N) |

Once a media file is transferred to a computer, the computer captures elementary metadata, including information about when an object was created, who created it, when it was last updated, the file size and the file type. For sound, this may include the sample rate, bit depth, duration and whether or not the recording is mono or stereo.

Other metadata needs to be documented manually. Metadata about the recording event itself includes a description of the event, information about the participants, their relationships to each other, age, and genders, the languages used and the relation of these to accepted language codes, the roles of onlookers, transcribers, translators and researchers, any tools or stimulus materials used, and camera angles. For analysis of verbal art it may be important to know additional information, such as the reasons for the performance. If you are doing phonetic studies you will want to know if the language examples were read or spoken. Metadata about cultural rights and use includes whether or not the recording is open, closed, restricted, and any family, bereavement and gender-related restrictions. Administrative metadata includes such things as when the record was made, who made the record, whether transcription or translation has been undertaken, whether archiving and permission processes have been completed and copies returned to the community.

For written texts the following basic metadata should be documented: writer(s), translator(s), compiler(s) and/or editor(s) name(s), where written, when written, publishing details, typescript and genre.

---

**Exercise 1  Deciphering metadata**

Look at the image of an old analogue tape in Figure 4.1. What metadata can you extract from what you can see? What other questions would you like to ask about this recording? What could go wrong if the label falls off?

---

### 4.2.4 Where to keep your metadata

Once you have assembled all the metadata, you need to work out where to keep it. As seen in Figure 4.1, fragments of metadata were once attached, written onto or stuck to an object such as a cassette tape, even if the code to decode their content was not always evident. With digital data the link between any persistent identifier such as a file name and all the rest of the information about the recording must be systematically stored somewhere. There are several approaches to this. The first, appropriate for simple data sets, is to use text files or spreadsheets such as Excel. The second is to create a relational database using database software such as FileMaker Pro. The data in such databases can be exported in various formats. Figure 4.2 shows an example of some of the categories that can be included (see Thieberger & Berez, 2012, p. 107).

**SayMore**, a language documentation tool built by SIL, can also be used for tasks including organising metadata, auto-segmentation of media, and transcription and translation, although it currently only operates in a Windows environment.[4] Whatever system you choose, remember to back-up your catalogue!

Figure 4.1
Metadata attached to a recording made on a cassette tape

Figure 4.2
A simplified view of the structure of a relational database for keeping track of metadata
See also Thieberger & Berez, 2012, p. 107 (Illustration: Jennifer Green)

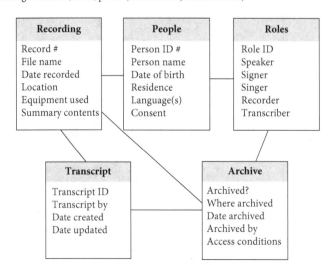

## 4.3 TRANSCRIPTION AND ANNOTATION

**Transcripts** are a tool of the linguistic trade, and the term usually refers to some type of graphic representation of an utterance. To make one you may employ a dedicated notation system such as the International Phonetic Alphabet (IPA) (for phonetic or phonological transcription), or a script such as the Latin, Chinese or Arabic one. Although sign languages are not generally written down, some transcription systems that have been developed for them are discussed briefly in §8.7 (see also Johnston, 2010, p. 110).

The choices you make about what you transcribe depends on your research questions, and what the transcript is to be used for. Ochs (1979, p. 44) writes that "a more useful transcript is a more selective one" reflecting the fact that only certain dimensions of language can be represented in any particular transcript at one time without it becoming overloaded with detail. The extent to which a transcript can and should accommodate multiple research interests and goals varies. What everyone agrees about, however, is that transcription is very time consuming. A very general rule is that one hour of audio recording can take up to ten hours to transcribe. Of course this varies depending on how well you know the language, how complex the language on the recording is (e.g. multiple speaker conversation vs single speaker word elicitation) and what level of transcription you require. Transcribing at the word level will be less time consuming than making a phonetic transcription. Transcriptions using Conversation Analysis methodologies, where, for example, the length of pauses are indicated, will also take longer.

Broadly speaking, **annotation** refers to the addition of other layers of interpretation to primary data. This may include a standard written form, but in addition many other aspects of language including phonological structure, morphological glosses, parts-of-speech, and information structure categories. The list goes on and, again, depends on your research interests (see Schultze-Berndt, 2006).

### 4.3.1 Time-aligning transcriptions and annotations

It is impossible to overstate the advantages of **time-aligning** transcriptions and annotations to the media itself. In the old days, transcriptions may have been made by hand into notebooks, or into text files on a computer, with time codes for segments of speech or other relevant information optionally noted down. Nowadays multimedia annotation software makes it possible to gain instant access to the exact place in the recording because transcriptions and media can be time aligned. Another huge advantage is that this significantly reduces double handling of the data – for example by having to type up hand-written transcriptions, and then time-align them to the media at a later date. Although it may take a little time to learn how to use these tools, the benefits are enormous. These tools are developed with researchers in mind, and they are improving all the time as new functions are added to meet the demands of the research community. Below we lay out some of the dimensions of several well-known tools that are used for transcription and annotation.

## 4.3.2 Software tools

Various software packages are used to assist with segmenting, transcribing and annotating speech, and some of these are also designed to work with video. Note that not all software runs on all computer platforms. For example, SIL International software no longer works on Macs except in a virtual PC environment and even then functionality may be limited. Another consideration may be how easy it is to learn to use the program and how readily data can be moved to another program that may have additional features that you require in your workflow. A question worth asking is whether the program is widely used and whether there is a support group to assist you if you get into trouble using it. It is good to ask around, look at online forums and see what support systems are close at hand for learning how to use the new tools. Note that some software is **open source** and freely available to use and even modify if you have the skills and inclination, whereas others are **proprietary** and can only be opened by related programs with access to the source code restricted.

ELAN[5] is one of a suite of tools that has been developed by The Language Archive at the Max Planck Institute for Psycholinguistics in Nijmegen, the Netherlands (Wittenburg et al., 2006). Up to four video clips can be imported into ELAN and synchronised prior to annotation. ELAN enables the user to design their own annotation tiers, and any annotations entered into these are time-aligned to the visual and audio media. ELAN supports imports from various script systems, and allows exports to Shoebox/Toolbox, CHAT, Praat and to tab-delimited text files, interlinear text and subtitles text. ELAN enables searches using regular expressions, either within a single annotation file or across multiple files that have been defined and saved as a search domain. It is also possible to export selections of media and their annotations from ELAN as discrete media clips. Although ELAN was designed with video users and sign language and gesture researchers in mind, it is possible to use it simply to annotate audio files. ELAN is supported by a detailed manual outlining its many functions, and a forum where users can post queries about any issues they encounter when using it.

Some of ELAN's basic features are shown in Figure 4.3. You are already familiar with the recording set-up for this session of Kaytetye sand story narration, which can be seen in §3.3.3. Now we can see that the video and audio from that session have been imported into ELAN. The video viewer allows you to look at the video; the waveform viewer gives a view of the sound and the media controls allow you to move backwards and forwards in the timeline. The tiers are the visible part of the template. A template can be re-used across your data set, and shared with others. In this example we show a simple template with only two tiers – one for the transcription of speech, and the second for a free translation of the speech. If you want to read more about the example shown in Figure 4.3 see §11.7. Finally, the timeline viewer is where you enter your annotations. In Figure 4.3 you can see three sets of annotations in the timeline viewer. In the right-hand side of the screen you can see that a total of seven annotations have been added to the Text-Speaker tier. You can also see their time codes displayed in the window. A more detailed discussion of some of the features of ELAN and its use in sign and gesture research and a more complex example of a template is shown in §8.7.

**Figure 4.3**
Representation of a screenshot from an ELAN annotation file with a video clip and an audio file imported (Illustration: Maxine Addinsall)

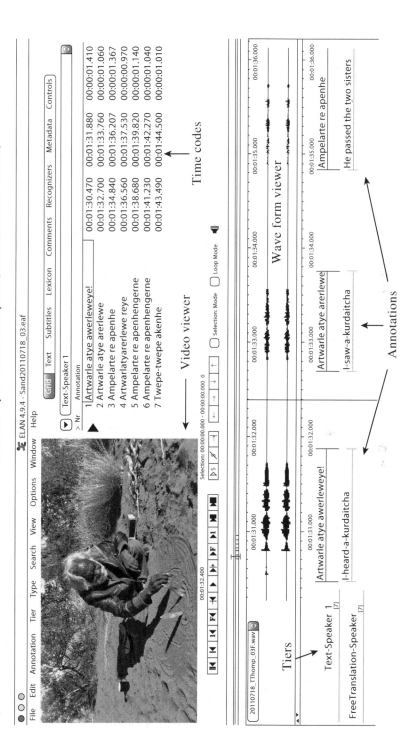

**CLAN**[6] is an annotation and statistical analysis tool that has a large community of users in language acquisition (§9.4.1) and Conversation Analysis. The coding and search capabilities of CLAN also make it a powerful tool for quantitative studies of variation and language contact (§10.4.2). It was developed as a part of the CHILDES (Child Language Data Exchange System)[7] project whose aim was to build a large database of homogenously formatted, accessible and analysable child language corpora from a variety of languages (MacWhinney, 2000). Currently there are around 130 corpora in the CHILDES database, covering a range of languages including English, German, Afrikaans, Catalan, French, Japanese and Cantonese. It consists of two main components: the annotation software, CHAT, and the associated statistical package, CLAN. CHAT can be used without CLAN; however, CLAN is dependent on well-formatted CHAT transcripts. An example of a CLAN file can be seen in §1.4.

CLAN has sophisticated search capabilities. The %mor tier allows simultaneous coding of part-of-speech, language (if it is a multilingual setting), morphological gloss and other features such as animacy, information structure category, grammatical relation etc. This means that large-scale quantitative searches can be done instantly using either CLAN functions or Python scripts. Because CLAN is formatted as UTF-08, it is possible to edit multiple files in a text-editing program such as **TextWrangler**.

Despite these advantages over ELAN, the CHAT file itself allows less complexity in relating different types of annotation in comparison with ELAN files. Unlike ELAN, CLAN tiers have a direct one-to-one correspondence with the speaker tier, which allows less flexibility in relating the tiers to the media file. A difference between the two is that whereas ELAN can deal with multiple video files, CLAN only has the capacity to import one.[8]

Other less complicated options for transcription include **Simple-ELAN**, which allows for transcription of audio or video on a single layer (i.e. on a single tier), and **F4transkript**. The latter has the advantage of having an optional plug-in foot pedal for fast typing (see review by Jones & German, 2016).[9] **Transcriber** is another free and easy to use tool.[10] All of these are good for doing a first parse of orthographic transcription.

### 4.3.3 Segmentation

In the ELAN example shown in Figure 4.3 you can see three distinct sets of annotations that have been added to the time line. You can also see that there are seven items visible in the pane on the right-hand side of the screen. The process of deciding how long to make each annotation is called segmentation. Decisions about the segmentation of data, where it is sound (speech and song) or forms of action (gesture and sign), are fundamental to the annotation workflow. Segmentation of data in each modality raises its own specific issues and the choices you make, and the level of granularity you require will depend on your research questions. It is generally accepted that some sort of utterance level unit is fundamental. In speech, intonation is recognised as performing a "basic delimiting function across languages"; even as the reliable coding of speech into intonation units (IUs) is a complex exercise in itself (Himmelmann, 2006, pp. 258–270). Although it is generally agreed that there is no single criterion sufficient for isolating IUs, significant pauses, pitch movement and vowel lengthening have all been suggested as criterion for the delineation of IU boundaries.

In the example, segments have been broadly selected on the basis of extended pauses between instances of speech. This is one good reason to include the wave form in your ELAN file, even though you can hear any sound recorded by the video camera – the inclusion of the wave form means that stretches of sound and silence are easy to see. For phonetic analysis of speech the units of segmentation are going to be much shorter, and the program **Praat** is designed specifically for this purpose.[11]

### 4.3.4 Transcription techniques

Transcription can be very tiring work, requiring persistence and concentration. That said, it is also a great opportunity to learn the language by careful, repeated listening. You should try to do as much transcription as you can in the field to give yourself the opportunity to check transcriptions with speakers. There is nothing worse than arriving home and trying to transcribe without such expert feedback. It is often less onerous if you work in a team (see §8.5.1 for an example of how teams of people with different skills can effectively work together, and §9.4.1.6 about team transcription and triaging transcription tasks). Invest in comfortable headphones, audio-splitters or quality speakers to make the task more enjoyable. As there are sure to be segments that you don't understand at first parse, it is a good idea to use a consistent symbol to identify these segments so that you can easily search for them later (e.g. \*\*\* in ELAN and & in CLAN). Make sure the symbol you choose isn't meaningful in the transcription program. If there are differing interpretations of what was said, additional tiers can be used to keep track of this variation or different speakers' opinions – variation can sometimes be the key to unravelling a puzzle. Lastly beware of tiring everybody out!

## 4.4 ARCHIVING

Long-term preservation of primary data is one of the central tenets of language documentation practice, and a core component of the documentation workflow (Gippert, Himmelmann, & Mosel, 2006, p. v). An archive can be defined as "a trusted repository created and maintained by an institution with a demonstrated commitment to permanence and the long-term preservation of archived resources" (Johnson, 2004, p. 153). A box of documents, tapes or hard drives kept under the bed or in a cupboard is not an archive; neither is your computer! All the terms used by Johnson above point to the need for researchers and communities to make informed judgements before committing to a destination for their research materials. How do you know whom to *trust*? How is the commitment to *permanence* assessed? What is meant by *long-term*? And should you archive everything that you record in the field anyway? It is also helpful to make a clear distinction between the short-term care of data, which begins as soon as the data is generated, and the notion of long-term archiving where research materials are kept for posterity.

---

### Why archive?

For myself and many colleagues, a major incentive to engage with digital archiving was to seek a strategy for coping with an ever-increasing private collection of audio and videotapes, originating from various research projects over the years, materials for which it became ever more difficult to find a machine that would allow the data to be used in the future. Increasingly, there are also recordings, usually audiotapes, produced and kept by members of the speech community, but they frequently get recorded over after a while or are lost in closed collections.

(Widlok, 2013, p. 4)

---

Before the end of the twentieth century, physical objects such as notebooks, photographs and analogue recordings on wax cylinders or magnetic tapes were generally donated or bequeathed to museums, libraries, universities and to dedicated archival institutions. Gaining access to these records now often involves a lengthy processes of negotiation, and frequently entails journeys to view material on site. The fieldworker often mediates such journeys, and these links between communities and archives are upheld by real or imagined expectations of ongoing personal connections. The inevitability of the fieldworker's passing, a lack of resources (or desire) to return to field sites, and many changes in personal and political circumstances all add up to a perception that some archives are not really for the people whose cultural materials they house (Ingram, in press; Seeger, 2004).

The question of who uses an archive and for what purposes is a very important one, and the answers will vary from community to community, and over time. Modern archives may engage diverse audiences, including community members, scientists of language and other related disciplines, and the general public (Conathan, 2011; Woodbury, 2014, p. 21). Whereas linguists may access archives of primary data in order to test out particular theoretical questions, speakers of endangered languages may look to an archive for very different reasons. Of most value may be the sound of a long-lost relative's voice, a fragment of a song that almost everybody has forgotten, an account of an historical event or a photograph (see Holton, 2012; Wasson, Holton, & Roth, 2016, p. 649).

Since about 2010, developments towards participatory models for linguistic archiving have attempted to break down traditional boundaries between depositors, users and archivists and to expand the audiences and uses for archives. The importance of the involvement of speaker communities in archival processes has gained increasing recognition (Henke & Berez-Kroeker, 2016, p. 428). This may entail

_Data management, annotation and archiving_  85

devolution away from the large archival institutions and the formation of smaller, locally based derivative archives. Such models may enable more direct interactions between the archive and community of origin (Ingram, in press; Seeger, 2004; Treloyn & Emberly, 2013). This reflects an increasing desire and expectation that collecting institutions will strive to empower speech communities and allow them a greater role in the direction and management of cultural collections. Nowadays there are various options to access materials online, and these bring great opportunities as well as new challenges.

### 4.4.1 Exploring archives

One way to begin to understand what is involved with archiving is to become an archive user yourself. Look at the practices in place for accessing records of various languages, and see what particular archives say about their processes for depositing data and for enabling access to the archive. Is it by registered users only or is it open access? Do any conditions put in place have a built-in expiry date? Do the archives have a catalogue, and if so how easy is it to use? What language, or languages is the metadata in? Find out if there are costs involved to get copies of the data out of the archive again, either for you, for people from the community you work with, or for complete outsiders; and whether or not archives have a long-term plan if funding to support their functions is not guaranteed into the future. Below we give brief descriptions of some archives, beginning with large archives with a more global scope, and then moving to examples of archives that have a more regional or language-specific focus.

#### ELAR (Endangered Language Archive)[12]

ELAR is a digital archive for materials on endangered languages, based at SOAS, the University of London. ELAR supports the preservation of digital materials, including audio and video recordings, of endangered languages from around the world. Much of the material at ELAR has been generated by the ELDP (Endangered Languages Documentation Program), which provides funding in annual grant rounds to enable scholars to undertake documentation of disappearing languages. ELDP also trains grantees and local scholars in language documentation methods. As an example of an ELAR corpus see the Gurindji Kriol documentation project (§10.2.3).[13]

#### TLA (The Language Archive)[14]

TLA was established in 2011 at the Max Planck Institute for Psycholinguistics in Nijmegen (the Netherlands) to house the materials created by documentation projects and to develop linguistic resources and tools. It holds linguistic data from over 60 languages generated by programs such as the DoBeS program, which was funded by the Volkswagen Foundation. For an example of a TLA corpus, see the Chintang/ Puma DoBeS documentation project (§9.2).

## PARADISEC (Pacific and Regional Archive for Digital Sources in Endangered Cultures)[15]

PARADISEC was founded in 2003. As of 2017, PARADISEC holds more than 7,000 hours of audio recordings, and represents over 1,080 languages. Depositors can specify conditions on the access and use of their data, and only registered users can access primary records. Access is password protected and users have to click an agreement detailing conditions of access.

## ANLA (Alaska Native Language Archive)[16]

ANLA is the main repository for information relating to the Native languages of Alaska. The archive serves researchers, teachers and students, as well as members of the broader community. Prior to the founding of the Alaska Native Language Center by state legislation in 1972, linguistic documentations for these languages were scattered in archives, libraries, and attics across the globe. These materials include original manuscripts from the Russian-American era and wordlists collected by early arctic explorers. In addition, the archive serves as a repository for educational materials developed by Alaska Native speakers and linguists. Parts of the collection are accessible via web portals tailored to individual languages. The archive also continues to partner with Native organisations to facilitate local access in remote regions.

## C'ek'aedi Hwnax Ahtna Regional Linguistic and Ethnographic Archive

C'ek'aedi Hwnax is located in the Copper River valley of south central Alaska. It is the first OLAC-compliant, Indigenously administered digital language archive in North America. It represents the Ahtna community's desire for local control over decades' worth of irreplaceable linguistic and cultural recordings, and represents a model of distributed linguistic archiving. The University of Alaska Fairbanks provides permanent off-site backup of the Ahtna collection on its servers and allows C'ek'aedi Hwnax full administrative control over access to the collection at the university. In this model, the responsibility for administration of language materials traditionally held in a central location is apportioned to different parties according to their needs and resources (Berez, Finnesand, & Linnell, 2012).

## AILLA (Archive of the Indigenous Languages of Latin America)[17]

AILLA houses audio and video recordings in a wide range of genres including narratives, chants, oratory, conversations and songs from many of the hundreds of severely endangered Indigenous languages spoken in Latin America. Many recordings are transcribed and translated into Spanish, English or Portuguese. The collection includes grammars, dictionaries, ethnographies, field notes and teaching materials for bilingual education and language revitalisation programs (Woodbury, 2014).

## AIATSIS (Australian Institute of Aboriginal and Torres Strait Islander Studies)[18]

AIATSIS holds the world's largest collection dedicated to Australian Aboriginal and Torres Strait Islander cultures and histories. Over 500 cultural groups are represented within the collection. The AIATSIS sound collection houses approximately 40,000 hours of audio, most of which is unique and unpublished. The film collection contains more than 5,000 video titles and 6.5 million feet of film and includes published film and video titles as well as prints of historical ethnographic films and other documentaries.

---

### Bush potatoes – the mother of all archives!

One way to conceptualise the ways that archives work is to think about the ways that some of the larger, well-resourced archives may act as the major repository for collections of linguistic data, yet at the same time spawning related smaller archives or local access systems. This is sometimes referred to as a "hub and spokes" model (Wasson, Holton & Roth, 2016, p. 659). Let's return to the semantically rich terminology used by Alyawarr people when talking about *anaty*, a species of bush potato from Central Australia, and the subject of the cover design for this book (see Chapter 1). In Central Australia, Indigenous people value this type of yam as a food source. If the *amikw* or mother yam is dug up the lifeline to some of the *akwerrk* or baby yams is cut. The converse is not so, and baby yams can be harvested without restraint. This metaphor from the domain of plants provides a way of thinking about the relationship between major archives and derivative ones (Figure 4.4).

Figure 4.4
Bush potatoes as an illustration of a "hub and spokes" model of archives (Drawing: Jennifer Green, 1978)

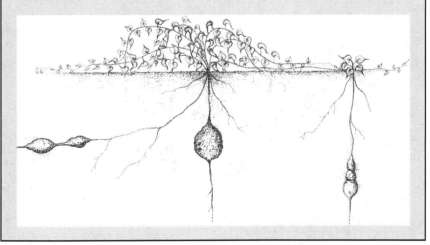

---

## 4.4.2 Depositing in archives – when, where, what and how?

It is generally recommended that, subject to ethical issues, "data should be archived immediately and often" (Thieberger & Berez, 2012, p. 100). However, it is important to consider what to archive, and to curate your collections in a principled way. Archives should not be treated as data dumps. Remember to archive the instructions, for example permission forms that should include cultural considerations such as future access (§2.5.2), and the colour code for your pens (§3.3.4), as well as the objects themselves. Imagine your archive deposit as a collection that contains all the keys to the original information: this may include field notes, particular fonts and details of the technologies used. It is best to look carefully at the requirements of the archive of your choice, as preferred formats for different types of archiveable materials may vary. Keep in mind that higher quality uncompressed versions or media are best for archival purposes, while lower resolution versions may be the only practical way for data to be accessed, particularly if access is online (§7.7.2). Some archives also have different requirements for legacy and 'new' materials, as well as for the structure of the metadata and the naming of files. Make sure you keep a record of all the materials you deposit.

At the community level, you may also encounter situations where archiving instructions conflict. For example, some may ask you to destroy a recording or photo for cultural reasons, such as in response to bereavement, but others in the community may anticipate that in the future these same recordings will be much sought after and valued by descendants of the speaker. These issues are not easy to resolve, but it is helpful to document people's intentions at the time you make recordings. It is important to try to keep in touch with research participants, even if on "the other side of the digital divide" (Singleton, Martin, & Morgan, 2015, p. 15).

---

**Exercise 2  Making a corpus accessible to the speech community**

You work in a community which does not have electricity or access to the internet. The community wants to make use of your work in the school. How do you ensure that a corpus is useful in a community that does not have access to the online corpus?

---

## 4.4.3 Landing pages and access platforms

Another way that access to linguistic and related materials can be improved is by carefully designed landing pages that provide a guide to archival collections. These may be envisaged as a kind of 'meta-documentation' or a user's guide to the collections you have curated (Woodbury, 2014, p. 25). Topics may include descriptions of your research, its design, methods and outcomes, as well as other more extensive treatments of the standard details of the participants and stakeholders that are already included in your metadata (§4.2). Chances are that you have already partly written this as a requirement of your research proposal! All of this contextual information can help others interpret your data in the future, and provide a user-friendly way into the heart of the collections. An example of a comprehensive description of a documentation project is one featuring the Ikaan language, spoken in two villages in southwestern Nigeria (see Salffner, 2015).[19] This research was designed to look at phonetic and phonological variation among speakers, but was based on a documentary corpus about knowledge of food, food production and farming amongst the Ikaan. A landing page for the Daly languages of northern Australia includes an interactive map, lists of language resources and links to archival deposits.[20]

### 4.4.4 Challenges for archives and their users

We know that the linguistic diversity of the world is diminishing rapidly. Some estimates are that between 50 per cent and 90 per cent of all currently spoken languages may disappear within the next four to six generations. A lesser known fact is that a high proportion of existing recordings about little known languages and cultures may also be lost over the next few decades unless something is done to preserve them. Most analogue recordings are at risk, but even digital material needs a lot of effort to ensure lasting availability. Digital file types and hardware become obsolete as technology evolves. Consequently, digital files created now may not be accessible in the future unless files stored on hard drives are updated as technology progresses. Everybody wants to avoid what some have termed 'data graveyards', one consequence of format obsolescence and the lack of capacity to keep up. Modern archives face immense challenges as the amount of digital material generated is rising exponentially. They also bear the onerous responsibility of migrating digital materials from one format to another. Although this has always been the case, in fact, "the crisis we have now is the time between the technological obsolescence of one format to another is much shorter than it used to be" (de Souza et al., 2016, p. 27). It is also abundantly clear that archives that may have been established with language in mind are being used for purposes that were not originally envisioned by their creators (Wasson, Holton & Roth, 2016, p. 646). Some of the challenges for archives and collections in the digital age are:

- enabling long-term sustainability for the future safeguarding of materials;
- finding expanded storage capacity solutions, including distributed preservation models;
- maintaining digital platforms, websites and online portals for digital access and display;
- determining preservation priorities and standards in a rapidly changing digital environment;
- determining acquisition policies in the face of increased born-digital and community-generated context;
- uneven distribution of communications technologies and infrastructure in remote and regional locations.

(after de Souza et al., 2016, p. 27)

The challenge for fieldworkers is to adequately reflect archiving options to the communities they work with, and to make sure that metadata, including that which details cultural rights to materials, is comprehensive and forward thinking. This is no easy task, as the profiles and possibilities of archives change in our lifetimes, as do community expectations about access to materials. It is also the case that many of the most highly endangered languages are found in communities that are the least connected to global networks, and this notion of the 'digital divide' reflects a somewhat paradoxical situation. If you are working in such communities, it is important that you don't bring outsider assumptions to the task, and that you do a bit of local scoping to assess the most appropriate ways of returning the results of your research to the people you work with. Also keep in mind that part of the fieldwork process should involve providing community-relevant copies of research materials in ways that suit particular local capacities – whether this be in the form of copies of materials on USB sticks, on CDs or in printed forms.

---

### Tip – Everybody does not have power!

Although the academic documentarian may see a suitable electronic archive as the best way of preserving and disseminating material, for local Third World community members, such an electronic product is rarely of direct value. When community members have no access to electricity, let alone technical equipment, computers and the internet, an electronic archive serves no practical use at all in the short to medium term (Bowden & Hajek, 2006, p. 46).

---

### 4.4.5 Scholarly recognition and transparency

There is growing recognition of the work that goes into archiving in a responsible way and of the value that collections of linguistic data have for future generations of language communities and language scholars alike. What everybody also knows about is the enormous amount of work that can go into curating, annotating and translating even small amounts of data. At times this objective may be at odds with the aims of your research questions, even as it provides many unforeseen benefits. All scholars need to strike a balance between producing traditional outputs – theses/dissertations, academic papers – and following the directions of their host communities in terms of community outputs. The conversation has begun about appropriate academic recognition for archives of primary data, alongside more traditional scholarly outputs such as grammars, dictionaries and text collections. Although there are well-established systems that recognise publications as scholarly outputs, as yet there are no agreed upon metrics for assessing primary data and curated collections of recordings (Thieberger et al., 2016).

### **4.4.6** The open access question

There is increasing pressure from the scientific community, and from those who generously support the development of archives, to make as much linguistic data as possible openly accessible. There are several reasons for this. For a start, citable, transparent data makes for an open academic community that is able to share data and investigate corpus-based claims about languages from across the world. Being able to share your own data and access that of others makes sense in terms of the research dollar invested in projects. Providing easy access to data sets can encourage others to get involved in working on a more diverse range of languages rather than on more well-known languages that have more documentation and larger corpora.

Another reason is that, for archives themselves, managing complicated access restrictions into the future is time-consuming, logistically challenging and expensive. Most archives simply do not have the resources to follow up contacts that may be outdated, difficult to locate or may have simply disappeared. The default go-to person is usually the researcher who made the recording in the first place, but clearly the practicality of this has an inbuilt end-date.

Nonetheless, one argument against open access is that rapid changes in technology may enable access to data for uses that may not have been imagined when the research took place and the consent and access were discussed. For example, before online access to archives was possible, consultations about keeping linguistic materials safe may have been put in terms of archives that were seen as being much like libraries. The possibility that materials could be viewed and downloaded from the internet may not have been imagined.

Knowing that linguistic records are destined for open access may skew the kinds of language it is possible to record in the first place. While elicitation of grammatical paradigms may be uncontroversial, naturalistic recordings of conversation and interaction may be otherwise, as they are often personal by nature. The more relaxed the filming sessions and the closer they approximate some 'naturalistic' goal, the more likely it is that people may say or do things on camera that are not intended for posterity or for public viewing (Margetts & Margetts, 2012, p. 15). The issue may become even more acute for particular types of language, such as ritual language. Linguistic records may also contain information that can be viewed as controversial and contentious in some circumstances. For example, in some countries records of language created in a linguistic context may contain materials that prove to be relevant to legal processes such as substantiating claims to traditional lands. Created in one context, the records can take on a life of their own in others. Another factor is that people may change their views over time. In Indigenous Australia we have seen, for example, a rapid change in opinions about whether images of the deceased can be viewed, and their voices heard. Whereas once this was highly taboo, at least for a considerable time after a person's passing, nowadays many people have changed their views about this and access is more open.

On the other hand, some records of what seems to be knowledge in the public domain can become more restricted over time. For example, John Haviland (2016) returned to a community in Northern Queensland with a film he had made some 40 years earlier to find out what the descendants of those featuring in the film wanted to do with it. The film was about traditional methods of preparing *gambarr*, a tar-like substance used for manufacturing spears and spear throwers. The descendants of those who made the film decided *not* to include the film in their local archive.

Some of these concerns can be addressed by discussing access to the fieldwork data very thoroughly during the consent process (§2.5) and by fostering ongoing relationships between the archive and the community (Ingram, in press; Seeger, 2004). Reviewing your data by playing it back to people after they have had time to consider the implications of making their language materials available to others is also important. It is also a very good idea to seize any opportunity to explore archives with the people you are working with. Many people are genuinely delighted and proud to see that their language can be viewed and appreciated the world over, and most see archives as a safeguard against the loss of valuable cultural knowledge. Others may, however, decide that they want to place some restrictions on access, and these requests must be honoured.

## 4.5 SUMMARY

Travelling to a new field site, meeting people to work with, and making the first recordings is a very exciting experience. What may seem to be less glamorous are the careful processes of data management that will in the long run ensure that your work practices are efficient, that you don't lose or misplace recordings and, finally, that your recordings are archived in appropriate ways so that future generations will benefit from your research. This chapter has dealt with the nuts and bolts of some of these processes – file naming, metadata and techniques for transcription and annotation. We also discussed some of the issues involved in archiving, and accessing archives.

## 4.6 FURTHER READING

Further discussions of workflow and technical aspects of language documentation can be found in Margetts & Margetts (2012) and Thieberger & Berez (2012). For discussions of research methods in sign language recording, and annotation of sign languages, see Crasborn (2015) and Perniss (2015). See Barwick (2012) for research methods in recording music. The SIL International website contains a wealth of information about tools for language documentation.[21] See also the RNLD website[22] and the First Voices website.[23] Henke & Berez-Kroeker (2016) provide a very useful overview and annotated bibliography of archiving in a language documentation context and Wasson, Holton & Roth (2016) give an overview of different models for archives as well as a discussion of the diversity of the needs of their users. For a discussion about citation and attribution of linguistic data see Berek-Kroeker et al. (2018).

## NOTES

1 www.language-archives.org/ Accessed 17 August 2017.
2 www.mpi.nl/IMDI/documents/documents.html Accessed 17 August 2017.
3 The 15-element Dublin Core Metadata Initiative (DCMI) can be seen at http://dublin-core.org/documents/dces/ Accessed 17 August 2017.
4 http://software.sil.org/saymore/ Accessed 23 August 2017.
5 https://tla.mpi.nl/tools/tla-tools/elan/download/ Accessed 23 August 2017.
6 http://childes.talkbank.org/access Accessed 31 August 2017.
7 http://childes.talkbank.org Accessed 31 August 2017.
8 A review of CLAN is given in Meakins (2007) and a CLAN CHeAT sheet to get started has been developed by David Osgarby and Tom Ennever, www.dynamicsoflanguage.edu.au/research/resources-for-linguistic-tools/ Accessed 28 August 2017.
9 http://hdl.handle.net/10125/24701 Accessed 25 August 2017.
10 http://trans.sourceforge.net/en/usermanUS.php and https://sourceforge.net/projects/trans/files/transcriber/1.5.1/Transcriber-1.5.2-ElCapitan.dmg/download Accessed 10 Janury 2018
11 www.fon.hum.uva.nl/praat/ Accessed 23 August 2017.
12 www.elar-archive.org/about/ Accessed 23 August 2017.
13 https://elar.soas.ac.uk/Collection/MPI171874 Accessed 23 August 2017.
14 https://tla.mpi.nl/home/history/ Accessed 23 August 2017.
15 www.paradisec.org.au Accessed 23 August 2017.
16 www.uaf.edu/anla/about/ Accessed 23 August 2017.
17 www.ailla.utexas.org Accessed 23 August 2017.
18 https://aiatsis.gov.au/collections/using-collection/search-collection Accessed 23 August 2017.
19 The collection can be found at https://elar.soas.ac.uk/Collection/MPI636676 Accessed 17 August 2017.
20 www.dalylanguages.org Accessed 25 August 2017.
21 www.sil.org/language-culture-documentation Accessed 17 August 2017.
22 www.rnld.org/node/149 Accessed 17 August 2017.
23 www.firstvoices.com/en/home Accessed 17 August 2017.

## REFERENCES

Barwick, L. (2012). Including music and the temporal arts in language documentation. In N. Thieberger (Ed.), *The Oxford handbook of linguistic fieldwork* (pp. 166–179). Oxford: Oxford University Press.

Berez, A., Finnesand, T., & Linnell, K. (2012). C'ek'aedi Hwnax, the Ahtna Regional Linguistic and Ethnographic Archive. *Language Documentation & Conservation*, 6, 237–252.

Berez-Kroeker, A. L., Gawne, L., Kung, S. S., Kelly, B. F., Heston, T., Holton, G., Pulsifer, P., Beaver, D.I., Chelliah, S., Dubinsky, S., Meier, R. P., Thieberger, N., Rice, K. & Woodbury, A. C. (2018). Reproducible research in linguistics: A position statement on data citation and attribution in our field. *Linguistics, 56*(1), 1–18. https://doi.org/10.1515/ling-2017-0032

Bird, S., & Simons, G. (2003). Seven dimensions of portability for language documentation and description. *Language*, 79(3), 557–582.

Bowden, J., & Hajek, J. (2006). When best practice isn't necessarily the best thing to do: Dealing with capacity limits in a developing country. In L. Barwick & N. Thieberger (Eds.), *Sustainable data from digital fieldwork* (pp. 45–55). Sydney: Sydney University Press.

Bowern, C. (2015). *Linguistic fieldwork: A practical guide*. Basingstoke (England): Palgrave Macmillan.

Conathan, L. (2011). Archiving and language documentation. In P. Austin & J. Sallabank (Eds.), *The Cambridge handbook of endangered languages* (pp. 235–254). Cambridge: Cambridge University Press.

Crasborn, O. A. (2015). Transcription and Notation Methods. In E. Orfanidou, B. Woll, & G. Morgan (Eds.), *Research methods in sign language studies: A practical guide* (pp. 74–88). London: Wiley Blackwell.

de Souza, P., Edmonds, F., McQuire, S., Evans, M., & Chenall, R. (2016). *Aboriginal knowledge, digital technologies and cultural collections: Policy, protocols, practice*. Melbourne Networked Society Institute Research Paper 4.

Gippert, J., Himmelmann, N., & Mosel, U. (Eds.), (2006). *Essentials of language documentation*. Berlin & New York, NY: Walter de Gruyter.

Haviland, J. B. (2016). Maing gambarr: It belongs to me, I belong to it. In J.-C. Verstraete & D. Hafner (Eds.), *Land and language in Cape York Peninsula and the Gulf Country* (pp. 455–579). Amsterdam & Philadelphia, PA: John Benjamins Publishing.

Henke, R., & Berez-Kroeker, A. L. (2016). A brief history of archiving in language documentation, with an annotated bibliography. *Language Documentation & Conservation*, 10, 411–457.

Himmelmann, N. P. (2006). The challenges of segmenting spoken language. In U. Mosel, N. P. Himmelmann, & J. Gippert (Eds.), *Essentials of language documentation* (pp. 253–274). Berlin & New York, NY: Mouton De Gruyter.

Holton, G. (2012). Language archives: They're not just for linguists any more. In F. Seifart, G. Haig, N. P. Himmelmann, D. Jung, A. Margetts, & P. Trilsbeek (Eds.), *Potentials of language documentation: Methods, analyses, and utilization* (pp. 105–110). Hawai'i: LDC Special Publication.

Ingram, C. (in press). "Each in our own village": Insights from a fieldworker/archivist on sustainable interactions with communities. In B. Woods, F. Gunderson, R. Lancefield (Eds.), The Oxford Handbook of Musical Repatriation: Oxford University Press.

IRCA. (2015). *Audio and metadata usage guidelines: Physical and digitised media* (pp. 1–14). IRCA. Indigenous Remote Communications Association. www.irca.net.au/projects/archiving/reference-group

Johnson, H. (2004). Language documentation and archiving, or how to build a better corpus. *Language Documentation and Description*, 2, 140–153.

Johnston, T. (2010). From archive to corpus: Transcription and annotation in the creation of signed language corpora. *International Journal of Corpus Linguistics*, 15(1), 104–129.

Jones, C., & German, A. (2016). Review of F4transkript, a simple interface for efficient annotation. *Language Conservation and Documentation*, 10, 347–355.

MacWhinney, B. (2000). *The CHILDES project: Tools for analyzing talk*. Mahwah, NJ: Lawrence Erlbaum Associates.

Margetts, A., & Margetts, A. (2012). Audio and video recording techniques for linguistic research. In N. Thieberger (Ed.), *The Oxford handbook of linguistic fieldwork* (pp. 13–53). Oxford: Oxford University Press.

Meakins, F. (2007). Computerized Language Analysis (CLAN) from the CHILDES project. *Language Documentation & Conservation*, 1(1), 107–112.

Ochs, E. (1979). Transcription as theory. *Developmental Pragmatics*, 10(1), 43–72.

Perniss, P. (2015). Collecting and analyzing sign language data: Video requirements and use of annotation software. In E. Orfanidou, B. Woll, & G. Morgan (Eds.), *Research methods in sign language studies: A practical guide* (pp. 55–73). London: Wiley Blackwell.

Salffner, S. (2015). Guide to the Ikaan language and culture documentation. *Language Documentation & Conservation*, 9, 237–267.

Schultze-Berndt, E. (2006). Linguistic annotation. In J. Gippert, N. Himmelmann, & U. Mosel (Eds.), *Essentials of language documentation* (pp. 213–251). Berlin: Mouton de Gruyter.

Seeger, A. (2004). New technology requires new collaborations: Changing ourselves to better shape the future. *Musicology Australia*, 27(1), 94–110.

Singleton, J. L., Martin, A. J., & Morgan, G. (2015). Ethics, Deaf-friendly research, and good practice when studying sign languages. In E. Orfanidou, B. Woll, & G. Morgan (Eds.), *Research methods in sign language studies: A practical guide* (pp. 7–20). London: Wiley Blackwell.

Thieberger, N., & Berez, A. L. (2012). Linguistic data management. In N. Thieberger (Ed.), *The Oxford handbook of linguistic fieldwork* (pp. 90–118). Oxford: Oxford University Press.

Thieberger, N., Margetts, A., Morey, S., & Musgrave, S. (2016). Assessing annotated corpora as research output. *Australian Journal of Linguistics*, 36(1), 1–21.

Treloyn, S., & Emberly, A. (2013). Sustaining traditions: Ethnomusicological collections, access and sustainability in Australia. *Musicology Australia*, 35(2), 159–177.

Wasson, C., Holton, G., & Roth, H. S. (2016). Bringing user-centered design to the field of language archives. In M. A. Shepard, G. Holton, & R. Henke (Eds.), *Emergent use and conceptualization of language archives* (pp. 641–681). Hawai'i: LDC Special Publication.

Widlok, T. (2013). 1. The archive strikes back: Effects of online digital language archiving on research relations and property rights. In M. Turin, C. Wheeler, & E. Wilkinson (Eds.), *Oral literature in the digital age: Archiving orality and connecting with communities* (Vol. 2, pp. 3–19). Cambridge: Open Book Publishers.

Wittenburg, P., Brugman, H., Russel, A., Klassmann, A., & Sloetjes, H. (2006). ELAN: A professional framework for multimodality research. In *Proceedings of LREC 2006, Fifth International Conference on Language Resources and Evaluation*. Genoa, Italy.

Woodbury, A. (2014). Toward making endangered language documentations people can read, use, understand, and admire. *Language Documentation and Description*, 12, 19–36.

# 5

# Phonetics and phonology

## 5.1 INTRODUCTION

Phonetics is the representation of human speech sounds, which are defined independently of any language. Each phonetic sound or **phone** is represented by a unique symbol defined by the International Phonetic Association (IPA). This means that you can transcribe sounds in any language unambiguously. The IPA has a website explaining all these symbols with corresponding sound files.[1] Phonology, on the other hand, is the interpretation of speech sounds in a particular language: the structure of sounds that produce meaningful contrasts. The segments of phonology are called **phonemes**. As field linguists, we want to record and analyse as much speech as possible in order to understand how speech sounds pattern in a given language.

A good phonological analysis rests on quality phonetic transcriptions of a sizable corpus of recordings from a range of language speakers. As Hayes (2011, p. 55) notes, "a really solid phonemicisation is often the result of years of hard work, carried out by linguists with good ears and extensive experience with the target language". In this chapter we discuss the issues, methods and preparation needed for working out the phonology of a language to ensure you are getting the most out of your fieldwork and not wasting the time (and patience!) of language consultants. For methodology in phonological analysis, we refer to Gussenhoven & Jacobs (2011) and Hayes (2011). These include exercises to improve your skills in phonological analyses, which is essential preparation for fieldwork on the sounds of a language.

Before you begin fieldwork, you should have clear objectives about what you wish to achieve in your phonological analysis. For example, do you want to identify all the contrastive sounds of a language (the phonological segmental inventory), determine the syllable structure, or describe the degree of variation associated with each contrastive sound? You should also be explicit about how much detail you are representing in transcription of sounds. In your early transcriptions of an unfamiliar language, you will want to include as much detail as possible, but once you have a grasp of the language you may choose to ignore sounds that are not meaningful or those whose patterns are now understood. As an example, English 'cat' often has a short burst of air after the 'c' and a narrow phonetic transcription would be [kʰæt]. However, once we have understood the aspiration rule, [kæt] might suffice and indeed be preferable (see Gussenhoven & Jacobs 2011, p. 16). (In English, aspiration occurs when the stop is the only segment in an onset of a stressed syllable.) Thus, it is

*Phonetics and phonology*   97

important to document whether your transcription is a **narrow** or **broad phonetic transcription**.

Some older written records do not document whether their transcriptions are narrow or broad, which can make it very difficult to interpret them. Furthermore, some early records do not use the modern IPA and so the fieldworker must do some detective work to try to understand their transcription system. For example, retroflex consonants used to be written with a dot diacritic underneath the consonant but now the IPA symbol has a right-inflecting tail, e.g. [ṭ]. Finally, it is very important not to confuse a phonemic representation with an orthographic representation. As we will see in §5.11, there are often irregularities in the relations between letters used in a spelling system and the phonemic segments in a language.

Although there may be no description of the language you are going to work on, there may be existing research on the phonology of related languages, or languages in the same geographic region. While this does not guarantee what the sound system will be like, such preparation will put you in a better position to help identify and understand the sound system of the language. It will also help you to work out whether or not your analysis is what you would expect from languages of this region or type. If it isn't, deviations from analyses of related languages will alert you to either the need to provide strong justification for your analysis or the need to reconsider your analysis.

You should observe any metalinguistic terms relating to the sounds of a language. Speakers may have ways of referring to different sounds or distinguishing between close contrasts. For example, in the Sino-Tibetan language Mueshaungx, Morey (2014, p. 660) notes that speakers have words for the tonal contrasts which translate as 'half-tone' (glottal), 'soft-tone' (tone 1), 'middle-tone' (tone 2) and 'hard-tone' (tone 3). As noted in Chapter 2, care should be taken to test the reliability of such intuitions. Be aware that native speaker intuitions about phonology may be based solely on their 'careful speech register', which may not apply to pronunciations in more casual speech. Most American English speakers would, for example, deny the existence of 't' in 'else' [ɛlts], yet we find this in casual pronunciations. Similarly, do not automatically assume that a native speaker's use of a phonemic orthography is always right.

It is well-worth observing what speakers do with their phonology in songs, poetry and language games, also known as 'ludlings'. These often count phonological units such as syllables or morae, and make patterns with the onsets or rhymes of syllables (e.g. alliteration or assonance). Gussenhoven and Jacobs (2011, p. 3) give a great example where the mora rather than the syllable is counted when translating English songs into Japanese. Native speakers well-versed in their poetic and music traditions usually have intuitions about what sounds good and bad, and thus the studies of metrics and phonology often go hand in hand (Halle & Keyser, 1971; Jakobson, 1960; Kiparsky, 1977). This has led a number of phonologists to regard the study of verbal art (see Chapter 11) and ludlings as 'applied phonology'.

You should pay attention to basic morphological structure, e.g. what constitutes a stem, and derivational and inflectional processes (§6.7.10), as morpho-phonemic affixes (§6.7.10). Earlier we saw how the phonological environment (consonant type,

# Phonetics and phonology

syllable structure, stress) can cause sound changes such as aspiration in English 'cat' [kʰæt]. Other environments to pay attention to are word and morpheme boundaries. For those primarily interested in syntax or semantics, transcription of anything longer than a word will be impossible until you have a good grasp of the phonology, and for this you need to begin with words in isolation.

One of the questions often asked is how many words you need to record to work out the phoneme inventory of a language. Crowley (2007, p. 97) estimates, on average, 300–400 words are needed while Chelliah & de Reuse (2011, p. 252) estimate 500–700. However, really it depends on the complexity of the sound system. In some languages there may be rare phonemes that are only encountered once a large vocabulary has been collected. Furthermore, having the ideal number of vocabulary items is only one part of the equation. In languages that use phonological contrasts that do not exist in the languages spoken by the linguist, a major challenge is being able to identify and 'hear' these contrasts. Some common sounds English speakers have difficulties hearing when working on a new language include aspiration, ejectives and nasalisation, palatal stops, initial velar nasals and glottal stops (for further examples see Bowern (2015, pp. 44–45)).

The simplest tools to help with this task are a pair of good ears and eyes to pay careful attention to the speaker's articulation. You should watch a speaker's mouth, as some articulations can be seen more easily than others, and may provide important information about phonological contrasts, for example lip-rounding and articulation of the tongue tip. You should also observe a speaker's responses to your attempt to articulate the sound and consider any native speaker's intuitions on contrasts. After the elicitation session you might use phonetic analysis tools to look at the acoustic properties (e.g. spectral and waveform analysis) or you might have colleagues or students who can put their ears to the task too. You might also consider making instrumental recordings, some of which we discuss in §5.10.

## 5.2 RECORDING DATA

Your first fieldwork session might involve eliciting vocabulary items from within a simple semantic domain, as discussed in §3.4. In this section we discuss how to analyse these words to understand the sound system of a language. Note too that these words will inform the beginning of a dictionary (§7.5). Simple elicitation provides comparable data for phonological analysis as it consists of words said in isolation by the same speaker and is likely to consist of words that are of the same parts of speech, often nouns. When conducting the first fieldwork session you will be getting to know your speaker, watching your recording equipment, listening and trying to write down the words. You should also be thinking about the sounds you are hearing and asking yourself questions about these. For example:

- Is there a voicing or geminate contrast in the stops?
- Is there a contrast between nasalised and oral vowels, short and long vowels?
- Are there ingressive, ejective, glottal or click sounds?
- How many coronal contrasts are there?

*Phonetics and phonology* 99

- Can words begin and end with a vowel or a consonant?
- What consonant clusters are there?

## 5.3 PHONETIC TRANSCRIPTION

Phonetic transcription is a time-consuming but necessary activity, especially when the language is new to you. But even if you are a speaker of the language, orthographic and phonemic knowledge can get in the way of hearing the sounds accurately. If there are existing recordings of the language, you should familiarise yourself with the sounds of the language and begin to attempt phonetic transcription of these before going into the field. Even if they have already been transcribed, this will be good practice. Attempt your own transcriptions before looking at any existing transcriptions: a comparison of your transcriptions with those of other linguists may turn out to be revealing. Begin your transcription with words said in isolation. Only once you have a handle on transcribing single word utterances will you be able to tackle longer utterances, as you will be better equipped to identify word boundary cues.

When you begin, aim to make your phonetic transcriptions as detailed as possible. Bowern (2015, p. 43) recommends sticking a copy of the IPA chart in the front of your notebook and we recommend taking a digital or print copy of the Handbook of the IPA (International Phonetic Association, 1999). Be careful not to leave out any diacritics and write as clearly as possible as your field notes will be digitised and no doubt read by others in the future. Don't be afraid of writing multiple alternative transcriptions for a word you hear, especially when the language is new to you. These alternatives can reveal much about the phonology of your own language and the sounds of the target language. Similarly, it is wise not to erase a transcription in your notebook; simply put a line through it and write the correction next to it. Make a note of any transcriptions you are unsure about. Conversely, keep a record of all those you are confident about. If you have prior experience in spectral or waveform analysis you can play your recordings in spectrogram software such as Praat to see what the acoustic properties are.[2]

Once you are in the field, you should spend a good two hours daily doing careful phonetic transcriptions of your recordings. Have your notebook out with your handwritten transcriptions from your field session and work in a time-aligned software such as ELAN or CLAN (§4.3.1) with your field recordings. When typing make sure the IPA font conforms to the Unicode Standard. In ELAN, make sure the Unicode IPA font will display by checking the Font Browser utility. Make a note of any sounds you are having difficulty transcribing. Search for multiple tokens of the same word or sound across your transcriptions (you can do this in ELAN by creating a 'phonetic tier', for example). You can then play multiple tokens side by side in Praat to see their phonetic features.

In the next sections we outline how to begin your phonological analysis. In practice, transcription and phonological analysis go hand in hand: you first transcribe, then chart and compare sounds and form hypotheses, then transcribe more, add to your charts and compare and test your hypotheses.

## 100 Phonetics and phonology

---

**Exercise 1  Word elicitation**

- Divide the Swadesh wordlist (Swadesh, 1950) into semantic domains and chose a semantic domain (see §7.2).
- Choose a language you can find a speaker of who is happy for you to practise elicitation with them. Add and remove words within your semantic domain in relation to the sorts of vocabulary that might exist in this culture (consider climate, flora/fauna, social structure etc.). Your list should contain between 20 and 30 words.
- Elicit these words with a speaker of the language, paying particular attention to all the recording and elicitation techniques identified in §3.4. If some words were easier to elicit than other words, why might this be? Was the speaker equally confident about all words and how would you represent any such differences in your field notes?
- Now do an IPA transcription of these words in a notebook. Make a table of all the phones in your transcription, identifying any that you are unsure about. Make a table with columns headed by each phone. Type these up using a Unicode font such as Doulos SIL. Add the words in the relevant columns.
- What segments and allophones can you identify? Are there any homophones or minimal pairs?

For teachers of a field methods class, the entire list of semantic domains can be divided among the students. Following each student's elicitation and transcription, a combined wordlist can be created. Do any of the same words appear in different elicitation sessions? What are the differences between students' transcriptions? Might the variation reflect a different first language?

---

## 5.4 PHONOLOGICAL ANALYSIS

---

In this section we suggest how to organise and analyse your data to work out the phonemes and identify variation. Now that you have done some transcription you will need to take stock of all the sounds you have and their distribution.

Compare each sound in all its different contexts (e.g. word-initial, word-medial, word-final; stressed, unstressed), as contrasts may not occur in all available positions. For example, chart all instances of nasalised vowels preceded by a stop. Keep track of the charts of sounds you make. Keep your analysis in a diary or at least separate from your fieldwork notes, as it is important to keep a track of your analysis. As you produce your charts and analysis, you should ask yourself if there are any gaps in the inventories. For example, does the velar nasal appear in all positions in a word? Are there pairs of voiced and unvoiced stops for all places of articulation? Are all homorganic nasal stop clusters attested, or is one place of articulation missing? Identify the phonological categories with the most segmental contrasts and

_Phonetics and phonology_ 101

those with the least. Are there any rare sounds? If so, consider whether these could be onomatopoeic words, ideophones, words from another speech register, or even loanwords. For example, perhaps your data has both voiced and unvoiced stops at all places of articulation except for alveolar, or perhaps stops are represented in all positions of the word, while taps and laterals are only attested intervocalically. We will now consider some data and walk through the process of phonemic analysis, drawing on Hayes (2011) and Gussenhoven & Jacobs (2011).

### 5.4.1 Minimal pairs and near minimal pairs

A minimal pair is two words with different meanings that differ in one sound in the same location, as in _fig_ /fig/ [fɪg] and _pig_ /pig/ [pɪg] in English (forward slashes represent a phonemic representation of a word while square brackets represent a phonetic representation of a word). Minimal and near-minimal pairs have long been used as evidence that two sounds are separate phonemes. The discovery of a minimal pair is an exciting moment for the field linguist. A common notation for minimal pairs is to use an underlined blank for the contrasting sound, with the invariable sounds flanking this, e.g. /b_t/ is the phonological context that provides evidence for Australian English vowel phonemes such as those in _bat, bit, bot, bite_. Such frames can reveal minimal triplets, quadruplets etc.

Some minimal pairs provide better evidence for a phonological distinction than others. The best minimal pairs are members of the same word class. Minimal pairs where one is a function word and the other a lexical word are not ideal. Given that the prosodic contexts in which these two different types of words occur are unlikely to be the same, this is a bit like comparing apples with oranges. For example, native speakers may not recognise a function word as being similar in sound to a lexical word. Similarly, some minimal pairs may include a word from another register or language (e.g. a borrowing), and these too may not be recognised as similar by a native speaker.

---

**Exercise 2  Minimal pairs that do the most work**

Below is a list of Bilinarra (Pama-Nyungan, Australia) words. What minimal pairs do they show and which ones are better minimal pairs than others? Note that a superscript vertical line is the IPA symbol for a stressed syllable.

| | | | |
|---|---|---|---|
| _gadaj_ | /ˈgɐdɐɪ/ | coverb | 'cut' |
| _bad_ | /bɐd/ | coverb | 'feel about' |
| _gardaj_ | /ˈgɐɖɐ/ | coverb | 'strangle' |
| _garru_ | /ˈgɐrʊ/ | verb | 'will' |
| _ngaba_ | /ˈŋɐbɐ/ | noun | 'big brother' |
| _garu_ | /ˈgɐɹʊ/ | noun | 'child' |
| _dad_ | /dɐd/ | coverb | 'on top' |
| _ngaja_ | /ˈŋɐɹɐ/ | conjunction | 'admonitive' |

## Phonetics and phonology

Some phonologically distinctive sounds might not be contrasted in a minimal pair. The absence of a minimal pair is therefore not evidence for a lack of a phonemic contrast. This may be more common in languages with long words and large phoneme inventories. In such cases it is necessary to look for near-minimal pairs, which are pairs that would be minimal except for some irrelevant difference. In English, for example, it is difficult to find a minimal pair for [ð] and [ʒ]; yet there exists a number of near minimal pairs such as 'heathen' [ˈhiðən] and 'adhesion' [ædˈhiʒən]. Once all reasonable hypotheses concerning allophone environments have been discounted, near-minimal pairs can be used as evidence for there being two contrastive phonemes. A hypothesis that [ð] becomes voiced [ʒ] following an unstressed syllable with a coda (as in [ˈhiðən] and [ædˈhiʒən]) would not be reasonable, as there is no phonetic motivation for this. Assembling large numbers of near minimal pairs should reveal whether a phonetic environment determines which of two segments appear or not, the latter being evidence for a case of two separate phonemes.

Keep track of all the minimal pairs you encounter as evidence for proposed segmental, stress or tonal categories. In addition to keeping a list of minimal and near-minimal pairs in your diary (and as a digital file), it is useful to make a note of these in the dictionary database, where you can refer to all other exemplars of the minimal pair, triplet etc. This is especially useful for language learners and the dictionary entry may describe this information as "sounds similar to X" or "not to be confused with X" (see also §7.6).

### 5.4.2 Identifying allophones

To work out if two sounds are allophones of the same phoneme, you need to establish that they are in complementary distribution rather than in free variation. Free variation is when two phones occur in the same environment without causing a change in meaning. There are no linguistic principles that govern the distribution of free variants, yet there is usually a sociolinguistic factor that affects the selection of one variant over the other, such as gender or age, as well as the particular speech register (e.g. formal or informal) and speed of delivery.

If two sounds are in complementary distribution, they only occur in certain environments, and so the task is to work out in which environments they occur. To do this, construct charts of the local environments. We do this in two stages. First, label each column with the target sounds and assemble all the words that these sounds occur in from your data. As an example, consider the ten Kaytetye words in Table 5.1. Assemble these into target sounds, in this case vowels, as in Table 5.2. It is a good idea to put the data in numerical order so that you can locate examples easily.

From this, you can then create a chart of local environments. Reduce each word to the sound preceding and following the target sound, noting any word boundaries. Use a number to cross-reference the word in your transcript. Table 5.3 shows the local environment for the ten words in Table 5.1 (you can omit the square brackets representing IPA for this task, as we have done, as this is assumed from the transcriptions made in Table 5.2).

**Table 5.1**
Ten Kaytetye words from an elicitation session, 20151029MT

| (1) [ɐˈʎepə] | 'soft, quiet' | (6) [ɐˈlɪŋə] | 'tongue' |
|---|---|---|---|
| (2) [eˈɾemə] | 'type of cricket' | (7) [ɐˈkɪcɐɾə] | 'language name' |
| (3) [ɐˈŋepə] | 'crow' | (8) [ɐˈˈnɪjələ] | 'later' |
| (4) [ɐˈɾemə] | 'louse' | (9) [ɪˈʎemə] | 'mouse' |
| (5) [ˈcɐkə] | 'smart' | (10) [eˈnɐpə] | 'echidna' |

**Table 5.2**
Elicited words assembled by vowel sounds (underlining marks the relevant vowel)

| [a] | [e] | [ɪ] | [ə] |
|---|---|---|---|
| [ɐˈʎepə] (1) | [ɐˈʎepə] (1) | [ɐˈlɪŋə] (6) | [ɐˈʎepə] (1) |
| [ɐˈŋepə] (3) | [eˈɾemə] (2) | [ɐˈkɪcɐɾə] (7) | [eˈɾemə] (2) |
| [ɐˈɾemə] (4) | [ɐˈŋepə] (3) | [ɐˈˈnɪjələ] (8) | [ɐˈŋepə] (3) |
| [ˈcɐkə] (5) | [ɐˈɾemə] (4) | [ɪˈʎemə] (9) | [ɐˈɾemə] (4) |
| [ɐˈlɪŋə] (6) | [ˈcɐkɐɾə] (5) | | [ˈcɐkə] (5) |
| [ɐˈkɪcɐɾə] (7) | [eˈnɐpə] (10) | | [ɐˈlɪŋə] (6) |
| [ɐˈˈnɪjelə] (8) | [ɪˈʎemə] (9) | | [ɐˈkɪcɐɾə] (7) |
| [eˈnɐpə] (10) | | | [ɐˈˈnɪjələ] (8) |
| | | | [ɪˈʎemə] (9) |
| | | | [eˈnɐpə] (10) |

**Table 5.3**
Chart of local environments of vowel sounds

| [ɐ] | [e] | [ɪ] | [ə] |
|---|---|---|---|
| #__ɾ (4) | #__ɾ (2) | #__ʎ (9) | p__# (1), (3), (10) |
| #__ʎ (1) | #__n (10) | ˈk__c (7) | m__# (2), (4), (9) |
| #__l (6) | ˈʎ__p (1) | ˈn__j (8) | ɲ__# (6) |
| #__k (7) | ˈʎ__m (9) | ˈl__ɲ (6) | ɾ__# (7) |
| #__ŋ (3) | ˈɾ__m (2), (4) | | k__# (5) |
| #__ˈn (8) | | | j__l (8) |
| c__ɾ (7) | | | |
| ˈc__k (5) | | | |
| ˈn__p (10) | | | |

## 104 Phonetics and phonology

At this stage, inspect the columns to see if there are any general patterns. We can see that [ɐ] in column one occurs in the most environments and that there is no general pattern to the environment it occurs in. Looking at column two, we can see that [e] has fewer environments. It occurs in word-initial and only stressed medial positions. Comparing columns one and two we can see a minimal pair environment in the first row (2) and (4) and so [ɐ] and [e] must be separate phonemes. Looking at column three we can see that [ɪ] only occurs before a palatal sound [ʎ], [c], [j] and [ɲ], whereas [e] in column two never does. Therefore [ɪ] and [e] are in complementary distribution and so are likely to be allophones. Looking at column four, [ə] occurs overwhelmingly in word-final position but it also occurs in medial unstressed position in (8), as does [ɐ] in (7). The sounds [ɐ] and [ə] contrast in medial unstressed position and must therefore belong to two separate phonemes. The schwa occurs in word-final and unstressed positions, whereas [e] occurs in word-initial and stressed environments, thus they are in complementary distribution; [ə] is thus an allophone of [e]. The environments of the four vowel sounds are written as follows. Two vowel phonemes can be proposed:

| /ɐ/ | /e/ |
|---|---|
| [ɐ] everywhere (no allophones) | [ɪ] / _ Cpal |
| | [ə] / _ #, unstressed |
| | [e] / elsewhere |

By comparing columns of sounds in this way, it should soon become clear whether the sounds are in complementary distribution or not. While adjacent sounds are the basis for much allophonic variation, other environments also give rise to it (e.g. vowel harmony). Charting these environments is time-consuming, but you will be at an advantage as you gain more experience with different languages because many of the same rules crop up across languages.

Target sounds should also be arranged into phonetic charts based on place and manner of articulation. That way you can see whether phonological rules apply to all sounds that share a particular phonetic feature or set of features, which is usually the case. For example, voiced laterals and nasals are both sonorant sounds and in some languages they can cause the adjacent segment to become voiced. When making charts to see the distribution of voiced and unvoiced consonants, pay attention to the distribution of such sounds. Of course, languages make use of different sounds and so the exact sounds that constitute a 'natural class' will vary from language to language.

---

### Exercise 3 Stops exercise

Below is a list of words in the language Yélî Dnye, spoken on Rossel Island, PNG, grouped roughly by semantic domain. Note that the stressed syllable is marked with a superscript vertical line. The colon is a long vowel (thus V vs V:) and ~ marks nasalisation.

_Phonetics and phonology_ 105

1. Make a row of each stop and tap sound and list the words in columns as per Table 5.2 (we will not analyse vowels, nasals or word stress in this exercise).
2. Construct a table of the local environments for each stop and tap sound, as per Table 5.3.
3. Chart any complementary distribution and describe which sounds are in complementary distribution.
4. Identify any allophony rules and propose a set of stop phonemes and allophones. Explain your motivation for selecting which ones are phonemes and which are allophones.

| | | | | | |
|---|---|---|---|---|---|
| 1 | /ˈkɛbi/ | crayfish type | 18 | /t̪ɔ̃ː/ | septum |
| 2 | /ˈŋaːŋgaː/ | shark type | 19 | /ˈtiɽə/ | sister |
| 3 | /ˈpaɽaɽa/ | sea urchin type | 20 | /ˈŋgwebi/ | sorcerer |
| 4 | /ˈt̪æːɽi/ | snail type | 21 | /kaː/ | picture |
| 5 | /ndi/ | cicada | 22 | /taː/ | high up |
| 6 | /ˈtubu/ | vine type | 23 | /ˈtədə/ | place |
| 7 | /kaː/ | fan palm | 24 | /ˈpəːɽuu/ | pull |
| 8 | /ˈmbala/ | bread fruit | 25 | /t̪aː/ | get dry |
| 9 | /ŋgaː/ | sago pulp | 26 | /ˈpibi/ | pouring something |
| 10 | /kiːː/ | banana | 27 | /ˈkugu/ | washing something |
| 11 | /t̪ɛː/ | yam type | 28 | /ˈŋgəŋgə/ | leaking |
| 12 | /po/ | tree type | 29 | /ndɛː/ | drinking |
| 13 | /tiː/ | thorn | 30 | /ˈŋgɛːɽe/ | dancing |
| 14 | /ˈpɔɽu/ | rope | 31 | /ˈpæːpæː/ | pulling |
| 15 | /mbu/ | mountain | 32 | /ˈtaːguu/ | turtle |
| 16 | /puː/ | hole | 33 | /ˈt̪æːɽuu/ | long |
| 17 | /paː/ | body | 34 | /ˈpəbə/ | lying down |

## 5.5 NATIVE SPEAKER INTUITIONS ON PHONOLOGY

If the language has contrasts you are not used to, it may be difficult to decide if two words are minimal pairs or homophones (see §7.6). In some cases you may get a reliable response by asking speakers if they think the two words sound the same or different, but it is not always clear what speakers are responding to in their judgements. Some speakers may claim that two words sound different simply because their semantics differ or because the two words usually have different intonation patterns (especially if the pair of words are from different parts of speech).

A helpful technique to distinguish pairs of words is to play recordings of the two potential homophones back to a speaker and ask which word has which meaning. If the response is consistently 'different', then the words are probably a minimal pair. In this case, check again in Praat for any phonetic differences. If the responses are not consistent, the two words may well be homophones. Try to do this with as many speakers as possible to get independent judgements.

A general technique used by Ladefoged (2003) to check pronunciation is to ask, "(w)hich of the versions of the word sounds better" (rather than "correct"), holding up one or two fingers each time, for the speaker to answer "first" or "second". If you are working with a speaker who is also highly literate in their language, it can be helpful to ask them to spell the words. The best solution is to collect multiple occurrences of the two words in natural speech and compare these carefully.

---

### Exercise 4 Voiceless stops in English

In English, voiceless stops are typically aspirated when they occur as the only consonant in the onset of a stressed syllable. That is, voiceless stops such as [p], [t], and [k] are aspirated in *pin, tin and kin*, but not aspirated in a cluster such as *spin* and *skin*. However, the situation is more complex. Design a wordlist to target the effects of stress, simple vs complex onset, intervening glide or liquid between stop and vowel, and simple vs complex coda. Record a native English speaker and transcribe the words phonetically. Organise your data using the principles above and prepare a hypothesis about the aspiration rule based on your data.

---

## 5.6 PHONEMIC TRANSCRIPTION

Once you have phonetic transcriptions from multiple speakers, chart these, as in Table 5.4. From these you can put forward a phonemic analysis, as in the final column of Table 5.4. Phonemicisation is an iterative process of proposing, testing and refining hypotheses about segmental and prosodic tonal contrasts.

As your data increases and you engage in this process again and again, you should come to a working phonemicisation from which you can move to a phonemic transcription, as this will enable you to transcribe data more efficiently (unless your fieldwork aims are solely phonetic). In ELAN, you can always go back and add a

*Phonetics and phonology* 107

Table 5.4

Comparing different Kaytetye speakers' pronunciations of the same words – superscript 'h' represents aspiration and the small circle devoicing

| file name | Speaker 1 20100426LB | Speaker 2 20100427TR | Speaker 3 20100429AP | phonemicisation |
|---|---|---|---|---|
| 'dog' | [ɐˈlekɐ̥] | [ɐˈlekʰ] | [ɐˈlekə̥] | /ɐləkə/ |
| 'bird' | [ˈʈɐŋgən] | [ˈʈɐŋgənə̥ʰ] | [ˈʈɐŋgənə̥] | /ʈɐŋkənə/ |
| 'woman' | [ɐˈɹ̊elɐ̥] | [ɐˈɹ̊elə̥ʰ] | [ɐˈɹ̊elə̥] | /ɐɹələ/ |

phonetic transcription tier to do more targeted analysis if your aim is phonetic analysis. Don't move to a phonemic transcription until you are sure of the phonology, because if what you represented as a phoneme actually turns out to be two contrastive sounds, this will require much more work to fix. Note that if you make subsequent changes to your representation system, this should be documented, including the date in which the change is introduced. Use your notebook to keep track of your data and analyses.

## 5.7 IDENTIFYING TONE

Identifying the number and the nature of tonal categories is a complex task that may vary between dialects of a language and between different analysts. A useful resource for fieldwork on a tonal language is Morey (2014). A tonal language is one where pitch enters into the lexical realisation of at least some lexical items. The minimum number of tonal categories in a language is two while the maximum so far attested is twenty. It is important to first document uninflected words, as the tonal category of a word can change when inflected. Morey recommends identifying tonal contrasts in words before exploring the phonetics of tone in detail, as the acoustic properties of tonal categories can be complex and varied. For example, a category may be based on a combination of pitch, phonation, duration and intensity and different speakers may realise pitch categories differently.

Native speaker intuitions about a tonal category of a word can provide evidence for your analysis. Beware, however, as different speakers may take the initial or final pitch of a tone as the point of comparison. It is useful to distinguish the analyst's perception of a tonal category from that of a native speaker's perception of a tonal category in a word. One way of checking the tonal category of a word with a native speaker is to whistle it. Morey (2014, p. 647) describes another method where he (SM) repeats a word, each time with a different tonal category, and asks the speaker (Aije Let) to identify the correct category (Figure 5.1).

Tonal categories are not always carried across in related languages. However, whether they are or aren't tends to be consistent across all cognate words (Morey, 2014, p. 639), so make sure you compare many words that have a given tonal

## Phonetics and phonology

**Figure 5.1**

Drawing on native speaker intuitions about tone in Tai Phake
Source: Morey 2014, p. 647

| SM: | ma$^5$ | kin$^6$ | sen$^6$ | san$^6$ | pen$^2$ | | | | |
|---|---|---|---|---|---|---|---|---|---|
| | neg | neg.eat | sound | which | be | | | | |
| | "And *not eat* is which tone?" | | | | | | | | |
| Aije Let: | kin$^6$ / | kin$^1$ | kin$^2$ | kin$^3$ | kin$^4$ | kin$^5$ | kin$^6$ | kin$^6$ / | hok$^1$ |
| | "*Not eat*? | kin$^1$ | kin$^2$ | kin$^3$ | kin$^4$ | kin$^5$ | kin$^6$, | it is number six." | |

category, not just one or two. Be aware that the functional load that tone plays can vary between closely related languages and tonal categories may diminish if the language is in contact with non-tonal languages.

Morey (2014) identifies and discusses four ways that tone can be represented in analysis, noting that above-vowel diacritics are recommended by the IPA. Practical orthographies mark tone in different ways, including underspecifying some contrasts or not marking tone at all. Some use diacritics, while others combine vowel and tone into a single symbol.

## 5.8 STRESS, PHONOTACTICS AND PROSODY

In some languages **stress** is fixed (regular), while in other languages it is contrastive as in English (*PERmit*, the noun; versus *perMIT*, the verb). Stressed syllables can be longer, louder and higher in pitch than unstressed syllables, but not all languages make use of all these features. There may also be secondary stress, determined by several different factors, including syllable weight, the number of syllables in the word and its morphology. As soon as you start transcribing, you should mark which syllables you think are stressed. Words may have different stress when appearing in phrases. Thus in working out the lexical stress patterns (if the language has lexical stress), you need to transcribe words in isolation first. Pay careful attention to vowels. These often have different qualities in stressed and unstressed syllables. Morphology also often (though not always) affects stress.

Phonotactics is the distribution of sounds in a word. For example, English disallows [ʒ] and [ŋ] words initially. Don't try to tackle the phonotactics and the phoneme inventory at the same time. These tasks require making different charts and so you are better off leaving phonotactics until after you have an understanding of the segmental phonology of the language. This principle applies also for working on the suprasegmental features of a language (intonation, rhythm, tone, stress). To work out the phonotactics, you will need to identify the syllabic template, e.g. $C_1V_1C_2V_2$ and make different segmental inventories for each position. To work out the syllable structure of the words, count the syllable nuclei and identify the syllable types

Phonetics and phonology 109

within the words (e.g. open vs closed; simple vs complex; onset vs no onset) and the relative frequency of these structures and types. Similarly, you will need to chart all open syllables, complex consonant positions etc.

Prosody is the intonational system of a language. Until recently, such analyses have been drawn directly from field data elicited for other purposes. Chelliah & de Reuse (2011, p. 275) observe that you should make notes and try out the intonational contours of different sentence types, such as commands, statements, interrogatives and different focus constructions such as clefts. You should also investigate the relationship between contours and discourse type, such as arguments, teasing, baby-talk and complaints. See Himmelmann & Ladd (2008) for a detailed discussion of fieldwork on prosody and ways to obtain controlled data designed specifically for intonational research.

## 5.9 EXPERIMENTAL DESIGN

After you have done an initial analysis of the sounds in a language, you may have a list of variants for which you are not sure if there is a conditioning environment or whether they are simply free variants. For example, you might not be sure whether the tap [ɾ] and [t] are allophones or free variants produced by different speakers; or you might have different vowel lengths and want to know what factors condition their allophony. You might therefore design a task that aims to get speakers to say words that have these sounds while controlling the linguistic environment in which they are said. Like all experiments, these tasks have a **dependent** variable and one or more **predictors** (or **independent** variables). For example, the dependent variable might be vowel length and two predictors might be the type of syllable (open or closed) and its position in the word (e.g. stressed/unstressed, initial/medial/final). The experiment would aim to measure the effects of the predictors (syllable type and word position) on the dependent variable (vowel length). While these experiments require reasonable numbers of speakers to produce statistical results, as discussed in §9.4.2 and §10.4.5.1, they can also be done with just one or two speakers to gain an understanding of an individual speaker's sound system.

Your analysis of categories should first look to the stressed position to find the maximal number of contrasts, as contrasts are often reduced in unstressed positions. Develop a hypothesis about what is triggering a particular variation; for example, are geminates and singletons dependent on preceding vowel length? Do nasals become prestopped in a stressed/unstressed environment? Do stops become voiced following a sonorant consonant? Does a three-way tonal contrast reduce in an unstressed position?

You will need to prepare a list of all words that contain the target sound which can confirm or refute the hypothesis. As an example, take the hypothesis that stops become voiced following a sonorant consonant. To test this, you will need to record words that have a sequence of a sonorant plus stop, as well as non-sonorant plus stop in them, including intervocalically and word-initially. You will

## 110  Phonetics and phonology

**Table 5.5**

Gap in the attested consonant clusters in a hypothetical language: is /ɾk/ non-permissible or an accidental gap?

|  | labial | | velar | |
| --- | --- | --- | --- | --- |
| non-apical stops | /p/ | /m/ | /k/ | /ŋ/ |
| tap + non-apical stop | /ɾp/ | /ɾm/ | ? | /ɾŋ/ |

need to devise an experiment consisting of a list of target words as well as some filler words to 'throw the speakers off the scent' of what you are trying to do. If the speaker knows what you are doing, this can create a bias in the result. Filler words also act as proxy hearing tests (in places where hearing problems are common) and help to monitor the continued attention of a participant (see §9.4.2.1 for further discussion on rigorous experimental design including numbers of participants).

Ideally, the target sound should be in the same position in the word and surrounded by the same sounds; and the words themselves should be made up of the same number of syllables. You may be able to use nonce or 'wug' words, made up words that adhere to the sound system of a language used for linguistic elicitation. In this way you can tap into a speaker's phonological awareness (Gallagher, 2013).

Note too that you might have a gap in the consonant clusters such as that illustrated in Table 5.5. Just imagine there are words in the language [kaɾpa], [piɾma], [miɾŋa] but no words with a sequence [ɾk]. To test whether this is an accidental gap or not you might make up a word [piɾka], say it to a speaker and ask what it means. If they say it back to you, then that's good evidence that it is a licit sequence in the language, even if they say there is no such word. However, it may be that speakers do not respond in a way that enables you to differentiate whether it is a non-permissible word or sound sequence in the language.

The selection of target words in experiments needs careful thought; it may be that nonce words can distract and even upset speakers. You also want to avoid words that are likely to lead to speakers making errors. This includes rare words, and if the participants are bilingual includes words common to both languages (through either inheritance or borrowing), which may induce a higher rate of errors.

To control the conditioning environment in which the target word is said, you will need to use a carrier phrase. This means asking a participant to embed each target word in the same sentence structure. Some common carrier phrases are "I know what an X is" or "I'm saying X" or "I saw X". You will need to record enough tokens of each target word to produce statistically significant results, which is usually between 5 and 10 tokens per participant. Rather than getting a participant to repeat these, you can randomise the target words so that they are not repeating them one after the other. Using a carrier phrase and randomising the repetitions of the experiment will also help to control for 'list intonation' – that is, a set intonation pattern where the preceding and last word in a list have different phonetic features. For example, the final word of a list or repetition may have a lower pitch and longer duration than words in the other positions. This can be especially problematic if working on a language with tonal or durational contrasts. Make sure the participant knows that the word will come up again a number of times so that they do not think they have made a mistake when it recurs.

You will need to devise some way to prompt the speaker to say the target word in the carrier phrase. If the participant is literate, you could have them read it. If they are not literate, you can make a recording of the phrase first and then use this as a prompt. That is, ask the consultant to repeat after they hear each utterance. The benefit of using a pre-recorded frame is that it will be the same for every consultant and every repetition of the token throughout the experiment. If possible, make the recording with a native speaker and add visual prompts (see Figure 5.2). This will certainly make the task less boring for the speakers.

You should consider whether you need a mix of different ages (for example in cases of language shift), as well as men and women (if sociolinguistic variation seems to be at play). This will depend on the research questions you are asking.

Figure 5.2
An example of one of the 35 Kaytetye target words and corresponding images (here 'in the scrub' [ɐˈʈɳeŋ]) in a carrier phrase 'Say X!', pre-recorded by a native speaker
Sources: Harvey, Davies et al., 2015; Harvey, Lin et al., 2015

artnenge

Unless the questions relate to gender and age, it is better to keep the participant group as homogenous as possible to avoid additional variables in the analysis. If you are investigating interdental consonants, you should avoid working with anyone who is missing front teeth! Pay close attention to views within the community about anyone who is said to have a 'bad tongue' or other comments that might suggest someone with unusual speech. Ideally, the speakers would also be monolingual or mother-tongue speakers, although this is not practical in many cultures where multilingualism is the norm.

In explaining the task, you might want to say that different people say words a bit differently, and that you want to make sure you record all the ways in which people say a word. Even if people understand why you want to do these sorts of experiments, they are not always easy for speakers to do. In free word order languages, it can be very difficult for speakers to fix the position of the target word. Asking speakers to use a test frame also adds to the many factors that make such elicitation an unnatural activity and thus may lead to increased speech errors. Therefore training speakers in using the carrier phrase is highly valuable. To help put speakers at ease, it can be useful to turn the training activity into a fun group activity.

## 5.10 INSTRUMENTAL PHONETIC FIELDWORK

In this section, we give a brief overview of basic acoustic recording techniques for phonetic fieldwork. Instrumental phonetic fieldwork employs a range of specialist equipment and software for processing data. These are beyond the scope of this book and we refer readers to Ladefoged (2003).

When making phonetic recordings, it is crucial to avoid background noise. If you are recording indoors, it will be necessary to reduce echo. This can be done by putting foam (e.g. mattresses) or blankets on the wall and by minimising the distance between the mouth and microphone. Butcher (2013, p. 65) recommends a head-mounted microphone positioned approximately 5 cm from the lips and slightly to the side (§3.2.2). If using a freestanding microphone, Butcher recommends these be placed 10–15 cm from the lips and put on a shock mount fixed to a boom arm that can be clamped to a table. A foam box or 'Porta-Booth' put around the microphone can also reduce reverb. With the small distance between mouth and microphone, you will need to do a 'dry run' with each speaker to set the recording level to capture the loudest signal level without distortion. Butcher (2013, p. 65) also recommends paying "particular attention to the presence of '50 Hz hum' (60 Hz in the United States) resulting from interference from the power supply". Running the equipment on battery power can resolve this, but if the problem persists, you may need to invest in a 'hum eliminator' (otherwise known as a galvanic isolation transformer).

When recruiting participants, men may be better for some kinds of acoustic research because their Fundamental Frequency, or F0, is lower than in women, thus providing richer information about formants. If you want to pursue fieldwork on specific aspects of articulation, you should be aware of the following tools of instrumental phonetics that can be taken into the field:

- Oral and nasal airflow masks can be used to record the amount of airflow and/or pressure from the nose and mouth.
- Ultrasound and electropalatography are used for studying how the tongue moves during articulation.
- Static palatography is used for studying where articulations are made and with which part of the tongue.
- Layryngeography or glottography (EGG) is used for measuring the timing of vocal fold vibration and distinguishing phonation types such as breathiness and glottalisation (Butcher 2013, p. 75).

For the area of perceptual phonetic fieldwork, see Butcher (2013). We also recommend Ladefoged (2003), who discusses the use of these methods in the field. As well as the tools mentioned above, it is also possible to innovate and use non-specialised equipment to make measurements, as Jesse Stewart describes.

---

### Using earbuds to measure nasality – Jesse Stewart

In 2012, I was in grad school taking a field methods course on Guaraní and looking to reanalyse the classic phonological explanation of nasal harmony (the spread of nazalisation to other segments) using acoustic correlates. One evening I was lying on my couch twirling my earbud earphones as I was staring at nasal harmonics in Praat. Bored out of my mind, I shoved the earbuds up my nose (because that's what people do when they're bored, right?). Eureka moments are an odd thing with wires dangling from your nostrils. I then plugged them into the recording jack and started spouting off French at my computer as Praat's sound meter jumped every time I made a nasal sound. You can imagine my excitement the next day as I explained to my professor what I had discovered. He entertained the idea for approximately half a second before forbidding me from sticking stuff up the consultants' noses. The promise of instant nasality faded just as quick. Fast forward six months to a café in Ecuador where I met Martin Kohlberger for the first time. As we chatted over coffee, he mentioned how he had borrowed nasal airflow measuring equipment from the Max Planck Institute for Evolutionary Anthropology in Leipzig to document the use of nasality in Shiwiar. Ecuadorian Customs, however, wouldn't let him take the equipment into the country without paying a hefty import tax. Leaving the equipment at Customs, he was trying to decide how to get alternative nasality measures. Half-jokingly, I recommended he ask his consultants if he could place earbuds under their noses and record them speaking. As it turned out that's exactly what he did and the earbuds method was born (Nevins & Coelha da Silva, 2017; Stewart & Kohlberger, 2017) (see Figure 5.3).

**Figure 5.3**
Limbardo Payaguaje, a Shiwiar speaker, demonstrates the use of the earbuds. The updated methodology positions just one earbud *under* (rather than *in*) the nose and one next to the mouth. Limbardo was keen to demonstrate the original positioning which he found humorous (Photo: Eduardo Portilla, used with permission of Limbardo Payaguaje)

## 5.11 ORTHOGRAPHY

Some endangered languages have never been written down, while many that have been are not written in any standardised way. This can be addressed by creating an orthography, a set of conventions for writing a language. As well as stipulating the rules for spelling, an orthography can include rules about hyphenation, capitalisation, word breaks and punctuation. An orthography can be useful for the community for a number of reasons. The community may wish to read and write their language, especially if they are literate in another language. An orthography can also assist in language teaching, especially in revitalisation contexts and when the language is being taught as a second language. Having a written form can also enhance the prestige and value of a language, both within and outside of the community. Written forms of the language are often used proudly on signs, as names for sports teams, rock bands and as tattoos, and can be found on the internet, social media and in church. However, it may be that some people do not want their language written down, as they may see it as having a standardising effect on their oral language or lead to weakening of memory skills. Broncho suggests it can also

*Phonetics and phonology* 115

be a "path for outsiders to potentially exploit cultural knowledge intended only for Native people".[3] If the community wants an orthography, there are socio-political factors as well as phonological arguments to consider when developing one. If you are starting from scratch, you will need to approach this differently than if you are working with an existing but perhaps poor orthography.

### 5.11.1 Phonological considerations

From a purely linguistic perspective, the orthography should be based on the phonemic principle that there is a one-to-one correspondence between the phonemes and the graphemes used to represent them. Such an orthography is easier to learn than one that is not (such as English). Suprasegmental features such as stress are usually not represented in an orthography, although when it comes to tone there are different views on whether tone should be taken into account, as there is evidence to suggest that exhaustive marking of phonemic tone reduces fluency in literacy (Koffi, 2014). Similarly, some other phonemic contrasts in some languages may be difficult for speakers to use correctly. This can be the case when the contrast is neutralised in various contexts. For example, in many Australian languages the alveolar / post-alveolar contrast does not apply in all positions of the word and thus an orthography that requires their distinction in all positions is likely to reduce reading fluency and accuracy.

### 5.11.2 Grapheme or literacy considerations

If you are starting from scratch, choose a script and alphabet that is already in use by the community and one that is easy to use on a keyboard. If the phoneme inventory of the main language of literacy in the community is very different from the language you are working on, it will probably be the case that more than one glyph needs to be used to represent some sounds. That is, you will need to devise digraphs such as 'ng' for [ŋ] or even a trigraph (although combinations of three or more glyphs are not ideal as these take longer to read and write). Another option is to use a diacritic, for example an underline can be used to distinguish a retroflex from an alveolar consonant. If choosing a digraph this is usually represented with 'r', for example the phonemes [t] and [ʈ] can be distinguished orthographically as 't' and 'rt' or 't' and 'ṭ'. Similarly, aspiration can be represented with an 'h' or an apostrophe following the consonant. Generally digraphs are preferred over diacritics as diacritics are cumbersome to type, so they tend to get left out. They can also be misread on a dirty computer screen.

If there is a whole series of sounds, you might consider representing these systematically. For example, in many Australian language spelling systems 'r' is used before a consonant to represent retroflexed phonemes e.g. 'rd', 'rt', 'rn', 'rl' for [ɖ], [ʈ] [ɳ] and [ɭ] respectively. Similarly, 'y' is used to represent palatalisation systematically, e.g. 'ty', 'ny', 'ly' for [c], [ɲ] and [ʎ] respectively. Note, though, there is little evidence that such consistency improves fluency in literacy; in fact it may be that overuse of a letter for different sounds may reduce literacy

# 116 *Phonetics and phonology*

fluency and be associated with errors such as metathesis. For homorganic consonant sequences it is common to reduce any digraphs required, e.g. [ɲc] is often written 'nty' rather than 'nyty', unless of course there is a contrast between [ɲc] and [nc].

### 5.11.3 Socio-political considerations

Decisions about orthography are rarely only about phonology. Bird (2001, p. 21) notes that "linguistic analysis alone does not provide an adequate foundation for an orthography, nor does it provide adequate impetus for orthographic change". A successful orthography is one that the community gains fluency in and is adopted by all sectors of society. Whether or not this can occur is more than just a phonological matter. Many linguists who have been caught in the cross-fire of orthographic arguments advocate collaboration with other researchers, such as sociologists. What may seem to be a trivial matter, for example deciding how a particular word should be spelt in the language, can for speakers be a highly emotive matter that exposes contentious issues about who has power when it comes to making decisions about spelling. Note that these arguments may never end and so should not delay the production of a dictionary or community literacy resources. Furthermore, there may be phonological issues that are unresolved and as Mosel (2011, p. 342) points out "it should not be forgotten that dictionary work on an endangered language and culture is frequently under severe time pressure".

Some people have preferences for spelling systems that do not seem at all 'scientific' or neatly consistent to linguists and are not based on phonemic principles. They may prefer orthographies they are used to, or ones associated with a particular religion and liturgical materials in old spelling systems that nevertheless have significant historical value for a community. Some language communities may even prefer spelling systems that distinguish them from their neighbours, even if the words are identical, because they see this as a way of asserting their unique identity. While it is important to point out the implications of having to learn two orthographies (assuming the language communities interact with one another), language speakers should be able to decide on the form of the orthography, as in the long run they will be the ones using it. Unless a speech community 'owns' the orthography, it is unlikely to stand the test of time. Furthermore, orthographic change is an expensive business as existing books, signage and websites need to be replaced and people taught a new system.

In language communities where there is a pre-existing and well-used orthography it is a good idea to work with this, even if it is not based on the phonemic principle, or if a new phonological analysis supersedes the one on which the current orthography is based. Generally, people do not like changing their orthography. More importantly, orthographies are a symbol of identity, as there is a tendency for people to equate the orthography with the language itself. Any suggestion to improve the orthography may be seen as an attempt to change their language. As a linguist, you may be asked for your opinions about spelling, but don't get upset if at times your view is not the prevailing one!

## Phonetics and phonology    117

If you are working with an orthography that is not phonemic and under-differentiates the phonetic form, this will make looking up a word in a dictionary cumbersome (though not impossible). If this is the case, it is useful to have a field in the dictionary for the phonemic or phonetic form (in the SIL Multi-Dictionary Formatter (MDF) field marker \ph is used for this (§7.6)). An example of this can be seen in §7.6.3 from the Kalam Dictionary. In communities where there are multiple orthographies, a possibility is to have a field in the dictionary for the alternate orthography(s). If using SIL dictionary-making software such as Toolbox or FLEx (§7.7) you will need to add a field for this.

---

**Exercise 5  Dealing with multiple spelling systems: Western Aranda, Arrernte or Arrarnta**

Below are six words in Western Arrarnta, a language for which there are three different spelling systems in use, as described by Kenny (2017, p.273). The main context in which literacy is used is the Church. German missionaries developed the first spelling system over 100 years ago and it has been used by language speakers for many years, though it is not phonemic (column one). Both new orthographies have been modified to take into account a number of phonemic contrasts that the early missionaries did not hear. The new missionary orthography (NM) is now used in the Church while the new secular orthography (NS) is also used by a neighbouring language group, associated with a different religion.

| Early Missionary (EM) c. 1880s–1980s | New Missionary (NM) 1990/2006 | New Secular (NS) 1980s/2000 | English gloss |
|---|---|---|---|
| 1 aldola | alturla | alturle | west |
| 2 Jabalpa | Yaparlpa | Yaperlpe | Glen Helen (place name) |
| 3 kwara | kwaarra | kwarre | girl |
| 4 kwata | kwaarta | kwarte | egg |
| 5 knulja | kngulya | kngwelye | dog |
| 6 mankama | maangkama | mangkeme | grow |

1. Chart the different letters for each word as follows:

| word | EM | NM | NS | Difference |
|---|---|---|---|---|
| 1 | aldola | alturla | alturle | d (EM), t(N) |
|   | aldola | alturla | alturle | o (EM), u(N) |
|   | aldola | alturla | alturle | l (EM), rl (N) |
|   | aldola | alturla | alturle | e# (NS), a# (M) |
| 2 | etc. | | | |

2. Compare the orthographies and make a numbered list of (a) the differences in consonants (b) the differences in vowels as follows:

| letter(s) | EM | NM | NS | word |
|---|---|---|---|---|
| (i) d (EM), t (N) | aldola | alturla | alturle | 1 |

3. What are the differences between the orthographies, considering first (a) consonants and then (b) vowels. Suggest reasons for these differences, including whether some pairs of letters might be digraphs.
4. All speakers feel strongly that the orthography they use is the best one. What would you do if you were asked to print a dictionary of the language? Would you use three spelling systems, select one, or print three different dictionaries? Discuss the reasons for your answer. Can you think of a digital solution to this dilemma?

## 5.12 SUMMARY

In this chapter, we have discussed how to transcribe and analyse words to work out the sound system of a language. Listening and watching speakers closely will put you in good stead to make the most out of the elicitation sessions. Organising sounds in their different environments meticulously will help to find patterns in the data and enable you to ask key questions and better design elicitation sessions. This is an iterative process of adding data, charting sounds, identifying gaps, forming hypotheses and eliciting more data. We also described how to design and run experiments to ascertain the effects of neighbouring sounds, stress and phonotactics. We briefly introduced a number of instrumental recording techniques and equipment for phonetic analysis. This chapter also outlined factors to keep in mind when developing an orthography from scratch, including the phonemic principle, co-opting an existing script and symbols, and taking into consideration factors influencing literacy fluency. The success of an orthography was also discussed in terms of non-linguistic factors as well as phonological ones.

## 5.13 FURTHER READING

There are excellent chapters on doing fieldwork on the sound systems of a language in Chelliah & de Reuse (2011, Chapter 10) and Bowern (2015, Chapter 5); and a good checklist in Sakel & Everett (2012, p. 159). For general guidelines for fieldwork on phonology see Van de Veen & Medjo Mvé (2010) and for fieldwork on the phonology of tonal languages see Morey (2014). A good introduction to phonological analysis is Gussenhoven & Jacobs (2011) as well as Hayes (2011). For fieldwork in phonetics see Ladefoged (2003), Himmelmann & Ladd (2008) and Butcher (2013). For issues in developing an orthography see Bird (2001).

## NOTES

1 www.internationalphoneticassociation.org/content/full-ipa-chart Accessed 30 August 2017.
2 Praat is software developed by Paul Boersma & David Weenink (2017).
3 www.britishcouncil.org/voices-magazine/how-do-you-learn-language-isnt-written-down Accessed 31 August 2017.

## REFERENCES

Bird, S. (2001). Orthography and identity in Cameroon. *Written Language & Literacy*, 4(2), 131–162.

Bowern, C. (2015). *Linguistic fieldwork: A practical guide*. Basingstoke (England): Palgrave Macmillan.

Boersma, P. & Weenink, D. (2017). Praat: doing phonetics by computer [Computer program]. Version 6.0.28, retrieved 23 March 2017 from www.praat.org/.

Butcher, A. (2013). Research methods in phonetic fieldwork. In M. Jones & R.-A. Knight (Eds.), *The Bloomsbury companion to phonetics* (pp. 57–78). New York, NY: Bloomsbury Academic.

Chelliah, S., & de Reuse, W. (2011). *Handbook of descriptive linguistic fieldwork*. Heidelberg: Springer.

Crowley, T. (2007). *Field linguistics: A beginner's guide*. Oxford: Oxford University Press.

Gallagher, G. (2013). Speaker awareness of non-local ejective phonotactics in Cochabamba Quechua. *Natural Language & Linguistic Theory*, 31, 1067–1099.

Gussenhoven, C., & Jacobs, H. (2011). *Understanding phonology*. London: Routledge.

Halle, M., & Keyser, J. (1971). *English stress: Its form, its growth and its role in verse*. New York, NY: Harper and Row.

Harvey, M., Davies, B., Lin, S., Turpin, M., Demuth, K., & Ross, A. (2015). Two types of prestopping in Kaytetye. In *Proceedings of the 49th Annual Meeting of the Chicago Linguistic Society*, 145–152.

Harvey, M., Lin, S., Davies, B., Turpin, M., Ross, A., & Demuth, K. (2015). Contrastive and non-contrastive pre-stopping in Kaytetye. *Australian Journal of Linguistics*, 35(3), 1–19.

Hayes, B. (2011). *Introductory phonology*. Oxford: Wiley-Blackwell.

Himmelmann, N. P., & Ladd, D. R. (2008). Prosodic description: An introduction for fieldworkers. *Language Documentation & Conservation*, 2(2), 244–274.

International Phonetic Association. (1999). *Handbook of the International Phonetic Association: A guide to the use of the International Phonetic Alphabet*. Cambridge: Cambridge University Press.

Jakobson, R. (1960). Closing statement: Linguistics and poetics. In T. A. Sebeok (Ed.), *Style in language* (pp. 350–377). Cambridge, MA: MIT Press.

Kenny, A. (2017). Aranda, Arrernte or Arrarnta? The politics of orthography and identity on the Upper Finke River. *Oceania*, 87(3).

Kiparsky, P. (1977). The rhythmic structure of English verse. *Linguistic Inquiry*, 8, 189–247.

Koffi, E. (2014). Towards an optimal representation of tones in the orthographies of African languages. *Linguistic Portfolios*, 3(12), 165–190.

Ladefoged, P. (2003). *Phonetic data analysis: An introduction to fieldwork and instrumental techniques*. Oxford: Blackwell.

Morey, S. (2014). Studying tones in north east India: Tai, Singpho and Tangsa. *Language Documentation & Conservation*, 8, 637–671.

Mosel, U. (2011). 17 Lexicography in endangered language communities. In P. Austin & J. Sallabank, *The Cambridge handbook of endangered languages* (pp. 337–353). Cambridge: Cambridge University Press.

Nevins, A., & Coelha da Silva, M. A. (2017). Maxakalí nasality and field recording with earbud microphony. *Revista de estudos da linguagem*, Belo Horizonte, 25(3), 1011–1042.

Sakel, J., & Everett, D. (2012). *Linguistic fieldwork: A student guide*. Cambridge: Cambridge University Press.

Stewart, J., & Kohlberger, M. (2017). Earbuds: A method for analyzing nasality in the field. *Language Documentation & Conservation*, 11, 49–80.

Swadesh, M. (1950). Salish internal relationships. *International Journal of American Linguistics*, 16, 157–167.

Van de Veen, L., & Medjo Mvé, P. (2010). Theory and practice of data collection for phonological analysis. www.ddl.ish-lyon.cnrs.fr/fulltext/Van%20Der%20Veen/2_Steps_phonological_analysis.pdf

# 6

# Morpho-syntax

By now you will have done a lot of single word elicitations and have a grasp of the phonology. The next step is to tackle phrases and clauses and get underway analysing the morpho-syntax. If you are a community member or have been working on the language for many years, you may have a comprehensive corpus that you can mine for an outline of a grammar, which will in turn provide the basis for further morpho-syntactic interrogation. For linguists new to the language and community, narratives, conversation etc. are often too complex a place to start. Speakers often want to train you up in the language to an extent that they consider you a worthy interlocutor or listener. So clause-based elicitation is often a good starting point.

---

**Exercise 1  Recording stories as a 'newbie' to the community**

Imagine you only have a few more days in a speech community before you have to head home. You have only been able to perform formal elicitation with the speakers. You plan to return but the speakers are elderly and you are worried that the elicitation you have done is not very dynamic. There is also a chance that your recordings may be the final record of the language. How do you create situations where speakers will tell narratives?

---

This chapter will focus on 'formal' elicitation as a methodology for digging deeper into the structure of a language. Formal elicitation operates at the clause or phrase level, and involves testing out structures incrementally to understand the function of different parts of the grammar. This type of elicitation may not be appropriate for all types of language, for example it may be impossible to do formal elicitation (at least initially) with languages that have a low status, such as many contact languages (see §10.4.1 for further discussion). Formal elicitation also does not help elucidate the variable use of grammatical elements (unless the variation is categorical and driven by grammatical cues). For example, elicitation will not help you arrive at an explanation for when English speakers use *of* to express possession instead of the *s*-genitive (§10.3.3). Other types of elicitation, such as director-matcher tasks, which use picture-prompts, may be more appropriate methods (see §7.5 and §10.4.4.1). A final word of caution – formal elicitation is not for everyone and some individuals and cultures might find the intense question-answer nature of elicitation irritating.

# 122 *Morpho-syntax*

## 6.1 THE VALUE OF FORMAL ELICITATION FOR GRAMMATICAL DESCRIPTION

There is an ongoing debate about the kind of data you need to do grammatical description. This debate is closely tied to the shift from **descriptive linguistics**, which is characterised by the classic Boasian trilogy of grammar, dictionary and text collection, to **language documentation**, which emphasises recording a broader range of language, using methodologies which allow for different types of potential analyses, including grammatical description (Himmelmann, 1998) (§1.2.4). The language documentation approach has formal elicitation at one extreme and free-ranging conversation at the other. Both have advocates who claim one or the other is the preferred data for grammatical description. Elicited data is often not considered 'real' language because it is constructed and relatively context free. Language is, of course, a dynamic and interactive system. On the other hand, conversational data is often fragmented and not revealing of the potential grammatical range of a language because people often don't talk to each other in full sentences. The reasonable mid-position for grammatical description is a combination of narrative, conversation, procedural and elicitation data. It is also important to remember that you will never find out what is ungrammatical without elicitation because the absence of a structure in a corpus might just relate to its rarity rather than to its grammaticality.

---

### Exercise 2  Elicitation versus conversation

What types of data might be good to get a grasp of the following and why?

- Grammatical relations i.e. subjects and objects?
- Number marking in pronouns?
- Focus markers?
- The anaphoric use of pronouns or demonstratives?
- An inverse system where inanimates > animates?
- Variation in the use of a case-marker?

---

Data from formal elicitation can prove highly insightful in trying to tease out what parts of a clause are contributing to various meanings. But where possible, it should be backed up with naturally occurring data from conversation or narrative. Note that this is not always possible. Some constructions are rare and your corpus may not capture them. For example, Nash (1996) discusses the possible orders and combinations of pronoun clitics in Warlpiri (Pama-Nyungan, Australia). He established through formal elicitation that it is possible to use a sequence of four pronouns, even though he was unable to find this sequence in spontaneous speech.

> The approximately 60,000 lines of Warlpiri material available in machine-readable form conform absolutely to the generalisation that *-rla-jinta* cannot follow any (non-zero)

*Morpho-syntax* 123

non-subject pronominal clitic [FM: i.e. four pronouns are not possible]. Yet several Warlpiri speakers on different occasions have agreed that such a combination is well-formed and interpretable.

(Nash, 1996, p. 132)

Explorations of morpho-syntactic phenomena such as Warlpiri pronouns reveal differences between what people *do* say (e.g. in narratives and conversation) and what they *can* say (which is best revealed by elicitation).

## 6.2 WHAT LANGUAGE TO PERFORM ELICITATION IN?

If you are an 'insider' linguist, the question of which language to perform elicitation in requires no answer. Clearly you would operate in the language under investigation because you speak it. If you are an 'outsider' linguist, the same question is less straightforward. Ultimately using the target language for elicitation is best practice. This approach is called 'monolingual fieldwork' (cf. Everett, 2001) and was long advocated for by Ken Hale (1983) who, in anticipation of a comparative Arandic dictionary for Central Australia, gained mastery of Arandic languages with his usual legendary speed and used one Arandic language to elicit other related languages. Indeed in some communities who do not speak a regional language such as English, French or Spanish, this is the only approach possible.

It might not be practical or possible to do monolingual fieldwork due to factors out of your control, for example your prowess as a second language learner. It is wrong to think that all linguists are good language learners. Not all of us are (and this does not make you a bad analyst of language)! It also might be hard to learn the language if it is highly endangered and is only spoken by older members of a speech community. For example, if you are working on a language in Vanuatu and living with a family, the language of interaction in the household might be Bislama (an English-based creole language) rather than the target language. You have a better chance of becoming a good Bislama speaker than learning the target language. If you do use an intermediary language such as English, Spanish or a contact language as the language of elicitation, there are many checks you can perform to make sure you are understanding the structures of the target language correctly, such as 'back translation' (§6.6.2).

---

### Tip – Using a creole language in elicitation

Not all speech communities like outsiders using their creole or indigenised variety of a European language such as English or French. These are often considered 'insider' languages and you may be interpreted as making fun of them. Follow the lead of the community members. If you use the creole with someone and they reply in English or French, continue the conversation in English or French. As you are accepted by the community more and more, the language of conversation and elicitation will no doubt change. See also §10.3.6.

## 6.3 WHAT EQUIPMENT TO USE?

Formal elicitation produces data with the least contextual information (i.e. discourse context or real world information) and therefore requires the least equipment. Some people advocate using video for all types of language recordings in all contexts to make sure every recording is potentially of use to many different research areas such as gesture studies (e.g. Seyfeddinipur, 2012). For most formal elicitation, except a few areas of grammar such as spatial relations (§6.7.5) and for all sign language elicitation (§8.4.4), a notebook and pen (§3.3.4) plus an audio recorder (§3.2.1 and §3.3.2) and a lapel microphone (§3.2.2) will suffice. After the recording session, you can also use a transcription program such as CLAN or ELAN to transfer your notes into a sound-linked digital form (§4.3.2). Note that if you are writing down sentences as the speaker says them, the speaker might talk slowly and in a fragmented manner to accommodate your learner status in their language. It might be best to wait until you are at the point you can discard the notebook as a transcription tool and just try out sentences on speakers orally and more fluently. That's a good point to start using ELAN or CLAN to transcribe audio recordings after elicitation sessions. The sound-linked utterances will then be a good source of example sentences for a multi-media dictionary (§7.7.5) or even a sound-linked grammar (§6.8).

## 6.4 ESTABLISHING PARTS OF SPEECH

Working out what part of speech a particular word belongs to is a fundamental task for both the grammar and dictionary. In the dictionary, parts of speech are usually shown directly after the headword as an abbreviation e.g. "jacket *n*." or "run *v*." (see §7.7.2 for more on dictionaries). In the grammar, parts of speech are often discussed in the chapter after the phonology chapter and before the morpho-syntax chapters. The morpho-syntax chapters are often organised according to parts of speech so this analysis is crucial to the overall structure of the grammar.

Establishing parts of speech is essentially an exercise in grouping words which pattern similarly in terms of their morpho-syntax. Writing rules of syntax would be very long-winded if we had to describe each word separately. We find that some words behave very similarly, and we group them as a part of speech.

It is important to determine parts of speech according to morpho-syntactic criteria rather than semantic criteria. For example, adjectives may be description words, but in many languages they are formally indistinguishable from nouns (e.g. Warlpiri in Australia) or verbs (e.g. Mohawk in North America), and therefore not a separate part of speech. Morpho-syntactic criteria can be based on word order (e.g. verbs come second), phrase structure (e.g. noun phrases are headed by determiners) or combinatory principles in the word's morphological structure (e.g. nouns are inflected for case). Table 6.1 provides some common criteria for distinguishing different word classes.

**Table 6.1**
Tips for determining some common word classes

| Part of speech | Common morpho-syntactic criteria |
|---|---|
| Nouns | • Open class<br>• Can distinguish case (§6.7.1), number (§6.7.6), gender (§6.7.8)<br>• Often modified by articles and adjectives to form noun phrases<br>• Can include adjectives, interrogatives and demonstratives |
| Verbs | • Open or closed class<br>• Usually distinguish tense, aspect and mood, and agreement categories (§6.7.2)<br>• Common difficulty is that many languages have complex predicates (serial verb constructions, light verb constructions, secondary predicates etc.) with different types of verbs. These types can be distinguished by their ability to take inflections and their semantic richness or bleaching |
| Adjectives | • Open or closed class<br>• Modify nouns to form noun phrases and may have particular ordering with respect to nouns<br>• Common difficulty is that many languages do not have adjectives but instead group descriptive words with nouns or verbs |
| Adverbs | • Usually a closed class<br>• Modify verbs, nouns or other adverbs and may have particular ordering with respect to these other parts of speech<br>• Common difficulty is that many languages do not have adverbs but instead group them with nouns or verbs |
| Interrogatives | • Closed class<br>• Often occur clause-initially for information structure reasons |
| Articles | • Closed class<br>• Combine with a noun to form a NP or DP<br>• Can distinguish definiteness, number, case, gender |
| Particles | • Closed class<br>• Usually uninflected |
| Demonstratives (§6.7.5) | • Closed class<br>• Often actually nouns and/or adverbs formally<br>• Distinguish deixis, e.g. from speaker, or anaphora, e.g. referents in discourse<br>• Can distinguish case, gender and other noun categories |
| Pronouns (§6.7.4) | • Closed class<br>• Stand in for nouns i.e. "The boy walked in. He was tall"<br>• Usually distinguish first, second and third person<br>• Can distinguish clusivity, gender, case<br>• Common difficulty is distinguishing bound pronouns from agreement marking |
| Conjunctions | • Closed class<br>• Join words or clauses which have the same or similar function in a sentence |
| Pre/postpositions | • Closed class<br>• Form a unit with a noun or pronoun (prepositional phrase), and this unit modifies a noun, verb or adjective |

126 *Morpho-syntax*

## 6.5 GETTING STARTED WITH CLAUSE-LEVEL ELICITATION

The key to good grammatical elicitation is changing the prompt sentences incrementally. This is a similar principle to the use of minimal pairs in phonology to establish contrastive sounds, i.e. phonemes (§5.4.1). In the case of grammar, minimally different clause structures establish meaningful units in the morpho-syntax. The trick with grammatical elicitation is not to change more than one category at a time because these categories might be interdependent. For example, if you are interested in the way the ergative marker works in an Indo-Iranian language, such as Hindi, you don't want to change both the transitivity and perfectivity of the sentence because both of these affect the use of ergative marking (ergative case is used on subjects of transitive verbs marked for perfective aspect).

In the following English examples you can see how sentences are changed incrementally to reveal grammatical relations, tense and number. The bolded parts show the changes in the clauses:

(1)   **He** cried          (he=subj+sg, cry=intransitive+past tense)

       **He** hugged her      (he=subj+sg, hug=**transitive**+past tense, her=obj+sg)

       He hugged **him**     (he=subj+sg, hug=transitive+past tense, him=**obj**+sg)

       He **hugs** him      (he=subj+sg, hug=transitive+**present** tense, him=obj+sg)

       He hugs **them**     (he=subj+sg, hug=transitive+present tense, them=obj+**pl**)

       **They** hug them     (they=subj+**pl**, hug=transitive+present tense, them=obj+pl)

From these sentences alone, we learn that English is a nominative-accusative language, at least in the pronoun system (subjects of transitive and intransitive verbs are the same) (see §6.7.1) and that verbs inflect for the number of the subject and for tense (see §6.7.2). These sentences give clues for where you should take elicitation next.

---

**Exercise 3  Discovering more categories through elicitation**

Thinking about (1), how would you continue the elicitation sequence to see if (i) verbs inflect for number with first and second person pronouns, and if (ii) nouns inflect for grammatical relations (subjects and objects)? Give some examples of sentences you would use.

---

At the end of each elicitation session, write up your current ideas on the grammatical categories of the language and devise follow-up sentences which explore particular categories in more depth.

*Morpho-syntax* 127

## 6.6 SUGGESTIONS FOR SUCCESSFUL ELICITATION

### 6.6.1 General tips

- When you are testing out sentences, **use limited vocabulary**, and only use vocabulary that you are confident with (e.g. from your single word elicitation sessions when you were establishing the phonology of the language). If you don't, speakers will get caught up in the semantics of the new words and you'll lose the flow of the grammar interrogation.
- Only **use semantically and pragmatically plausible sentences**. Sometimes creating minimally different clauses can lead to nonsensical sentences. For example, if you are interested in the animacy hierarchy effects on direct-inverse systems (§6.7.1), it might be tempting to test out the two sentences 'The dog bit me' and 'I bit the dog'. While it is possible to construct scenarios where the second sentence is possible, it will probably be met with resistance from a speaker.
- Elicitation can be boring! Yes, really! **Take breaks regularly** (provide tea and biscuits or whatever is appropriate) and don't wear people out. Alternate grammatical elicitation with another task, such as translating stories, to keep it fresh.
- **Plan ahead** as it's hard to think of the right examples on the spot. Plan at least twice as much as you think you will need. Some examples will work and others won't and it is difficult coming up with alternatives spontaneously.
- **Familiarise yourself with grammatical descriptions of related or neighbouring languages** to give yourself an idea of what structures might be present. Design sentences around the structures of these languages, but don't be limited to previous work or analyses.
- **Grammaticality judgement tests can be unreliable**. Don't just say a sentence yourself and ask if it is correct or not. Positive responses to a test sentence may mean that the clause is correct, but it also might mean that speakers think you've given it a good shot and need encouragement. Negative responses are also difficult to interpret. The sentence might be ungrammatical, but it might also just be semantically weird.
- **Determining grammaticality** is done more reliably by getting speakers to repeat a sentence. Especially in early stages of fieldwork, you should always have the speaker utter the relevant sentence before you can consider it acceptable. They will usually repeat it word for word if it is correct, but will correct it if not. It goes against the grain for anyone to repeat something which is ungrammatical. Another option is to give the translation in the intermediary language, or use a prompt of some sort (e.g. pictorial) and have the speaker utter the sentence themselves.
- The 'gavagai' problem or **the indeterminacy of translation** (cf. Quine, 1960). It is often difficult to tell whether a word (or construction) means quite what you think it means. If someone points to a rabbit and says *gavagai*

128 *Morpho-syntax*

are they referring to the whole animal, part of it, its action or an exclamation "Hey a rabbit!"? Put the word in a sentence, and try inflecting it as a noun or verb.

- **The use of a vernacular language**, such as a colonial English or variety or creole, can be problematic. As an L2 learner of the variety, you need to be careful that words mean what you think they mean. For example, if someone exclaims "Oh here comes that cheeky dog!" in Australian Kriol – adopt a defensive pose. Don't try to pat the dog! *Cheeky* means 'dangerous' in Kriol. And in general, **make sure you record translations of these words using proper translations** not pseudo-English/French/Spanish etc. which doesn't distinguish the semantics of the standard and vernacular varieties. Don't assume that the vernacular language forms have the same semantics as the standard form of the language.
- When you are fairly certain of your analysis and you start glossing examples, **use the Leipzig Glossing Rules**,[1] and where morphemes do not have a gloss, use the conventions developed by other linguists for languages in the same language family or region. **Do not invent new glosses** (even if your analysis of the category is slightly different from others, in which case you should describe this in your grammar). It causes no end of headaches for other linguists and community members reading these grammars trying to figure out your category if you invent new terms.

### 6.6.2 Back translation

Back translation is a process whereby a different speaker or team of speakers translates a previously translated sentence or text from the 'target' language (the language you are documenting) back into the 'elicitation' language (the mutually understood language, often the contact or vernacular language, you are using for elicitation). Back translation is the time-honoured method of SIL International linguists for ensuring quality translations. It is a good technique for figuring out if you have understood the functions of particular language structures, but requires you to have a good knowledge of the language. You can use it to check sentences you have constructed, or to check other speakers' sentences (but be careful not to come across as if you are checking how good the other speaker is etc.). It is a particularly useful method for when you know you are operating on the edge of what is grammatically acceptable. This method is also discussed in §8.4.5.

---

**Tip – Checking sentences from other speakers**

If you think a speaker said something ungrammatical by mistake, but you don't want to make them look bad, you could pretend you have found it written down in your notebook, but you're not sure if you got it right or not, so then if it's wrong it looks like it's your fault.

---

### 6.6.3 A culturally embedded grammar

Although the focus of formal elicitation is on the morpho-syntax of the language, you should carefully consider the semantic content of the sentences you are creating. Linguistic categories, although highly abstract on the one hand, are also imbued with cultural practices and principles. For example, many Australian languages have highly complex kinship systems which are encoded in the grammar, referred to as 'kintax' by Evans (2003). Murrinhpatha (Southern Daly) has a (non)sibling distinction in the pronoun system (Blythe, 2010) and Arandic languages (Pama-Nyungan) encode kin relations in their pronouns (Wilkins, 1989). This is another reason it is always better to use example sentences which originate with the speakers of a language themselves (for example from narrative or conversation) rather than elicitation (see also §6.1). These examples reflect better the world which shaped the language. Epps, Webster, & Woodbury (2017) worry that there is a trend away from these types of sentence examples:

> Hill (2006:609) lists, among ways that a linguist might 'write culture in grammar,' the use of '[e]xample words, constructions, and sentences in the grammar [that] implicitly reflect culturally-appropriate usage ... because they were drawn from a corpus of texts.' She concludes that while Boas, Sapir, and other earlier-period writers did just this, that – in spite of notable examples to the contrary – 'there is an increasing tendency in American grammars to favour the transparent representation of grammatical phenomena over the cultural interest of the example sentences,' implying as well a lesser reliance on textual attestations as examples.
>
> (Epps, Webster, & Woodbury, 2017, p. 51)

When you come to writing up your grammar, where possible, try to use example sentences from your corpus that reflect that culture of the speech community. Of course you will need to resort to elicited examples for rare constructions (§6.1).

### 6.6.4 Mindful elicitation

One of the problems with publishing some of the sentences made up by linguists is that they become instantiations of culture and may perpetuate negative stereotypes about often already marginalised people. For example, grammars are full of sentences exemplifying transitivity using verbs that denote violence. 'Hit' is a classic transitive verb, but so is 'hug' or 'carry'. When you construct sentences for elicitation, avoid topics that refer to violence, sex, alcohol, drugs (including smoking), child abuse or neglect, as these may upset people down the track. Also bear in mind that descendants of the speakers may read the grammar in years to come, or may be an audience member in a presentation using data you collected. Imagine that you are trying to re-construct your language and the only verb in the corpus is 'hit'!

---

**Perpetuating negative stereotypes of communities – Al Harvey**

My name is Al Harvey, I am of Saibai Island descent and am currently working on a project to preserve, document and protect the Top Western Torres Strait Island dialect of Kalaw Kawaw Ya (KKY).

Today KKY, like many other Australian Indigenous languages, is endangered. The loss of languages is more than just the loss of spoken word. It has always been explained to me that languages are a reflection of a people's soul and way of living in the world. Speakers and descendants of a language have a role to play in the preservation and maintenance of that language but so too do people who work with those languages, including linguists. It's important that linguists are cognisant of the role they play in acting as a facilitator in the preservation of languages. Linguists also need to be aware that language data gathered is presented in a way that reflects the good faith in which it was given.

I was at a linguistics workshop recently where the presenters offered sentences from an Aboriginal language. One of the sentences presented in the targeted language translated into English as 'The man hit the woman'. For the purpose of the exercise it seemed to me to be an unnecessary display of a negative stereotype in a forum of predominately non-Indigenous linguists.

Thinking of language data beyond something to be scientifically analysed and being cognisant that the language you're working with comes from the soul of a people would surely go some way to avoiding such unnecessary representations.

## 6.7 AREAS OF GRAMMAR TO FOCUS ON

Human languages are similar in some ways, but incredibly diverse in others. Making sense of this diversity is one factor that drives field linguists to document language after language. The discovery of new linguistic categories and the different instantiations of well-known categories contribute much to understanding the design space of language. This section covers many of the major linguistic categories that most languages encode – core grammatical relations, verb distinctions, pronoun distinctions, spatial relations, number and information structure; as well as major language family-specific categories such as noun classes and evidentiality. We also discuss major morphological categories such as clitics vs affixes and derivation vs inflection. Throughout these sections, we give references to key typological works which provide cross-linguistic surveys of particular constructions and parts of speech. Other excellent resources are the World Atlas of Language Structures (WALS)[2] and the Atlas of Pidgin and Creole Structures (APiCS).[3] Also helpful is Tim Shopen's (2007) classic series 'Language typology and syntactic description' and Thomas Payne's (1997) *Describing morphosyntax: A guide for field linguists*. Another great resource is the 'Typological tools for linguistic research' questionnaire series developed by the MPI for Evolutionary Anthropology in Leipzig.[4] Use these references, as well as grammatical descriptions of related or neighbouring languages, to give yourself a sense of the potential categories and distinctions that you might find in the language you are working on.

### 6.7.1 Grammatical relations

All languages mark core grammatical roles in some way and it is important to establish this early into elicitation because other structures in the language follow from it. Core grammatical roles are the subject of an intransitive clause (S), subject of a transitive clause (A) and object of a transitive clause (O). To find out how the language distinguishes these roles, you need to elicit sentences that show the full range of transitivity, such as:

**(2)** (a) The woman sleeps.
(b) The child sleeps.
(c) The woman hugs the child.
(d) The child hugs the woman.
(e) She hugs him.
(f) He hugs her.
(g) He sleeps.

The main ways nouns distinguish grammatical roles are by word order (e.g. English), case-marking (e.g. Finnish) or both word order and case-marking (e.g. German). Pronouns, which are a closed class, often distinguish roles using different forms i.e. suppletive case-marking (e.g. English) rather than regular case-markers (§6.7.4). Usually either A or O is marked the same as S (through word order, morphology or form). When A and S are grouped together (typically unmarked), and O is distinguished by case-marking or form, you have an **accusative** system. When O and S are grouped together (typically unmarked), and A is distinguished by some kind of marking or form, you have an **ergative** system (Figure 6.1).

For example, in German, grammatical relations are marked through case in the determiner system. German is an accusative language because A and S determiners have the same form e.g. *der* (masculine) 3(a) and (c). Word order also helps. German is a verb second language and the subject usually comes before the verb but it can also come after the verb 3(c). Follow the bolded determiners in (3) to see how they group subjects and distinguish the object from subjects.

**Figure 6.1**
Groupings of A (transitive subject), S (intransitive subject) and O (object) in an accusative system (non-dotted line) and ergative (dotted line) system

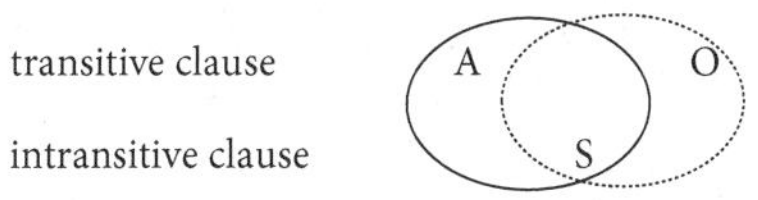

## 132 *Morpho-syntax*

(3) German (Germanic, Indo-European, Germany)

   (a) **Der**        Hund schläft                 (intransitive)
        the.M.NOM    dog    sleeps
        The dog sleeps.

   (b) **Der**        Hund beißt **den**           Mann    (transitive)
        the.M.NOM    dog    bites    the.M.ACC     man
        The dog bites the man.

   (c) **Den**        Mann beißt **der**         Hund    (transitive)
        the.MASC.ACC   man    bites    the.MASC.NOM   dog
        The dog bites the man.

English groups A and S through word order (both are preverbal). Other languages such as some Berber, Cushitic, Omotic (East Africa), Yuman (California) and Austronesian languages mark A and S morphologically and leave O unmarked. These languages are called **marked-s** or **marked-nominative languages** (Handschuh, 2015). In contrast, Pitjantjatjara shows an ergative pattern because S and O are unmarked, and A is marked morphologically.

(4) Pitjantjatjara (Western Desert, Pama-Nyungan, Australia)

   (a) **Papa**         ngura-ngka     nyina-nyi    (intransitive)
        dog             camp-LOC      sit-PRS
        The dog is sitting in camp.

   (b) **Wati-ngku papa**   nyanga-nyi            (transitive)
        man-ERG dog      see-PRS
        The man sees the dog.

---

### Exercise 4   If English were ergative?

If English pronouns patterned in an **ergative** configuration, which pronouns would be the same and which would be different if speakers were to say these sentences:

(5) 3sg is dreaming.

(6) 3sg is carrying 3sg.

---

Some languages have internal splits between accusative systems and ergative systems (but see Goddard, 1982). Silverstein (1976) explains ergativity splits based on the inherent lexical content (with relevant features being person and animacy) of a referring expression. Pronouns are more likely to pattern as accusative and nouns are more likely to pattern as ergative (Figure 6.2).

Figure 6.2
Silverstein's hierarchy and ergative/accusative splits

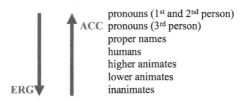

To find out whether the language marks these roles differently depending on the Silverstein hierarchy, the following sequence of elicitation sentences can be useful:

(7) (a) She cut the grass. (3rd person)
   (b) I/you cut the grass. (1st and 2nd person)
   (c) Sally cut the grass. (proper noun)
   (d) The woman cut the grass. (human)
   (e) The dog bit the child. (higher animate)
   (f) The mosquito bit the child. (lower animate)
   (g) The grass cut me. (inanimate)

Other argument relations systems to look out for are **direct-inverse systems**, common in Algonquian and Athabaskan languages (Klaiman, 1992). These systems consist of two configurations – the direct construction, usually unmarked, is used when the subject of the transitive clause outranks the object in the person hierarchy, and the inverse is used when the object outranks the subject. Sentences (7)(d)–(g) can help determine whether this system is found in the language.

Case may also be optionally marked in some languages, with the grammatical relation of the referring expression unaffected. **Optional ergativity** is common in Tibeto-Burman and Australian languages and is often driven by animacy, information structure and perfectivity (McGregor, 2010b). Objects may also be optionally marked (or receive different case-markers) and this is called **differential object marking**, for example Hindi (Indo-Aryan, India) marks human objects with the accusative case suffix *–ko*, but only optionally marks non-human objects. Where non-human objects are marked they are definite (de Hoop & de Swart, 2008). You will need to use different techniques other than elicitation to sort out this type of variation (see §10.3.3 for some methods).

### 6.7.2 Verb distinctions

Languages carve up time in different ways and the verb is one place where this is most apparent. Verbs have inherent **Aktionsart** or 'lexical aspect', with tense, aspect and mood (TAM) marking interacting with Aktionsart. The forms of

**Figure 6.3**
Some Aktionsart categories

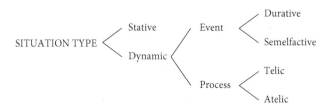

inflected verbs also often differ, forming different conjugations or verb classes. Voice and directional categories such as **hither, thither** and *associated motion* (see §6.7.5) are also often marked on verbs. Verbs can also combine with other verbs, forming complex predicates such as serial verbs. This section deals with each of these categories in turn.

Aktionsart is often categorised according to the kinds of situation types seen in Figure 6.3. You can try eliciting the following types of sentences to determine the Aktionsart of verbs (but note that not all tests will be available in all languages). Unlike **dynamic** verbs e.g. *drive, hit, sneeze, learn, write*, **stative** verbs e.g. *be, have, remain, know, love, fear* will not combine with a progressive marker (8)(c) and generally can't be used in imperatives (8)(d). **Semelfactive** verbs, as opposed to **durative** verbs, refer to an event which takes an instant to accomplish and can be elicited using punctual adverbials (8)(e). Time-span adverbials can be used to distinguish **atelic** from **telic** verbs.

(8) (a) I am running to work. (dynamic)
    (b) I know Swahili. (stative)
    (c) *I am know**ing** Swahili. (stative)
    (d) *Know Swahili. (stative)
    (e) The mine blew up **at 4 o'clock**. (semelfactive)
    (f) He coughed **all night**. (durative)
    (g) I ran the race. (telic)
    (h) I ran **for an hour**. (atelic)

Aktionsart interacts with grammatical **aspect** which is used to pick out some temporally specifiable part of a situation. Simplified aspectual contrasts can be represented as in Figure 6.4.

**Habitual** aspect expresses the occurrence of an event or state as characteristic of a period of time e.g. *I eat dinner*. **Perfective** aspect describes the situation as a whole with no reference to how it unfolds in time. It 'telescopes' a situation to a point e.g. *I ate dinner*. **Imperfective** aspect attends to the internal temporal structure of a situation e.g. *I am eating dinner*.

Figure 6.4
A simplified aspectual schema

**Tense** is probably the most common category marked on verbs cross-linguistically. Some languages make a two way morphological tense distinction, usually past/non-past as in English or Finnish, or future/non-future as in Dyirbal (Dixon, 1972). Other languages have a three-way distinction – past, present and future. Use adverbials to discover these distinctions:

Some languages carve up time in more detail, making distinctions between remote and recent past and future. Some languages make no tense distinctions, instead distinguishing between **realis/irrealis** mood. They indicate that a certain situation or action is (not) known to have happened at the time the speaker is talking. Often languages have a combination of tense and realis distinctions and these can be quite hard to tease out, for example future tense and potential mood often have a lot of overlap, and often it is difficult to figure out whether a language has a future/non-future tense or an irrealis/realis mood distinction. Other types of **mood** categories which languages can encode are subjunctive, conditional, imperative, dubitative and hortative. Payne (1997) provides good contexts and example sentences for sorting out these distinctions.

Often the pattern of inflection in a language categorises verbs into groups, referred to as **conjugation classes**. Like noun classes (§6.7.8), verbs of the same conjugation class have a particular pattern of inflection i.e. members of a given class typically inflect in the same way (take the same set of inflections) as one another. Eliciting all of the conjugations for every verb can seem like a daunting task, but often conjugations are minimally different and there is frequently one form which distinguishes them. For example in Bilinarra, the potential or imperative inflections are the best distinguished so you can categorise a verb on the basis of one example (see Table 6.2).

136  *Morpho-syntax*

**Table 6.2**

Verb conjugations in Bilinarra, which has five major classes of verbs and a number of irregular verbs

|  | Class 1 'put' | Class 2 'cook' | Class 3 'look' | Class 4 'talk' | Class 5 'go' |
|---|---|---|---|---|---|
| **IMPerative** | *yuwarra* | *gamba* | *nyangga* | *manyja* | *yanda* |
| **PaST(PERFective)** | *yuwani* | *gambarni* | *nyanya* | *marni* | *yani* |
| **PaST IMPerFective** | *yuwanirra* | *gambanirra* | *nyanyarra* | *marnirra* | *yanirra* |
| **POTential** | *yuwarru* | *gambawu* | *nyanggu* | *malu* | *yan.gu* |
| **PReSent** | *yuwarra* | *gambala* | *nyanga* | *mala* | *yana* |
| **INFINitive** | *yuwanu* | *gambarnu* | *nyangu* | *marnu* | *yanu* |

Source: based on Meakins & Nordlinger, 2014, p. 272

---

### Tip – Don't use *be* or *go* to elicit verb conjugations

Highly frequent verbs such as *be* or *go* are often a bad choice for establishing conjugation classes because they are often irregular e.g. *be, is, was* or *go, went*.

---

### Tip – Try a range of verbs to elicit conjugations

Verb conjugations are often based on transitivity or phonological characteristics such as syllable structure or codas so try a range of verbs – transitive, intransitive, ditransitive, one syllable stems, two syllable stems etc. to ensure that you have discovered the full range of verb classes.

---

**Voice** alternations which affect transitive clauses are also encoded on the verb. Active voice e.g. *I held the book* is the unmarked configuration of the subject and object. Passive voice promotes the patient to subjecthood, often demoting the agent to an optional element and marking the verb in some way e.g. *The book was held by me.* Middle voice is another way to express a transitive verb where there is a sense that the agent is acting on itself e.g. *The book flipped open.* On the other hand, the antipassive in ergative languages removes the object from core argument structure. See some examples from Choctaw (Muskogean, Mississippi/Oklahoma) and Kabardian (Abkhaz–Adyghe, Caucasus) in (10) and (11).

**(10)**  Choctaw (Foley & Van Valin Jr, 1985, pp. 322–323)

Bill at　　　okhisa　an　　　tiwwih.

Bill **SUBJ**　door　　OBL　　he_opens_it

Bill opens the door. (Active voice)

Okhisa　　at　　　tinwah.

door　　　**SUBJ**　open-**MID**

The door opens. (Middle voice)

**(11)** Kabardian (Moravcsik, 1978, pp. 259–260)

Fie-m qʷʼpsfie-r je-dzag'e
dog-**ERG** bone-ABS TR-bite
The dog bites the bone. (Active voice)

Fie-r qʷʼpfie-m je-w-dzag'e
dog-**ABS** bone-INST TR-**ANTIPASS**-bite
The dog gnaws on the bone. (Antipassive voice)

**Complex predicates** are single verbal predicates such as light verb constructions and serial verbs which are encoded in two or more types of verbs. The literature on complex predicates is riddled with a confusion of constructions and terminology, often specific to particular language families (and even plenty of variation within the literature on families). If you come across complex predicates, read Butt (2003), who provides some useful navigational tools through this "jungle" of terminology, as she calls it. Several general volumes which are also useful are: Aikhenvald and Dixon (2006) and Amberber, Baker & Harvey (2010).

### 6.7.3 Possession

Every language has a way of expressing possession. Some good overviews of the way that possession is marked across the world's languages include McGregor (2010a) and Dixon & Aikhenvald (2015). Sometimes possession is also marked through pronouns (see §6.7.4). Possession is often expressed by marking the dependent of a noun phrase with **genitive case** (or often dative case) i.e. *John's book*; or by marking the head of the noun phrase with **possessive suffix** i.e. *John book-his*.

Some languages divide nouns into different types based on the possessive construction they participate in. For example a distinction is often made between alienable and inalienable possessums (the possessed object). Cross-linguistically, inalienable nouns tend to be body parts and close kin, and alienable nouns are all nouns which do not participate in a part-whole relationship (Chappell & McGregor, 1995).[5] Try out these types of sentences and see how speakers express possession:

**(12)** (a) Maria drove Juan's car. (classically alienable)
(b) Maria met Juan's mother. (close kin)
(c) Maria met Juan's mother-in-law. (in-law kin)
(d) Maria fed Juan's dog. (higher animate)
(e) Maria borrowed Juan's spade. (tools)
(f) The reindeer's liver was infected. (attached body part)
(g) The reindeer's liver was delicious. (detached body part)

Commonly, alienable relationships are indicated on nouns through genitive case or possessive suffixes, and inalienable possession is unmarked, but the dependent noun in the possessive phrase is cross-referenced by a pronoun.

## 6.7.4 Pronoun distinctions

In describing a new language, you will inevitably have to come to grips with pronouns. Typically pronouns exist either as **free forms** or **bound forms** (which may be affixes or clitics – see §6.7.11 for the distinction). Some languages have both. In many languages, bound pronouns are obligatory and occur in conjunction with full nouns, cross-referencing number or other properties of the noun. In these cases, the pronouns are often analysed as agreement markers (similar to –s in the English *He sleeps*). Pronouns typically mark different features:

- Person
  - first, second and third person
  - Sometimes first person pronouns distinguish inclusive (including the hearer) and exclusive (excluding the hearer) categories

---

### Tip – The deictic centre problem

A classic problem with pronoun elicitation goes a bit like this:

Linguist: How do you say "You talked to me"?
Speaker: "I talked to you".

This problem is generally unavoidable. Some speakers are good at deictic switches and others aren't. Start with third person pronouns *s/he/it* and *them* before moving onto first and second person pronouns, then just account for the way the speaker is conceptualising the task. This might be hard to do at first but slowly in conversation you will realise if you have first and second person pronouns flipped.

---

- Gender
  - e.g. no gender distinctions
  - e.g. masculine and feminine in third person pronouns
  - e.g. animacy.

To elicit gender distinctions in pronouns, you will need to take advantage of their anaphoric function (unless gender is encoded in the first and second person pronouns also). Try a sequence like (13). This sequence changes gender, but you can use it for other categories e.g. animacy.

**(13)** (a)  The man went to the shop and PRO bought an apple.
   (b)  The woman went to the shop and PRO bought an apple.
   (c)  The bus went to the shop and PRO brought lots of people.

- Case (see §6.7.1)
  - e.g. nominative, accusative, dative
  - e.g. subject, non-subject (inc. oblique)
  - e.g. non-core cases – oblique (sometimes dative), locative, allative etc.

To elicit case distinctions in pronouns, use similar methods suggested for grammatical relations above. This sequence changes the transitivity and voice of verbs and therefore the grammatical role but you can use it for other categories. Again start with third person because it is less confusing:

**(14)** (a)  PRO slept.                          (intransitive, subject)
    (b)  PRO bought an apple.              (transitive, subject)
    (c)  Juan bought PRO.                   (transitive, object)
    (d)  Juan went to PRO.                  (transitive, adjunct)
    (e)  Maria gave PRO an apple.           (ditransitive, indirect object)
    (f)  Maria gave Juan PRO.               (ditransitive, direct object)
    (g)  Juan was given an apple by PRO.    (transitive, passive)

- Number (see also §6.7.6)
  - singular and plural systems are common (and sometimes dual and trial, e.g. Larike (Central Moluccan, Ambon Island, Indonesia) (Laidig & Laidig, 1990))
  - minimal, unit augmented (i.e. minimal+1) and augmented systems are less common. They have *three* inclusive forms in the first person forms, covering the minimal (= two people – speaker and hearer), unit augmented (= three people – speaker, hearer and one other) and augmented (= speaker, hearer and two or more others) categories.

---

### Tip – How to spot a minimal-UA-augmented system!

It is easy to assume that the language you are working on is just like other members of the same language family. When Rachel Nordlinger and Felicity Meakins were documenting Bilinarra (Pama-Nyungan, Australia), they assumed that it had a singular – dual – plural system like other Ngumpin-Yapa languages such as Warlpiri (Table 6.3). As such they didn't try to elicit a 'you + me + one other person' pronoun. It was only when *ngaliwula* turned up in conversation that they realised they had a minimal-UA-augmented system on their hands (perhaps the result of Bilinarra calquing its pronoun system on unrelated northern languages such as Jaminjung which have this system (Schultze-Berndt, 2000)) (Table 6.4).

## 140  Morpho-syntax

Table 6.3

Bilinarra pronouns assumed to be a singular – dual – plural system

|   | SINGULAR | DUAL | | PLURAL | |
|---|---|---|---|---|---|
| 1 | *ngayi* | INC<br>*ngali* | EXC<br>*ngayirra* | INC<br>*ngaliwa* | EXC<br>*ngandiba* |
| 2 | *nyundu* | *nyunbula* | | *nyurrulu* | |
| 3 | *nyandu* | *nyanbula* | | *nyarrulu* | |

Table 6.4

Bilinarra pronouns as a minimal-UA-augmented system with the crucial pronoun highlighted

|   | MINIMAL | UA | AUGMENTED |
|---|---|---|---|
| 1exc | *ngayi* | *ngayirra* | *ngandiba* |
| 1inc | *ngali* | ***ngaliwula*** | *ngaliwa* |
| 2 | *nyundu* | *nyunbula* | *nyurrulu* |
| 3 | *nyandu* | *nyanbula* | *nyarrulu* |

Source: Meakins & Nordlinger, 2014, p. 217

Other relevant categories for pronouns are possession (§6.7.3), reciprocals ('they hugged each other') and reflexives ('he hugged himself'). Two useful typological overviews are Nedjalkov (2007) and Evans et al. (2011). If you are interested in working in more depth on reciprocals, good stimulus materials can be found on the MPI (Nijmegen) website.[6]

### 6.7.5  Spatial relations

Spatial relations, or the way an object (figure) is located with respect to another object (ground), constitute an important conceptual system which finds its expression in a number of places in a language – adpositions, case-marking, demonstratives, verbs expressing deixis, fixed bearing systems and of course gesture. The Language and Cognition Department at the Max Plank Institute for Psycholinguistics (Nijmegen, the Netherlands) has developed some useful stimulus materials and accompanying field manuals to explore areas of spatial grammar such as topological relations, motion events, spatial deixis and fixed bearing systems.[7] Elicitation on spatial relations should be videoed because gesture, pointing and context are important cues for this part of the grammar (§3.3.3).

Most basically, the position of a figure with respect to a ground is marked by adpositions or local case-markers in many languages e.g. *the man is in the house*. Common case-markers for marking spatial relations are the locative, allative,

*Morpho-syntax* **141**

ablative, inessive, elative, illative, perlative and terminative. See Blake (1994) for a good discussion of different types of local cases and their functional range.

---

### Tip – One case to rule them all!

Bear in mind that some cases, particularly datives, have a broad range of functions. For example, the dative in Bilinarra (Ngumpin-Yapa, Pama-Nyungan, Australia) can mark indirect objects, alienable possessors, animate goals, beneficiaries, purposes (Meakins & Nordlinger, 2014, pp. 130–134). So don't think you have solved the function of one case form when you discover a single function!

---

**Spatial deixis** expresses the relationship between speech participants (speaker, hearer) and referents in space. Demonstratives, for example *this* (proximal to the speaker) and *that* (distal from the speaker), are common linguistic cues for locating speech participants and referents. As discussed in Chapter 8, these words typically go with gesture, as the speech alone is insufficient to delineate the meaning of an utterance. Demonstrative systems carve up space in very different ways cross-linguistically (Himmelmann, 1996; Levinson et al., 2017). In some languages, verbs also express deixis. For example, in Pitta-Pitta (Pama-Nyungan, Australia) verbs can be marked by *–yangu* 'hither' and *–yaka* 'thither' to indicate motion to and from the speaker or some other reference point (Blake, 1979).

More exact angular relations between the figure and ground are often specified using (i) fixed bearings, e.g. *the man is **north** of the house*, (ii) the speaker's own body axis, e.g. *the man is to the **left** of the house*, or (iii) words which express the inherent facets of an object such as a front, back or side, e.g. *the man is **behind** the house* (Levinson, 2003, pp. 38–56). Languages make use of one or more of these systems in different scales of space. For example, English uses all three systems but favours fixed bearings (cardinal directions) in large-scale space, such as wayfaring, and left-right terms in small-scale space, such as describing the relative position of objects on a table. Fixed bearing systems vary enormously across languages, particularly those which do not have left-right systems. Tzeltal (Mayan, Mexico) expresses all spatial relations in relation to the slope of the land (Brown, 2006). Jaminjung (Mirndi, Australia) uses a river drainage system (Schultze-Berndt, 2006) and Yélî Dnye (Papuan, Rossel Island) expresses all spatial relations through a seaward/hillward system (Levinson, 2006). The use of cardinal direction systems in Australia to describe actions in small-scale space such as passing the salt at supper or putting on a seatbelt is by now quite famous (see Ronnie Wavehill's story in §1.4 and §7.6.1 for an example). Tasks such as the MPI (Nijmegen) 'Animals in a row' game and the 'Man and tree' game have been developed to elucidate the primary spatial relations speakers of different languages use. See §10.4.4.1 for a discussion of how the 'Man and tree' game works and §7.5 for more on director-matcher tasks.

## 142 Morpho-syntax

---

> **Exercise 5  Cardinal directions in the field**
>
> You have just discovered that cardinal directions are used prolifically in the language you are eliciting. A speaker wants to tell you a story about the places they hunt for game. What sorts of equipment should you use? What are some things you should take into consideration when you are setting up?

### 6.7.6 Number

Languages mark number in different parts of the grammar, typically as numerals, noun morphology or pronouns (see §6.7.3). A good overview of number systems is given by Corbett (2000). Number is not a major category in all languages. Some languages have no number morphology, such as Vietnamese.

Where a language marks number, it may make a singular/plural distinction as in many Indo-European languages such as English. Other languages make a three way singular/dual/plural number distinction, such as Jingulu (Mirndi, Australia) (Pensalfini, 2003).

(15)  (a)  I saw **a** bird.
      (b)  I saw **two** elephant**s**.
      (c)  I saw **a herd** of elephant**s**.

(16)  (a)  Jamarni wawa.              'That's a child.'
      (b)  Jama**bila**rni wawa(**bila**).   'Those two are children.'
      (c)  Jama**bala**rni wawa(**bala**).  'Those are many children.'

### 6.7.7 Information structure categories

Information structure categories, broadly topic and focus, are notoriously difficult to decipher and cannot be undertaken using formal elicitation methods, hence the brevity of this section. You need to elicit extended texts (narratives, conversations etc.) and use an audio recorder at the very least (to capture prosody). A good introduction to some field methods is given by Skopeteas (2010) and in general, the Potsdam Questionnaire for Information Structure (QUIS) is a useful starting point.[8]

### 6.7.8 Noun classes and gender

Gender permeates through the grammar of a language in different ways, including in third person pronouns, for example *him/her* in English (§6.7.3) and noun classification systems such as gender and noun classes. This section focuses on noun classification, which is common cross-linguistically, although not found in all languages. Good cross-linguistic overviews of gender and noun classes can be found in Corbett (1991) and Aikhenvald (2003). These books will give you a sense of what to expect if you begin to suspect that the language you're working on classifies nouns.

The distinction between gender and noun class systems is often talked about as being based on the presence of agreement, although this distinction has been problematised and gender can be thought of as a special kind of nominal classification (Corbett & Fedden, 2016). For example, Jingulu (Mirndi, Australia) distinguishes four genders: masculine, feminine, vegetable and neuter; and adjectives and demonstratives show agreement in gender with the head noun (Meakins & Pensalfini, 2016, p. 426):

**(17)** MASC  Bininj**a**      bardakurr-**a**     NEUT     Darrangku bardakurr-**u**
                 man(m)      good-**M**                      tree(n)      good-**N**
                 'A good man'                                 'A good tree'

        FEM      Nayu**rni**     bardakurri-**rni**    VEG      Karnariny**mi** bardakurri-**mi**
                 woman(f)    good-**F**                     spear(v)     good-**V**
                 'A good woman'                           'A good spear'

Languages differ as to the number of genders they distinguish. Many Romance languages have a two-way distinction which is sometimes marked on the noun, referred to as 'masculine' and 'feminine' because nouns referring to male and female animates divide into the two classes (and all other nouns are then obligatorily categorised in these classes). German has three classes, referred to as 'masculine', 'feminine' and 'neuter'. Note that gender is marked in the article rather than on the noun itself (*der* – M, *die* – F, *das* – N in the nominative). Bantu and Papuan languages have numerous noun classes, for example, Swati (Bantu, Swaziland and South Africa) has over a dozen classes, represented by prefixes, including (tone not represented):

**(18)**  *um(u)-*    persons             *umfana*    'boy'
       *li-*         body parts, fruit   *lidvolo*    'knee'
       *s(i)-*      instruments      *sitja*     'plate'
       *in-*        animals          *indʡa*     'dog'
       *bu-*      abstract properties *bubi*      'evil'
       *pha-*    locations         *phandle*  'outside'

Nouns are categorised into classes in different ways. Sometimes inherent semantic dimensions, such as biological gender and animacy, are relevant. For example, Tamil (Dravidian, Sri Lanka) has a purely semantic system with three classes that divide nouns into male humans, female humans and other. For other languages, semantics provides the basis for the system but other factors play a large role, for example German phonology gives a lot of clues as to noun class assignment. For instance, words ending in *-e* and *-ung* are more often than not feminine. One method for trying to determine what principles underlie the classification is to try borrowing words from the vernacular language into the system to see if the phonology or semantics play a role.

144  *Morpho-syntax*

## 6.7.9 Evidentiality

Evidentiality expresses the nature of evidence for a given statement, i.e. whether the speaker knows it as a fact, whether they heard it from someone else (hearsay), whether they witnessed it etc. In English, evidential categories are expressed through verbs and adverbs:

**(19)** (a)  I am happy                (direct evidence)
     (b)  Mary seems happy       (inferential)
     (c)  Mary looks happy        (visual evidence, inferential)
     (d)  Mary is happy, reportedly    (hearsay)
     (e)  I hear that Mary is happy    (hearsay)

Indicating the information source in English is optional; however, in some languages, particularly in South America, there is a distinct grammatical category of evidentiality that is required at all times. Without the evidential marker the sentence is ungrammatical! A good place to start with understanding evidentiality systems is Aikhenvald (2004). Some common evidential categories given by Aikhenvald are:

- Witness versus non-witness
  - first hand vs second hand vs third hand
  - sensory
    - visual vs non-visual (i.e. auditory, olfactory etc.)
  - inferential
    - information inferred by direct physical evidence
    - information inferred by general knowledge
    - information inferred because of speaker's experience with similar situations
    - past deferred realisation.
- Reportative
  - hearsay
  - quotative e.g. suffix meaning 'X said'
    - Assumed.

---

### Exercise 6  Eliciting evidentiality

What are the kinds of scenarios you would construct with speakers to figure out how evidentiality is encoded in the language? What sorts of sentences would you use?

---

Languages with grammatically encoded evidentiality range from two-term systems such as Jarawara (Arawakan, Amazon) through to five-term systems, for example Tariana (Arawakan, Amazon), which has the following categories – visual

**Table 6.5**
Evidentiality and tense marking in Tariana

| | present | recent past | remote past |
|---|---|---|---|
| visual | *-naka* | *-ka* | *-na* |
| non-visual | *-mha* | *-mahka* | *-mhana* |
| inferred 'generic' | - | *-sika* | *-sina* |
| inferred 'specific' | - | *-nihka* | *-nhina* |
| reported | *-pida* | *-pidaka* | *-pidana* |

Source: Aikhenvald, 2003

sensory, non-visual sensory, inferential (generic, specific), reportative – which fuse with tense forms (present, recent past, remote past) (Table 6.5).

### 6.7.10 Derivation vs inflection

Unless you are working on an isolating language, you will probably encounter plenty of morphology. In fact, if it turns out the language you are working on is polysynthetic, you will have a lot of verbal morphology (and accompanying morpho-phonological processes) to explain (although there's still plenty of syntax in NPs and at the clause-level to work out) (Fortescue, Evans, & Mithun, 2017). Although some theories of morphology do not make a distinction between inflectional and derivational morphology (instead allowing for morphological processes to occur solely in the syntax or lexicon) (see Anderson, forthcoming for an overview of morphological theory), most grammatical descriptions still utilise this distinction. Distinguishing inflectional and derivational morphology is not always straightforward, but here are some ideas and techniques that may prove helpful. In general, derivational morphology is said to create new lexemes and all other features derive from this process (see Bauer (2003) for a good overview). Try some of these tests:

- Does the morpheme change the word class?
  - Yes = probably derivation
  - No = inflection or derivation
- Is the morpheme productive? Can it combine with any member of a word class? e.g. if you have an inflectional past tense, you should expect every verb to have a form, and be very interested if one seems to lack a past tense. On the other hand, if you have a nominalisation which looks derivational, it won't be a surprise if its occurrence is patchy (because it is lexically specific)
  - Yes = inflection
  - Not really = derivation
- Does the morpheme have a regular meaning?
  - Yes = inflection e.g. plural *-s*
  - May not = derivation e.g. *-ette* on *flannelette* vs *suffragette*

146 *Morpho-syntax*

- Does the morpheme appear on the inside of a derivational morpheme closer to the root?
  - ○ Yes = derivation
  - ○ No = maybe inflection (although of course two or more derivations are possible)
  - ○ e.g. *palatal-is-ation-s* 'root-DER-DER-INFL'
- Is the morpheme specific to a closed class of words – i.e. can you borrow a word into the class?
  - ○ Yes = inflection
  - ○ No = derivation
- Is the morpheme obligatory?
  - ○ Yes = inflection
  - ○ No = derivation e.g. it is often possible to replace a form with a monomorphemic form e.g. *excitement* vs *joy*
- Is this morpheme relevant to syntax or the broader clause?
  - ○ Yes = inflection e.g. case, agreement (verb or noun)
  - ○ No = derivation or inflection e.g. gender, number.

Of course there are plenty of counter-examples, and these have formed the basis of much theorising about the distinction between inflection and derivation, whether morphemes really exist, and the place of 'morphology' in language. It is exciting to think that you may stumble over new forms in the language you are working on which may challenge current ideas about morphology.

## 6.7.11 Clitics vs affixes

In the process of documenting a language, you will probably come across parts of a word which are difficult to classify as *affixes* (prefixes, suffixes, infixes, transfixes, circumfixes etc.) or as *clitics* (proclitics or enclitics). Clitics are elements that have some features of a word and some features of an inflectional affix. In English many auxiliary and modal verbs have clitic counterparts:

**(20)** (a-i)  She **will** be here soon.  (modal verb)
    (a-ii)  She**'ll** be here soon.
    (b-i)  She **has** gone.  (present perfect)
    (b-ii)  She**'s** gone.

These types of clitics are called *simple* clitics and they are the easiest to distinguish from affixes because they have a corresponding full word form. *Special* clitics, such as the genitive *'s* in English, do not have a corresponding full word form, making them harder to distinguish from affixes. Some general rules of thumb developed by Anderson (2005) and Bauer (2003) are:

- Clitics can combine with many different word classes whereas affixes are usually restricted by word class.
  - ○ e.g. *The man I was talking to's got a cold* (preposition), *The cold you just caught's gotten worse* (verb), *The cure's really easy* (noun)

- Affixes attach to lexical categories whereas clitics can attach to phrasal categories. This means they interact with syntax more than inflectional affixes.
  - e.g. *Sophie'll go to town* (noun) vs *The queen of England'll go to town* (phrase)
- Clitics don't tend to have irregular forms whereas irregular (and suppletive) forms of inflectional affixes are common.
- There are no syntactic operations e.g. passivisation, which treat a word combined with a clitic as a unit. e.g. *The cat's just eaten the mouse* > *\*The mouse just been eaten by the cat's.*
- Further clitics can attach to clitics; however, inflectional affixes cannot attach to clitics i.e. clitics do not form new stems with their hosts. e.g. *The handle-**er-s=ve** forgotten to bring the animals.*

## 6.8 FINDING A HOME FOR YOUR GRAMMATICAL DESCRIPTION

Formal elicitation can form the basis of a number of fieldwork outputs, including formal or comparative typological treatments of the morpho-syntax, or a full descriptive grammar of the language. Many publishers are now open to innovative ways of incorporating your audio-visual corpus. For instance, Mouton has published the first sound-linked grammar of a language (Meakins & Nordlinger, 2014). If you go down this path, think carefully about copyright agreements with publishers. It is unlikely the speech community will want publishers to take copyright over their voices and stories (§2.4.4). There are also a number of options for producing a hypertext grammar which makes sense from the point of view of the user (grammars are rarely read from cover to cover!) (Nordhoff, 2012).

Learner's guides for non-linguists are also a useful by-product of grammatical analysis. Learner's guides are often requested in communities where the language is endangered and there are many non-speakers; or where they have large numbers of outsiders working in the community. Learner's guides, or parts of them, also sometimes find their home in dictionaries (see §7.5.3.7).

---

**Learning Lakota**

Lakota is a Siouan language spoken by Lakota people of the Sioux tribes in the states of North and South Dakota in the United States. It is one of the few First Nations languages of North America which continues to have a strong speaker base. The language was first written down by missionaries around the 1840s. The recent Lakota Grammar (Figure 6.5) from the Lakota Language Conservancy[9] is a learner's guide in that it has been written for pedagogical purposes, but it still has quite a bit of grammatical detail. The learner's grammar is a part of the Lakota Language Conservancy's efforts to standardise and professionalise Lakota language teaching in tribal and neighbouring schools.

**Figure 6.5**
Front cover of *Lakota Grammar Handbook*

> **Exercise 7  Linguistic terminology in learners' guides**
>
> Learners' grammars tend to be aimed at community members wanting to learn their language or outsiders working in the speech community who need to learn the language. Users typically do not have a background in linguistics, but the writers of these grammars need to bridge academic and non-academic worlds. If you plan to write a learners' grammar, you need to think about terminology. Do you go ahead with standard linguistic terminology or do you create more transparent layperson terms? Do you use the Leipzig rules to gloss example sentences or do you make up glosses that a non-linguist would understand? What would you call ergative markers? Evidentiality? Gender agreement? First person unit augmented pronouns?
>
> - Pick a small section of a grammar and have a go at turning it into a more user-friendly version that might appear in a learner's grammar.
> - Pick a small section in a learner's grammar and re-caste it in more standard linguistic form.

## 6.9 SUMMARY

Traditionally, writing a descriptive grammar of a language has been a primary goal for many field linguists. This chapter has provided the fundamental tools for getting started on this objective. It outlined the general technique of formal elicitation which involves eliciting sequences of minimally different clauses in order to understand the morpho-syntactic and functional categories of the language under investigation. The chapter then offered more specific methods for eliciting grammatical categories common to many languages such as pronoun and TAM distinctions, expression of grammatical relations and possession, as well as other common categories such as noun classification and evidentiality. These methods are also useful for work on contact languages (Chapter 9) and child language (Chapter 10), as they form a comparative basis for these types of projects.

## 6.10 FURTHER READING

Ameka, Dench & Evans (2006) and Nakayama & Rice (2014) contain a number of useful articles on different aspects of grammar writing. Shopen's (2007) classic series *Language typology and syntactic description* and Payne's (1997) *Describing morphosyntax: A guide for field linguists* provide good direction for sorting out morpho-syntactic categories. Bouquiaux & Thomas (1992) is a 700+ page English translation of the original 1971 French field manual which has a 6,400 sentence questionnaire – not for the faint hearted! Sebastian Nordhoff's (2009) grammar of Sri Lankan Malay is model for a hypertext grammar. The ebook version of Meakins & Nordlinger's (2014) grammar of Bilinarra contains sound links to example sentences.

## NOTES

1 www.eva.mpg.de/lingua/resources/glossing-rules.php Accessed 31 August 2017.
2 http://wals.info Accessed 31 August 2017.
3 http://apics-online.info Accessed 31 August 2017.
4 www.eva.mpg.de/lingua/tools-at-lingboard/questionnaires.php Accessed 31 August 2017.
5 Another sort of part-whole relationship is marked by **partitive case**, which is used for expressing that something is a part of a larger mass i.e. *a library of books*. Even if there is no specific partitive case, find out how speakers express this relationship e.g. the use of dative or ablative case is common.
6 http://fieldmanuals.mpi.nl/volumes/2004/reciprocals/ Accessed 31 August 2017.
7 http://fieldmanuals.mpi.nl/projects/space-project/ Accessed 31 August 2017.
8 www.sfb632.uni-potsdam.de/quis.html Accessed 31 August 2017.
9 http://lakhota.org Accessed 31 August 2017.

# REFERENCES

Aikhenvald, A. Y. (2003). *Classifiers: A typology of noun categorization devices*. Oxford: Oxford University Press.

Aikhenvald, A. Y. (2004). *Evidentiality*. Oxford: Oxford University Press.

Aikhenvald, A. Y., & Dixon, R. M. W. (Eds.). (2006). *Serial verb constructions: A cross-linguistic typology*. Oxford: Oxford University Press.

Amberber, M., Baker, B., & Harvey, M. (Eds.). (2010). *Complex predicates: Cross-linguistic perspectives on event structure*. Cambridge: Cambridge University Press.

Ameka, F., Dench, A., & Evans, N. (2006). *Catching language: The standing challenge of grammar-writing*. Berlin: Mouton de Gruyter.

Anderson, S. (2005). *Aspects of the theory of clitics*. Oxford: Oxford University Press.

Anderson, S. (forthcoming). A short history of morphological theory. In J. Audring & F. Masini (Eds.), *The Oxford handbook of morphological theory*. Oxford: Oxford University Press.

Bauer, L. (2003). *Introducing linguistic morphology*. Edinburgh: Edinburgh University Press.

Blake, B. (1979). Pitta-Pitta. In B. Blake & R. M. W. Dixon (Eds.), *Handbook of Australian languages* (pp. 183–242). Amsterdam: John Benjamins.

Blake, B. (1994). *Case*. Cambridge: Cambridge University Press.

Blythe, J. (2010). Self-association in Murriny Patha talk-in-interaction. *Australian Journal of Linguistics*, 30(4), 447–469.

Bouquiaux, L., & Thomas, J. (1992). *Studying and describing unwritten languages*. Dallas: SIL International.

Brown, P. (2006). A sketch of the grammar of space in Tzeltal. In S. Levinson & D. Wilkins (Eds.), *Grammars of space: Explorations in linguistic diversity* (pp. 230–271). Cambridge: Cambridge University Press.

Butt, M. (2003). *The light verb jungle*. Harvard Working Papers in Linguistics (Papers from the Harvard/Dudley House Light Verb Workshop) 9.

Chappell, H., & McGregor, W. (Eds.). (1995). *The grammar of inalienability: A typological perspective on body part terms and the part-whole relation*. Berlin: Mouton de Gruyter.

Corbett, G. (1991). *Gender*. Cambridge: Cambridge University Press.

Corbett, G. (2000). *Number*. Cambridge: Cambridge University Press.

Corbett, G., & Fedden, S. (2016). Canonical gender. *Journal of Linguistics*, 52(3), 495–531.

de Hoop, H., & de Swart, P. (2008). Cross-linguistic variation in differential subject marking. In H. de Hoop & P. de Swart (Eds.), *Differential subject marking* (pp. 1–16). New York, NY: Springer.

Dixon, R. M. W. (1972). *The Dyirbal language of north Queensland*. Cambridge: Cambridge University Press.

Dixon, R. M. W., & Aikhenvald, A. Y. (2015). *Possession and ownership*. Oxford: Oxford University Press.

Epps, P., Webster, A., & Woodbury, A. (2017). A holistic humanities of speaking: Franz Boas and the continuing centrality of texts. *International Journal of American Linguistics*, 83(1), 41–78.

Evans, N. (2003). Context, culture, and structuration in the languages of Australia. *Annual Review of Anthropology*, 32, 13–40.

Evans, N., Gaby, A., Levinson, S., & Majid, A. (Eds.). (2011). *Reciprocals and semantic typology*. Amsterdam: John Benjamins.

Everett, D. (2001). Monolingual field research. In P. Newman & M. Ratliff (Eds.), *Linguistic fieldwork* (pp. 166–188). Cambridge: Cambridge University Press.

Foley, W., & Van Valin Jr, R. D. (1985). Information packaging in the clause. In T. Shopen (Ed.), *Language typology and syntactic description* (Vol. 1, pp. 282–354). Cambridge: Cambridge University Press.

Fortescue, M., Evans, N., & Mithun, M. (2017). *The Oxford handbook of polysynthesis*. Oxford: Oxford University Press.

Goddard, C. (1982). Case systems and case marking in Australian languages: A new interpretation. *Australian Journal of Linguistics*, 2, 167–196.

Hale, K. (1983). A lexicographic study of some Australian languages: Project description. In P. Austin (Ed.), *Australian Aboriginal lexicography* (pp. 71–107). Canberra: Pacific Linguistics A-66.

Handschuh, C. (2015). *A typology of marked-S languages*. Berlin: Language Sciences Press.

Himmelmann, N. (1996). Demonstratives in narrative discourse: A taxonomy of universal uses. In B. Fox (Ed.), *Studies in anaphora* (pp. 203–252). Amsterdam: John Benjamins.

Himmelmann, N. (1998). Documentary and descriptive linguistics. *Linguistics*, 36, 161–195.

Klaiman, M. (1992). Inverse systems. *Lingua*, 88, 227–261.

Laidig, W., & Laidig, C. (1990). Larike pronouns: Duals and trials in a central Moluccan language. *Oceanic Linguistics*, 29, 87–109.

Levinson, S. (2003). *Space in language and cognition: Explorations in cognitive diversity*. Cambridge: Cambridge University Press.

Levinson, S. (2006). The language of space in Yélî Dnye. In S. Levinson & D. Wilkins (Eds.), *Grammars of space: Explorations in cognitive diversity* (pp. 157–203). Cambridge: Cambridge University Press.

Levinson, S., Cutfield, S., Dunn, M., Enfield, N., & Meira, S. (Eds.). (2017). *Demonstratives in cross-linguistic perspective*. Cambridge: Cambridge University Press.

McGregor, W. (2010a). *The expression of possession*. Berlin: Mouton de Gruyter.

McGregor, W. B. (2010b). Optional ergative case marking systems in a typological-semiotic perspective. *Lingua*, 120(7), 1610–1636.

Meakins, F., & Nordlinger, R. (2014). *A grammar of Bilinarra: An Australian Aboriginal language of the Northern Territory*. Boston, MA: De Gruyter Mouton.

Meakins, F., & Pensalfini, R. (2016). Gender bender: Disagreement in Jingulu noun class marking. In F. Meakins & C. O'Shannessy (Eds.), *Loss and renewal: Australian languages since colonisation* (pp. 425–450). Berlin: Mouton de Gruyter.

Moravcsik, E. (1978). Case-marking of objects. In J. Greenberg, C. Ferguson, & E. Moravcsik (Eds.), *Universals of human language* (pp. 249–289). Stanford, CA: Stanford University Press.

Nakayama, T., & Rice, K. (2014). *The art and practice of grammar writing*. Honolulu, HI: University of Hawai'i Press.

Nash, D. (1996). Pronominal clitic variation in the Yapa languages. In W. McGregor (Ed.), *Studies in Kimberley languages in honour of Howard Coate* (pp. 117–138). Munich: Lincom Europa.

Nedjalkov, V. (2007). *Reciprocal constructions*. Amsterdam: John Benjamins.

Nordhoff, S. (2009). *A grammar of Upcountry Sri Lanka Malay*. Utrecht: LOT.

Nordhoff, S. (2012). *Electronic grammaticography*. Honolulu, HI: University of Hawai'i Press.

Payne, T. (1997). *Describing morphosyntax: A guide for field linguists*. Cambridge: Cambridge University Press.

Pensalfini, R. (2003). *A grammar of Jingulu: An Aboriginal language of the Northern Territory*. Canberra: Pacific Linguistics.

Quine, W. (1960). *Word and object*. Cambridge, MA: MIT Press.

Schultze-Berndt, E. (2000). *Simple and complex verbs in Jaminjung: A study of event categorisation in an Australian language.* Wageningan: Ponsen and Looijen.

Schultze-Berndt, E. (2006). Sketch of a Jaminjung grammar of space. In S. Levinson & D. Wilkins (Eds.), *Grammars of space: Explorations in cognitive diversity* (pp. 63–114). Cambridge: Cambridge University Press.

Seyfeddinipur, M. (2012). Reasons for documenting gestures and suggestions for how to go about it. In N. Thieberger (Ed.), *The Oxford handbook of linguistic fieldwork* (pp. 147–165). Oxford: Oxford University Press.

Shopen, T. (2007). *Language typology and syntactic description* (Vols. 1–3). Cambridge: Cambridge University Press.

Silverstein, M. (1976). Hierarchy of features and ergativity. In R. M. W. Dixon (Ed.), *Grammatical categories in Australian languages* (pp. 112–171). Atlantic Highlands, NJ: Humanities Press.

Skopeteas, S. (2010). *Word order and information structure: Empirical methods for linguistic fieldwork.* Unpublished Work, Potsdam.

Wilkins, D. (1989). *Mparntwe Arrernte (Aranda): Studies in the structure and semantics of grammar.* PhD thesis: Australian National University.

# 7

# Semantic fieldwork and lexicography

## 7.1 INTRODUCTION

Once you have some grounding in the phonological and grammatical analyses of the language, you will need to start investigating how the language conveys meanings. This can be a very exciting process as you learn about different ways of describing, categorising and speaking that may seem very unfamiliar at first, at least if it's not your own language. In this chapter we consider methods and techniques to elicit the meanings of words. Different types of words require different types of investigation. For example, for kin terms, you will need to have an understanding of the social categories in the culture to elucidate their meanings. For plants and animals, it helps to have an understanding of the Linnaean system of classification or at least a reference guide with this information.

We can approach the issue of identifying meaning from two angles. We can start from a lexical form and explore its different meanings; or we can begin with a domain of meaning and explore all the different ways such meanings are expressed. For example, we can start with a body part term such as *nuu* 'throat' in Yélî Dnye and explore its occurrences in different contexts. The word *nuu* 'throat' combines with different verbs and nouns to express emotions in different ways as seen in the example *A nuu u tpile* "A thing I really like" (literally, "My throat its thing") (Levinson, 2006, p. 237). Alternatively, we can take a broader approach and begin with a semantic domain, such as 'emotion' where we find many lexical items (e.g. 'sad', 'happy'). Both strategies are useful when delving into semantics.

One of the most useful outcomes of linguistic fieldwork is a dictionary. Not only linguists, but other social scientists, the speech community and people working in the community in a diverse range of employment contexts may all benefit from access to a dictionary of the language. The basis of the dictionary is the lexical database, which is also an excellent way of compiling and organising the results of your fieldwork.

In this chapter, we first consider how to elicit vocabulary using a spoken language, where we cover semantic domains and taxonomies (§7.2); and then elicitation using non-linguistic stimuli such as pictures and videos (§7.3). We also consider how to elicit special register vocabulary (§7.4) and look at ways of making a simple dictionary (§7.5) before moving on to a discussion of the ways that more complex information can be included in dictionaries (§7.6). Finally, we consider digital tools available for making and displaying dictionaries (§7.7).

## 7.2 ELICITING VOCABULARY

In your first fieldwork session you might start by exploring some everyday well-known vocabulary such as greetings, kin terms and words for objects in the natural environment that are easily observable or readily at hand. Alternatively, you may try eliciting vocabulary items from a wordlist (§5.2). There are many short word-list questionnaires of basic vocabulary. The most well-known are the 100 and 200 word Swadesh (1950) lists. These were designed to enable cross-linguistic comparisons and thus they aim for universal and non-culturally specific concepts. There are also many geographically focused wordlist questionnaires which include culturally important vocabulary and omit irrelevant vocabulary. Some well-known regional lists are given below:

- Wordlist for Australian Languages (Menning & Nash, 1981; Sutton & Walsh, 1987)
- CALMSEA (Culturally Appropriate Lexicostatistical Model for South East Asia) (Matisoff, 1978)
- Sino-Tibetan Etymological Dictionary and Thesaurus word list questionnaire[1]
- Comparative African Wordlist.[2]

Most of these questionnaires are in English. These short wordlists can be useful if you only have limited time in the field or if you unexpectedly have a brief opportunity to record a speaker of a language for which there is little documentation. To obtain a much larger vocabulary and elucidate the semantics of the words, elicitation from longer wordlists grouped in semantic domains is required.

### 7.2.1 Semantic domains

A semantic domain is an area of meaning and the words used to talk about it. For example a domain that includes 'bird' will also include 'crow', 'fly', 'wing', 'egg' etc. Working in semantic domains can be an efficient way to get to a great deal of vocabulary very quickly because semantically related words are often used in the same context. SIL International has developed a list of 1,800 semantic domains grouped into nine broad categories.[3] There are also a number of regionally specific semantic domain lists, such as ones used for Indo-European languages,[4] for Native American languages[5] and for Australian languages.[6] Many systems use a unique letter for each domain and numbers to represent sub-domains within them (e.g. M 'plants', M1 'vines, M2 'grasses'). For an example of this see Figure 7.1.[7]

Using a semantic domain field in your elicitation lists and in your growing record of the lexicon will enable you to sort and compare data based on meanings, as well as refine your definitions. Semantic domain fields are also very useful for creating picture dictionaries (see §7.5.2). As well as these natural classes, you can use cross-cutting fields to mark functional categories such as food or medicine. For example, you might use a code for 'edible' alongside 'plant' for a word 'pencil yam' so that you can group all foods together and all plants together. Document your list of semantic domain codes and make sure that this documentation is part of your metadata

*Semantic fieldwork and lexicography*    155

**Figure 7.1**
AIATSIS list of semantic domains for Australian languages

| | |
|---|---|
| A: body parts and products | N: physical (dimensions, quantity) |
| B: human classification | O: non-physical (values, emotions, etc.) |
| C: language, mythology, ceremony | P: motion |
| D: human artefacts | Q: state |
| E: food, cooking and fire | R: vocalising & thought |
| F: water (fresh, salt, mud, etc.) | S: bodily function |
| G: elements (sky, topography, etc.) | T: impact and violence |
| H: mammals | U: holding and transfer |
| I: reptiles | V: locationals, temporals, directionals |
| J: birds | W: interrogatives |
| K: marine life | X: interjections |
| L: insects and spiders | Y: particles |
| M: plants | Z: pronouns |

(see §4.2.3). Mosel (2004, p. 45) proposes a method she calls 'active eliciting', where language consultants choose their own semantic domains – for example, terms for different types of food, food preparation and so on.

---

**Tip – Words that may offend**

Be aware of any taboo words or words that may be embarrassing for speakers, for example words for private body parts. If you are working with a speaker who is literate, referring discreetly to a written word may be less confronting than saying it out loud.

---

Before you go into the field, select the appropriate semantic domain codes for the region and expand each domain by adding concepts that you predict might be lexicalised in the language. Consider other possible categorisations. For example, the domain of 'birds' may not include emus and cassowaries because they don't fly, as is the case in many languages of Australia and Papua New Guinea. Conversely, some Australian languages class 'bat' and 'grasshopper' as 'birds'. Languages with noun classes or gender may make it possible to access these language-specific categorisations, for example, emus may not receive the same gender as other birds (§6.7.8).

Wordlist elicitation is often noun heavy, so pay particular attention to eliciting verbs that might collocate with these nouns (e.g. 'fish' and 'swim'). One strategy to find words is to use a dictionary of a related or neighbouring language to elicit

**Table 7.1**

An example of a semantically based elicitation list

| Semantic codes for body parts | Gloss | Speaker 1 | Speaker 2 | Speaker 3 | Speaker 4 |
|---|---|---|---|---|---|
| A1.2 | leg | | | | |
| A1.2.1 | knee | | | | |
| A1.2.2 | kneecap | | | | |
| A1.2.3 | thigh | | | | |
| A1.2.4 | calf | | | | |
| A1.5 | to bend (leg) | | | | |

words. However, make sure to cross-check this data with a range of speakers, as it is easy to introduce errors in this way and to over-state similarities between languages. Your ability to detect errors will improve if you have close collaborations with bilingual speakers and as you learn more about the language.

It is a good idea to use a spreadsheet and put each elicitation word into semantic domains or sub-semantic domains so that you can sort your data in different ways. An example is given in Table 7.1 where A1 is the code for body parts and A1.2 is the code for parts of the leg.

---

### Exercise 1  What is a leg?

A fun way to ascertain the denotation of body part terms is to give speakers an outline of a human or an animal body, and ask them to use different colours to colour in each body part term. For example, not all languages categorise 'legs' in the same way, as Majid, Enfield & van Staden (2006, p. 141) discuss:

> Most report segmentation of the limbs with reference to the discontinuity of joints. However, there is no necessary relationship between a perceptual discontinuity and the naming of a part. Savosavo has a category for leg beginning at the hip joint and encompassing the foot. Punjabi and American Sign Language (ASL) distinguish leg from foot, explicitly recognising the discontinuities of both the hip joint and the ankle. Yélî Dnye also has two terms, but unlike Punjabi and ASL it distinguishes upper leg from lower leg but ignores the ankle discontinuity by having a single category for lower leg plus foot. Jahai recognises all three parts, upper leg, lower leg, and foot.

Choose five dictionaries of diverse languages and compare their terminology for 'leg' and its different parts.

Semantic fieldwork and lexicography 157

One way to assess whether you have covered a semantic domain thoroughly is to compare the number of words you have found with that of a similar language. For example, in Oceanic languages you might compare the number of words in the domain of 'fish' in one dictionary with the number you find in the language you are working on (Pawley, 2012). This can be a quick way to work out where you need to do more research, but note that it is possible there are real differences in the size of the lexicon, even when comparing the languages of two similar cultures. The domain of kin terms is often one in which there is a large degree of non-equivalence cross-linguistically. If the kinship system is complex, it is a good idea to work out genealogies with research participants to help you map out the precise denotation of terms.

## 7.2.2 Taxonomies and other classification systems

Taxonomies are networks of generic (also called superordinate or hypernymic) and hyponymic (or subordinate) relations. For example, in English, 'woman', 'man' and 'spouse' are all hyponyms of 'person'. Taxonomies can be represented by tree diagrams, and it is common for some nodes in a taxonomy to be named while others are not. For example, in Hopi kinship terminology there are only names for every alternate node in the taxonomy of matrilineal descent (Voegelin & Voegelin, 1971, 306–310). Another common feature is the use of one and the same word at different levels of a taxonomy. For example, in many Romance languages, 'woman' and 'wife' are the same word.

Taxonomies are generally embedded in local cultural and social systems and reflect ethno-ontologies as they are often "based on an indigenous understanding of cultural connections between elements of the lexicon" (Cablitz, 2011, p. 228). Folk taxonomies often reflect information such as the fruiting patterns of trees and the habits of animals. Taxonomies may be based on different things, such as form, function, part-whole relationships, stages of growth or co-occurrence of species (Turpin et al., 2013). Functional categories include things such as food, medicine and 'indicator species', for example birds that bring bad news or flowers that herald the onset of spring. Some members of a taxonomic class are more prototypical than others and there may be speaker variation as to whether such peripheral members are included in the class. For example in Wayan *ika* 'fish (generic term)' can also include sea turtles, octopus and squid for some speakers (Pawley, 2012, p. 279).

A folk taxonomy is a vernacular naming system, which can be contrasted with a scientific taxonomy. Western scientific identifications (e.g. a type of plant or cloud) are vital if the community wish to communicate their knowledge to the broader public, and for comparative purposes (e.g. the Linnaean system provides a useful cross-linguistic comparative tool). If possible, team up with scientists who are specialists in the relevant subfield and geographic area. Their knowledge will help you to discover if there are gaps in the lexicon and whether some words may in fact cover a number of species. You might not think to ask what the word is for 'vestigial wings of an emu' (a flightless bird) or the stage of an edible grub when its 'nose' starts to grow unless you know a bit about the relevant flora and fauna. If you

# Semantic fieldwork and lexicography

can't find the relevant specialist to help you, you will have to rely on field guides, plant/animal checklists and photos (§2.7.4). Bear in mind though that the most reliable way of collecting words and meanings in the natural world domain is by first-hand observation and experience. A scientific identification based on showing a speaker a photo of a species and asking for its name is going to be less reliable than one based on a context where the speaker comes across the species in its natural environment and volunteers a name for it. The context, including habitat, sounds, smells, time of day etc., is often critical to people's ability to correctly identify species. Furthermore, being *in situ* often leads to more insightful information about meanings, lexical relations and vocabulary, as well as cultural and general knowledge. The example of the Alyawarr bush potato plant at the beginning of this book, and on the front cover, was drawn from on-the-ground experience – locating the plant, digging the tubers up, then cooking and eating them.

---

### What grub is that?

Determining the identification of a plant, animal or insect is not always a simple matter. For one thing, names in the target language, source language and the Linnaean system may not be in a one-to-one relationship. Kaytetye names 25 different 'edible insect larvae' (Turpin & Si, 2017) within one of the five generic food classes. Because scientific nomenclature is based on terms for the adult of the species, it was necessary to find out what sort of insects these larvae become when they grow up. As some larvae can take years to pupate, the only option was to test the DNA of the larvae specimens, which was possible by collaborating in the field with an entomologist (Yen, 2015). It turned out that some were moths and butterflies, some were beetles and many had not been identified (i.e. not given a Linnaean name). Rarely did the Kaytetye and the scientific classifications fully correspond. These targeted field trips revealed much knowledge about edible larvae. For example, while the clues to locating edible larvae were relatively well known (looking for cracks on the ground, frass at the base of the tree), it was only on these trips that Kaytetye speakers related how knowledge of topography plays a part in signalling which stands of trees are likely to have larvae: they are not found in low-lying flood-prone areas. In addition to working on the denotation of these terms, teaming up with entomologists meant that it was possible to understand the many words for different behaviours, stages of development and products relating to the semantic domain of edible insect larvae. Furthermore, the specimens collected were lodged in appropriate scientific collections with the standard metadata. This means that it will always be possible to track any divisions or new names that are given to these in the Linnaean system and map these to Kaytetye knowledge systems.

*Semantic fieldwork and lexicography*   159

Table 7.2
Literal names for the constellation *Ursa Major* in Alaskan languages

| Language | Family | Literal translation |
| --- | --- | --- |
| Aleut | Eskimo-Aleut | 'caribou' |
| Yup'ik | Eskimo-Aleut | 'caribou' |
| Siberian Yup'ik | Eskimo-Aleut | 'caribou' |
| Inupiaq | Eskimo-Aleut | 'caribou' |
| Tsimshian | Tsimshianic | 'spoon' |
| Haida | Haida | 'sea-otter-stretching-board' |
| Tlingit | Na-Dene | 'all stone' |
| Ahtna | Na-Dene | 'the one that moves above us' |
| Den'ina | Na-Dene | 'the one that turns over us', 'stars stretched' |
| Koyukon | Na-Dene | 'it rotates its body', 'according to it the year is measured' |
| Tanacross | Na-Dene | 'dipper' |
| Upper Tanana | Na-Dene | 'I'm sitting' |
| Gwich'in | Na-Dene | 'the seat' |

Source: Holton, 2012, p. 107

Other natural systems are interesting to explore for their ethno-categories. In many cultures, knowledge of the natural world is deeply embedded in religion and mythology. The Alaskan example in Table 7.2 is taken from the domain of astronomy and it shows the names many Alaskan languages use for the star constellation *Ursa major*. For the linguist, it can be very difficult to know what particular constellation is being named if a speaker points one out. Pictures or star charts can help when you are in the field, but if there is the opportunity to take one or more language speakers to a planetarium this can be a lot of fun.

---

### Exercise 2  Stargazing in Alaska

Consider the names for the constellation *Ursa major* in the Alaskan languages in Table 7.2. In the field how would you check that the Alaskan term does refer to this constellation and not some other? How would you investigate the basis for the names, that is, the basis for the polysemy? What information would you put in the dictionaries for this entry?

## 160 *Semantic fieldwork and lexicography*

So far we have discussed methods and techniques to help explore domains of meaning where the words are mostly concrete nouns. To explore the meanings of more complex words and phrases you will need to collect examples of language used in context. We discuss techniques for doing this in §7.3.

## 7.3 ELICITATION USING NON-LINGUISTIC STIMULI

Language used in more natural settings such as narratives, conversations and procedural texts (to name just a few genres) can provide crucial evidence about the meanings of words. These extended texts can also shed light on patterns of polysemy and taxonomies through collocations and the cultural information they may convey. Nonetheless they may not provide answers to some questions of semantic scope. Furthermore, a corpus of a lesser-known language rarely includes all the words in the lexicon and often there are not enough instances of the terms whose semantics are in question, making it difficult to extrapolate about meaning or grammar (Hellwig, 2006). In these situations, non-linguistic stimuli, such as visual prompts (pictures, videos and three-dimensional objects) and even those based on sounds, tastes or smells can be used either (semi-)experimentally or simply as prompts to collect data. The use of non-linguistic stimuli for elicitation is a good way to get at "the juicy semantic detail of the language" (Majid, 2012, p. 3). They can help delineate meanings, produce excellent illustrative examples, and even provide content for definitions that may later be used in dictionaries (§7.6.2). Such stimulus materials can be used across languages, thus creating corpora of comparable data for cross-linguistic semantic analysis.

Many (semi-)experimental tasks and stimulus sets have been designed by the Language and Cognition group at the Max Planck Institute for Psycholinguistics (MPI) in Nijmegen (the Netherlands) as a part of their research on semantic typology.[8] They include, for example, stimulus sets for investigating spatial cognition and demonstratives (§6.7.5), event categorisation, time, perception and emotion, tactile texture, taste, smell and colour. Descriptions of the tests and the stimulus materials can be found on the MPI website and can be used with permission and proper attribution.[9] Majid (2012) also provides an excellent chapter on the use of these materials. The advantage of these questionnaires and tasks is that they help elucidate both cross-linguistic differences between languages, and inter-speaker variation within a community. They have also been used to explore domains beyond semantics, for example morpho-syntactic distinctions such as reciprocals (§6.7.4).

The MPI stimulus sets are mostly conducted as director-matcher tasks which are designed around sets of stimuli, usually pictures or videos, that are minimally different to each other. The 'director' has a board with the pictures facing away from the 'matcher' who listens to the sentences (see §10.4.4.1 for a picture of a director-matcher task in action). The 'matcher' has a second set of free cards in front of her. The 'director' asks for a card, and the 'matcher' selects the matching card and gives

Semantic fieldwork and lexicography    161

it to her. The 'director' is required to be explicit in her description to differentiate the pairs of cards which are minimally different.

Other tasks involve video description, for example the 'put/take' project which investigated the extent to which speakers of different languages agree on whether, how and how finely to distinguish between placement and removal events of different kinds (Narasimhan et al., 2012, p. 3). A consortium of linguists applied the same stimulus set of 60 short video clips (3–4 seconds long) to 19 languages from different language families to better understand how different languages express information about 'putting' and 'taking'. In contrast to languages like English which use a light verb 'put' for many events involving manipulation and movement, many languages encode "suspension, adhesion, animacy, properties of the figure and the ground, manner, and force-dynamic notions such as control, force, intentionality" (Narasimhan et al., 2012, p. 10). For example, Yélî Dnye has verbs which distinguish between 'putting something on a body part' and 'taking something off a body part'.

You may also wish to innovate and create your own tasks to explore different semantic domains (see §10.4.4.1 for an example of a 'bespoke' director-matcher task used to study variable case-marking in a language contact setting). The design can be very simple, with eight to ten pictures stuck to an A3 piece of stiff cardboard which can then be laminated. The spare set of cards for the 'matcher' has Velcro on the back to allow them to be stuck to the picture on the board (also velcroed). More sophisticated versions of director-matcher tasks can be created using iPads which then allows sound to be aligned with target pictures. These might not be appropriate for non-tech savvy participants, or for use in places where there is intense sunlight because the screens will be hard to see! You could put together a set of animal, machine and human sounds to get an understanding of verbs of vocalisation, such as 'talk', 'hum', 'sing'. Go online and see if there are audio guides for birds, frogs and insects in the region where you work.

---

**Tip – Get your Velcro the right way around!**

Don't stick the hooked Velcro on the free pictures otherwise you will gather half the debris in the community! If the ripping sound of Velcro irritates you, try magnets (but be careful that they don't interfere with the microphones).

---

When creating a picture, video or object-based stimuli for elicitation make sure the content is easily identifiable to speakers. Aim for tasks that are fun – amateur videos with local content can be a good way of introducing variety to the fieldwork tasks, and if you are in them yourself even better! Well before you begin the tasks with speakers, you should trial the images with one or two speakers to ensure that people know what they represent. You may need to modify or reject

# 162 *Semantic fieldwork and lexicography*

certain pictures if speakers do not recognise them or are distracted by something in them. In some cases, drawings are better than photos because it is possible to modify them to make the feature of interest stand out. Include two or three stimulus items that are not part of the contrasts you are aiming to test to familiarise the participant with the task and the nature of the materials. Don't make the tasks too long – longer than half an hour for this type of repetitive exercise is too long.

Try to transcribe all the data. Some responses may not be based on a correct reading of the stimuli; other responses may be, but do not address the semantic issue you aimed to explore. You may want to code these utterances differently, in contrast to utterances which do address the target issue. There may also be multiple responses to the one stimulus. The first may be a short natural response, while subsequent responses may be more considered or reflective. Identify the constructions employed and how the semantic information is distributed over the clause. Transcription is the time to consider whether additional forms or constructions should also be brought into further elicitation tasks. Consider your data for the sorts of situations that call for descriptions of particular constructions or words. You can do this manually, but there are also statistical tools and methods, discussed in Majid (2012), that can be useful if you have a very large collection of data.

Stimulus sets can also be designed to explore semantic distinctions in non-experimental settings with just a few speakers. In these cases, the objects in the stimulus sets can just be used as prompts to better understand semantic categorisation without contributing to larger cross-linguistic studies or studies of interspeaker variation in a community.

---

**Exercise 3  Odd one out (or in!)**

You have developed a stimulus set of plant pictures to get an understanding of ethnobotanical categorisation in the language you are working on. Participants have been asked to group 'like' pictures together. Some people comment that some plants are "strangers" and others are "real". What kind of distinction could these words be referring to?

---

## 7.4 SPECIAL REGISTERS

During fieldwork you may encounter words that are only used in particular social settings. Such special ways of talking are referred to as 'special' or 'alternate' registers. For example, in many Australian languages a respect register, also referred to as 'mother-in-law' or 'avoidance' language, is prototypically used in the presence of, or to refer to, particular kin relations (particularly mothers-in-law and sons-in-law).

Semantic fieldwork and lexicography    163

These languages have specialised vocabulary that is used to refer to these relations, their actions and even everyday items with which they are associated, such as meat, fire and water. Other registers may be used in mourning or in ceremonial or religious contexts. In the Papuan language Kalam, there is a special register known as 'Pandanus language', which consists of around 1,000 words and phrases that are used when people are harvesting and cooking pandanus nuts (Pawley, 1992). As well as having unique vocabulary, these words may conflate semantic distinctions made in the everyday speech register. Everyday words may also have different meanings in special registers. For example, in formal registers plural pronouns may have singular reference.

It is very exciting to come across these specialised kinds of speech in your fieldwork. However, it is not always appropriate to record special registers in their natural context of use, which may be intensely personal and emotional, for example during bereavement. In such cases it may be more appropriate to record discussions about these registers. However, it is important to try to understand the social context in which they are used. A good starting point is to compile what has been written about these registers in similar cultures or languages. You are then in a much better position to ask sensible questions about the sorts of contexts one would and wouldn't use them in.

In highly endangered languages, special registers are often associated with practices that are at the core of people's cultural and social identity. As such, a documentation of respect or polite vocabulary, with demonstrations of how these words are used and in which situations, can be highly valued by the community. Documentation of these registers can be incorporated into language and culture programs, cross-cultural inductions and resources aimed at promoting the community's language and culture.

---

### Mountain language in Papua New Guinea

When the Awiakay of East Sepik Province in Papua New Guinea left their village or bush camps and went to the mountains, they used a different linguistic register, 'mountain talk', in which several lexical items are replaced by their avoidance terms. In this way the Awiakay would prevent mountain spirits from sending sickness or dense fog in which they would get lost on their journeys. Although this way of speaking is in decline, a new linguistic register similar in its form and function has sprung up. *Kay menda*, 'different talk', or 'hidden talk', is used when the Awiakay go to the town to sell eaglewood and buy goods. In the examples in Table 7.3 you can see how in Mountain language the ordinary word for 'termites' nest' is replaced by a word meaning 'old woman' and the ordinary word for 'tobacco' is replaced by the more general term 'the smoking thing' (Hoenigman, 2012, p. 197).

**Table 7.3**

A comparison of some words in Ordinary Awiakay and Mountain Awiakay

| Ordinary Awiakay | Mountain Awiakay |
| --- | --- |
| *ayŋgwaŋ* 'flying fox' | *apuria* 'type of bee' |
| *yaki* 'tobacco' | *emwi kolokolay* 'the smoking thing' |
| *muŋguma* 'termite nest' | *nam tapuka* 'old woman' |
| *awin* 'mountain bird, spirit of a dead man' | *tine pawiakay* 'red bird' |

## 7.5 LEXICOGRAPHY

The famous eighteenth-century chronicler of the English language, Samuel Johnson, once defined a lexicographer as a "harmless drudge" who is concerned with "detailing the signification of words". Contrary to this we argue that making dictionaries can be a lot of fun, even though there is undeniably a lot of hard work involved. Producing dictionaries is one of the ways that linguists can make a useful contribution to the communities they work with (Corris, et al., 2004, p. 34). Dictionaries can also have real symbolic value in communities. They may take on an authoritative role, promoting the perceived value of a language, as well as being a tool to teach and learn the language. Grammatical and other linguistic information found in dictionaries may be increasingly relied on as endangered languages are not passed on through processes of primary language socialisation (Kroskrity, 2015, p. 146). Dictionaries also provide a springboard and a reference for ongoing research on a language. Even if you don't plan to make a detailed dictionary of a language, an elementary dictionary makes your work useful and accessible to others who may build on this to make a more comprehensive one. With limited time and resources it is important to get something out rather than strive for the Holy Grail of all dictionaries! Nevertheless, there is no getting away from the fact that dictionaries are "artefacts of literate societies" (Corris et al., 2004, p. 34). This does present a paradox, as those with low-literacy levels may have difficulties using dictionaries in the ways anticipated by those who design them. Rarely will a single dictionary be able to serve a wide range of users, so there is plenty of scope for variety.

### 7.5.1 Types of dictionaries

There are many different types of dictionaries. Dictionaries of major languages tend to have much more information than those of minority, endangered languages (Kroskrity, 2015; Mosel, 2011). In general terms, dictionaries can be categorised based on the number of languages they contain. In a monolingual dictionary, all the material in the dictionary is in the same language, and the definition forms the central part of the entry. In contrast, bilingual dictionaries typically translate from one language to another. Bilingual dictionaries can be unidirectional, listing words of one language and translating these into another, or bidirectional, allowing translation to and from both languages. For endangered languages that are often the focus of fieldwork this other language is usually a major language such as English, Spanish or French. Sometimes a third language, such as the national language, is also included (see Figure 7.8). But even unidirectional bilingual dictionaries usually have a section, typically at the end, that reverses the direction of the two languages to some degree. This is known as a finder list or reversal (§7.6.6).

A dictionary can be published in either print or digital form. As long as your data and workflows are well structured, both options may be open to you. A print dictionary can be held in the hand and can have a powerful symbolic impact. You can also flick through a book to see non-adjacent words easily. A print dictionary may be the only practical option in communities with limited access to modern technologies (Mosel, 2011, p. 339), but the situation worldwide is changing rapidly. Digital dictionaries have a number of advantages. One is being able to search for words in multiple ways, reducing the dependency on alphabetical order as a search principle. It is now common for digital dictionaries to have a 'fuzzy search' function; where search results show multiple words even when the search text has been misspelt. A digital dictionary also has the advantage of being able to incorporate sound and video. And while the cost and size of print dictionaries may mean limiting the amount of information included, digital dictionaries are not constrained in this way so long as the images and audio are the right resolution. A digital dictionary can also be updated incrementally at low cost. If the internet is available, a digital dictionary can be disseminated widely on different types of devices, such as on mobile phones. Various digital interfaces for dictionaries are discussed in §7.7.2.

It is a good idea to get drafts of the dictionary out as soon as possible and circulated in the community to get feedback on layout, usability and of course errors. If most community members have poor eyesight, then you should also consider carefully the size of the font if making a print dictionary.

---

### Tip – Curly questions about fonts

Some fonts don't work well with particular orthographic choices that are made for languages. For example if a language has a retroflex distinction represented by an 'r' preceding another a consonant such as 'n' then, it is better to use a *sans serif* font (one without curlique extensions or 'serifs') or else the digraph 'rn' may end up looking like an 'm'. A *sans serif* font has been used in the example shown in Figure 7.2 and in the dictionary headwords in Figure 7.3.

Figure 7.2
A page from the *Central Anmatyerr Picture Dictionary* that illustrates some person terms
Source: Green, 2003, p. 3

## tyerrty map – people

**rrkwenty**

Rrkwentyel inem tyerrty map ngkwarl-penh.

**kwerltety**

Kwerltetyel kwer map kaltyel-anthem.

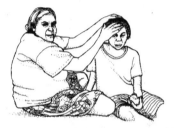

**ngangkar**

Ngangkarel angkwerrewem tyerrty rikert.

**theth**

Thethel tyerrty rikert map mpwarem.

**thakeman**

Artwang thakeman lhem nanth arlweletyek.

**ngkart**

Ngkartel kaltyel-anthem tyerrty map Altyerr-kenh angkety.

*Semantic fieldwork and lexicography* 167

---

**A dictionary of Bikol**

Not long ago I came across a nice example of how an encyclopedic or eth-nographic dictionary can serve as a data resource for future generations, centuries after it was compiled. Malcolm Mintz, an Austronesianist who specialises in Bikol, spoken in southern Luzon, a few years ago published a book about Bikol society around 1600 (Mintz 2011). His book contains chapters giving detailed accounts of food and society, war and conflict, crime and punishment, religion, childhood and the family, and rice and agricultural and marketing practices. Where did he get his data? Largely from a remarkable dictionary, compiled around AD 1600 by the Franciscan padre, Marcos de Lisboa (1754), who lived for ten years among the Bikol people.

(Pawley, 2015, p. 138)

---

## 7.5.2 Starting small

For many language communities there is no pre-existing dictionary. Producing a short, simple wordlist for use in schools and for other learners, or setting the groundwork for a bigger dictionary is something that a fieldworker can plan to do alongside other research objectives. Large encyclopaedic dictionaries require many years, and sometimes decades of work, but if your research is well designed you can envisage the results of your work as eventually contributing to these more ambitious projects. It is much better for all concerned to complete a small dictionary than to leave a large ambitious one languishing!

Smaller thematic publications can be a very satisfying outcome for researchers and communities alike (Mosel, 2011, p. 350). They can serve practical ends in health and education as well as being meaningful stepping-stones on the path towards the big dictionary. Suggested themes include flora and fauna (see Figure 1.4 for an example), food preparation, gardening, health or kinship. One approach to maximise collaboration is to team up and pool resources, such as photos and illustrations, that can then be used to make parallel publications in communities where related languages are found in similar environments or ecosystems. This was the approach taken in an Australian picture dictionaries project, which resulted in a series of 13 picture dictionaries based on a shared template and a core set of common images, in this case line drawings that were easily and economically reproducible in print. The *Central Anmatyerr Picture Dictionary* is organised in semantic domains (§7.2.1) and has short simple sentences for each word, along with the line drawings. Larger, so-called encyclopaedic dictionaries typically contain a lot more information (and fewer drawings!). Figure 7.2 shows a page from the *Central Anmatyerr Picture Dictionary*. It illustrates some terminologies for people – *rrkwenty* 'police', *ngangkar* 'traditional healer', *thakeman* 'stockman', *kwerltety* 'teacher', *theth* 'health sister' and *ngkart* 'priest'.

# 168 Semantic fieldwork and lexicography

Dictionaries of commonly used phrases and colloquial expressions such as the colloquial dictionary of Navajo (Navaho) (Young & Thompson, 1994) are handy for beginners, advanced bilinguals, as well as for linguists. Often smaller publications such as these can be spin-offs from much larger lexicographic projects.

We now discuss some of the core components of dictionaries – headwords, definitions, example sentences, and finder lists or reversals. We then move on to look at alternative ways to deliver and access dictionaries and at the tools that are useful for making them.

## 7.6 WHAT'S IN A DICTIONARY

Figure 7.3 shows part of a page of a bilingual dictionary of the Anmatyerr language from Central Australia, showing some of the types of information in a typical entry. Most prominent are the headwords, usually displayed in a distinctive font and arranged in alphabetical order. In this entry homonyms, words that are spelt and sound the same but have distinct meanings, are distinguished by superscript numbers. The entry contains an indication of the part of speech (§6.4), definitions or glosses for the headwords, and example sentences in Anmatyerr and translated into English. Dictionary entries also alert the reader to minimal pairs, or words that sound similar to each other (§5.4.1) and to words with related meanings to those of the headword. There is information about scientific classification if the word is in the biological domain.

### 7.6.1 Headwords

A **headword** is the first and most prominent word in a dictionary entry. Under the headword, dictionaries then typically list idioms and derived words. Alternatively, derived words can be written as separate headwords, thus leaving it up to the reader to determine any semantic relatedness to the previous or following entries.

A print dictionary relies on searching by alphabetical ordering; however, this may be problematic in languages that have variability at the start of words and for polysynthetic languages with a large number of prefixes. One decision to make is whether to use an inflected form as the citation form or an unnatural root form. Listing all possible forms is not practical as there may simply be too many, making the size of an entry span multiple pages, and making it difficult for the user to know where the entry for a headword starts and ends. For words that have many different inflected forms, you will need to decide which should be the main headword. For example, for verbs you may choose to have a form such as 'walk' as the main headword rather than 'walks' or 'walked'. You might want to include irregular inflected forms as 'signpost' entries to the main form. This can be done automatically in FLEx, a software package discussed in §4.3.2. If the forms are regular, it is useful to give an example of one fully inflected verb with the citation form bolded in the front matter of the dictionary or as an appendix. A similar decision needs to

**Figure 7.3**
A guide to the parts of a dictionary entry in the *Central & Eastern Anmatyerr to English Dictionary*
Source: adapted from Green, 2010, p. 411

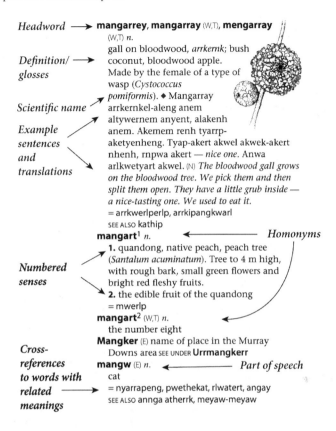

be made with variant forms. Remember there may be no right or wrong decision, as each dictionary entry style has pros and cons in terms of usability; the important thing is to make a decision, stick to it and get on with the job!

Next come meanings, and if a headword has more than one related meaning (or sense) these are generally numbered sequentially in the entry (see Figure 7.3). Superscript numbers are usually used to distinguish homonyms (words that sound identical but their meanings are not related). The issue of deciding whether words are homonyms or one word with related meanings is not always straightforward, even in a monolingual situation. For example, is "[siŋk]", a thing in the kitchen, related in meaning to "a low area or hole"? Further problems arise in bilingual dictionaries, where the division of meanings into distinct senses and the ordering of these senses may reflect polysemy found in either the source language or the target language (see Evans, 1997; Goddard & Thieberger, 1997). As a starting point it is useful to assume homophony unless there is strong evidence for a semantic relationship.

## 170 Semantic fieldwork and lexicography

---

**Exercise 4 How many meanings?**

Below are three meanings of the one phonological form in Kaytetye. How would you go about working out whether the words are homonyms, whether there is one or more polysemous words, or one word with a broad monosemous meaning?

**ampwernarrenke** *v.i.*

1. (of honey) to go hard and lumpy, due to cold weather
2. to be scared, shy or frightened
3. to shiver from cold.

---

### 7.6.2 Writing definitions

A **definition** is a core part of a dictionary. We all laugh when Baldrick defines a 'dog' as 'not a cat' in the Blackadder comedy skit that imagines the catastrophic loss of Dr Johnson's precious English dictionary manuscript. While this statement is undeniably *true*, nevertheless as dictionary users we also know that it is a very bad definition. Jokes aside, exactly how much information a definition should include, and what sort of language it is written in depends to some extent on who the users will be. Definitions should be succinct and accurate statements of the meanings of words. As well as single word translation equivalents or 'glosses', it is good practice to include more complex definitions. Equivalents can easily be misconstrued by users. For example, an English translation equivalent 'light' (as in 'not heavy') might also be misunderstood as meaning 'not dark'. Such misunderstandings can be minimised by including a definition as well as translation equivalents. Figure 7.4 is taken from the dictionary of the Alaskan Athabaskan language Koyukon (Jetté & Jones, 2000, p. 107). It shows definitions of some of the derived words under *daa'* 'horn' or 'antler'.

**Figure 7.4**
Definitions for some of the words derived from *daa'* 'horn' or 'antler' in Koyukon

---

**daa'** /horn/

**-daa', daa** (*n., inc., cmp.:* Ø) horn, antler, *especially referring to the whole antler structure*

**-daa' leł** (*n.; de*) velvet covering moose antlers from May to August, *lit.* 'horn skin'

**-daadeeken** (*n,;* Ø) base of the horns or antlers at their point of eruption from the skull; antennae or 'feelers' of insect

**-daaloyet** (*n.*) *L* tip of the point of moose or caribou antler

**-daaloghuze, -daahus** (*n.;* Ø) point of the tine of a moose or caribou antler, *lit.* 'thorns at the end of the horns'

---

### 7.6.3 Putting encyclopaedic and cultural knowledge in definitions

When writing dictionary definitions one of the major decisions is how much information to include. The **encyclopaedic definition** includes more information than a definition in a standard dictionary and this model should be considered if the users include people whose culture is highly endangered and has little or no written history. Consider the dictionary definition of the word 'SMI', the most significant ceremonial event in Kalam society, a non-Austronesian language from Papua New Guinea (Pawley & Bulmer, 2011, p. 528) (Figure 7.5). Encyclopaedic definitions such as these enable detailed semantic exploration and they are essential if one is to understand Kalam society. Furthermore, in endangered cultures it may never again be possible to record such meanings and so, without the dictionary, the full meaning of a word such as SMI might remain a mystery for ever.

### 7.6.4 Folk definitions

Another kind of definition, composed by a native speaker, is known as the **folk definition**. Casagrande & Hale (1967) recorded 800 folk definitions in Papago (now known as Tohono O'odham), a Native American language spoken in southern Arizona and north-western Mexico. Such definitions give priority to the ways speakers of that language elucidate, in their own words, difficult to translate concepts (Mosel, 2011). As rich records of native speaker knowledge, they are a valuable form of language documentation and they provide data that can be used for various purposes, be it lexicography, grammars, semantic typology or ethnography (Dingemanse, 2015). Such definitions can help elucidate patterns of polysemy and unravel the logic of local taxonomies where the connections between things are based on cultural or encyclopaedic knowledge (Evans, 1997, p. 150; Wilkins, 1997, p. 441).

Figure 7.5

The dictionary definition of the word 'SMI' in Kalam

---

**SMI** [sími·], **n.** The all-night dance-festival which a man (the **b smi** or **smi nop**) and his co-resident extended family may host as the climax of the ceremonial activity in which youths and, later, girls have their nasal septa pierced (compare **miuk puŋi-**), pigs are killed and cooked, and pork, axes and shell valuables are given to affinal groups. The dance is also attended by performers and spectators who are not kin of the hosts and who do not stay to receive gifts and participate in the feasting on the following day. Large quantities of taro are required to entertain guests, and the festivals are held from late July to early December, when taro has been harvested. The **smi** is the major ceremonial institution of Kalam society. It involves extensive economic preparation in planting gardens, building up pig stock and assembling gift valuables and personal ornaments; the building of special dance houses (**smi kopt**); the propitiation of dead kin (**cp kawnan**) and nature demons (**kceki**); the fulfillment, through gifts, of the obligations of kinship and affinity (compare **tusmen**); and as a measure of the prosperity, prestige and political influence of the host group and its leader.

---

**Warlpiri folk definitions.**

The following is a Warlpiri definition for the word *ngarlingarli*:

> *Ngarlingarli, ngulaji yangka kujaka ngunami jarda ngurlju-purdanji, ramarra-purdanji, yangka kakarrara-purdanji miyalu kurlirra-purda, manu purturlu yatijarra-purda, manu wirliya-jarra karlarra-purda, jurru kakarrara-purda. Yangka ngarlingarliji kujaka ngunami jarda miyalu-purdanji-wangu, purturlu-purdanji-wangu – ngarlingarliji.*

> **Ngarlingarli**, that's when one lies flank downwards, ribs downwards, when one is eastwards, stomach southwards, spine northwards, and both feet westwards, the head eastwards. So **ngarlingarli** is lying asleep, neither stomach downwards, nor back downwards – that's **ngarlingarli**.

Composed by Paddy Patrick Jangala for the Warlpiri dictionary (Laughren, Hale, & Warlpiri Lexicography Group, 1987).

---

**Exercise 5  What folk definitions reveal about a culture**

What do you think this very precise way of describing the way to lie down might show about Warlpiri cultural practices? Can you write a folk definition about something special from your own culture?

---

Another example is from the Teop encyclopaedic dictionary of marine life and fishing (Mosel, 2017). It has over a thousand entries and is an example of a dictionary that is focused on a single semantic domain. It includes line drawings and photos as well as many bilingual texts. An example taken from the entry for *bakubaku* 'shark' is below:

> *Bero a maamihu kaku bakubaku. A meha a beera sana to aniani aba nana. Amaa meha saka beera vira haari. Amaa meha amaa vaamanae, eara o aba to ani rae. A peha bakubaku na tei me nana bono buaku totoka o kekeetoo. O buaku matana, o meho buaku komanae, o meho buaku paana vihinae, o peho hee toon nae.*

> There are many kinds of shark. There is a very big one that eats human beings. Others are not very big. The young ones, it is us, the human beings, who eat them. A shark has seven fins. Two are in the front, two others at its belly, another two under its tail, and one on its back.

(Source: Sii 46W 145–150)[10]

### 7.6.5 Illustrative examples

**Example sentences**, also called **illustrative examples**, are another very important part of a dictionary entry. They demonstrate meanings by illustrating usage and exemplifying the grammatical frames in which a word occurs. A good illustrative example in a dictionary is short and natural and shows how the word is used in a sentence. As well as drawing on examples from texts of spontaneous speech, asking a speaker to make up a sentence to demonstrate how a word is used can also be a useful approach. Be aware, however, that you might end up with some sentences that would never actually be said in everyday interactions!

It is best to have some basic vocabulary and grammar under your belt and familiarity with the cultural context before seeking illustrative examples. It is a good idea to have one or two illustrative examples in the language (perhaps from your earlier recordings) which you can use to model what you would like in the elicitation session. You should also prepare some possible scenarios in which the word might be used beforehand to assist speakers if they appear stuck. In some cases, speakers can compose more interesting illustrative examples when working in pairs or in groups, and this approach can also be much more fun. Remember that the most interesting vocabulary often emerges in contexts where speakers themselves choose what to say, and where free-flowing conversations about the meanings of words can lead in unexpected but often illuminating directions:

> By working in the native language, taking full advantage of the metalinguistic capacity of the language and its speakers, we can create a snowball effect whereby speakers' commentaries reveal other features of the language, as well as translating into words their judgements of typical and proper usage.
>
> (Hanks, 2015, p. 34)

### 7.6.6 Finders and reversals

As we mentioned earlier in this chapter, many bilingual dictionaries include a section at the end of the dictionary called a **finder list** or **reversal**. These help a dictionary user to find the right headword in the main part of the dictionary. In a user study of some Australian Indigenous language dictionaries, Corris et al. (2004, p. 43) found that the English Finder lists played a very important role in locating the Indigenous language headwords, as English literacy was often stronger than literacy in the local Indigenous language.

Making a good finder list is an art in itself, and requires the lexicographer to put themselves in the shoes of a user who is trying to find a word in a dictionary. Pay particular attention to words where there is a high degree of mismatch between one language and the other. For example, the English pronoun 'we' has more than a dozen different equivalents in the Arandic languages of Australia. One solution is to create a hierarchy where a list of sub reversal words are nested under a main reversal word. An example of this from the kinship domain, drawn from the Anmatyerr dictionary, is shown in Figure 7.6. In this instance the main reversal word is 'uncle' and the English phrases in italics lead the reader to the equivalent terms in Anmatyerr. You can see that there is certainly more than one word for 'uncle' in Anmatyerr!

Other useful finder lists in dictionaries are specialised semantically organised ones such as alphabetical lists of scientific terminology for plants and animals, and lists of place names.

# Semantic fieldwork and lexicography

**Figure 7.6**
Part of the finder list entry for 'uncle' in the *Central & Eastern Anmatyerr to English Dictionary*
Source: Green, 2010, p. 719

**uncle**

| | |
|---|---|
| *mother's brother* | **amarl, kamern** |
| *father's brother* | **angey, anywek-anywek** |
| *father's elder brother* | **anawerr, pap anawey, pap aywa** |
| *father's elder brother (baby talk)* | **anawerr-anawerr, anawey, anawey-anawey** |
| *uncle (from English)* | **angkel** |
| *great-uncle (father's mother's brother)* | **aperl** |
| *great-uncle (father's father's brother)* | **arreng** |
| *great-uncle (mother's father's brother)* | **atyemey, rtartart** |
| *great-uncle (mother's mother's brother)* | **menh-menh, nyany, ipmenh** |

## 7.6.7 Front matter and end matter

Dictionaries include information at the front and end of the main dictionary to help people use the dictionary correctly. Dictionaries vary as to the extent that they include information about the grammatical structures and phonology of the language (Mosel, 2011, p. 342). At a minimum, the grammatical information necessary to be able to infer all the correct forms of a word should be included. This may include verb classes and their conjugations, pronoun tables and lists of inflectional morphology such as case-markers or gender agreement. A user-friendly pronunciation guide also helps readers get their tongue around words and assists them in understanding the orthography that has been chosen for the language. Other useful additions may be maps, and charts that represent important local cultural concepts such as kinship or terminology for seasons of the year. The introduction to the dictionary is also a great place to provide more general information about the language and its speakers, including links to key references about its documentation. Dictionaries also vary as to the extent to which they include various aspects of a language, such as intergenerational and dialectal variation, special registers that may occur in the language, and historical information about the language and its speakers.

## 7.6.8 What words to put in and what to leave out?

For the lexicographer a practical issue is which words to include in the dictionary. Lexicographers are charged with the task of balancing familiar notions of what dictionaries are and the levels of linguistic detail required to make a good dictionary, while at the same time honouring "indigenous notions of regulating cultural knowledge" (Kroskrity, 2015, p. 142). The dictionary database may include common borrowings from neighbouring languages, which should be marked as such, but speakers may decide to limit the dictionary to only those lexemes they consider as properly 'belonging' to their language.

It may be the case that certain other terms in the language you are working on should not be put in the dictionary. Some examples may relate to levels of restriction of cultural knowledge that may be either age- or gender-based. Speakers may also request that terms which they consider rude or offensive, such as words for private body parts, or particular vocabulary (such as swear words) be left out. There may be other words that you stumble across that are regarded by communities as riské or taboo and therefore that should not be made public. For someone who is not fully versed in local cultural practices that can be evoked by seemingly simple words, the items that should not be included in records for public consumption are not always apparent. It is best to ask!

## 7.7 TOOLS FOR MAKING AND DISPLAYING DICTIONARIES

Technology has come a long way since the first dictionaries were made using a pile of cards, a headword on each, and sorted alphabetically on the living-room floor. In this section we consider the pros and cons of the currently available dictionary-making tools and interfaces.

### 7.7.1 Tools for making dictionaries

A dictionary can be made from a well-structured text file or in custom dictionary-making software. A well-structured text file has the advantage that it can be read and edited in multiple platforms using a variety of software and exported to a range of different display options. On the down side, however, it requires rigorous consistency checking, and it is easy to make mistakes in the dictionary structure itself when entering data. Custom-made software is less flexible and will constrain input and thus reduce these types of errors.

If you are making a dictionary by using a text file it is a good idea to use **MDF (multi-dictionary formatter)** data field markers (Coward & Grimes, 2000).[11] These are internationally recognised data fields for dictionaries. MDF defines about 100 different data field markers, although the average dictionary compiler will only use about 20 to 30 of them on a regular basis. If you use the MDF system, then software such as Lexique Pro (see below) can automatically format your lexicon as a dictionary (including pictures and audio) as well as making a finder list. Some of the most commonly used MDF field markers are shown in Figure 7.7, an example of a directional noun entry from the *Gurindji to English Dictionary* (Meakins et al., 2013). The entry was derived from a narrative told by Ronnie Wavehill which was then transcribed in CLAN (see Figures 1.2 & 1.3 in §1.4). The use of MDF codes made it straightforward to produce both a print dictionary and an electronic multimedia dictionary[12] using Toolbox and Lexique Pro. As you can see in Figure 7.7, sound links are provided for the headword and example

## 176 Semantic fieldwork and lexicography

**Figure 7.7**
Example of the MDF codes used in an entry from the Gurindji to English Dictionary

| \lx | lexeme | kurlarnimpa |
|---|---|---|
| \sf | headword sound | Headword_Sound\VioletWadrill\kurlanimpa_VW.mp3 |
| \ps | part of speech | dir |
| \de | definition | up on the southside |
| \ge | English gloss | southside |
| \re | English reversal field | southside (up on) |
| \sd | semantic domain | V Space and Time |
| \xv | vernacular example | Kurlarnimpa, kula kajuparik nyila-ma kurlarnimpa ngarlaka-ma nganayirla-ma Ngangi-ma, Ngangi na ngarlaka No.17-ta kaarnimpa kuya. |
| \sfx | example sound | DICT_Audio\RonnieWavehill\kurlarnimpa_RW_eg2_Kurlarnimpa.mp3 |
| \xe | English translation of vernacular example | To the south, not close by, in the south and up the hill is Ngangi. Ngangi is that hill to the east of No. 17 |
| \rf | reference, source of the example sentence | RW: EC98_a027: Kujilirli: 14:14min |
| \cf | cross-reference | kurlarra |
| \nt | notes | FM changed from '(stationary) on the southern side of somewhere' |
| \dt | date | 03/Aug/2012 |

sentence in the online version of the dictionary. The reference (\rf) means the sentence is 'discoverable' in the Gurindji corpus. The word *kurlarnimpa* is also cross-referenced (\cf) to the entry for *kurlarra* 'south' which has all of the 24 inflected forms of 'south' included as sub-entries to show the paradigm for this cardinal term. The paradigms for each of the four cardinal directions are also included in the front matter of the dictionary.

---

### Exercise 6 Reverse engineering the *Nafaanra to English Dictionary*

Below are three entries in the SIL *Nafaanra to English Dictionary*, a language spoken in West Africa.[13] These have been exported from a text file that uses MDF fields. What fields have been used in these entries? (You will need to consult the full range of MDF fields at the SIL website.)

**fana** *verb*. mislead. **U u nyu yo na we pan tnumu nu, la, u ni fana.** He promised to come to work, but he misled me.

**fanaa** *noun*. deceit. **Ni n na fanaa kee chaa.** I do not want to be deceived.

**faŋga** *noun*. 1) strength. **Faŋgaa wa pɔ wre nu.** The child is strong and healthy. 2) grave, tomb. **Faŋga kre juari.** The grave is broken. *Pl:* **fanyi.**

**fawolo** *noun*. ancestors. **Kakala na o fawolo na yiri; praa sni yurɔ hlɛ na.** Our ancestors came from Kakala; they slept on animal skins.

---

Semantic fieldwork and lexicography 177

**Toolbox** is a free data management and analysis tool developed by SIL International for field linguists. It is especially useful for maintaining lexical data, and for parsing and interlinearising texts, but it can be used to manage virtually any kind of data. For ease of use, the Toolbox package includes prepared database definitions for a typical dictionary and text corpus. Toolbox offers powerful functionality, including customised sorting, multiple views of the same database, a browse view to show data in tabular form, and filtering to show subsets of a database. It can deal with any number of scripts in the same database. While Unicode is preferred, Toolbox can handle scripts in most legacy encoding systems. Toolbox also has powerful linguistic functionality. It includes a morphological parser that can handle almost all types of morphophonemic processes. It has a word formula component that allows the linguist to describe all the possible affix patterns that occur in words. It has a user-definable interlinear text generation system which uses the morphological parser and lexicon to generate annotated text. Interlinear text can be exported in a form suitable for use in linguistic papers. Toolbox has export capabilities that can be used to produce a publishable dictionary from a dictionary database.

**Lexique Pro**,[14] developed by SIL International, is a free lexicon viewer for dictionaries. It interfaces with Toolbox (or a formatted text file using MDF fields) to produce the dictionary and finder list. It can be used to view and edit an existing Toolbox database (or text file), and then finally export the dictionary to print or web-based formats (Guérin & Lacrampe, 2007). Audio and images can be included. It can be configured to display your Toolbox database in a user-friendly format so that you can distribute it to others. On the down side, note that it can only be used on Macs in a virtual PC environment.

**FLEx** (Fieldwork Language Explorer)[15] is another tool developed by SIL International to help field linguists with elicitation, dictionary creation and publication, and interlinearising text. It also only works in the Windows environment and on Linux. As the dictionary grows, FLEx suggests morphological parsing. FLEx also allows multiple users in different locations to contribute to the one dictionary database through its Send/Receive function. Figure 7.8 shows a headword *ájiita* from the Iquito dictionary (Zaparoan, Peru) in FLEx. The headword *ájiita* is a root (Spanish *raíz*), and it can be seen that the citation form is *ajiráani*. There are two related words, *ajiraákuma* and *ajiratíini*, as well as a derivational root, *ajíra*. There are reversal forms in both Spanish and English, *picar* and *pierce*, that lead back to the headword *ájiita*. Definitions of the various senses of this word follow (not shown here).

Two other off-the-shelf dictionary-making software packages are **Miromaa Community Dictionary Maker**[16] designed for Australian Indigenous languages and **TLex** (aka **TshwaneLex**), which has been adopted by some publishers, government organisations and individuals.[17]

### 7.7.2 Digital dictionary interfaces

There are many ways of displaying dictionaries in user-friendly digital formats, and some dictionaries may now be produced in both paper and digital forms. Much of the off-the-shelf dictionary-making software, such as FLEx and Lexique Pro, have

## Semantic fieldwork and lexicography

**Figure 7.8**

An example from the Iquito dictionary in FLEx, showing the headword information (citation forms, related forms, morphological type) and the beginning of the next section on meanings where reversal fields are located (Illustration: Maxine Addinsall)

Source: Michael & Beier (in press)

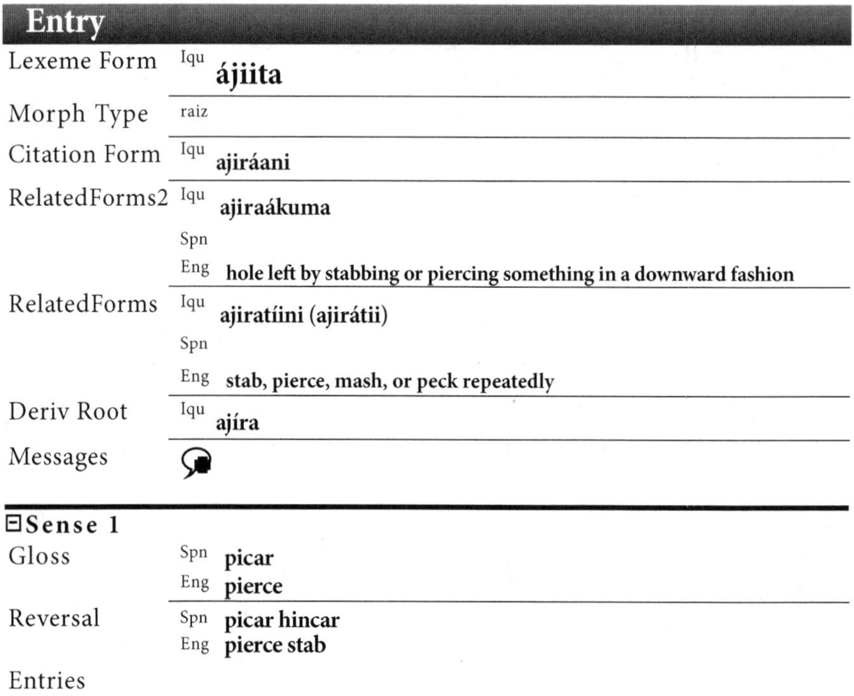

| Entry | | |
|---|---|---|
| Lexeme Form | Iqu | **ájiita** |
| Morph Type | raiz | |
| Citation Form | Iqu | ajiráani |
| RelatedForms2 | Iqu | ajiraákuma |
| | Spn | |
| | Eng | hole left by stabbing or piercing something in a downward fashion |
| RelatedForms | Iqu | ajiratíini (ajirátii) |
| | Spn | |
| | Eng | stab, pierce, mash, or peck repeatedly |
| Deriv Root | Iqu | ajíra |
| Messages | | 💬 |

**⊟ Sense 1**

| Gloss | Spn | picar |
|---|---|---|
| | Eng | pierce |
| Reversal | Spn | picar hincar |
| | Eng | pierce stab |
| Entries | | |

options for digital display as well as options for exporting print-formatted layouts. SIL International has a growing catalogue of free online dictionaries.[18] Some of these contain sophisticated search functions that allow a user to search the dictionary based on words in either language or by semantic domains or by parts of speech. Some, such as the *Lakota to English Dictionary*, come with language learning materials that can be downloaded and purchased online.[19] Another example of an online dictionary is the Tahitian dictionary, a bilingual dictionary searchable by either Tahitian or French (see Greenhill & Clark, 2011).[20]

Line illustrations or photos can be easily displayed in online dictionaries for elucidating the meanings of words or concepts that do not have ready equivalents in another language. For example, in the online version of the Archi-Russian-English Dictionary (a Lezgic language spoken by about 1,200 people in Daghestan), a photograph is used to illustrate the meaning of *t'uq'ˤ*, a 'stone post inside an underground sheepfold which supports the stone roof' (Figure 7.9).[21] The dictionary also includes audio links to inflected forms of the headword.

**Kirrkirr** is a program written in Java that displays a lexical database in innovative ways, such as showing semantic networks of words. It also provides useful tools for

Figure 7.9
An entry from the dictionary of Archi
Source: Chumakina, et al., 2007

non-technical end users. Kirrkirr has been used to display dictionaries of languages such as Nahuatl, an Indigenous language of Mexico; Biao Min, a language from southern China; as well as a number of Australian languages and even English. The lexical database needs to be in xml format and it requires a schema matching the dictionary fields to the Kirrkirr concepts (Manning, Jansz, & Indurkhya, 2001).[22]

A well-structured dictionary text file can also be displayed in a web browser, which can be locally hosted on a computer or on the web. In this format it is possible to update the display 'live', that is, as the database is changed. Some online dictionaries also use a 'fuzzy search' function whereby a word can be located even if it is misspelled by the user. The Yolŋu Matha Dictionary enables the dictionary user to spell out words using a set of filters that predict some of the orthographic symbols that represent sounds that may be misheard by some users, for example the difference between a retroflex or non-retroflex consonant, and whether or not some consonants are voiced or not.[23]

There are also now a large number of mobile phone dictionary apps in Indigenous languages, such as Tusaalanga, a dictionary of the Canadian language Inuktitut, and My Cree, which is aimed at Native youth wanting to learn how to speak Plains Cree. Design issues for mobile phone dictionary and learners apps include dealing with large file sizes that may not download or stream well, and finding ways to avoid cluttered screens on small devices.[24]

## Semantic fieldwork and lexicography

---

**Exercise 7  Making a dictionary entry**

Choose around five words from a particular semantic domain and draft dictionary entries for them. Include at least the following fields:

- Definition – ideally you would ask your consultant for his/her definition in the language concerned
- Gloss – simple one word/phrase English or other target language equivalents
- Grammatical information (e.g. if it is a noun, what classifier is used with it)
- Pragmatic information (e.g. what register it belongs to)
- Encyclopaedic information
- An illustrative sentence. It is best to use sentences a speaker has uttered (and approved); constructed examples are to be avoided
- Divisions into senses and sub-entries
- Semantic domain codes for each of the senses
- Reversal codes for the headword.

Use MDF codes to mark up your data.

---

## 7.8 SUMMARY

In this chapter we discussed ways to explore the meanings of words by eliciting vocabulary in semantic domains, using taxonomies and other classification systems. We also looked at the use of non-linguistic stimuli to elucidate meanings of words and to collect data on more complex areas of semantics. Dictionaries, even small ones, are a very useful output of linguistic fieldwork. This chapter outlined the main components of a dictionary and discussed ways to organise your linguistic data when planning for a dictionary. We also looked at currently available dictionary-making tools and ways of displaying dictionary content. A brief discussion of sign language dictionaries is found in §8.7.4.

## 7.9 FURTHER READING

For descriptions of semantic fieldwork techniques see Majid (2012). You can find many tools for semantic elicitation in the field at the Max Plank Institute's Language and Cognition Field Manuals and Stimulus materials site.[25] For more detailed information on the role of biological expertise in linguistic fieldwork see Conn (2012) and McClatchey (2012) and for astronomy see Holbrook (2012). Discussions of lexicography in Indigenous languages of Australia and the Pacific are found in Goddard & Thieberger (1997) and Thieberger (2015). Coward & Grimes (2000a) discuss techniques for dictionary making and further information about tools used for lexicography can be found on the SIL International website.[26]

# NOTES

1 http://stedt.berkeley.edu/questionnaires Accessed 27 August 2017.
2 http://comparalex.org/?page=stdlist&id=3 Accessed 27 August 2017.
3 http://semdom.org/ Accessed 27 August 2017.
4 https://lrc.la.utexas.edu/lex/semantic Accessed 27 August 2017.
5 http://siletz.swarthmore.edu/semantic_domains/ Accessed 27 August 2017.
6 www.anu.edu.au/linguistics/nash/aust/domains.html Accessed 27 August 2017.
7 www.anu.edu.au/linguistics/nash/aust/domains.html#2 (based on Sutton & Walsh, 1987) Accessed 28 August 2017.
8 http://fieldmanuals.mpi.nl/ Accessed 30 August 2017.
9 http://fieldmanuals.mpi.nl/regulations-on-use/ Accessed 30 August 2017.
10 http://dictionaria.clld.org/contributions/teopfish Accessed 21 August 2017.
11 This can be accessed online at http://downloads.sil.org/legacy/shoebox/MDF_2000.pdf Accessed 20 August, 2017.
12 http://ausil.org/Dictionary/Gurindji/ Accessed 31 August 2017.
13 http://downloads.sil.org/legacy/shoebox/Nafaanra.pdf Accessed 29 August 2017.
14 www.lexiquepro.com/ Accessed 29 August 2017.
15 http://software.sil.org/fieldworks/ Accessed 29 August 2017.
16 www.miromaa.org.au/miromaa.html Accessed 20 August, 2017.
17 http://tshwanedje.com/tshwanelex/ Accessed 20 August, 2017.
18 www.sil.org/dictionaries-lexicography/online-dictionaries Accessed 28 August 2017.
19 www.lakotadictionary.org/nldo.php Accessed 28 August 2017.
20 www.farevanaa.pf/dictionnaire.php Accessed 28 August 2017.
21 www.smg.surrey.ac.uk/archi-dictionary/ Accessed 17 August 2017.
22 https://nlp.stanford.edu/kirrkirr/ Accessed 31 August 2017.
23 http://yolngudictionary.cdu.edu.au/ Accessed 28 August 2017.
24 Many of these apps are reviewed at https://rising.globalvoicesonline.org/blog/2013/06/21/idecolonize-a-review-of-indigenous-language-learning-apps/ Accessed 28 August 2017.
25 http://fieldmanuals.mpi.nl/ Accessed 31 August 2017.
26 https://software.sil.org/shoebox/mdf/ Accessed 31 August 2017.

# REFERENCES

Cablitz, G. H. (2011). The making of a multimedia encyclopaedic lexicon for and in endangered speech communities. In G. Haig, N. Nau, S. Schnell, & C. Wegener (Eds.), *Documenting endangered languages: Achievements and perspectives* (pp. 223–262). Berlin: De Gruyter Mouton.

Casagrande, J. B., & Hale, K. L. (1967). Semantic relationships in Papago folk-definitions. In D. Hymes & W. Bittle (Eds.) *Studies in southwestern ethnolinguistics: Meaning and history in the languages of the American southwest* (pp. 165–193). The Hague and Paris: Mouton & Co.

Chumakina, M., Brown, D., Corbett, G. G., & Quilliam, H. (2007). A dictionary of Archi: Archi-Russian-English (Online edition). http://dx.doi.org/10.15126/SMG.16/2

Conn, B. J. (2012). Botanical collecting. In N. Thieberger (Ed.), *The Oxford handbook of linguistic fieldwork* (pp. 250–280). Oxford: Oxford University Press.

Corris, M., Manning, C., Poetsch, S., & Simpson, J. (2004). How useful and usable are dictionaries for speakers of Australian Indigenous languages? *International Journal of Lexicography*, 17(1), 33–68.

Coward, D., & Grimes, C. (2000). *Making dictionaries: A guide to lexicography and the multi-dictionary formatter*. Waxhaw, North Carolina: SIL International. http://elibrary.bsu.az/books_400/N_297.pdf

Dingemanse, M. (2015). Folk definitions in linguistic fieldwork. In J. Essegbey, B. Henderson, & F. McLaughlin (Eds.), *Culture and language use* (pp. 215–238). Amsterdam: John Benjamins.

Evans, N. (1997). Sign metonymies and the problem of flora-fauna polysemy in Australian linguistics. In D. Tryon & M. Walsh (Eds.), *Boundary rider: Essays in honour of Geoffrey O'Grady* (pp. 133–153). Canberra: Pacific Linguistics.

Goddard, C., & Thieberger, N. (1997). Lexicographic research on Australian Aboriginal languages. In D. Tryon & M. Walsh (Eds.), *Boundary rider: Essays in honour of Geoffrey O'Grady* (pp. 175–208). Canberra: Pacific Linguistics.

Green, J. (2003). *Central Anmatyerr picture dictionary*. Alice Springs: IAD Press.

Green, J. (2010). *Central & Eastern Anmatyerr to English dictionary*. Alice Springs: IAD Press.

Greenhill, S. & Clark, R. (2011). POLLEX-Online: The Polynesian Lexicon Project Online. *Oceanic Linguistics*, 50(2), 551–559.

Guérin, V., & Lacrampe, S. (2007). Lexique Pro. *Technology Review*, 1(2), 291–300.

Hanks, W. F. (2015). The Space of translation. In C. Severi & W. F. Hanks (Eds.), *Translating worlds: The epistemological space of translation* (pp. 21–49). Chicago, IL: Hau Books.

Hellwig, B. (2006). Field semantics and grammar-writing: Stimuli-based techniques and the study of locative verbs. In F. Ameka, A. Dench, & N. Evans (Eds.), *Catching language: The standing challenge of grammar writing* (pp. 321–358). Berlin: Mouton de Gruyter.

Hoenigman, D. (2012). *From mountain talk to hidden talk: Continuity and change in Awiakay registers*. Honolulu, HI: University of Hawai'i Press.

Holbrook, J. (2012). Cultural astronomy for linguists. In N. Thieberger (Ed.), *The Oxford handbook of linguistic fieldwork* (pp. 345–367). Oxford: Oxford University Press.

Holton, G. (2012). Language archives: They're not just for linguists any more. In F. Seifart, G. Haig, N. Himmelmann, D. Jung, A. Margetts, and P. Trilsbeek (Eds.), *Potentials of language documentation: Methods, analyses, and utilization* (pp. 111–117). Honolulu, HI: University of Hawai'i Press.

Jetté, J., & Jones, E. (2000). *Koyukon Athabaskan dictionary*. Fairbanks, AK: Alaska Native Language Center.

Kroskrity, P. V. (2015). Designing a dictionary for an endangered language community: Lexicographical deliberations, language ideological clarifications. *Language Documentation & Conservation*, 9, 140–157.

Laughren, M., Hale, K., & the Warlpiri Lexicography Group (1987). *Warlpiri–English dictionary: Body-part section*. Lexicon Project Working Paper 6. Cambridge, MA: MIT Centre for Cognitive Science.

Levinson, S. (2006). Parts of the body in Yélî Dnye, the Papuan language of Rossel Island. *Language Sciences*, 28, 221–240.

Majid, A. (2012). A guide to stimulus-based elicitation for semantic categories. In N. Thieberger (Ed.), *The Oxford handbook of linguistic fieldwork* (pp. 54–71). Oxford: Oxford University Press.

Majid, A., Enfield, N., & van Staden, M. (2006). Cross-linguistic categorisation of the body: Introduction. *Language Sciences*, 28(2–3), 137–147.

Manning, C. D., Jansz, K., & Indurkhya, N. (2001). Kirrkirr: Software for browsing and visual exploration of a structured Warlpiri dictionary. *Literary and Linguistic Computing*, 16(2), 135–151.

Matisoff, J. (1978). *Variational semantics in Tibeto-Burman: The "organic" approach to linguistic comparison*. Philadelphia, PA: Institute for the Study of Human Issues.

McClatchey, W. (2012). Ethnobiology: Basic methods for documenting biological knowledge represented in languages. In N. Thieberger (Ed.), *The Oxford handbook of linguistic fieldwork* (pp. 281–297). Oxford: Oxford University Press.

Meakins, F., McConvell, P., Charola, E., McNair, N., McNair, H., & Campbell, L. (2013). *Gurindji to English dictionary*. Batchelor, Australia: Batchelor Press.

Menning, K., & Nash, D. (Eds.). (1981). *Source book for Central Australian languages*. Alice Springs: IAD Press.

Michael, L., & Beier, C. (In press). *A dictionary of Iquito*.

Mosel, U. (2004). Dictionary making in endangered speech communities. In P. Austin (Ed.), *Language Documentation and Description* (pp. 39–54). London: SOAS.

Mosel, U. (2011). Lexicography in endangered language communities. In P. K. Austin & J. Sallabank (Eds.), *The Cambridge handbook of endangered languages* (pp. 337–353). Cambridge: Cambridge University Press.

Mosel, U. (2017). Teop encyclopedic dictionary of marine life and fishing. *Dictionaria*, (2), 1–1014.

Narasimhan, B., Kopecka, A., Bowerman, M., Gullberg, M., & Majid, A. (2012). Putting and taking events: A crosslinguistic perspective. In A. Kopecka & M. Bowerman (Eds.), *Events of putting and taking: A crosslinguistic perspective* (pp. 1–18). Amsterdam: John Benjamins.

Pawley, A. (1992). Kalam Pandanus language: An old New Guinea experiment in language engineering. In T. Dutton, M. Ross, & D. Tryon (Eds.), *The language game: Papers in memory of Donald C. Laycock* (pp. 313–334). Canberra: Pacific Linguistics.

Pawley, A. (2012). What does it take to make an ethnographic dictionary? On the treatment of fish and tree names in dictionaries of Oceanic languages. In G. Haig, N. Nau, S. Schnell, & C. Wegener (Eds.), *Documenting endangered languages: Achievements and perspectives* (pp. 263–287). Berlin: De Gruyter Mouton.

Pawley, A. (2015). Review of 'Nicholas Thieberger (Ed). 2012. The Oxford handbook of linguistic field-work'. *Language Documentation & Conservation*, 9, 134–139.

Pawley, A., & Bulmer, R. (2011). *A dictionary of Kalam with ethnographic notes*. Canberra: Pacific Linguistics.

Sutton, P., & Walsh, M. (1987). *Wordlist for Australian languages*. Canberra: Australian Institute of Aboriginal Studies.

Swadesh, M. (1950). Salish internal relationships. *International Journal of American Linguistics*, 16, 157–167.

Thieberger, N. (2015). The lexicography of Indigenous languages in Australia and the Pacific. In *International handbook of modern lexis and lexicography* (pp. 1–16). New York, NY: Springer.

Turpin, M., Ross, A., Dobson, V., & Turner, M. K. (2013). The spotted nightjar calls when dingo pups are born: Ecological and social indicators in central Australia. *Journal of Ethnobiology*, 33(1), 7–32.

Turpin, M., & Si, A. (2017). Edible insect larvae in Kaytetye: Their nomenclature and significance. *Journal of Ethnobiology*, 37(1), 120–140.

Voegelin, C. F., & Voegelin, F. M. (1971). The autonomy of linguistics and the dependence of cognitive culture. In J. Sawyer (Ed.), *Studies in American Indian Languages* (pp. 303–317). Berkeley, CA: University of California Press.

Wilkins, D. P. (1997). Handsigns and hyperpolysemy: Exploring the cultural foundations of semantic association. In D. Tryon and M. Walsh (Eds.), *Boundary rider: Essays in honour of Geoffrey O'Grady* (pp. 413–444). Canberra: Pacific Linguistics.

Yen, A. L. (2015). Conservation of Lepidoptera used as human food and medicine. *Current Opinion in Insect Science*, 12, 102–108.

Young, R. W., & Morgan, W. (1994). *Colloquial Navaho. A dictionary.* New York, NY: Hippocrene Books.

# 8

# Sign and gesture

## 8.1 INTRODUCTION

Taking a broad view of language that encompasses more than just spoken language opens up many fascinating possibilities for fieldwork. Sign languages are the main medium of communication for some and documentation and analysis of the many sign languages of the world is a dedicated field of expertise. Linguistic research in the mid-twentieth century validated natural sign languages as fully-fledged languages in their own right. Gesture is ubiquitous and appears to occur whenever hearing individuals communicate in face-to-face spoken interactions (Kendon, 2004a). As well as speaking, people may point, make quick maps and diagrams, and interact with anything in reach, including small objects or props, and visual displays such as computer screens or whiteboards. There seems to be no culture in the world that does not employ forms of bodily action alongside speech. People even gesture when they are talking on the telephone and their interlocutor is not in sight! Some argue that using research methods that include gesture as a matter of course is good practice, not only if you are specifically interested in gesture, but for what gesture might reveal about speech itself (Seyfeddinipur, 2012). Other research questions are focused on understanding more about the common ground that sign and gesture share and what this can show about language in general.

To begin to understand what you might miss out on by not considering communicative actions that either accompany speech or replace it, imagine that you are reading a transcript of the spoken part of an interaction or of a narrative. Not only are expressive elements of speech, such as intonation and prosody (§5.1.8), routinely left out of such transcripts, but there are other gaps in the information needed to fully make sense of what is being conveyed. The text reads, "They went over *there*". But where, exactly, is there? She said, "The river was about *this* wide". But how wide? In these simple examples it is likely that actions that go with speech provide the missing link. While some types of words are well-known gesture-attractors, a close look at human communication shows that gesture and speech work together in all sorts of other interesting ways. Pointing tends to be closely melded to particular types of speech – for example Wilkins (2003) has shown how in Arrernte (Pama-Nyungan, Australia) demonstratives (words like 'here', 'there', 'this', 'that') go together with pointing gestures that are accurately anchored to cardinal directions and form what he calls "composite demonstrative signals" (see also §6.7.5). This is one example of how an utterance may be incomplete without considering the ways that speech and action work together.

There is some overlap in the research methodologies that can be used for both sign language and gesture. One reason for this is because both sign and gesture share the same kinesic/visual modality. Another comes down to the choices of language documentation tools towards which both sign language and gesture researchers gravitate. This chapter gives some background on studies of sign languages (§8.2) and gesture (§8.3) before discussing some of the research questions that arise in these fields of research (§8.4). We discuss particular methodological considerations for working with sign and gesture (§8.5), elicitation and filming techniques, and some of the tools that are used for annotation (§8.6 and §8.7), and then briefly look at various forms of representation of sign languages and gesture for theses and other publications (§8.7.3). As this chapter can only hope to touch the surface, at the end we direct the reader to some publications that deal in more detail with the many issues involved. Sign language dictionaries are briefly discussed at the end of the chapter (§8.7.4).

## 8.2 DIFFERENT TYPES OF SIGN LANGUAGES

There are many sign languages, including sign languages used by those who are deaf – which are sometimes referred to as **primary** or **natural** sign languages; and **alternate** or **secondary** sign languages, which may replace speech in some circumstances. There are also some **artificial sign systems** that encode speech in manual form (see Pfau, 2012).[1] All of these vary in terms of lexical and grammatical complexity. Estimates of the exact number of sign languages vary, but most suggest that the number is well over a hundred.[2]

While fully-fledged sign languages are the primary mode of communication for the deaf, other types of sign languages are used in particular cultural contexts, and these tend to have been developed and used by hearing people. For example, in Central and northern Australia, Indigenous sign languages are used alongside speech, gesture and other semiotic systems such as sand drawing. Sign may be used by hearing interlocutors when they are in view, but out of earshot; and sign is used, particularly by women, as a mark of respect when they are bereaved. Sign is also used in some ceremonial contexts. Although some signs may be in everyday use across the communities and learnt in early childhood, more complex repertoires are learnt later in life. These sign languages have been described as 'alternate' as they are not generally the main mode of communication in these communities, but rather used instead of speech in particular cultural circumstances (Bauer, 2014; Green & Wilkins, 2014; Kendon, 1988; Maypilama & Adone, 2013). Another example is found in North America where a conventionalised sign language emerged as a form of communication between First Nations communities that spoke many different languages (Davis, 2015; Farnell, 2009).

**Shared sign languages** are those that are used by both hearing and deaf members of a community. If a community is geographically isolated and has a large population of people who cannot hear, a common sign language that everyone learns may develop (Pfau, 2012). One of the most well-known examples of this was Martha's Vineyard Sign Language, once widely used on the island of Martha's Vineyard off the coast of Massachusetts in the United States. Other gestural communication systems have arisen in cloistered religious communities where speech is forbidden

(Quay, 2015), and yet others in workplaces, such as sawmills and fish markets, where speech is not practical because of noise or other environmental factors that get in the way of audible communication. Another system, known as **homesign**, may develop in a family context as a means of communication between deaf children and their immediate family network. Some research has shown how sign languages may emerge and develop once such children get together and form a cohort, typically in an educational context (Goldin-Meadow, 2005; Kegl, Senghas, & Coppola, 1999; Senghas, Kita & Özyürek, 2004).

Some recent research has focused on sign languages used in a range of non-Western contexts, including those found in small-scale rural or 'village' communities (de Vos, 2016; de Vos & Pfau, 2015; Jepsen et al., 2015; Nyst, 2007; Zeshan & Sagara, 2016; Zeshan & de Vos, 2012). The sociolinguistic profile of these village sign languages varies when compared to sign languages that have developed in industrialised societies, where sign languages often evolved in the context of schools for the deaf (Nyst, 2015, p. 108). In spite of recognition of the diversity and wealth of sign languages many are highly endangered – for deaf sign languages this may be driven by changes in technology, such as the availability of cochlear implants, and subsequent changes in the socio-cultural contexts of sign language use. In some communities, more prestigious sign languages may overshadow lesser known local ones (Nyst, 2015, p. 109). When it comes to 'alternate' sign languages, even though sign knowledge may be strong in some domains, it may be that some of the cultural practices that defined their use are less prevalent than they used to be. Although more elaborate knowledge of sign may be on the wane, new signs emerge to reflect the communicative needs of changing social circumstances.

## 8.3 GESTURE

Interest in gesture dates back to classical antiquity, when gesture was recognised as an important component of the art of rhetoric (see Kendon, 2004a, Chapter 3). While most studies of gesture have focused on manual gestures, others consider the role of movements of the head and torso, facial expressions, movements of the lips, the eyes and so on. Whereas an element of a sign language can be described as "a relatively stable, identifiable visual-gestural act with an associated meaning which is reproduced with consistency by native signers" (Johnston & Schembri, 1999, p. 117) gestures may be one-off and idiosyncratic, varying from one communicative event to another or between their users. Even so, some types of gestures may be conventionalised, and so have fairly consistent interpretations in a particular culture over repeated occurrences (see the example of gestures from South Africa below). There are also significant cross-cultural differences as to the way that various actions are understood, and even as to what types of actions are socially acceptable. It remains the case that much of what we know about gesture comes from laboratory-based studies. Studies of gesture used in small-scale language communities are not so common (but see, for example, Haviland, 2003; Le Guen, 2012; Wilkins, 2003). There is certainly plenty of useful and exciting work to be done in the field!

The question of what counts as 'sign' and what is 'gesture' is not a trivial one. Some have envisaged the range of visible human communicative actions as being on a continuum, with gesture at one end, and primary sign languages at the other (McNeill, 1992). However, as the term 'gesture' means different things in different contexts, and because this term is difficult to nail down with precision some prefer to not even use it at all. As Adam Kendon (2004b) has written, it is important to recognise "that 'gesture' is a term that covers a multitude of diverse activities" (2004b, pp. 98, 99). Some suggest that a 'gesture' must be *deliberately* expressive, which distinguishes gestures from other actions such as adjusting one's clothing, scratching the head, or jiggling the feet (Kendon, 2004a). Others discuss the degree to which various types of gesture that accompany speech involve the *conscious* intention of the speaker, or the communicator (see McNeill, 2015). Some consider that 'gesture', and in particular pointing, is also an important part of sign languages (Cormier, Schembri, & Woll, 2013; Johnston, 2014, p. 34).

One type of gesture is referred to as a **symbolic gesture**, an **emblem** or a **quotable gesture**, and these can be used independently of speech and tend to have stable meanings in a community (Kendon, 2004a, pp. 335–344).

### Quotable gestures in South Africa

In an urban residential area or 'township' outside Johannesburg in South Africa, gesture is a prominent feature of everyday communication among Black South Africans. A large repertoire of quotable gestures is in use. There are approximately 143 gestures that can function independently of speech, but the repertoire is changing, with some gestures falling into disuse and new ones emerging. Examples of these gestures include 'Phone', 'Soccer', 'Clever', 'Money', 'Sleep', 'Child', 'Bewitch' and 'Car' (Brookes, 2004).

Along with a young male co-researcher from the local community, Brookes collected approximately ten hours of video recordings of naturally occurring communicative interactions. These consisted of conversations amongst young men on street corners, in yards, inside houses and at larger social events such as parties. Using video is not always straightforward: "Although video recordings provide the most accurate data of gestural use, detailed written observations were an important source of data because instances of gestural communication and some gestures are often difficult to capture on video" (Brookes, 2004, p. 189). The research methods used in this study also included elicitation interviews and **decoding tests** (see §8.6.2).

Various attempts have been made to come up with other ways to classify different types of gestures (see Kendon, 2004a, Chapter 6 for an overview). Some terms that you may come across in the literature referring to co-speech gesture include **iconic**, **metaphoric**, **deictic** and **beat** (McNeill, 1992). Iconic gestures are those that are closely related to the meaning content of co-occurring speech (for example if someone is describing how to turn on a tap, and they make a turning action with their hand); metaphoric gestures refer to more abstract ideas or categories (for example, spoken space-time metaphors may be accompanied by gestures to the front, behind or to either side of the speaker). Beats have no propositional content but rather serve discourse functions as the hand moves "with the rhythmic pulsation of speech" (McNeill, 1992, p. 15).

Deictic or pointing gestures are highly context-dependent and usually associated with movements of the finger or hand, although directed nodding of the head, shifts of the torso, eye-gaze and lip-pointing may all be found (Enfield, 2009). People often augment manual pointing actions by using material objects – sticks, electronic 'pointers', computer cursors and so on. Pointing gestures can refer to objects in reach or to those that are further away, to abstract entities, such as referents in discourse, or to objects in virtual spaces. Some scholars are critical of attempts to draw hard and fast distinctions between types of gesture by showing that many of these semiotic properties can be combined. Thus various combinations of iconic, metaphoric, deictic and beat-like properties of an action may be found together.

## 8.4 SOME REASONS TO STUDY SIGN AND GESTURE

There are many compelling reasons to study sign languages. Research on sign languages contributes to explorations of many aspects of linguistic theory, and this is evident in debates focusing on the nature of the human language capacity, its relationship to other aspects of communication and cognition, and questions such as whether or not the diverse range of languages we see in the world today share some universal patterns of organisation (Evans & Levinson, 2009; Pinker, 1994). One of the key questions that research on sign languages can help answer is whether or not language universals are modality-specific (de Vos & Pfau, 2015; Palfreyman, Sagara, & Zeshan, 2015, p. 187).

Other research questions include understanding how sign languages emerge and change over time, and how children acquire sign (and how these processes compare with the spoken modality). Some investigate the nature of sign language contact with other signed languages or with other communicative systems, and the ways signers code-switch and vary their use of sign repertoires in particular sociolinguistic circumstances (Palfreyman, 2016). **Psycholinguistic** approaches to understanding how sign is produced and processed is another field of inquiry. Other researchers are trying to come to grips with questions such as how many sign language families there are in the world (Pfau & Zeshan, 2016). Descriptions of non-Western sign languages further our understandings of sign language typology, and this has implications for the field of language typology in general (Le Guen, 2012, p. 244). Some research compares actions used by signers and those used by non-signers. This may illuminate the ways that gesture may influence the development of sign language lexicons and the interplay between the spontaneous actions that accompany speech and the role of gesture in fully-fledged sign languages (Cormier et al., 2012). Sign language research can also have important practical outcomes, assisting in the creation of resources, such as dictionaries, that help people learn and maintain sign languages, as well as raising general community awareness of sign (§8.7.4).

Looking at gesture and its relationship to speech provides an opportunity to get under the 'cognitive hood' and explore many aspects of language and thought (for an overview of some experimental studies see Goldin-Meadow & Alibali, 2013). Some studies have investigated the correlation between the grammatical structures and semantic categories of a language, and the types of co-speech gestures produced by speakers of those languages. For example, by comparing the gestures of English, Turkish and Japanese speakers, Kita & Özyürek (2003) concluded that the semantic categories of a language do have an influence on what is displayed in gesture (see also Akhavan, Nozari, & Göksun, 2017).

---

### Looking at gesture and speech in Avatime

Some have wondered about whether serial verb constructions (SVC) refer to single or multiple conceptual events. Defina (2016) examined the co-speech gestures that went with these and with other complex clauses in Avatime, a language spoken in the Volta region of Kwa (Ghana). The data were utterances taken from narratives and procedural descriptions. Where SVCs occurred, she found that single gestures overlapped the entire construction, whereas other complex clauses were accompanied by distinct gestures overlapping each verb. The Avatime speakers' use of single gestures with SVCs therefore suggests that these particular constructions refer to single conceptual events rather than multiple ones (Defina, 2016).

---

Gesture is also important in studies of language acquisition (see Chapter 9). When children first begin to use spoken language, and even before they speak, they also employ bodily movements that may be socially recognised as gestures or as potential signs (Hoiting & Slobin, 2007; Tomasello, Carpenter, & Liszkowski, 2007). Gesture may be very good at doing some things that speech does not do so well – for example indicating with precision aspects of spatial location and direction, and depicting the size and shape of objects (Streeck, 2010).

Gesture is also a significant element of the pragmatics of an interaction, helping to coordinate speech between interlocutors, and moderating the outcome of ongoing conversation. In addition, gesture (and sign) may be important in songs, poetry and other forms of the verbal arts (Chapter 11). Lastly, taking a multimodal approach to the recording of spoken languages, and paying attention to the actions that go with speech can provide a new perspective on the meanings of words, as well as inevitably uncovering new vocabulary. This can often be a revelation, as the action tells you something about the meaning of an utterance that was not clear if you only *listened* to what was being said and did not *look* as well.

> **Exercise 1  Including gesture in the written grammar of a language**
>
> Do you think that the gestures of speakers of a language should be described in the grammar of that language? Are there any particular parts of a grammar that you think might benefit from this approach?

## 8.5  SOME CONSIDERATIONS WHEN WORKING ON SIGN LANGUAGES

### 8.5.1  Working in teams

Hearing researchers who take on research on primary sign languages need to be particularly aware of their status as 'outsiders' (§1.2.2) and reflect on possible impacts their research may have on the deaf community (Singleton, Martin, & Morgan, 2015, p. 8). As is discussed in §2.4, it is always preferable to work collaboratively with experts in the language you are studying. This is also the case for sign – and if you are not a native signer of the language you are studying it is strongly advised that you work closely with collaborators or research assistants who are (Nyst, 2015, p. 112). You may find that there are opportunities to learn some of the basics of the sign language you are working on before you start, although the chances of finding teachers of little-documented sign languages in your home-base may be remote. Otherwise make every effort to learn as much as you can while you are in the field. Your mistakes as a learner can often be very instructive for all! Teamwork has many advantages – it speeds up time-consuming processes, provides opportunities for training and engagement, and recognises the complementary skills that all bring to bear.

> **A team approach to annotation of Adamorobe Sign Language (AdaSL)**
>
> Adamorobe Sign Language is a village sign language used in Adamorobe, an Akan village in eastern Ghana. Deaf and hearing members of the community use the sign language. A team approach was developed in the annotation of sign data.
>
>> (W)hen there are no deaf or hearing native signers with the necessary literacy and language and computer skills, an alternative solution is to form annotation teams in which each member has a complementary skill. Thus I worked with three people on the annotation of AdaSL data: one hearing native signer, bilingual in AdaSL and Akan; one non-signer, literate in Akan; and one non-signer, literate in Akan and English. The signer voiced the translation in Akan, which was written down in notebooks by the non-signer literate in Akan, which in turn was translated into English by the third member. The notebooks served as a support for my own annotations of the data.
>>
>> (Nyst, 2015, p. 118)
>
> The notebooks were then scanned, typed up and their contents then imported into ELAN.

## 8.5.2 Speech effects on sign language

In environments where it is likely that many people are to some extent multilingual or practising bi- or multi-modals, the importance of untangling the **observer effect** has an additional layer of complexity (see also §10.4.3). One observer effect is the tendency of signers to skew their signing towards the structure of the ambient spoken language if they are signing with, or in the presence of, hearing signers. As we will discuss below, it is important to consider these effects when deciding on research methodologies for sign languages.

## 8.5.3 Number of participants

Other considerations when documenting sign are the selection of participants, and deciding how many are needed for certain types of study. A crucial factor to consider is the high degree of variation in deaf signing communities due to interrupted language transmission across generations, educational practices, and language contact, all of which make studies based on just a few signers problematic. Research on sign languages also needs to accommodate the signer's cultural and literacy practices, which may vary immensely from one field context to another (Padden, 2015, p. 152). Working in groups can be a great way to approach documentation of sign, particularly in contexts where knowledge of sign is fragile and endangered.

## 8.5.4 Informed consent

In §2.5.2, we discussed the issue of informed consent for research projects and the importance of reaching a mutual understanding of consent between the researcher and the participant. Although this issue pertains to any research situation and to any multilingual situation where research participants and researchers do not share a common language, for sign research there are additional steps that may need to be taken. The use of sign interpreters is strongly advised (§2.5.2). Informed consent may be documented either by video in the relevant sign language or in written form in the ambient spoken language. Remember to archive the evidence of consent along with your field recordings.

## 8.5.5 Anonymity

When it comes to sign language and gesture research there are additional considerations that may need to be addressed in formal ethics applications (§2.5). The first has to do with the nature of the documentation and the use of video, which makes it virtually impossible to anonymise the research participants. In reference to video recordings of New Zealand Sign Language, McKee & McKee (2013, p. 518) have written that "(v)ideo clips are embodied linguistic performance by individuals who have social identities and styles that are immediately recognizable to their own language community". In some communities the identity of people is also read from other cues – the shape of their hands, characteristic scars or body markings, and clothing etc.

Some research institutions suggest that videos be 'anonymised' by either blurring, pixelating or blocking out parts of participant's faces. While this may not have the desired effect, as people may still be recognisable, in sign language research this leads to a potential masking of important linguistic information such as facial expressions, eye-gaze and movements of the lips and brows. Apart from the identification of particular individuals, another consideration is the effect that disclosing the location of field sites may have on the community (Kusters, 2012, pp. 45, 46). For example identifying a fascinating or 'exotic' research site might result in an increase in visitors, either well-meaning health professionals, linguists or other researchers. They may not stay long enough to engage with community expectations of reciprocity, and may end up being seen as a burden rather than a plus. There are additional ethical considerations if you have a sign language acquisition project in mind and plan to record children signing (see §9.2.3).

### 8.5.6 Metadata for sign languages and gesture

In §4.2.2 we discussed the importance of metadata in general terms, and the need to make primary research data machine-readable, locatable and searchable. Research projects on sign and gesture are likely to generate large volumes of video data, and if you are using more than one camera, then it is even more important to make sure you are well organised and have a good system in place right from the start. As well as all the categories of metadata discussed in §4.2.2, in sign language and gesture research it is important to include information about the number of cameras used, the configuration of the cameras and their viewpoint, and the presence and visibility of interpreters (on or off camera). If you are interested in spatial aspects of sign or gesture it is essential that the ways that the participants are facing when you are making a recording are noted carefully, and this becomes part of your metadata. If you don't have a good sense of direction (and some linguists who are interested in space do not!), a compass is a useful addition to your field kit. Or use your smart phone!

Particular metadata that refers to the language situation of signers in a research project includes their language background, hearing status, education, age of sign acquisition and literacy practices. Other metadata can help keep track of the sign sub-systems used, such as sign supported speech, fingerspelling and air-writing, although you may well decide to code for these in your annotation system. A detailed discussion of metadata categories for sign language corpora can be found in Crasborn & Hanke (2003).

## 8.6 RESEARCH METHODS FOR DOCUMENTING GESTURE AND SIGN

As is the case for spoken languages, a broad distinction can be made between naturalistic methods, which attempt to find out how sign or gesture is used in face-to-face interaction (§8.7.2), and elicitation and (semi-)experimental methods which are effective in targeting certain domains, and also in providing data

# Sign and gesture

that is comparable across languages (§8.6.1). Not all of these methods will be practical in the field. On the other hand, getting out of laboratory-based situations is important if knowledge of gesture and sign language diversity is to be advanced. A discussion of some of these methods for sign languages is given in Nyst (2015, pp. 115, 116).

---

**Studying sign on suburban trains in Mumbai**

In the suburban trains of Mumbai, deaf commuters tend to travel in train compartments that are reserved for people with disabilities because these spaces allow them to communicate in sign language, which is impossible in the other overcrowded compartments. One of these commuters reflects on the communicative advantages of this space:

> In the general compartments it was so crowded that when there was a deaf person with you, you could sign only small signs above people's heads. Now I feel free. I have space to communicate.
>
> (Kusters, 2009, p. 45)

Deaf people of different backgrounds, ages and genders meet each other in these compartments, and this practice has in turn strengthened links in the Mumbai deaf community. The "handicapped compartment" is the most central place for deaf people in Mumbai to exchange news and gossip and discuss various deaf-related issues. Annelies Kusters investigated multimodal communication between deaf and hearing strangers and acquaintances in public spaces in Mumbai (such as markets, shops, streets, food joints, public transport). Her research focused on the everyday use of space, employs a **participant observation** methodology, and has also resulted in several films created with and for the communities she worked with. This is a good example of producing tangible, useful and valued work that directly benefits the community.[3]

---

## 8.6.1 Elicitation and other methods

Eliciting lexical data in sign languages is useful for the purposes of cross-linguistic comparison, for phonological analyses of sign, and for creating filmed materials for sign language dictionaries (Nyst, 2015, p. 116). This may involve working from questionnaires or lists such as those discussed in §7.1.2, but those compiled by previous researchers on related sign languages may also be a useful starting point. Some typological studies of sign languages focus on particular semantic domains (§7.3) such as kinship, colour terms and number (Palfreyman, Sagara & Zeshan, 2015; Zeshan & Sagara, 2016). The flora and fauna domain may also be a useful one to explore. As is the case with spoken language elicitation methods, it is important to have a plan of what you aim to do – but also to be flexible and responsive to suggestions from the team you are working with. Experience shows that some of the most fruitful and rich recording sessions and perhaps some of the most interesting theoretical insights happen when the unexpected occurs.

It may be preferable to use pictures and props rather than written words from a spoken language, but again this depends of the levels of literacy in your research team. It is likely that tasks that rely on some form of written literacy will yield very different results from those that do not. Also be aware that some image-based stimuli may be difficult to use in signing communities, as the interpretation of images may require forms of literacy that participants are not familiar with (Nyst, 2015, p. 116). An elicitation set can be made by uploading pictures of local objects to a laptop computer and presenting this as a slide show. If using pictures of people that are locally known, make sure there are no gender-specific constraints about showing photos in public (Padden, 2015, p. 144).

In §7.5 we discussed various non-linguistic stimuli that are used to explore semantic and grammatical dimensions of languages. Many of these tasks, for example director-matcher tasks and the use of video clips as stimuli, can be used for sign language research. Signers may be asked to watch a video and then describe it to another signer who then repeats the description (Padden, 2015, p. 148). For example, an animated colour cartoon series called Canary Row, which formed the basis of studies of gesture in the McNeill laboratory, has also been used by sign language researchers (see Emmorey et al., 2008). The cartoon stimulus is shown to a participant and they then have to recount the story to a 'listener' who has not seen the cartoon. The wordless picture story, *Frog, Where Are You?* (Mayer 1994 [1969]), has also been used to elicit narratives in sign (see also §9.3.2.3 and §10.4.4.3). Elicitation can target particular domains, such as possessive, reciprocal or locative constructions, or it can be used to explore sign order in multi-sign utterances.

The Language and Cognition group at the Max Planck Institute for Psycholinguistics in Nijmegen has designed a suite of prop-based tasks, including the 'Man and Tree' game and the 'Animals in a Row' task (Levinson et al., 1992). These have also been used in sign language research (see de Vos, 2012).[4] If you are interested in exploring the gestural repertoires of a speech community, choose gesture-rich topics. Discussions about route finding, and procedural or 'how to' texts, such as talking about ways to cook a meal or fix a car, may all yield rich data that has a lot of action in it (Seyfeddinipur, 2012).

---

### Exercise 2 Eliciting signs for kin

Your research is in a community where there is a shared sign language as well as several spoken languages, and you are trying to find out more about signs for kin terms. The signers are literate in English, but not in the heritage language of the community. The terminology of the kinship systems is very different between all of these languages. What sort of tasks could you design to help determine what signs are used for kin terms and what they mean?

One fascinating research question is investigating how different languages and cultures conceptualise time. Cultures differ with respect to the spatial metaphors they use, and in some cases these metaphors may be represented in ways other than in speech. For example, English speakers often gesture to the left when talking about the *past*, and to the right when referring to the *future*. When asked to perform a temporal ordering task, English speakers tend to lay out time as proceeding from left to right. Arabic speakers, who read written forms of language from right to the left, do the opposite. The Kuuk Thaayorre from Cape York in northern Australia predominantly rely on a cardinal system (roughly aligned with north, south, east and west) rather than left and right. In an experimental study, it was found that the Kuuk Thaayorre lay out time as proceeding from east to west (Boroditsky, Gaby, & Levinson, 2008). In Yucatec Maya spoken language from Mexico "sequential events are expressed with a rolling gesture that implies cyclicity rather than linearisation of events or orientation of time flow". The absence of a metaphorical time line in Yucatec Maya gesture is also apparent in Yucatec Maya Sign Language (YMSL) (Le Guen, 2012, p. 210).

---

### Exercise 3 Time, gesture and orientation

You are not sure how to understand the ways that people gesture about time in the language you are working on. You notice that when people talk about 'morning' they point in one direction, and when they talk about 'afternoon' they point to another. You are not sure whether this action is anchored to the body and thus shows a left/right distinction or whether the speakers/signers are using an absolute frame of reference (i.e. fixed bearings such as north, south, east, west). How could you test these possibilities further? What else should you look out for if you are working inside a building?

---

## 8.6.2 Quizzes and decoding tests

If part of your research agenda is trying to understand the complex relationships between different modalities and the ways they contribute to the meaning of an utterance, there are various tasks that can assist. One way to do this is to isolate the input of one modality (say speech or action) in order to find out how the output in the other works (although this will not help if they truly work together). In the study of quotable gestures from South Africa, mentioned above, Brookes (2004, pp. 192, 193) attempted to find out which elements of the gestural repertoire had more conventional meanings by presenting videos of the gesture action, without speech, and asking consultants to provide written glosses. This 'decoding test' helped to delineate the repertoire of gestures that were 'quotable' by canvasing the opinions of a range of research participants.

Another application of this sort of methodology was used in a study of sand stories from Central Australia (Green, 2014). In sand drawings, a small set of graphic symbols drawn on the ground have conventionalised meanings, but one research question was to investigate the extent to which the graphic symbols alone would have shared meanings to those who are familiar with the practice. To investigate this, a 'sand quiz' was developed by selecting a set of films of the drawing action, the bird's-eye view in the video data (see §4.3.3), into three small movies for use as an elicitation tool. The aim was to test the extent to which particular sand drawing forms have meanings that are independent of context, and to thus provide insights into how dynamic graphic information is understood by interlocutors. The use of 'visual questionnaires' to achieve layered interpretations of communicative events is recognised by some as being an important technique in ethnographic data collection. It also highlights the importance of participant involvement in determining the meanings of different types of action.

### 8.6.3 Filming gesture and sign

While many technical issues about using film in a language documentation context have been discussed in §3.3.3, in the following sections we will look at some particular considerations when working on gesture and sign languages. We will also expand on the discussion of approaches to the annotation and coding of various types of visual linguistic data. If sign or gesture is being filmed for the purpose of analysing the form of the action, then you need to pay particular attention to the film set-up. Make sure that you film the full extent of the sign or gesture articulation, and be aware that typical sign or gesture spaces vary cross-culturally. Some signs or gestures may involve the hands extending way above the signer's head, and unless your camera angle is wide enough crucial details of these kinds of actions, such as the handshape at the apex of the action, may be lost. Although it is not typical, some signers (for example Indigenous people from Arnhem Land in Australia) may employ the lower leg for the articulation of some signs (even if they are standing up!). If signers are being filmed seated on chairs it is advisable to choose, if possible, chairs without arms, as arm-rests on chairs can get in the way and skew the normal articulation of signs.

Although being proscriptive about clothing may not be advised and could be seen by some as being an imposition, as discussed in §3.3.3, some types of patterned clothing don't look good on film. Backdrops for filming sign can be useful if one of the purposes of the research is to make filmed records of sign that show different aspects of sign articulation clearly. A quick browse of some online sign dictionaries of the world shows variation in the colour of the backdrops used for filming. The online dictionary of Auslan (Australian Sign Language)[5] uses blue, whereas others may opt for grey, green or mauve. The point is that either stark white or black backgrounds are not flattering and will skew the light reading of your camera one way or the other, resulting in either under-exposure or over-exposure of the faces and hands of the participants (§3.3.3). Also note that boldly patterned backdrops may make sign articulation harder to discern clearly. When recording alternate sign languages in Central Australia we found a length of uncrushable blue fabric that presented a smooth mono-tonal surface even after it had been used repeatedly and carried in the back of a truck for many thousands of kilometres. Figure 8.1 shows a mobile studio (the blue curtain is inside the tent) that provided a comfortable space for filming sign in remote conditions. Such methods may be adapted to suit particular field circumstances, and even without the tent a portable length of fabric may be useful. Remember to pack the gaffer tape!

Another consideration is the way that signers orient themselves to the camera. Direct interaction of a signer with the camera as a default 'interlocutor' may be advantageous for filming examples of sign for a website or online sign dictionary, where simulating eye contact with imagined online audiences is the aim, but in other contexts direct continuous eye contact with the camera may seem very unnatural. If you are interested in more natural interactions then it is much better to film several people together, angled towards each other and at a slight angle to the camera. If you have two cameras, then it is possible to arrange them so that each films either the signer or the addressee. A top-down view is useful if you want to know more precise details of sign articulation in relation to the body. The top-down view can be filmed by attaching a camera to a tripod, a lighting stand (see §3.3.3) or even improvised solutions such as strapping the camera to a plank tied to a garden ladder. Keep in mind that you don't need to have three cameras! Natural conversational interactions, either signed or spoken, that are filmed less laboriously with one camera can also provide valuable data for linguistic analyses.

As discussed earlier, with all recordings it is important to keep note of the context. Sketch maps or photographic records of community layouts, or if inside, of the

Figure 8.1
Documenting alternate sign languages in Central Australia with Anmatyerr women Clarrie Kemarr and Eileen Perrwerl, and linguist Gail Woods. The blue curtain is hung inside the tent 'studio' (Photo: Jennifer Green 2012)

orientation and physical features of a room can be useful down the track and can be added to your field notebooks (§3.3.4). If, for example, you are trying to find out how space is used to encode time, then knowing whether or not a signer or gesturer is pointing to external spaces (outside a room), or to a clock on the wall inside is a crucial piece of information that may tip your analysis in one direction or the other.

## 8.7 ANNOTATING SIGN LANGUAGES AND GESTURE

The software ELAN is currently the tool of choice for many who work on sign languages and gesture (Crasborn & Sloetjes, 2008). One of the signature features of ELAN is the way it allows users to design their own **template** for data annotation. Each level in a template is called a **tier**, and in Chapter 4 we discussed a simple template which had only two tiers (§4.3.2). Tiers have a range of attributes that can be chosen when the tier is first designed. These include the hierarchical relationships between tiers (what is the 'parent' tier and which tiers are dependent i.e. the 'child' tiers). It is also possible to add controlled vocabularies to the attributes of a tier and thus limit the entry values of the annotations that can be added to a particular tier in the time-line. So for example you may want to set up a controlled vocabulary that defines values for grammatical categories, or the range of hand shapes that are used. As discussed in (§4.3.3), choices have to be made about segmentation of the data and this will influence the design of your template. Although it is possible to use a simple template that only has one or two levels to annotate sign or gesture, many projects allow for very detailed annotation of sign or gesture forms. It all comes down to what the research questions are.

Another popular tool used for annotation of sign and gesture is ANVIL, originally developed for gesture research in 2000. It offers multi-layered annotation based on a user-defined coding scheme. During coding, the user can see time-aligned and colour-coded elements on multiple tracks. ANVIL can import data from phonetic tools like Praat, and it can display wave forms and pitch contours. A feature of ANVIL that is not offered by ELAN is that it supports 3D viewing of motion capture data (Kipp, 2014; see Perniss, 2015, p. 69).

### 8.7.1 What to annotate first

Once you have filmed a session, transferred the film from the camera(s), named the files, started working on your metadata and set up an ELAN file, the next question is where to begin with the process of annotation. Annotation is normally done in a series of steps or parses, first selecting the broadest units and then moving on to the more finely grained levels (Johnston, 2014, p. 6). Over time, continuing work on annotation and transcription of the corpus will enable it to be searched on a variety of parameters. We give several examples below.

If you are studying sign or co-speech gesture the first issue is to decide on your system for identifying units of action. When somebody gestures or signs, their hands may move from a default or rest position, into the air (or to some other location) and then back again. This excursion of the hands has been described as a gesture-unit or a 'G-unit' in gesture studies (Kendon, 2004a). A G-unit comprises phases of **preparation**, **stroke**, **hold** and **recovery** or **retraction** (Kendon, 2004a; McNeill, 1992). The phase when an articulator moves from a resting position and approaches the 'apex of the excursion' is called the preparation. The phase where the dynamics of the movement and expression are executed most clearly or most forcefully is called the stroke. Then there may be a hold, or a brief moment of rest in the air after the stroke. When the hand retreats back to a position of rest it is called the recovery or retraction phase. This position of rest is identified by observation and will vary with postural changes of the narrator. If your study of gesture is about fine-tuned timing of gesture in relation to speech, you may want to incorporate these gesture phases into your ELAN template. If you are working on sign this level of granularity may not be relevant to your research questions, and different criteria may be employed to identify the beginnings and ends of sign actions.

Figure 8.2 shows three screenshots from a video of Ngaatjatjarra linguist Lizzie Marrkilyi Ellis working with her mother Tjawina Porter. Tjawina is showing the way men spear kangaroos. The figure illustrates the phases of preparation, as Tjawina's hands leave their position of rest. Then comes the stroke where the action reaches its apex with an emphatic index figure action that coincides with an expressive sound we have written as *prrrrrr*. This represents the sound that the spear makes when it enters the kangaroo's body. At this point Lizzie joins in. Finally, in the recovery phase, Tjawina's hands return, in silence, to a resting position.[6]

The transcription of the speech that goes with this action is shown in Figure 8.3, which zooms in on a short segment of an ELAN file that is used for this sequence.

Figure 8.2
Phases of an action that accompanies speech. Ngaatjatjarra linguist Lizzie Marrkilyi Ellis works with her mother Tjawina Porter, Alice Springs, Northern Territory, Australia, 2012 (Video stills: Jennifer Green)

Figure 8.3
An ELAN template that allows for annotation of the phases of an action, and for morphological glossing of the co-occurring speech

| Speech [2] | Wati pirni-lu tjurti-ralpi | | | | Wati-witja-nku nyangka marlu. Prrrrrr | | | | |
|---|---|---|---|---|---|---|---|---|---|
| Word [7] | wati | pirni-lu | tjurti-ralpi | | wati-witja-nku | nyangka | marlu | prrrrrr | |
| WordGloss [7] | man | many-ERG | loaded.woomera-and | | across-go-FUT | while/when | kangaroo | SOUND | |
| RH-Action [1] | | | | | | | | | |
| ActionPhase [3] | | Preparation | | | | | | Stroke | Recovery |
| SpeechTrans [2] | The men put their spears into the woomeras | | | | As the kangaroo goes across. 'Prrrrr'. | | | | |

The template has tiers for speech, for segmentation at the word level, for morphological glosses, and for the action that accompanies the speech. It shows clearly that the action and speech co-occur, and overlap in interesting ways.

> **Exercise 4  Is it a sign or a gesture?**
>
> Look again at Tjawina's example in Figures 8.2 and 8.3. Do you think that the expressive action shown is a sign or a gesture? What else would you need to know about the communicative practices of Ngaatjatjarra people in order to answer this question?

If your research question is about the relationship between speech and the actions that accompany it you may want to include various gesture types as a controlled vocabulary in your ELAN template, even as you keep in mind the fact that it is at times difficult to be categorical about identification of the types (§8.3). As seen in Figure 8.4 these will then appear as a drop-down menu item when you go to add a value to the selected annotation. Using controlled vocabularies in ELAN is one way to eliminate variation that is caused by spelling things badly, and of course this makes searches for annotation values more efficient.

An example of a more complex sign language ELAN template is the Auslan (Australian Sign Language) one, which has over 40 tiers. This template includes

Figure 8.4
A screenshot from ELAN, showing the controlled vocabulary option which enables you to set the values for an annotation

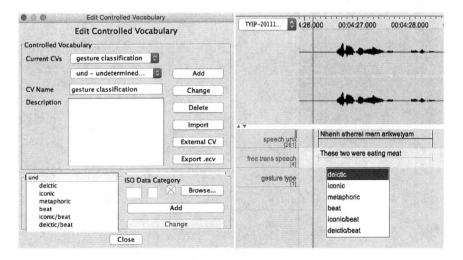

separate tiers for the right and left hands; tiers for aspects of sign action such as handshape, orientation, location and movement; and tiers for non-manual aspects of signing such as mouthings and movements of the face and brows (Johnston, 2014). Controlled vocabularies in ELAN may be used to show whether an action is a lexical sign, a depicting sign, an instance of pointing and so on. For sign languages, sign ID glosses, free translations, grammatical tags and other features of the sign action and function may be added in. **Sign ID glosses** are usually keywords in a spoken language that partially reflect the meaning of the sign (Johnston, 2010, p. 123). It is important to note that they are not full translations of the sign's meaning, but rather unique and succinct identifiers of the sign (§7.6.2). The convention in sign language studies is to represent sign ID glosses in capital letters.

Figure 8.5 is a screenshot taken from an ELAN annotation file for a video of NGT (Sign Language of the Netherlands) (Crasborn et al., 2004).[7] You can see that at least three cameras have been used, and the images that are visible in Figure 8.5 (from CAM 2 and CAM 3) give a distant and closer view of the signer. In the right hand panel of the frame you can see a series of sign ID glosses (in Dutch) that have been added to the annotation tier. These include HOND 'dog', SLAGER 'butcher', VLEES 'meat' and BOT 'bone'. Sign ID glosses are also visible in the timeline viewer. Translations of the signed utterance are shown in both Dutch and English. '*Een hond liep op zijn gemak ...*' 'A dog was walking around ...'. Although only part of the template is visible, it has 19 tiers, including those for translations of the Dutch ID glosses into English, a tier for mouth

Figure 8.5
Representation of a screenshot from an ELAN annotation file, showing sign ID glosses in Dutch (Illustration: Maxine Addinsall)

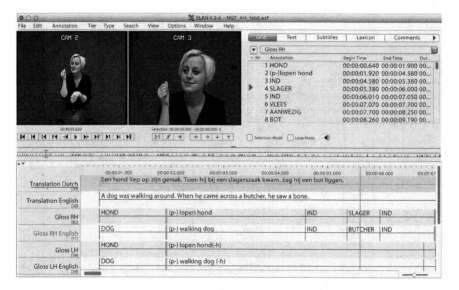

actions, movements of the eyes and brows and many more. Compare this to the template illustrated in §4.3.1.

If there are a lot of tiers in your ELAN template and they get in the way they can be hidden from view to give you more computer screen space to work with (simply right click on the tiers and choose which ones you want to either hide or reveal). The tiers can be brought out again when needed. It is better in the long run to do this rather than being tempted to make a simpler template, especially if you are working in a group that shares a template, and you have a long-term aim of making a searchable corpus. Depending on the level of detail you want to go in to, annotation of sign and gesture can be very time-consuming. One way to lighten the load is to work in teams (see also §8.5.1).

### 8.7.2 Building a corpus of sign

**Corpus methods** are gaining increasing importance in sign language research as both researchers and communities recognise their value. Auslan (Australian Sign Language) led the way, and in 2004 researchers began to compile a corpus (Johnston, 2010, p. 127). Since then other sign languages have followed. As is the case for spoken languages, a modern sign language corpus can be described as "a collection of written and spoken texts *in a machine readable form* that has been assembled for the purposes of studying the type and frequency of constructions in a language" (Johnston, 2010, p. 209 emphasis in original). Such corpora should be as representative of as many different types of sign use as possible, and be well-described by associated metadata (§4.2.2). Building a corpus as a basis for research can help avoid some problems inherent in generalising from small numbers of signers who are not truly representative of the larger community. One of the keys to effective corpora is consistency, and this applies to the methods that are used to annotate data (see §4.3) as well as the ways that language is collected, or the sampling methods used. The language activities that may be represented in a corpus include narratives, ordinary conversation, games and elicitation using various props and stimuli.

---

#### Exploring the use of space in Kata Kolok

Kata Kolok is a rural sign language that is the primary mode of communication for many in the northern Bali village of Bengkala, where a high percentage of residents are deaf. In a research project that aimed to explore the nature of sign-spatial mappings in Kata Kolok a corpus of almost 100 hours of archived video data was developed. The activities represented in the corpus include conversations, story retellings, stimulus-based elicited data – including some of the tasks from the Nijmegen Space Games and the Language of Perception tasks, and tasks exploring the functions of pointing in Kata Kolok (de Vos, 2012, p. 62).

### 8.7.3 Representing gesture and sign in publications

Although sign and gesture are not usually written down in the ways that speech is, there is still a call for ways to demonstrate aspects of both in various forums, including traditional paper or text-based publications. Just as spoken languages have the IPA to represent sound (§5.1.3), various systems have been designed for annotating the features of sign, even though they are not widely used for writing down larger texts. Stokoe, a pioneer of sign language linguistics, devised a sign notation system that used symbols to represent the location, hand shape and movement of signs (Stokoe, Casterline, & Croneberg, 1965). Other notation systems have since been developed and used in sign language dictionaries, including the Hamburg Sign Language Notation System (HamNoSys) (Prillwitz & Schulmeister, 1987) and SignWriting.[8] Kendon based his 'Rdakardaka' notation system, used for the 'alternate' sign languages of Aboriginal Australia, on that of Stokoe and his colleagues, although he added some symbols and modified others (Kendon, 1988, pp. 462–473).

---

**A sign written in three notation systems**

The sign MOTHER from Anmatyerr sign language uses a horn hand shape. Look at these different ways of representing the sign action (Figure 8.6). Firstly, you can see a line drawing of the sign action. Secondly you see the sign shown in three different 'phonetic' scripts: first Rdakardaka, then HamNoSys and finally in SignWriting. Some elements of these scripts are clearly iconic. For example the handshape, with the second and fifth fingers extended, is represented differently in each of the systems. If you were planning to use such a script practical considerations include how accessible the script is and whether or not it is used widely. If you want to see this sign in action go to Iltyem-iltyem, an online dictionary of Central Australian alternate sign languages.[9]

**Figure 8.6**
The Anmatyerr sign MOTHER (illustration: Jenny Taylor)

Transcripts of multimodal data can assist in visualising patterns of co-occurrence between modalities and should be closely associated with explicating your research questions. Ideally, transcripts should be possible to generate without too much fuss, and be a direct product of the annotation file (e.g. of an ELAN file) and not the result of laborious updating by hand. For the purposes of reproduction and citation in linguistic theses and texts such a transcript needs to be graphically replicable (i.e. won't lose too much if it is photocopied in black and white), easy to understand, and not overloaded with information.

There are existing conventions used for representing, as transcript, the interaction of gesture and its co-occurring speech. There is no standard, and the systems vary both in terms of the graphic conventions used and the underlying assumptions about what can be deduced from such representations. Some may use, for example, boldface type to indicate speech that co-occurs with a gesture stroke, and underlining to indicate a hold phase. Kendon (2004a) uses symbols placed below the line of speech script to show phases of gestural action. For example, 'P' shows preparation, '....' shows a stroke, and 'H' shows a hold. Another way is to represent co-speech gesture by numbers above the transcript line of spoken text (see case study below). There are also varying uses of line drawings, still shots from video footage, and verbal descriptors to illustrate aspects of gestures that co-occur with speech (see for example Enfield, 2009; Haviland, 2000; Streeck, 2010).

In academic papers about sign languages either still photos or screenshots of sign action or line drawings are used, and these static images may be enhanced by the addition of arrows that indicate motion. Still frames that are overlaid to show snapshots of the transformation of an action over time are also common. Line drawings may reproduce well in academic texts, but lose out on some contextual information; on the other hand, video stills may be too detailed and context-rich to clearly make a point. None capture the complexity and infinite richness of the real thing and this brings us face-to-face with the conundrum of trying to represent multidimensional action in static form. It is also common to provide links in academic publications to online video examples, and this is in general part of a principle that linguistic data should be cited and searchable (§4.4.6). If using videos or photos, remember that it is important to check with research participants that it is acceptable to reproduce images of this kind in a public context. In some contexts a line drawing may be more acceptable as it is slightly more anonymous than a photo of a person is.

The example shown in Figure 8.7 is from a community language resource that uses photos and embedded QR codes (Quick Response Code). It shows the sign for *lukarrarra* (*Portulaca filifolia*) a species of plant used by Mudburra and Jingili people from northern Australia. An arrow that indicates one aspect of the sign action (one hand sweeps across the back of the other) has been added to a still photograph, and there is a QR code linked to a video clip (Raymond et al., 2017).[10]

**Figure 8.7**
Pompey Raymond demonstrates the sign for *lukarrarra* (*Portulaca filifolia*), Elliott, Northern Territory, 2017 (Photo: Jennifer Green, Video: Felicity Meakins)

### A transcript of a sand story

In sand stories from Central Australia drawing on the ground is accompanied by speech, and sometimes sign (see Figure 3.3 for the field recording set-up for filming sand stories). Between episodes in a story told in this manner the ground is wiped clean before the narrator begins to draw again. This example shows how interlinear transcription of speech can be linked to graphic representations of six actions that accompanied speech in a small extract from a sand story. In Figure 8.8a four graphic units represent 'shade' (1), 'person' (2), 'dish' (3) and 'digging stick' (4). The fifth action is the conventional sign HUSBAND/WIFE and the sixth a deictic gesture. Then the first frame is erased and another begun by a drawing that represents 'windbreak' (1), 'person' (2) and then 'fire' (3) (Figure 8.8b).

In the transcript the line above the speech gives an approximate idea of the temporal relationship between speech and different types of action in the story. The medium in which the actions are enacted is also indicated.

For example |......| shows that it occurred on the ground (drawing); and |^^^^| in the air (gesture and sign). The convention |====| indicates erasure of the drawing space. Figure 8.9 shows part of the action of the Anmatyerr sign HUSBAND/WIFE (see also Green, 2014, pp. 96–98).

**Figure 8.8**
A schematic representation of graphic units drawn on the ground: (a) the first sequence; (b) the second sequence

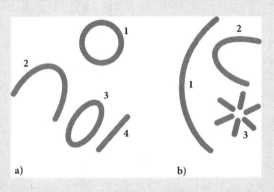

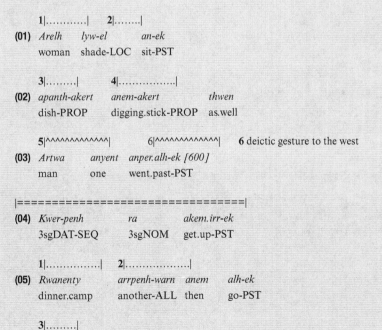

1|............|    2|........|
(01) *Arelh*    *lyw-el*    *an-ek*
     woman    shade-LOC    sit-PST

     3|........|    4|................|
(02) *apanth-akert*    *anem-akert*    *thwen*
     dish-PROP    digging.stick-PROP    as.well

         5|^^^^^^^^^^^|    6|^^^^^^^^^^^|    **6** deictic gesture to the west
(03) *Artwa*    *anyent*    *anper.alh-ek [600]*
     man    one    went.past-PST

|================================|
(04) *Kwer-penh*    *ra*    *akem.irr-ek*
     3sgDAT-SEQ    3sgNOM    get.up-PST

     1|..............|    2|..................|
(05) *Rwanenty*    *arrpenh-warn*    *anem*    *alh-ek*
     dinner.camp    another-ALL    then    go-PST

     3|........|
(06) *Rwa*    *amp-em*
     fire    burn-PRS

*A woman was sitting in the shade of a tree with her digging stick and dish. A man, [her] husband, went past in a westerly direction. Then the woman got up and went to another dinner camp. A fire is burning.*

**Figure 8.9**
The Anmatyerr sign HUSBAND/WIFE (Illustration: Jenny Taylor)

---

**Exercise 5  Get your multimodal palette together!**

It is now time to see if you can go through the steps of making an audio-visual recording right through to a preliminary analysis of several short utterances. In this task you will:

- make a short video recording
- get the files off the camera, name the files and create a set of basic metadata
- design an ELAN template or choose a simple ready-made one
- annotate the data
- decide how you would represent and cite several examples in a linguistic text.

### 8.7.4 Sign language dictionaries

Dictionaries of sign languages are highly valued by communities. They can help facilitate communication between sign language users and the surrounding spoken language community, and help promote the status of the sign language. Nowadays many of these are online, although there still may be a place for paper-based resources that use video stills, line drawings or photographs.

As we have discussed above, sign languages are not written languages, although there have been some forms of notation developed to represent them. Although such systems may occasionally be used to represent the headwords (§7.6.1) in sign language dictionaries, to a large extent most of the additional information in sign dictionaries is in written forms of a spoken language. Some sign dictionaries enable searches based on parameters such as handshape, although a usage study of one such dictionary suggested that even if this option is available, searching by a written form of an ambient spoken language may be the most commonly used strategy (Vale, 2017). SIL International is currently developing and testing a program called SooSL which is designed to support the creation of video-based dictionaries for sign languages of the world.[11] New technical developments are also giving rise to different tools that complement sign language dictionaries, for example Word-Net-like lexical databases such as ASL-Lex (Caselli et al., 2016).[12]

---

**Multilingual and bimodal: A dictionary of NZSL (New Zealand Sign Language)**

The Online Dictionary of NZSL is a multimedia digital resource designed for use by learners and teachers of NZSL, deaf people, families and associates of deaf people, interpreters, researchers, and public agencies. The dictionary is a reference tool that allows users to search for NZSL vocabulary through either English / Te Reo Māori words or by the visual features of signs themselves. Te Reo Māori translations have been added to each entry, making the dictionary accessible in the three official languages of New Zealand. It contains over 4,300 lemmas (McKee & McKee, 2013).[13]

---

Some technical issues with online dictionaries of sign – for example the need to enable smooth display of sign videos in different online environments – are also considerations for dictionaries of spoken languages that aim to include audio or video, and for other multimedia language resources. As is the case with other dictionary projects, a team working on a sign language dictionary needs to think carefully about the relationship between the dictionary and the underlying corpus on which it is based. As discussed in the case study below, this includes issues such as whether or not to create discrete clips for the dictionary, or whether to extract them by time code from the primary archival files.

### An online dictionary of an alternate sign language in Central Australia

The Iltyem-iltyem project is an online dictionary of some Central Australian sign languages.[14] The dictionary was based on semantic domains that had previously been used in the Anmatyerr picture dictionary, one of the spoken languages in the region (§7.5.2). A key challenge for this project was to design a workflow which identified suitable sign utterances from longer video recordings and then extracted them and their associated metadata for presentation on a website. There are two main approaches to undertaking this. The first is to select relevant sections in a media file by start and end time codes and then call them up as 'snippets' (e.g. by HTML 5), and stream them from a host server which holds a repository of archival files, which remain intact. The alternative is to create 'clips' – a suite of secondary files that are then presented as independent items (or segmented files). Clips are small and more manageable for media streaming, especially over slow internet connections which are typical in some remote Australian communities.

This was the approach we chose for this project, even though creating clips can potentially lead to data management problems by replicating media and creating secondary files. Although perhaps not regarded as best practice in language documentation, we found it to be appropriate in this context given the limits on internet speed in the user communities. Managing the large number of secondary files requires a workflow design that maintains provenance between archived media and the clips created for online publication.

Figure 8.10 shows how the project workflow takes divergent paths after the video capture stage (ii). These paths have different outputs: Path A is an editing workflow, in which media files are compiled and edited using proprietary media compilation software to make films for various purposes. Path B is a workflow for creating sets of preservation files and for selecting media to present online on the Iltyem-iltyem website. Path B comprises the following stages: (i) record, (ii) transfer video, (iii) create media repository, (iv) transcribe & annotate, (v) export and (vi) build website posts (Carew & Green, 2015).

**Figure 8.10**
The Iltyem-iltyem sign language project workflow

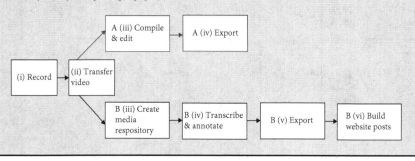

## 8.8 SUMMARY

Going beyond speech to look at communicative actions opens up a new view of language and can lead to many insights that may not be possible if a mono-modal approach is taken to the ways that human languages are used. This chapter has given an introduction to sign languages and gesture, and discussed some of the common ground they share. We considered some of the particular issues that research on these entails, before looking at practical matters such as filming techniques, and tools that are used for annotation. The chapter concluded with a brief discussion of sign language dictionaries.

## 8.9 FURTHER READING

Guides to a range of issues in research methods in sign languages include Orfanidou, Woll & Morgan (2015), and Pfau, Steinback & Woll (2012). Transcription and annotation of sign languages is found in Crasborn (2015), Johnston (2014) and Perniss (2015). Singleton et al. (2015) discuss ethics in sign language research. For perspectives on theory and methodologies in Deaf Studies see Kusters, De Meulder & O'Brien (2017). The SIL website has useful links to resources and publications on sign.[15] An overview of studies of gesture is found in Kendon (2004a) and a discussion of methodologies in gesture research in Seyfeddinipur (2012). Multimodal perspectives on the role of body movement in language and communication, and chapters on gesture research methods are found in Müller et al. (2013). For overviews of the state of the art in sign language lexicography see Zwitserlood (2010) and McKee & Vale (2016).

## NOTES

1. One convention is to capitalise the term *Deaf* when referring to communities of individuals who identify with aspects of Deaf culture, and to use lower case 'd' when speaking solely about hearing loss. However, there is regional and personal variation as to how this convention is applied.
2. Ethnologue lists 142 sign languages www.ethnologue.com/subgroups/sign-language Accessed 21 August 2017. ISO codes are either registered or under review for 107 of these. See www.evertype.com/standards/iso639/sgn.html Accessed 21 August 2017.
3. https://vimeo.com/172930705 Accessed 27 August 2017.
4. http://fieldmanuals.mpi.nl/volumes/1992/man-tree-space-games/ Accessed 31 August 2017.
5. See www.auslan.org.au Accessed 27 August 2017.
6. Source: SIGN20121031-JP&EG-02-JG1.mov (02:34–02:40 min).
7. www.ru.nl/sign-lang/projects/completed-projects/echo/ Accessed 20 September 2017.
8. www.signwriting.org/ Accessed 5 December 2017.
9. http://iltyemiltyem.com/sign/anmatyerr/mwek/ Accessed 17 August 2017.

10   To view the film clip download a QR Code Reader to your mobile device.
11   www.sil.org/about/news/new-technology-supports-language-development-signed-languages Accessed 27 August 2017.
12   www.asl-lex.org Accessed 22 August 2017.
13   http://nzsl.nz Accessed 27 August 2017.
14   http://iltyemiltyem.com/sign/ Accessed 22 August, 2017.
15   www.sil.org/sign-languages/sign-language-resources Accessed 3 August 2017.

## REFERENCES

Akhavan, N., Nozari, N., & Göksun, T. (2017). Expression of motion events in Farsi. *Language, Cognition and Neuroscience*, 32(6), 792–804. https://doi.org/10.1080/23273798.2016.1276607

Bauer, A. (2014). *The Use of Signing Space in a Shared Sign Language of Australia* (Vol. 5). Berlin: De Gruyter Mouton and Ishara Press.

Boroditsky, L., Gaby, A., & Levinson, S. C. (2008). Time in space. In A. Majid (Ed.), *Field manual* (Vol. 11, pp. 52–76). Nijmegen: Max Planck Institute for Psycholinguistics.

Brookes, H. (2004). A repertoire of South African quotable gestures. *Journal of Linguistic Anthropology*, 14(2), 186–224.

Carew, M., & Green, J. (2015). Making an online dictionary for Central Australian sign languages. *Learning Communities: International Journal of Learning in Social Contexts. Special issue: Indigenous sign languages*, 16, 40–55.

Caselli, N. K., Sehyr, Z. S., Cohen-Goldberg, A. M., & Emmorey, K. (2016). ASL-LEX: A lexical database of American Sign Language. *Behavior Research Methods*. https://doi.org/10.3758/s13428-016-0742-0

Cormier, K., Quinto-Pozos, D., Sevcikova, Z., & Schembri, A. (2012). Lexicalisation and de-lexicalisation processes in sign languages: Comparing depicting constructions and viewpoint gestures. *Language & Communication*, 32(4), 329–348.

Cormier, K., Schembri, A., & Woll, B. (2013). Pronouns and pointing in sign languages. *Lingua*, 137, 230–247.

Crasborn, O. (2015). Transcription and notation methods. In E. Orfanidou, B. Woll, & G. Morgan (Eds.), *Research methods in sign language studies: A practical guide* (Vol. 6, pp. 74–88). London: Wiley-Blackwell.

Crasborn, O., & Hanke, T. (2003). Metadata for Sign Language Corpora. Background Document for an ECHO Workshop. Radboud University, Nijmegen, 8–9 May 2003.

Crasborn, O., & Sloetjes, H. (2008). Enhanced ELAN functionality for sign language corpora. In O. Crasborn, T. Hanke, E. Efthimiou, I. Zwitserlood, & E. D. Thoutenhoofd (Eds.) *Construction and exploitation of sign language corpora. Proceedings of the Third Workshop on the Representation and Processing of Sign Languages* (pp. 39–43). Paris: ELDA.

Crasborn, O., van der Kooij, E., Nonhebel, A., & Emmerik, W. (2004). ECHO data set for Sign Language of the Netherlands (NGT). Department of Linguistics, Radboud University Nijmegen.

Davis, J. (2015). North American Indian Sign Language. In J. B. Jepsen, G. De Clerck, S. Lutalo-Kiingi, & W. B. McGregor (Eds.), *Sign languages of the world: A comparative handbook* (pp. 911–931). Berlin: De Gruyter Mouton and Ishara Press.

de Vos, C. (2012). *Sign-spatiality in Kata Kolok: How a village sign language in Bali inscribes its signing space*. Nijmegen: Radboud University.

de Vos, C. (2016). Sampling shared sign languages. *Sign Language Studies*, 16(2), 204–226.

de Vos, C., & Pfau, R. (2015). Sign language typology: The contribution of rural sign languages. *Annual Review of Linguistics*, 1(1), 265–288. https://doi.org/10.1146/annurev-linguist-030514-124958

Defina, R. (2016). Do serial verb constructions describe single events?: A study of co-speech gestures in Avatime. *Language*, 92(4), 890–910.

Emmorey, K., Borinstein, H. B., Thompson, R., & Gollan, T. H. (2008). Bimodal bilingualism. *Bilingualism: Language and Cognition*, 11(1), 43–61.

Enfield, N. J. (2009). *The anatomy of meaning: Speech, gesture, and composite utterances.* Cambridge; New York, NY: Cambridge University Press.

Evans, N., & Levinson, S. C. (2009). The myth of language universals: Language diversity and its importance for cognitive science. *Behavioral and Brain Sciences*, 32(5), 429–448.

Farnell, B. (2009). *Do you see what I mean?: Plains Indian sign talk and the embodiment of action.* Lincoln, NE: University of Nebraska Press.

Goldin-Meadow, S. (2005). *The resilience of language: What gesture creation in deaf children can tell us about how all children learn language.* New York, NY: Psychology Press.

Goldin-Meadow, S., & Alibali, M. W. (2013). Gesture's role in speaking, learning, and creating language. *Annual Review of Psychology*, 64(1), 257–283.

Green, J. (2014). *Drawn from the ground: Sound, sign and inscription in Central Australian sand stories.* Cambridge: Cambridge University Press.

Green, J., & Wilkins, D. P. (2014). With or without speech: Arandic sign language from Central Australia. *Australian Journal of Linguistics*, 34(2), 234–261. https://doi.org/10.1080/07268602.2014.887407

Haviland, J. B. (2000). Pointing, gesture spaces and mental maps. In D. McNeill (Ed.), *Language and gesture* (pp. 13–45). Cambridge: Cambridge University Press.

Haviland, J. B. (2003). How to point in Zinacantán. In S. Kita (Ed.), *Pointing: Where language, culture, and cognition meet* (pp. 139–169). New York, NY: Psychology Press.

Hoiting, N., & Slobin, D. I. (2007). From gestures to signs in the acquisition of sign language. In S. D. Duncan, J. Cassell, & E. T. Levy (Eds.) *Gesture and the dynamic dimension of language: Essays in honor of David McNeill* (pp. 51–65). Amsterdam: John Benjamins.

Jepsen, J. B., De Clerck, G., Lutalo-Kiingi, S., & McGregor, W. B. (2015). *Sign languages of the world: A comparative handbook.* Berlin: Mouton de Gruyter and Ishara Press.

Johnston, T. (2010). From archive to corpus: Transcription and annotation in the creation of signed language corpora. *International Journal of Corpus Linguistics*, 15(1), 104–129.

Johnston, T. (2014). Auslan Corpus Annotation Guidelines [June version]. Sydney: Macquarie University. www.auslan.org.au/about/annotations/

Johnston, T., & Schembri, A. (1999). On defining lexeme in a signed language. *Sign Language & Linguistics*, 2(2), 115–185.

Kegl, J., Senghas, A., & Coppola, M. (1999). Creation through contact: Sign language emergence and sign language change in Nicaragua. In M. DeGraff (Ed.), *Comparative grammatical change: The intersection of language acquisition, creole genesis, and diachronic syntax* (pp. 179–237). Cambridge, MA: MIT Press.

Kendon, A. (1988). *Sign languages of Aboriginal Australia: Cultural, semiotic and communicative perspectives.* Cambridge: Cambridge University Press.

Kendon, A. (2004a). *Gesture: Visible action as utterance.* Cambridge: Cambridge University Press.

Kendon, A. (2004b). Review of "Hearing gesture: How our hands help us think" by Susan Goldin Meadow. *Gesture*, 4(1), 91–101.

Kipp, M. (2014). Anvil: The video annotation research tool. In J. Durant, U. Gut, & G. Kristofferson (Eds.) *The Oxford Handbook of Corpus Phonology* (pp. 420–436). Oxford: Oxford University Press.

Kita, S., & Özyürek, A. (2003). What does cross-linguistic variation in semantic coordination of speech and gesture reveal?: Evidence for an interface representation of spatial thinking and speaking. *Journal of Memory and Language*, 48(1), 16–32.

Kusters, A. (2009). Deaf on the lifeline of Mumbai. *Sign Language Studies*, 10(1), 36–68.

Kusters, A. (2012). Being a deaf white anthropologist in Adamorobe: Some ethical and methodological issues. In U. Zeshan & C. de Vos (Eds.) *Sign languages in village communities: Anthropological and linguistic insights* (pp. 27–52). Berlin: De Gruyter Mouton and Ishara Press.

Kusters, A., De Meulder, M., & O'Brien, D. (Eds.) (2017). *Innovations in Deaf Studies: The role of deaf scholars*. Oxford: Oxford University Press.

Le Guen, O. (2012). An exploration in the domain of time: From Yucatec Maya time gestures to Yucatec Maya Sign Language time signs. In U. Zeshan & C. de Vos (Eds.) *Sign languages in village communities: Anthropological and linguistic insights* (pp. 209–250). Berlin: De Gruyter Mouton and Ishara Press.

Levinson, S. C., Brown, P., Danziger, E., De León, L., Haviland, J.B., Pederson, E., & Senft, G. (1992). Man and tree and space games. In S. C. Levinson (Ed.), Space stimuli kit 1.2: November 1992 (pp. 7–14). Nijmegen: Max Planck Institute for Psycholinguistics.

Mayer, M. (1994) [1969]. *Frog, where are you?* China: Puffin.

Maypilama, E., & Adone, D. (2013). Yolŋu sign language: An undocumented language of Arnhem Land. *Learning Communities*, (13), 37–44.

McKee, R. L., & McKee, D. (2013). Making an online dictionary of New Zealand Sign Language. *Lexikos*, 23(1), 500–531.

McKee, R. L., & Vale, M. (2016). Sign language lexicography. In P. Hanks & G.-M de Schryver (Eds.), *International handbook of modern lexis and lexicography*. (pp. 1–22). Heidelberg: Springer Verlag.

McNeill, D. (1992). *Hand and mind: What gestures reveal about thought*. Chicago, IL: University of Chicago Press.

McNeill, D. (2015). *Why we gesture: The surprising role of hand movements in communication*. Cambridge: Cambridge University Press.

Müller, C., Cienki, A., Fricke, E., Ladewig, S. H., McNeill, D., & Teßendorf, S. (Eds.) (2013). *Body-language-communication:An international handbook on multimodality in human interaction*. Berlin: Walter de Gruyter.

Nyst, V. (2007). *A descriptive analysis of Adamorobe sign language (Ghana)*. Utrecht: Netherlands Graduate School of Linguistics.

Nyst, V. (2015). Sign language fieldwork. In E. Orfanidou, B. Woll, & G. Morgan (Eds.), *Research methods in sign language studies: A practical guide* (pp. 107–122). London: Wiley-Blackwell.

Orfanidou, E., Woll, B., & Morgan, G. (2015). *Research methods in sign language studies: A practical guide*. London: Wiley-Blackwell.

Padden, C. A. (2015). Methods of research on sign language grammars. In E. Orfanidou, B. Woll, & G. Morgan (Eds.), *Research methods in sign language studies: A practical guide* (pp. 141–155). London: Wiley-Blackwell.

Palfreyman, N. (2016). *Variation in Indonesian sign language*. Berlin: De Gruyter Mouton and Ishara Press.

Palfreyman, N., Sagara, K., & Zeshan, U. (2015). Methods in carrying out language typological research. In E. Orfanidou, B. Woll, & G. Morgan (Eds.), *Research methods in sign language studies: A practical guide* (pp. 173–192). London: Wiley-Blackwell.

Perniss, P. (2015). Collecting and analyzing sign language data: Video requirements and use of annotation software. In E. Orfanidou, B. Woll, & G. Morgan (Eds.), *Research methods in sign language studies: A practical guide* (pp. 55–73). London: Wiley-Blackwell.

Pfau, R. (2012). Manual communication systems: Evolution and variation. In R. Pfau, M. Steinbach, & B. Woll (Eds.), *Sign language: An international handbook* (pp. 513–551). Berlin: De Gruyter Mouton.

Pfau, R., Steinbach, M., & Woll, B. (2012). *Sign language: An international handbook* (Vol. 37). Berlin: De Gruyter Mouton.

Pfau, R., & Zeshan, U. (2016). Positive signs: How sign language typology benefits deaf communities and linguistic theory. *Linguistic Typology*, 20, 547–559.

Pinker, S. (1994). *The language instinct: How the mind creates language*. New York, NY: William Morrow and Company.

Prillwitz, S., & Schulmeister, R. (1987). *HamNoSys: Hamburg Notation System for Sign Languages. An introduction*. Hamburg: Zentrum Für Deutsche Gebärdensprache.

Quay, S. (2015). Monastic sign language from medieval to modern times. In J. B. Jepsen, G. De Clerck, S. Lutalo-Kiingi, & W. B. McGregor (Eds.), *Sign languages of the world: A comparative handbook* (pp. 871–900). Berlin: De Gruyter Mouton and Ishara Press.

Raymond, P., Dixon, P., Dixon, S., Dixon, R., Dixon, J., Dixon, E., Raymond, M., Dalywaters, H., Collins, J., Woods, R., Peterson-Cooper, E., Meakins, F., Pensalfini, R., & Wightman, G. (2017). *Jingulu and Mudburra plants and animals: Biocultural knowledge of the Jingili and Mudburra people of Murranji, Marlinja, Warranganku (Beetaloo) and Kulumindini (Elliott), Northern Territory, Australia*. Batchelor, Australia: Batchelor Press.

Senghas, A., Kita, S., & Özyürek, A. (2004). Children creating core properties of language: Evidence from an emerging sign language in Nicaragua. *Science*, 305(5691), 1779–1782.

Seyfeddinipur, M. (2012). Reasons for documenting gestures and suggestions for how to go about it. In N. Thieberger (Ed.), *The Oxford handbook of linguistic fieldwork* (pp. 147–165). Oxford: Oxford University Press.

Singleton, J. L., Martin, A. J., & Morgan, G. (2015). Ethics, deaf-friendly research, and good practice when studying sign languages. In E. Orfanidou, B. Woll, & G. Morgan (Eds.), *Research methods in sign language studies: A practical guide* (pp. 7–20). London: Wiley-Blackwell.

Stokoe, W., Casterline, D., & Croneberg, C. (1965). *A Dictionary of American Sign Language on linguistic principles*. Washington, D.C.: Gallaudet College Press.

Streeck, J. (2010). *Gesturecraft: The manu-facture of meaning*. Amsterdam: John Benjamins.

Tomasello, M., Carpenter, M., & Liszkowski, U. (2007). A new look at infant pointing. *Child Development*, 78(3), 705–722.

Vale, M. (2017). *Folk definitions as a model for sign language dictionary definitions: A user-focused study of the Online Dictionary of New Zealand Sign Language*. Doctoral Thesis. Victoria University of Wellington.

Wilkins, D. (2003). Why pointing with the index finger is not a universal (in sociocultural and semiotic terms). In S. Kita (Ed.), *Pointing: Where language, culture and cognition meet* (pp. 171–215). Mahwah, N.J.: L. Erlbaum Associates.

Zeshan, U., & de Vos, C. (Eds.). (2012). *Sign languages in village communities: Anthropological and linguistic insights* (Vol. 4). Berlin: De Gruyter Mouton and Ishara Press.

Zeshan, U. & Sagara, K. (Eds.) (2016). *Semantic fields in sign languages: Colour, kinship and quantification*. Berlin: De Gruyter Mouton and Ishara Press.

Zwitserlood, I. (2010). Sign language lexicography in the early 21st century and a recently published dictionary of sign language of the Netherlands. *International Journal of Lexicography*, 23(4), 443–476. https://doi.org/10.1093/ijl/ecq031

# 9

# Child language acquisition

## 9.1 INTRODUCTION

The great comedian W. C. Fields is credited with the quip, "Never work with animals or children!" Fieldwork on language acquisition, the study of how children learn language(s), brings with it the usual excitement and challenges, but there are also some specific considerations to think about if you do want to work with children. This chapter provides some helpful advice for people considering an acquisition study, including funding requirements (§9.3.1), choosing a field site (§9.3.2), whether documentation of the adult language already exists (§9.3.3), ethics and consent (§9.3.4), potential gender problems (§9.3.5), health considerations (§9.3.6) and recruitment (§9.3.7). We then give a snapshot of some of the standard methodologies used in acquisition research and how they can be adjusted for the field, with a view to understanding where compromises can be made to take into account some of the difficulties of field research (§9.4).

The field of language acquisition in general also has many good methodological overviews for how to conduct studies (Blom & Unsworth, 2010; Ingram, 1989; Rowland, 2013; Stoll, 2015). Nonetheless, field studies of child language acquisition present many unique challenges, such as the level of funding required to undertake longitudinal studies requiring repeat fieldwork, the extent to which the target language has been documented and the time it takes to transcribe children's speech (even you are an L1 speaker of the language!). These challenges come on top of the usual considerations for language documentation (see Chapters 2–4) and are discussed in more detail in Kelly, Kidd et al. (2015) and Eisenbeiss (2006). How do you aim for best practice in child acquisition research, given the additional challenges posed by fieldwork? In this chapter, we discuss various issues and methodological challenges in the context of three case studies of field acquisition projects – Chintang, Murrinhpatha and Light Warlpiri.

## 9.2 WHY DOCUMENT CHILD LANGUAGE ACQUISITION?

Language acquisition is one of the most important sub-disciplines of linguistics because it offers a unique window into the nature of the human faculty for language. The generativist tradition has used acquisition studies to argue that humans possess an innate module dedicated to language, called a Language Acquisition Device (LAD). This device is said to consist of a number of organising principles of grammar, such as anaphora resolution and recursion, with language-specific parameters such as head direction and pro-drop (Chomsky, 1981). More recently, it has been replaced with a single principle of 'recursion' (Fitch, Hauser, & Chomsky, 2005) and, since then, with 'merge' (Yang, Crain, Berwick, Chomsky, & Bolhuis, 2017).[1] Other theories, such as the constructivist approach of Tomasello (2003), claim that general cognitive mechanisms such as pattern finding, joint attention, imitation and statistical learning are sufficient for children to piece together language from surrounding speech. All of these approaches assume that children learn language through an interplay of innate mechanisms, whether specific to language or domain-general, and the input of adult language.

To investigate how children learn language, we need acquisition studies from a diverse range of languages to determine what is common in how children acquire these languages and how acquisition situations differ. We currently only have acquisition studies from around 2 per cent of the world's 6,000–7,000 languages, and only corpora from 0.1 per cent. Most of these studies and corpora also only come from a sample of Indo-European languages from Western Europe, such as English, French, Italian and German (Lieven & Stoll, 2013; Stoll, 2015). As a result, theories of acquisition have been biased towards the quirks of these languages, such as relative pronoun constructions, e.g. *the cat that ate the mouse*, which are actually rare in the world's languages.

Another problem with the current state of play is that many Western European languages do most of the work of grammar in their syntax rather than by their morphology. For example, in the sentence *The boys hugged Mary*, we know that it was *the boys* who hugged Mary because subjects come before verbs in English. English and other Western European languages have relatively simple morphological structures, so many theories of acquisition have proposed rule-based learning processes to account for how children acquire inflectional morphology such as plural suffixes, e.g. *boys* (Berko, 1958), or past tense inflections, e.g. *hugged* (Pinker & Ullman, 2002). But the acquisition task is different if you are a child acquiring a polysynthetic language such as Chintang. Chintang expresses the subject, object and tense on the verb, so children acquiring Chintang need to learn many more verb forms than English children before they fully master the language – up to 4,000 distinct forms compared with just four in English i.e. *hug, hugs, hugged, hugging* (Stoll, Mazara, & Bickel, 2017)! The question then becomes, do children learn the rules first and then build up the verb (*hug + ed = hugged*); or do they learn the whole verb first as an unanalysed chunk and develop the rules as they acquire more and more verb forms (*hugged, chopped, sipped* = [*hug, chop, sip*] + *ed*)?

### Chintang Language Acquisition Project

The Chintang project formed a part of the larger Chintang/Puma DoBeS documentation project (§4.4.1). Chintang belongs to the Kiranti subgroup of the Sino-Tibetan language family. It is spoken by around 6,000 people in Eastern Nepal on a lower foothill of the Himalayas. Chintang is still learnt as a first language by most children in the community, but children also grow up surrounded by Nepali, which is the dominant language of Nepal. Nepali is the medium of instruction in schools, so children's knowledge of Nepali strengthens when they enter school.

Chintang is a polysynthetic language which means something that requires a whole sentence to say in English can be said in a single verb in Chintang! The verb is very rich in morphology, encoding the usual sorts of verbal categories (e.g. tense, aspect, mood), as well as information about the subject and object (e.g. person, number). Nouns are also morphologically complex, inflecting for case and number, but they are not obligatory, and hence sentences are verb heavy.

(1) Gakkaŋ       yogoi?       **na-khaŋ-ce-ke**
    after.a.while  over.there   3A.2[SG]P-see-DUAL[A]-NONPAST
    "After a while they (dual) see you (singular) over there." (Stoll et al., 2012)

A longitudinal acquisition corpus was created by video recording four Chintang children (girl 2;0, boy 2;0, girl 2;11, boy 3;0), who all lived in the same village, but in different households. To create the corpus, focus children were recorded for four hours per month over a period of 18 months. The four hours were recorded within a single week, but the recordings often took place over many sessions. The recordings were conducted by a Nepalese researcher in collaboration with local assistants who spoke Chintang. A total of 220 hours of recordings were transcribed, morphologically annotated and translated into Nepali and English in ELAN by the local Chintang assistants, who received training throughout the project. For a good description of the methodology of this project, see Stoll et al. (2012) and Lieven & Stoll (2013).

What is needed is a more diverse sample of languages to be able to answer some of these questions about acquisition and the human faculty for language. Sabine Stoll (2015), who has worked on Russian, German and Chintang acquisition, states that this is the "top priority for the field of acquisition". Studies of how children learn less well-known languages have already expanded our knowledge of how children learn language. For example, the emphasis that Chintang places on the verb presents problems for one dominant idea in the acquisition literature – the existence of a universal noun bias. This idea suggests that children learn nouns first because their referents are more concrete and it helps them bootstrap into language (Gentner, 1982). But what happens in languages such as Chintang where nouns are grammatically optional and also comparatively rare compared with verbs in children's input (Stoll et al., 2012; see also Tardif, 1996 for a study showing Mandarin children first learn nouns and verbs equally)? Stoll & Bickel's (2013b) study of Chintang has also raised questions about the way that children learn ergative languages, which group intransitive subjects and objects, bringing into question the notion of the 'agentivity bias' in acquisition.

The agentivity bias was originally proposed through studies of languages, such as English, which group transitive and intransitive subjects (cf. Pinker, 1984). Work on lesser-known languages is already demonstrating some of the similarities and differences in how children learn languages across the world (ultimately providing a window into how language works in the human mind).

Of course, these reasons for studying language acquisition come from the point of view of linguistic research. If you are an 'insider' linguist studying your own language, you might have different motives for conducting an acquisition study. For example, if your community has a school where children are taught in their own language, you may wish to gain a better understanding of the order in which children acquire different aspects of your language. It also may be useful for teachers to know what language skills children bring to school and what areas of their language require greater attention within the framework of a formal curriculum. Being able to establish the norms of acquisition in your language can also help identify children who are struggling and might require extra support. If your language is endangered, a language acquisition study may help identify aspects of language which need prioritising.

## 9.3 SPECIAL CONSIDERATIONS FOR ACQUISITION WORK

Luckily you aren't the first person to conduct a field study of language acquisition! There are some great studies that you can read to help you get started. Some of the more substantial acquisition studies have been Elinor Ochs' (1988) work on Samoan (Polynesian, Samoa), Penny Brown's (1998, 2001) work on Tzeltal (Mayan, Mexico), Katherine Demuth's (1992) corpus of Sesotho acquisition and Shanley Allen's (1998, 2013) research on Inuktitut (Eskimo-Aleut, Canada). As we discuss the specifics of field methodologies, we give you a snapshot of the Chintang, Murrinhpatha and Light Warlpiri acquisition studies. These innovative case studies provide some interesting 'work arounds' to accommodate some of the difficulties of acquisition studies in the field.

> **Exercise 1  Archiving child language corpora**
>
> Pick one of the field studies of acquisition mentioned above. Where are the recordings archived? Is the video available? Is the audio available? Are the names anonymised?

### 9.3.1 Funding

Field studies of acquisition are very expensive, and should not be undertaken without considerable financial support. Longitudinal studies of children learning their first language (§9.4.1) require the children to be recorded at regular intervals which means repeat trips to a field site or employing a local researcher for considerable lengths of time to conduct the recording sessions. In addition, more funding is also often required for participant payments than in other types of projects because transcription usually needs to be done with caregivers in addition to field assistants because caregivers are the best interpreters of their own children's utterances (§9.4.1.6). Experimental studies can also be very expensive because they require a corpus in the first place to help design the research questions, and also require large numbers of participants (§9.4.2). If you are interested in an acquisition project, it is a good idea to look out for advertisements for PhD students at large institutes, centres or within well-funded projects. Or if you have a field site in mind, pitch an idea to a potential supervisor. The design of acquisition projects has been developed over decades and is necessary to ensure interpretable (and ultimately publishable) results. Such results cannot be achieved with small studies which may leave too many unanswered questions.

### 9.3.2 Choosing a field site

Choosing a field site might be a no brainer if you are a member of the speech community wanting to study how children acquire your language, but if you are an 'outsider' linguist, there are a number of factors you need to consider before launching into an acquisition study which are outlined in this section.

There are two approaches we recommend to choosing a field site. The first method is theoretically motivated. Think about what assumptions or predictions in current acquisition theories might be explained by the phonological, morphological or syntactic peculiarities of particular languages, as opposed to the process of acquisition itself. For example, remember that in the introduction to this chapter we observed that the rule-learning theories of generativists are largely the product of studying the acquisition of inflectionally light languages. If you are interested in these questions, choose a language which has a very different grammatical architecture to see if those assumptions or predictions can be generalised to a language with a different typological profile. This was the approach taken by the Chintang project (and also the Murrinhpatha project, §9.3.3). It addressed theoretical questions in the literature about whether nouns are learnt first and whether morphology is acquired via rules or whole words, using polysynthetic languages which are verb-orientated and morphologically complex.

Another approach is to choose a language which maximises the diversity of languages for which we have acquisition studies. Choosing a language on this basis is a great contribution to the data available for theoretical work on acquisition. Currently there are only 37 languages publicly available in CHILDES,[2] which is the largest online database of acquisition studies, and ten languages in ACQDIV.[3] Other studies can be found in other online archives, for instance the Chintang acquisition study is housed in the TLA (The Language Archive) (§4.4.2).[4] Smaller cross-linguistic studies were also published in a series of four volumes edited by Dan Slobin (2004). To broaden the available data, Stoll and Bickel (2013a) have developed a method called Maximum Diversity Sampling which can also help you identify potentially interesting languages to conduct acquisition studies on.

### 9.3.3 Existing documentation

One question that is important to consider is whether the adult language of a community has been well documented already. Without a comprehensive documentation of the adult speech, it is impossible to know what children are targeting in their own speech production. Eisenbeiss (2006) recommends integrating the collection of child language data into documentation projects. The Murrinhpatha project takes this approach, in what Rachel Nordlinger (2015) refers to as a "Multigenerational Documentation Project", where the adult, youth and child language are studied simultaneously by a team of researchers. At the very least, search for languages which already have extensive documentation and analysis. Indeed, in the past decade, many language documentation projects have greatly expanded our knowledge of typology (linguistic structure and variation between languages), which means there are more languages which could support acquisition studies.

> **Murrinhpatha acquisition project (LAMP)**
>
> LAMP formed a part of a larger Multigenerational Documentation Project focused on Murrinhpatha, a polysynthetic non-Pama-Nyungan language spoken in Wadeye in northern Australia by 2,700 people. Murrinhpatha is the main language of the community and is one of the few Australian Indigenous languages still learnt by children. Nonetheless, most of the organisations in Wadeye operate in English. Children are schooled in English, and many other government services, such as health and welfare, are also only provided in English.
>
> A longitudinal acquisition corpus was created by video-recording five children (1;9-4;3, four female, one male) over two years. The focus children were recorded over four field trips of two-three months duration. Each child was recorded twice during each field trip. The recordings were conducted by a PhD student and team-transcribed in ELAN by the student in conjunction with Murrinhpatha grandmothers and mothers of the children. A total of 33 recordings representing 34 hours were made, of which approximately 12 hours were annotated in this way. For a good description of the methodology of this project, see Forshaw (2016) and Kelly, Forshaw, et al. (2015).

If you are working in highly endangered language situations where a community is undergoing language shift, additional documentation of the target language might be required. In these cases, the only existing documentation may be of an older variety, no longer the dominant language of the community or the target of acquisition. In these cases, extensive documentation of the target language might be required. Indeed this was the case when Carmel O'Shannessy started her work on the acquisition of ergative marking in Light Warlpiri and Warlpiri in Australia (§9.4.2). The ergative marker in both Light Warlpiri and the variety of Warlpiri spoken in the community had not been described sufficiently to begin an acquisition study. In this case, O'Shannessy documented the use of the ergative marker in both the adult language and by children simultaneously (Meakins & O'Shannessy, 2010; O'Shannessy 2011). For suggestions on how to document languages in language shift scenarios, see §10.4.

### 9.3.4 Ethical considerations

Working with minority communities has many more ethical considerations compared with other populations (see §2.5); however, working with children requires even more care to ensure that your research does not affect the children's health and safety in any way. All university ethics committees will require extra documentation to demonstrate how children's wellbeing will be taken into consideration.

**Informed consent** for a child will need to be given by their official caregiver. If you have a continuing relationship with the community, you should consider redoing the consent forms when the child comes of age – 16, 18 or 21 in most countries. Also note that all participants who are recorded need to sign consent forms, not just the caregivers.

---

**Exercise 2 Consent dilemmas**

What would you do in the following situation? You have obtained from the archive someone else's corpus of videos which was made 20 years earlier. The consent forms show that the parents gave permission on behalf of their children for other researchers to use these recordings. You return to the community to find the families. One of the focus children, now an adult, wants their videos deleted. Should they have a say in how these recordings are used, archived and accessed?

---

**Background police checks** are required by law in many countries before you begin working (paid or unpaid) with children to ensure that you have not previously committed a crime against a child. For example, in Australia, these are called a 'Working with Children Check' or 'Working with Vulnerable People' and successful applicants are issued with a 'blue card' or 'ochre card' depending on the jurisdiction. In Canada, anyone working with children has to get a 'Criminal Record and Vulnerable Sector Check' from the police. It is also worth getting familiar with any **local welfare policies** such as the mandatory reporting of suspected child neglect or abuse.

**Payment** should be appropriate to the country and community you are working in (§2.5). Although it is illegal to pay children directly in many countries, the caregiver should be compensated for the child's time (and no doubt their own). If payment is inappropriate you may contribute to the children in other ways such as by assisting with educational costs, or providing home goods (bedding etc.), food or toys. Your university may have policies about what they will and won't cover, so make sure you talk to the right people before such arrangements are made.

**Archiving and access** also requires extra consideration in language acquisition projects. Videos may contain images of naked children, a normal everyday occurrence in some communities and climates, but nevertheless something which should not be available via the internet, even in password protected archives. In many communities, caregivers may only wish for the audio or the transcripts to be available (and not the video), even where there is nothing compromising on the videos. Other requests from caregivers for anonymity, gossip to be deleted etc. should be abided by, as is the case for all recordings.

### 9.3.5 Gender of researcher

As a researcher, your gender needs to be taken into consideration in acquisition projects. Child rearing in most cultures is a largely female-dominated activity, even in the case of male children. For many communities, it is considered odd (or even suspicious) for a male to be interested in working with children. It may also cause problems within families in the community if a man works with young mothers. The research project might be misinterpreted as a hunt for a wife! So if you are male, it might be worth garnering the opinion of people (either locals or outside researchers) who have worked in the target community to figure out how appropriate it is for you to work with children. It may be the case that you cannot conduct an acquisition project, but sometimes all that is required is extra attention to respectful behaviour. Gender was a serious consideration when Bill Forshaw started working in Wadeye on the acquisition of Murrinhpatha.

> (T)he nature of this project meant that I was required to have working relationships with the mothers of the various focus children. These were young women of a similar age to me. It was culturally inappropriate for me to spend time alone with these women. Consequently initially all my contact with these women was through the primary RA [research assistant] who was a mother or mother-in-law of these women. Over the life of the project these women have become more comfortable in interacting with me, however, during transcription and recording sessions it was always important that there be another adult present.
> 
> (Forshaw, 2016, p. 125)

### 9.3.6 Health considerations

Some children live in countries which have poor access to immunisation programs, sanitation, nutritious food and clean water. These conditions make them susceptible to many illnesses 'outsider' linguists may not have experienced before, such as diphtheria or cholera. Many children also grow up in areas rife with mosquito-borne diseases such as malaria, dengue fever and different forms of encephalitis. All of these illnesses affect children more severely than adults. Researchers need to be mindful that illness may prevent children and their families from participating in the project at particular times. As a researcher, it is also important to ensure that you don't further exacerbate the ill health of children by bringing additional disease to the community. Make sure that you are healthy when you set off on fieldwork, and ensure that you have had all relevant vaccines such as flu shots, diphtheria, cholera etc. (§2.7). Also be aware of your health in the field. Something as minor as a strep throat in an adult can develop complications, such as rheumatic heart fever, in a child.

Other children are members of minority groups within colonised countries. Aboriginal communities and Indian reservations in Australia, Canada and the United States have First World conditions in many respects i.e. they have housing, electricity, access to health clinics, and have high rates of immunisation for many childhood illnesses such as measles, mumps and rubella (MMR), Hepatitis B, flu and whooping cough. However, in many other respects, Indigenous peoples in colonised countries live in Third World conditions. For example, houses can be overcrowded and sewage systems are often blocked with overuse, all of which means that disease spreads fast. Diseases which are not seen elsewhere in these countries may be common in these places. For example, tuberculosis has mostly been eradicated in Australia, except in some Aboriginal communities. In the case of children, chronic ear infections are common and can result in hearing impairment in the crucial acquisition years (Galloway, 2008). In these cases, it is important to test children's hearing at various times during the project to ensure that acquisition sequences are not being confounded by temporary deafness.

### 9.3.7 Recruitment of project team

Local researchers are crucial to the success of an acquisition study in the field. You may be that person yourself, or you may be an 'outsider' linguist who needs to recruit from the speech community. Research teams might be structured differently in different places. In the case of the Chintang project, a Nepalese research assistant made all of the recordings with assistance of local assistants who spoke Chintang and could liaise with the families. The Murrinhpatha situation consisted of a PhD student coordinating the families with a local research assistant who was the grandmother of one of the focus children. So how do you recruit local researchers? You could start by asking the advice of linguists who might already work in the community, perhaps on documenting the adult language, or approach organisations which have a language program such as schools and language centres (see Chapter 2).

Once you have established the core language team, you can begin recruiting children and their families. If you live in the community yourself, you might want to start with your own family and then recruit via those networks. If you are an 'outsider' linguist, there are a number of ways you could begin the process of recruitment. The language team might have suggestions as to which families have children of the right age who might be interested in participating. This was the approach taken by the Murrinhpatha project. A linguist already working in the community introduced the student to a community member who then helped establish the acquisition project.

Another alternative might be to approach relevant organisations such as a school, kindergarten or crèche. Obviously children who are already school-aged are too old for an acquisition project, but they may have younger siblings. These organisations may also be interested in the results of your project. Sometimes caution needs to be taken with state-based organisations such as schools. It is worth finding out how well integrated the organisation is in the community. In many countries, the medium of instruction is in the official language of the country, for example in the Chintang and Murrinhpatha communities, the schools teach in Nepali and English, respectively. Sometimes this means there can be a tense relationship between state-based organisations and the communities which requires some political navigation on the part of the researcher. This approach will also typically require another layer of institutional ethics and consent.

## 9.4 METHODS IN ACQUISITION RESEARCH

Now that you have established the language team and a cohort of children and their families, the next step is to start your study. Acquisition studies fall into two categories – (i) longitudinal studies of small cohorts of children and (ii) cross-sectional experimental studies of large numbers of children. Both types of studies have advantages and disadvantages and work well in tandem. Usually longitudinal studies expose interesting areas of acquisition which can be pursued in more depth with experimental work.

In the next section we provide an overview of the state-of-the-art in child language acquisition studies and suggest some modifications that take into account some of the difficulties posed by undertaking such a study in the field. Be warned that some of the methods standard to language acquisition research are also prohibitively difficult for many remote field sites. When preparing your timeline for the study, take into account extra time for transcription, as children's speech is much more difficult to transcribe than adult speech. Most acquisition study methods were developed for major languages which have large numbers of children available, are often close to major universities with labs, and have plenty of native-speaker transcribers available. Depending on your aims, you may be satisfied with a pilot-level study, but high standards in data collection and analysis are expected by major international journals such as *Journal of Child Language*. This issue is discussed in detail for studies of smaller languages in an issue of *First Language* (Kelly et al., 2015).

### 9.4.1 Creating a longitudinal corpus

Longitudinal acquisition studies record children in naturalistic situations. Children are recorded at home and in other familiar places interacting with their caregivers, so they can be observed spontaneously in their own environment with familiar interlocutors. These studies usually involve small groups of children, recorded from an early age, over a long period of time. They provide the most detailed data for individual children.

The earliest longitudinal studies involved parent researchers recording children's utterances in diaries (summarised in Ingram, 1989, pp. 7–11). These studies have the advantage of catching interesting early utterances, usually grammatical errors, that reveal stage-specific strategies underlying a child's language production. But as children become more and more talkative, it is increasingly hard to record every utterance, which makes it impossible to conduct quantitative studies. Also caregiver utterances are generally not noted down which means that a child's utterance is usually recorded out of context and it is not clear what utterances are spontaneous and what are imitations. Good imitations of adult sentences may give the impression that a child has reached a morphological milestone when they have not!

Modern longitudinal studies of language acquisition now rely on audio-visual corpora of individual children sampled at regular intervals. Using video means that the context of utterances is captured, including caregivers' prior utterances and the visual field of the child. Many corpora have been developed using CLAN (see §4.4 and Carmel O'Shannessy's Light Warlpiri project in §9.4.2) and are now held in the CHILDES database, although the Chintang and Murrinhpatha projects discussed in §9.1 and §9.3.3 use ELAN (see §4.3.2).

Developing a corpus is a huge undertaking and there are many factors to take into consideration to produce a representative corpus. Stoll (2015) cautions the researcher to pay particular attention to (i) choosing representative children (number, age span), (ii) the context of recording (place, number and type of people present in the recordings), and (iii) the intervals between recordings and their length. We will look at each of these in turn and also discuss issues of transcription.

### 9.4.1.1 How many children?

A vital question when setting up an acquisition project is how many children you should record. Most non-field studies recruit around 4–6 children for longitudinal studies, and both the Chintang and Murrinhpatha projects applied this standard. It is vital to recruit this many children because we know that children vary enormously in language development. For example, in a cross-sectional study of American-English children, it was found that children who scored in the 10th percentile of the MacArthur-Bates Communicative Development Inventories (CDI) comprehended fewer phrases at 16 months than did children who scored in the 90th percentile at 8 months (Fenson et al., 1994, p. 33).

---

**Exercise 3  Between recruitment and recording comes ...**

A local research assistant has introduced you to a number of families and you are keen to get started recording. You set up all of your gear and start recording. For the first hour the child sits mutely and the caregivers nervously try to get the child to speak. Before leaping into recording, what sorts of things can you do to make recording a comfortable scenario for everyone involved?

Bear in mind that there will be some natural attrition over the course of the project so this means you need to over-recruit at the beginning of the project. Another issue lies in representativeness. Even when you choose a cohort of six children, how do you know that these children are representative of the population? Stoll & Gries (2009) developed a method which involves conducting a series of incremental comparisons between a child and his/her caregivers. This method can be applied as the corpus is being collected, and it gives you a sense of whether you have the right children in your sample.

### 9.4.1.2 What age to start recording at?

The age at which you begin to record depends on your research question. Based on the MacArthur-Bates CDI, word comprehension starts at 8–10 months, word production at 8–16 months, and grammatical production at 20–36 months (for an overview see Bates, Dale, & Thal, 1996). Because there is such variation in the onset of grammar, children are usually selected for studies on the basis of 'mean length of utterance' (MLU) rather than age, i.e. how many (analysable) morphemes they are producing in a single utterance (Rice, 2010). These ages are based on English-speaking children and might actually be quite late, particularly for grammatical production. Both the Chintang and Murrinhpatha studies showed that children learning polysynthetic languages acquire grammar quite early because all verb stems are bound, i.e. they don't exist on their own without inflections, unlike English verbs. Nonetheless both studies recruited children within the age range recommended by other major studies – 24 months in the case of Chintang and 21 months in the case of Murrinhpatha. Another approach is to stagger the age at which you start recording children. The Murrinhpatha project recorded two older children at the beginning of the project, as well as the younger children, to get a better sense of language development.

### 9.4.1.3 How to record children?

Once you have established a cohort of children, you need to capture their language use in the most naturalistic way possible. Most studies of major languages involve recordings of (usually) mother-child dyads during activities such as play, eating and dressing. But not all cultures raise their children in the same way and it is important to account for these differences. The Murrinhpatha project began with Western style set-ups using toys and adult-child dyads, but shifted quite quickly to more natural interactions involving everyday activities such as food preparation and eating which included more interlocutors and had no toys (Kelly, Forshaw, et al., 2015). The reason for this shift in methods was because Murrinhpatha children lived in large, intergenerational households where caregiver-child dyads were unusual. Mothers are usually the centre of young children's lives, but children are also cared for by people from different generations, as well as older children. Adults do not usually play with children, but interact with them constantly in day-to-day routines. In the case of Chintang, an ethnographic study of child rearing was conducted first which helped determine who the children interacted with the most and in what contexts. Similar to the Murrinhpatha study, large differences between these and more familiar Western contexts were observed, for example in the amount of child-directed speech, the demographics of the interlocutors, the fact that adults did not play with children, and the paucity of toys (Lieven & Stoll, 2013).

Once you have established the best way to record the children, you can now get underway with setting up your equipment. In general, the specifications for video (§3.2.5) and audio (§3.2.1) settings should be followed. In the case of the Murrinhpatha project, children were recorded using two video cameras (one on the general scene and another one on the focus children). One camera had a shotgun microphone and the other a wireless microphone receiver (§3.2.2). The children wore wireless microphones in backpacks. It was possible to mic up two focus children at a time, with one lapel microphone recording through the left channel of the stereo audio track and the other through the right channel. The receivers were then 'mounted' on the camera using zip ties (because these cameras typically only have one shoe). The boom mic was connected to the camera via an XLR cable through the R channel. This camera also had a shotgun microphone mounted on it running through the L channel. The backpacks were necessary because Murrinhpatha children don't always wear shirts due to the constant heat. The backpacks meant good audio was recorded and children could roam freely because the wireless microphones had a 50 metre radius. Of course recording in this way is data hungry, requiring a lot of available storage and a good workflow to keep track of all of the data 'objects' associated with each recording session (see §4.2.1).

---

**Exercise 4  Recording sessions and media 'objects'**

Read the passage on the Murrinhpatha camera and microphone set-up. How many media objects will result from this session? How many separate video and audio recordings are happening simultaneously? How would you label each of these objects?

---

An alternative is the Chintang set-up which has one camera with a 'fish-eye' lens and a shotgun microphone which produces just one media 'object' and requires less initial set-up time. There is also no need to set up radio microphones, which require level checks and balancing. All of this can be time-consuming and difficult for a solo researcher. The 'fish-eye' lens captures much of the action, and is an alternative to an additional roaming camera for active children.

If there is no electricity available, recording devices which use disposable batteries can be used. No video cameras use disposable batteries, but some audio recorders do. For roaming children, the device can be put in a backpack or bumbag (fanny pack) and worn by the child. In the worst case scenario, a diary style study can be undertaken (see §9.4.1). This sort of study might be effective in field situations where it is common for the researcher to live with a family, such as in Melanesia or Papua New Guinea.

### 9.4.1.4 Where to record children?

Corpus methods also need to take into account the context of the recordings, particularly the interlocutors given that children adjust their speech depending on who is talking to them. Most corpora consist of simple child-mother dyads (which makes transcription a lot easier than multiple people talking at once!), but of course children grow up with many more interlocutors. Recordings should also try to capture a variety of contexts including meal times, play, joint reading and other daily activities and routines. Often these situations involve many interlocutors, making transcription very difficult. The Murrinhpatha project solved this problem by driving participants to a location a distance away from the community of Wadeye to limit the number of interlocutors and thus increase the feasibility of transcription. Focus children (usually two in a recording session) and a number of people were taken to a nearby bush location to look for bush foods, have a picnic and go fishing. Participants were limited by number of seats in a car!

### 9.4.1.5 Frequency and regularity of recordings?

Finally, the timing and length of recordings needs to be considered. Traditionally children were recorded anywhere between once a week to once a month; however, Tomasello & Stahl (2004) find that this method is not suitable for characterising the development of a child's speech, potentially missing rare phenomena. Instead, they recommend recording once a month for five hours, although the five hours can be distributed over a number of recording sessions in a single week. Other studies have recorded children for ten hours per week. At the extreme end is the Human Speechome Project which continuously recorded one child from birth (Roy, 2009). The Chintang project followed the recording guidelines recommended by Tomasello & Stahl (2004) because the data collection was conducted by a local researcher. In the case of the Murrinhpatha project, the collection was coordinated by the PhD student who was based in Melbourne (two days air travel away). As a result, recordings were more sporadic. They also depended on weather conditions as recording is not possible during the monsoon season due to the noise of wind and rain. Nonetheless, because verbs occur in almost every Murrinhpatha utterance, small numbers of recordings still yielded large amounts of relevant data. Having fewer recordings is more problematic for rarely occurring constructions. For example, in O'Shannessy's (2011) study of the acquisition of ergative marking, she needed to create picture-prompt tasks to stimulate the use of nouns, which are not grammatically obligatory in Light Warlpiri or Warlpiri (§9.4.2.3).

### 9.4.1.6 Who does the transcription?

It is important to allocate lots of time for transcribing your recordings. All language documentation projects face a bottleneck of transcription in their workflow (§4.3). Recordings are easy to make compared with transcription, which can often take 50 hours per one hour of recording of two speakers (Travis & Torres Cacoullos, 2013). Acquisition data is even harder to transcribe. It is easier if you are an 'insider' linguist who speaks and writes the language which is the target of acquisition but, if not, you are faced with the double difficulty of learning the target language and then deciphering the children's rendering of it! The Chintang project was fortunate to be able to recruit many native speaker transcribers who also translated utterances into Nepali and English. The Murrinhpatha project took a team transcription approach with the PhD student transcribing utterances and with mothers and grandmothers assisting. This was a much slower process which meant that less transcription was possible. The solution for the Murrinhpatha project was to 'triage' the recordings, i.e. choose places where children talked the most. Allen & Crago (1996) also discuss this approach, where dense sections of recordings are selected for transcription. Both projects also emphasise the importance of transcribing children's utterances as soon as possible after the recording while it is fresh in the minds of the primary caregiver or older children, who are usually the focus children's best interpreters.

### 9.4.2 Cross-sectional experimental studies

The other main method for examining questions about language acquisition involves experiments. Often corpus studies throw up interesting data that can only be examined in more detail with experiments. Experimental work generally examines one linguistic feature of interest across a larger group of children of different ages. The use of different age groups, usually children from the same MLU groups (see §9.4.1.2), makes the assumption that the synchronic snapshot of children at different ages (or MLUs) represents diachronic language development. In this respect, it is similar to the concept of 'apparent-time' in Variationist Sociolinguistics (see §10.3.3). For a good overview of experimental methods used in acquisition research, see Ambridge & Rowland (2013) and Blom & Unsworth (2010).

All experimental work requires considerable preparation. Tasks must be age-appropriate and sufficiently interesting and motivating for children to cooperate. The experimental tasks must also be well-constructed. Thought needs to be put into the choice of novel items (i.e. 'wug' or novel words), the number of trials of a task, fillers used during the task (to test for continued attention from the child) and their timing in tasks. Images on screens need to be counter-balanced and their order of presentation randomised. Appropriate numbers of participants (usually 10–12 per age group) are also required for statistical modelling of results, so over-recruiting is necessary to account for drop-outs and children who cannot complete tasks.

The Chintang and Murrinhpatha projects did not adopt experimental methods, but one good example of their use in a field study of acquisition comes from O'Shannessy's (2011) study of the acquisition of argument disambiguation in Light Warlpiri.

---

**The acquisition of Light Warlpiri**

Light Warlpiri is a mixed language which is spoken at Lajamanu in northern Australia, and is similar in structure to Gurindji Kriol (see §10.2.3). Lexically, it combines nouns from Warlpiri (Pama-Nyungan) and Kriol (an English-based creole language), with verbs that are mostly from Kriol. The grammar is derived from both languages – the noun phrase structure, including case-marking, is derived from Warlpiri and the verb phrase structure comes from Kriol.

O'Shannessy targeted Light Warlpiri for an acquisition study because argument disambiguation (who is doing what to whom, see §6.7.1) is expressed through a complex interaction of word order and case-marking. Case-marking systems are hypothesised to be easier to learn than word order systems because nominal case-marking is more transparent as a cue than word order (Slobin, 1982). O'Shannessy first created an audio-visual corpus of 45 hours of Light Warlpiri and 16 hours of Warlpiri from Lajamanu children which was sound-linked (ethics approval was not obtained for public display of video, see §9.3.4), transcribed in CLAN (§4.3.2) and housed in The Language Archive (§4.4.1). She then further investigated argument disambiguation patterns in her corpus data with comprehension tasks. She used different experimental and semi-experimental tasks to explore how children at Lajamanu learn to disambiguate arguments.

---

### 9.4.2.1 How many children to test?

In the case of experimental work, many more children are needed than in corpus studies. Usually at least 12 children per age group are required to produce data which can be modelled using current statistical methods. O'Shannessy had success with using nine children in each category, but again, over-recruiting was key (see also §9.4.1.1). Experimental work with children is notorious for the high number of children who fail control items in test conditions, which is another reason for over-recruiting.

### 9.4.2.2 Methods for exploring perception or comprehension

Corpus studies are only really useful when a child has started talking. To get an understanding of a child's comprehension of language before they start producing language, ingenious methods, such as the 'non-nutritive sucking paradigm', have been instrumental in providing a window on the child's development of phonological categories. This method records changes in the rate of sucking of a pre-linguistic infant on an electronic dummy or pacifier in response to particular linguistic stimuli (Eimas et al., 1971). Other comprehension methods include 'act-out' which involves children performing sentences with puppets or toy props to elucidate their understanding of aspects of grammar such as argument structure (who did what to whom?). 'Picture-choice tasks' can be used with children who are too young to act out scenarios, but nevertheless can point. In these tasks, children point to one of two pictures presented on a split screen which they think best matches an auditory stimulus. For even younger children, their comprehension of grammatical structures can be examined using implicit eye-movement methods such as the 'intermodal preferential looking paradigm'. This is similar to the pointing task, but instead the length of time children spend looking at either of two pictures is interpreted as an indication of their comprehension of the auditory stimulus. A similar task which uses auditory targets instead of pictures is the 'conditioned head-turn preference procedure'.

> **Exercise 5  Experiments in the field – what's possible and what's not?**
>
> Many of the tasks described above require laboratory conditions which are not possible in the field. Think about each of the methods and why they might work or not work in field conditions. Can you think of ways of adjusting some methods so they will work in the field, or what additional equipment you might need to make them work?

To test the respective influence of case-marking and word order in Lajamanu children's comprehension of argument roles, O'Shannessy (2011) devised a picture-choice task using images of one animal doing something to another animal e.g. *kissing, holding, washing* (Figure 9.1). The short videos were designed

Figure 9.1
A 'picture-choice' task used with Warlpiri children

by O'Shannessy to be culturally appropriate and were turned into videos by a Chinese animation company and run in a web browser.[5] The presentation of pairs of videos and pairs of actors and patients were counter-balanced, and their order of presentation randomised and interspersed with controls. Children aged 5;0, 7;0 and 9;0 and a control group of adults saw paired, animated events simultaneously on video and heard a transitive sentence spoken where the word order and the use of ergative marking was variable. There were four possibilities for subject marking (SV, -ERG; SV, +ERG; VS, +ERG; VS, -ERG). Children were then asked to point to the picture which best matched the sentence they heard in order to determine whether word order or case-marking was the primary cue for argument disambiguation. O'Shannessy found that initially children used both case-marking and word order strategies, but they used case-marking more often as they grew older, matching adult-strategies.

### 9.4.2.3 Methods for eliciting speech

When children begin producing speech, other methods are used. Elicited production methods can include relatively unstructured methods such as asking children to describe videos or books. The *Pear Story* silent video (Chafe, 1980) and *Frog Story* wordless picture book (Berman & Slobin, 1994) are the most well-known of the cross-linguistic comparative studies which use these methods (see also §10.4.4.3). More controlled tasks involve picture descriptions, but with experimenters directing children's responses with more directed questioning. For example, to elicit verbs, experimenters might ask *What's X doing?* Or to elicit passives, experimenters might ask *What happened to the man?* Children may also be induced to produce target constructions by imitation or syntactic priming methods.

Sometimes the standard picture books, such as the *Frog Story*, are culturally opaque to children (but don't presume so – children are very creative!) or perhaps they just do not elicit the language structures of interest for the acquisition study. Picture description tasks can also elicit more tokens of constructions or parts of speech which are rare in the corpus. Higher numbers of tokens make it easier to understand the development of structures in children. O'Shannessy (2004) devised a series of picture books where the actors performing different actions changed from page to page, forcing children to explicitly say the actor (despite nouns being grammatically optional in Light Warlpiri and Warlpiri). This series consists of seven books which contain culturally specific and modern themes for the Warlpiri. Most of the stories are about hunting, monsters, collecting bush medicine and usually involve extended family groups and minor disasters. The books were ingeniously created by photographing cut-out scenes with small dolls and other everyday objects (Figure 9.2). The stories are quite simple and are appropriate for children, and accessible for re-use by researchers. O'Shannessy created the pictures by making backdrops and positioning dolls and other objects. Facial expressions were photoshopped. Books were laminated and bound with wire so they can be used multiple times.

**Figure 9.2**
A scene from 'The Guitar Story'
Source: O'Shannessy, 2004

## 9.5 SUMMARY

There is currently much scope for acquisition studies of lesser known languages to make major contributions to acquisition theory, and linguistic theory more broadly. Understanding acquisition provides a crucial piece of the puzzle of the human language capacity. Acquisition projects can also contribute a lot to a speech community where the target language is endangered. For example, projects of this kind can help understand which parts of the language to target in revitalisation efforts.

## 9.6 FURTHER READING

For a general discussion of field methods for acquisition, see Eisenbeiss (2006) and Kelly, Forshaw et al. (2015). For discussions on standards for corpus building, see Stoll (2015). For good descriptions of field studies of acquisition, see Ochs (1988) on Samoan, Brown (1998, 2001) on Tzeltal, Demuth (1992) on Sesotho, and Allen (1998, 2013) on Inuktitut. For a good overview of experimental methods used in acquisition research, see Ambridge & Rowland (2013), O'Shannessy (2013) and Blom & Unsworth (2010).

## NOTES

1  For an overview of this field see Ambridge and Lieven (2011).
2  http://childes.talkbank.org/browser Accessed 31 August 2017.

3  www.acqdiv.uzh.ch/en.html Accessed 31 August 2017.
4  www.clrp.uzh.ch Accessed 31 August 2017.
5  Flash is freeware for using content created on the Adobe Flash platform, including viewing multimedia and streaming video and audio.

## REFERENCES

Allen, S. (1998). Categories within the verb category: Learning the causative in Inuktitut. *Linguistics*, 36, 633–677.

Allen, S. (2013). The acquisition of ergativity in Inuktitut. In E. Bavin & S. Stoll (Eds.), *The acquisition of ergativity* (pp. 71–105). Amsterdam: John Benjamins.

Allen, S., & Crago, M. (1996). Early passive acquisition in Inuktitut. *Journal of Child Language*, 23(1), 129–155.

Ambridge, B., & Lieven, E. (2011). *Child language acquisition: Contrasting theoretical approaches*. Cambridge: Cambridge University Press.

Ambridge, B., & Rowland, C. (2013). Experimental methods in studying child language acquisition. *Wiley Interdisciplinary Review of Cognitive Science*, 4(2), 149–168.

Bates, E., Dale, P., & Thal, D. (1996). Individual differences and their implications for theories of language development. In P. Fletcher & B. Macwhinney (Eds.), *Handbook of child language* (pp. 96–151). Oxford: Blackwell.

Berko, J. (1958). The child's learning of English morphology. *Word*, 150–177.

Berman, R., & Slobin, D. (1994). *Relating events in narrative: A crosslinguistic developmental study*. Hillsdale, NJ: Lawrence Erlbaum.

Blom, E., & Unsworth, S. (2010). *Experimental methods in language acquisition research*. Amsterdam: John Benjamins.

Brown, P. (1998). Children's first verbs in Tzeltal: Evidence for an early verb category. *Linguistics*, 36(4), 713–753.

Brown, P. (2001). Learning to talk about UP and DOWN in Tzeltal: Is there a language-specific bias for verb learning. In M. Bowerman & S. Levinson (Eds.), *Language acquisition and conceptual development* (pp. 512–543). Cambridge: Cambridge University Press.

Chafe, W. (Ed.). (1980). *The pear stories: Cognitive, cultural, and linguistic aspects of narrative production*. Norwood, NJ: Ablex.

Chomsky, N. (1981). Principles and parameters in syntactic theory. In N. Hornstein, & D. Lightfoot (Eds.), *Explanation in linguistics: The logical problem of language acquisition* (pp. 32–75) London: Longman.

Demuth, K. (1992). Acquisition of Sesotho. In D. Slobin (Ed.), *The cross-linguistic study of language acquisition* (Vol. 3, pp. 557–638). Hillsdale, NJ: Lawrence Erlbaum.

Eimas, P., Siqueland, E., Jusczyk, P., & Vigorito, J. (1971). Speech perception in infants. *Science*, 171, 303–306.

Eisenbeiss, S. (2006). Documenting child language. *Language Documentation and Description*, 3, 106–140.

Fenson, L., Dale, P., Reznick, S., Bates, E., Thal, D., Pethick, S. (1994). Variability in early communicative development. *Monographs of the Society for Research in Child Development*, 59, 1–185.

Fitch, T., Hauser, M., & Chomsky, N. (2005). The evolution of the language faculty: Clarifications and implications. *Cognition*, 97, 179–210.

Forshaw, W. (2016). *Little kids, big verbs: The acquisition of Murrinhpatha bipartite stem verbs*. PhD Thesis. University of Melbourne.

Galloway, A. (2008). Indigenous children and conductive hearing loss. In J. Simpson & G. Wigglesworth (Eds.), *Children's language and multilingualism: Indigenous language use at home and school* (pp. 216–234). New York, NY: Continuum.

Gentner, D. (1982). Why nouns are learned before verbs: Linguistics relativity versus natural partitioning. In K. Hirsh-Pasek & R. Golinkoff (Eds.), *Action meets word: How children learn verbs* (pp. 544–564). Oxford: Oxford University Press.

Ingram, D. (1989). *First language acquisition: Method, description and explanation.* Cambridge: Cambridge University Press.

Kelly, B., Forshaw, W., Nordlinger, R., & Wigglesworth, G. (2015). Linguistic diversity in first language acquisition research: Moving beyond the challenges. *First Language, 35*(4–5), 286–304.

Kelly, B., Kidd, E., Wigglesworth, G., Forshaw, W., Nordlinger, R., O'Shannessy, C. (2015). Special Issue: Indigenous children's language: Acquisition, preservation and evolution of language in minority contexts. *First Language, 35,* 279–285.

Lieven, E., & Stoll, S. (2013). Early communicative development in two cultures: A comparison of the communicative environments of children from two cultures. *Human Development, 56,* 178–206.

Meakins, F., & O'Shannessy, C. (2010). Ordering arguments about: Word order and discourse motivations in the development and use of the ergative marker in two Australian mixed languages. *Lingua, 120*(7), 1693–1713.

Nordlinger, R. (2015). Mapping morphological complexity in Murrinhpatha. Presented at the Linguistics Association of Great Britain conference, UCL, London.

Ochs, E. (1988). *Culture and language development: Language acquisition and language socialization in a Samoan village.* Cambridge: Cambridge University Press.

O'Shannessy, C. (2004). *The monster stories: Picture stimulii to elicit lexical subject NPs.* Nijmegen: Max Planck Institute for Psycholinguistics.

O'Shannessy, C. (2011). Competition between word order and case-marking in interpreting grammatical relations: A case study in multilingual acquisition. *Journal of Child Language, 38*(4), 763–792.

O'Shannessy, C. (2013). Methods in researching children's acquisition of sociolinguistic competence. In J. Holmes & K. Hazen (Eds.), *Research methods in sociolinguistics: A practical guide* (pp. 304–324). Chichester, England: John Wiley & Sons.

Pinker, S. (1984). *Language learnability and language development.* Cambridge, MA: Harvard University Press.

Pinker, S., & Ullman, M. (2002). The past and future of the past tense. *Trends in Cognitive Sciences, 6*(11), 456–463.

Rice, M. (2010). Mean length of utterance levels in 6-month intervals for children 3 to 9 years with and without language impairments. *Journal of Speech, Language and Hearing Research, 53*(2), 333–349.

Rowland, C. (2013). *Understanding child language acquisition.* Abingdon, England: Routledge.

Roy, D. (2009). New horizons in the study of child language acquisition. *Proceedings of Interspeech 2009,* Brighton (England).

Slobin, D. (1982). Universal and particular in acquisition. In E. Wanner & L. Gleitman (Eds.), *Language acquisition: The state of the art* (pp. 128–170). Cambridge: Cambridge University Press.

Slobin, D. (2004). The many ways to search for a frog: Linguistic typology and the expression of motion events. In S. Strömqvist & L. Verhoeven (Eds.), *Relating events in narrative* (Vol. 2, pp. 219–257). Hillsdale, NJ: Lawrence Erlbaum.

Stoll, S. (2015). Crosslinguistic approaches to language acquisition. In E. Bavin & L. Naigles (Eds.), *The Cambridge handbook of child language* (pp. 107–133). Cambridge: Cambridge University Press.

Stoll, S., & Bickel, B. (2013a). Capturing diversity in language acquisition research. In B. Bickel, L. A. Grenoble, D. Peterson, & A. Timberlake (Eds.), *Language typology and historical contingency: In honor of Johanna Nichols* (pp. 195–216). Amsterdam: John Benjamins.

Stoll, S., & Bickel, B. (2013b). The acquisition of ergative case in Chintang. In S. Stoll & E. Bavin (Eds.), *The acquisition of ergativity* (pp. 183–207). Amsterdam: John Benjamins.

Stoll, S., Bickel, B., Lieven, E., Banjade, G., Bhatta, T., Gaenszle, M., Paudyal, N., Pettigrew, J., Rai, I., Rai, M., Rai, N., (2012). Nouns and verbs in Chintang: Children's usage and surrounding adult speech. *Journal of Child Language*, 39(2), 284–321.

Stoll, S., & Gries, S. (2009). An association-strength approach to characterizing development in corpora. *Journal of Child Language*, 36, 1075–1090.

Stoll, S., Mazara, J., & Bickel, B. (2017). The acquisition of polysynthetic verb forms in Chintang. In M. Fortescue, M. Mithun, & N. Evans (Eds.), *The Oxford handbook of polysynthesis* (pp. 495–514). Oxford: Oxford University Press.

Tardif, T. (1996). Nouns are not always learned before verbs: Evidence from Mandarin speakers' early vocabularies. *Developmental Psychology*, 32(3), 492–504.

Tomasello, M. (2003). *Constructing a language: A usage-based theory of language acquisition*. Cambridge, MA: Harvard University Press.

Tomasello, M., & Stahl, D. (2004). Sampling children's spontaneous speech: How much is enough? *Journal of Child Language*, 31(1), 101–121.

Travis, C., & Torres Cacoullos, R. (2013). Making voices count: Corpus compilation in bilingual communities. *Australian Journal of Linguistics*, 33(2), 170–194.

Yang, C., Crain, S., Berwick, R., Chomsky, N., & Bolhuis, J. (2017). The growth of language: Universal grammar, experience, and principles of computation. *Neuroscience & Biobehavioral Reviews*. https://doi.org/10.1016/j.neubiorev.2016.12.023

# 10

# Contact languages

## 10.1 INTRODUCTION

Contact languages such as creole varieties can be studied like any other language. They have their own phonology, lexicon and grammatical rules so the field linguist can create a corpus of the language, compile a dictionary or write a grammar. But there are also specific questions that relate to contact languages which make them an interesting object of study in and of themselves. For example, is simplification or morphological reduction a feature of language contact; what is the respective role of universal constraints, typological (mis)matches and community norms on language mixing; and how does the degree of bilingualism in a community or individual affect contact outcomes? And of course language contact is not restricted to spoken language, but also occurs in other modalities such as sign language (see Chapter 8). This chapter discusses special considerations that field linguists should think about before embarking on documenting a contact language (§10.3) and methods particular to these linguistic varieties (§10.4).

### 10.1.1 What are contact languages?

Contact languages originate in individuals who speak more than one language. The lexicons and grammars of those languages start influencing each other in the mind of the bilingual – even partial bilinguals. For example, many of us know people who don't speak fluent German who use *über-* from German in their English: "She's such an über-mother!" As significant numbers of these new structures propagate through a speech community, so a contact language is born. The result is a language which is difficult to position on a traditional family tree due to its dual parentage. Classic types of contact languages are pidgin and creole languages (§10.2.1), stabilised code-switching (§10.2.2), mixed languages (§10.2.3) and language shift varieties (§10.2.4).

Contact languages are often difficult to document because, for a number of reasons, they are rarely held in high esteem by speech communities. In some cases, they are reminders of the waning use of a valued heritage language. In this sense, they often fall victim to the grief surrounding language loss. In other cases, they are spoken by repressed minorities such as indigenous peoples, and by association are held in low regard. Sometimes they are associated with younger generations (even where older people speak them) which adds to their low prestige. Of course older generations grumbling about the way young people speak is universal! The result is that contact languages are often not named, but have descriptive labels, such as 'young people's X' or 'our X', and sometimes these reflect their low status or lack of recognition as a distinct language, for example, 'rubbish talk', 'light X', 'lingo' or 'patois' (see §10.3.7 for a discussion of naming practices).

Some linguists have also perpetuated the view of community leaders or the regional majority by not considering contact languages worthy objects of linguistic research. This is despite the fact that they are often the dominant language of a speech community! Garrett's (2009) paper 'Contact languages as "endangered languages": What is there to lose?' argues that contact varieties have been largely invisible to documentary linguistics. Indeed discussions of them in field methods courses often involve techniques for avoiding confusing structures in semi-speaker or contact varieties for the 'real' grammar. Archives are also full of recordings with metadata about heritage languages under investigation, but with no record of contact languages, despite the fact that they are often the *lingua franca* of recording sessions.

### 10.1.2 Why document a contact language?

Documenting contact languages is often politically fraught and obviously the wishes of the community must be adhered to. Older members of the speech community may not want the language documented. Documenting a contact language may put it in the public domain and undermine the speech community's self-presentation as speaking a strong heritage language. In addition, the community may not want precious funding and resources directed to documenting a new language at the expense of a more endangered, heritage language. A compromise might be to document (aspects of) both the heritage and new varieties in parallel if the time and scope of your project allows. This approach has the dual benefit of recording crucial community heritage for posterity, as well as understanding the development of the new variety better.

Where communities are interested in documenting these varieties, it may be an empowering experience for younger members of a speech community to have their way of talking recognised as distinct and valid, and possessing the properties of established languages, such as grammatical rules. Working with speakers of contact languages can be a wonderful experience for the fieldworker. For the fieldworker who is a member of the speech community wanting to maintain or revitalise their heritage language, documenting newer varieties can mean beginning to understand which parts of the language are undergoing change most rapidly and where to target community language programs. Chances are, if you are an 'insider' linguist, you are young, and it is also a great opportunity working with your peers in creative ways which value the speech of your generation. If you are an 'outsider' linguist recently graduated, chances are you are also young, and documenting a contact language can mean working with people your own age, which can be a lot of fun!

Contact languages also have immense scientific value. Contemporary language change can help us understand how historical change occurs. For example, linguists can observe language change underway in processes such as grammaticalisation, borrowing and second language influence, and better understand how these processes may have shaped languages historically (where often these processes require reconstruction using historical linguistic methods, e.g. the comparative method). Understanding contemporary sociophonetic or grammatical variability may also help linguists map deeper historical changes which led to splits in family trees, i.e. linguistic diversification. Studying languages in contact can also teach us more about synchronic linguistic structures. For example what is permissible in borrowing or code-switching often relies on the respective typological match of the languages in contact. Unexpected switches or borrowings may lead to the reanalysis of a linguistic structure.

## 10.2 TYPES OF CONTACT LANGUAGES

It is important to gain a good understanding of what type of contact language is spoken in the community. Often the socio-historical circumstances of its genesis will give you a good clue, as will some features of the language – although categories of contact languages tend to be very typologically diverse.

### 10.2.1 Pidgin and creole languages

Pidgin and creole languages typically emerge in situations of mass migrant labour, particularly forced slavery, and trade. They are generally associated with the European colonisation of the African continent, the Indian subcontinent, South-East Asia, the Atlantic and the Pacific. They find their origins in population displacement and the emergence of new communities which occurred as these areas underwent European expansion. Generally the lexical source of pidgin and creole languages is a European language: English, French, Dutch, German; or Arabic. Phonologically and semantically, these languages often reflect the heritage languages, called 'substrate' languages. Structural influence is also found, although disagreements exist about the extent of influence wielded by the substrate languages.

> **Tip – Pidgin or creole – what's in a name?**
>
> Some communities speak a creole but call it "Pidgin", for example in the Solomon Islands. If you want to find out if the language is a creole or a pidgin, try to find out if the language has child speakers or if it is just used for limited purposes such as trade. Some communities also call their creole "Creole", but may spell this differently e.g. Kriyol (Guinea-Bissau), Kwéyól (Sant Lucia) and Kriol (northern Australia).

Pidgins are not used as the native language of a speech community, but function as a *lingua franca* between a number of groups, which otherwise do not have a shared language. Typologically, they are characterised by a highly reduced vocabulary and structure, which reflects their limited communicative use. On the other hand, creoles have a large base of first language speakers. As a result, they are more complex grammatically and more fully expressive. See Winford (2003) for a good overview of these languages and read Diana Guillemin's reflections on returning to Mauritius after many decades to document her first language, a creole (see also Guillemin, 2011).

### Documenting Mauritian Creole – Diana Guillemin

Forty years after leaving Mauritius, I returned as a linguist to collect data on the *lingua franca*. Though spoken and understood by most, Mauritian Creole remains a low prestige language, despised by the educated Mauritians, who also speak French. An acrolect had emerged in the last few decades with francophones emulating a French accent and turns of phrase when speaking creole. I needed informants who had spoken only creole all their lives, and whose speech had not been tainted by French, the dominant language of the media. My relatives fail to understand my need to venture in a remote community to hear creole speakers articulate their vulgar jargon, and I am made to feel like a traitor of my French heritage.

My informants are two women, direct descendants of African slaves, also known as 'creoles'. Margo is around 40 and Marie is 80 years old and both had lived in the same fishing village since birth. Creoles have been marginalised and made to feel worthless by the likes of whites and coloureds like me and they have every reason to distrust me. Furthermore, my digital audio recorder and paperwork give me an air of unwelcome authority. My first hurdle thus is to reassure them that I have no ulterior motives and that my interest is purely linguistic. They find this surprising given that they have been made to believe that theirs is not even a real language.

I soon realise that the ethical clearance forms are useless as they are both illiterate. I resort to verbal consent, which I record and play back to them. Since I am a native speaker, I decide that spontaneous conversation would be more relaxing, and also more productive than eliciting discourse by showing them a set of picture prompts that I have also brought along. I start by recounting my own youth in Mauritius, expressing my nostalgia at the changes that I have noticed since returning, especially the large number of hotels built on the coast. This is a topic close to their hearts and, seeing that I share their concerns, they soon start to speak freely about their resentment at the loss of their beach now reserved for tourists.

Marie is happy that someone is interested in her past. Though it stirs up painful memories it seems that she has accepted these hardships as her lot. We occasionally stop to play back her stories and she giggles at the sound of her own voice recalling how hard it was to work in the sugarcane fields without protection in the midday sun, how the cane leaves cut their skin. She also remembers some happy times, such as walking barefoot to the mountains to dance *segas* around a bonfire every Saturday night and returning back home at sunrise.[1] They were self-sufficient then, growing their own vegetables, and at dusk the men would throw a fishing line into the sea to catch their dinner, now no longer possible since they have been denied access to the beach.

I am exhilarated at the wealth of data that I am collecting. I note the lack of copulas, the frequent use of resumptive pronouns, the specificity marker and of course the prosody of this language so different from French. I am fortunate to speak their language but this makes me sensitive to their anger and frustration. It is difficult to not become emotionally involved and to not feel guilty for my privileged position. I hope nonetheless that we have all been enriched by the experience and that they will value the records of their stories for their children and grandchildren.

### 10.2.2 Normative code-switching

Code-switching is a language contact process as well as an outcome. For example it has developed into a community-level practice in many Spanish-English communities in the United States (Torres Cacoullos & Travis, 2016) or the French-Dutch community of Brussels in Belgium (Treffers-Daller, 1994). Code-switching usually involves either inserting vocabulary (and sometimes different parts of grammar) from one language into another language; or changing languages between sentences or parts of sentences, for example prepositional phrases or subordinate clauses. Code-switching can remain quite variable, shaped by discourse cues, for example a change in topic or the use of direct speech. It can also be shaped by grammatical constraints, for example no switching of inflectional morphology (case, TAM affixes, agreement marking etc.) in other communities. Code-switching can also stabilise in different ways. Vocabulary from one language often becomes a permanent part of another language, called 'loanwords'. Code-switching can also lose its pragmatic function over time with the shape of the mixing increasingly determined by grammatical constraints. At the extreme end of this cline are mixed languages. See Poplack (2015) for a good overview.

#### Romani-Turkish code-switching

The Romani community of Thrace in Greece is a trilingual community which speaks Romani (Indo-Aryan), Turkish (Turkic) and Greek (Hellenic). The Roma had arrived in the Byzantine Empire by 1200, now Turkey and Greece (Matras, 2002). At present, approximately 200,000 Roma live in Greece (Bakker, 2001). Thrace Romani is under threat by Turkish and Greek to different degrees in different places. Although it is still learnt by children in some areas, language shift can be seen in the parent generation. All children have access to bilingual education in Greek-Turkish in primary school, although secondary education is strictly in Greek, also the language of administration and services. In practice children tend to attend Greek schools and many of them do not complete their schooling.

A Thrace Romani-Turkish-Greek corpus consisting of 5,816 words was collected between 2007 and 2010 with 21 Roma speakers in the Drosero neighbourhood at the outskirts of the city of Xanthi. This community has approximately 4,000 people of low socio-economic status. The corpus consists of Romani with 15 per cent Turkish words and 4 per cent Greek words mixed within Romani sentences. In the sentence below, *afu* is from Greek, and the verb and its inflections are Turkish, but the rest of the sentence is Romani. It is the use of the inflected Turkish verb, unusual in cases of language contact, which prompted the collection and the corpus.

(1) Latʃo afu gadal dyʃym-ijor-sənəs te dʒavtar mange
    good since this_way think-PROG-2PL COMP go.1SG.DIR me.DAT
    Fine, since this is what you think, I'll leave.

(Adamou & Granqvist, 2015, p. 526)

The corpus was collected through storytelling interviews with the field linguist Evangelia Adamou, and in-group conversations between the Roma participants. This productive data was further investigated experimentally using reaction-time tasks to determine whether mixed Romani-Turkish sentences have higher processing costs than unilingual L2-Turkish sentences (Adamou & Shen, 2018).

### 10.2.3 Mixed languages

Mixed languages are the result of the fusion of two languages and develop from community bilingualism. This is one way they differ from pidgin and creole languages – in the case of pidgin and creole languages, there is usually an uneven access to the colonial language. Mixed languages also differ from pidgin and creole languages in that their genesis is a product of expressive rather than communicative needs. That is, pidgin and creole languages are born out of the need for communication between people of a number of language groups, whereas mixed languages are created in situations where a common language already exists and communication is not at issue. Thus the mixed language serves as an expression of an altered identity, be it new, or differing significantly from an older identity. Mixed languages usually develop from code-switching, but show more stability i.e. predictability in the sites of switches and newly developed structures not reflected in either source language. See Meakins (2018) for criteria for distinguishing mixed languages from other contact varieties.

> **A mixed language – Gurindji Kriol**
>
> Gurindji Kriol is a mixed language spoken in the Gurindji communities of Kalkaringi and Daguragu in northern Australia. It formed through multiple processes of code-switching, language shift and creolisation. These changes can be seen across generations. Older generations continue to speak traditional Gurindji (Pama-Nyungan), but code-switch into Kriol (English-lexified creole), which originally derived from a pidgin English variety. People under the age of 40 years speak Gurindji Kriol, a mixed language, which is now the first language of younger people.
>
> The linguistic practices of the Gurindji are closely tied to their social circumstances. Before colonisation the Gurindji were multilingual, speaking the languages of neighbouring groups with whom they had familial and ceremonial connections. The establishment of cattle stations by colonisers saw the introduction of the cattle station pidgin (which later developed into Kriol) into the linguistic repertoire of the Gurindji. In the 1970s, code-switching between Kriol and Gurindji was the dominant language practice of Gurindji people. It is likely that this code-switching provided fertile ground for the formation of the mixed language.
>
> Gurindji Kriol derives its lexicon relatively evenly from both languages. Structurally, Kriol contributes much of the verbal grammar including TAM auxiliaries, and Gurindji supplies most of the nominal structure including case and derivational morphology. In the sentence below, Gurindji elements are in italics.
>
> (2) Samantha   *yawu-ngku* i   bin   *turrp*   im    *wartan*
>     NAME       fish-NOM  it   PST   jab       her   hand
>     A (cat)fish jabbed Samantha in the hand.
>
> The documentation of Gurindji Kriol has occurred in tandem with the documentation of Gurindji. Over a number of projects an 165-hour (405,027 words) annotated sound-linked corpus of Gurindji Kriol now exists which represents language from 157 speakers (Meakins, 2013). The corpus is transcribed in CLAN (§4.3.2) and much of it is housed in ELAR and PARADISEC (§4.4).[2]

## 10.2.4 Language shift varieties

Language shift varieties form in situations where speech communities are undergoing a shift from a local language, often to a more regionally dominant language. Sometimes the new speech variety stalls half-way through the shift process and stabilises, even just within a generation, as has happened with English in the Middle Ages and many German diaspora varieties in the United States more recently. In other cases, a shift to the regionally dominant language goes to completion and the heritage language is no longer used. This obsolescence process often occurs across different domains of discourse at different rates. For example, often ritual contexts are the last domain where an endangered language is still spoken. The use of Latin in churches in Germany before Martin Luther wrote the *Deutsche Messe* is one example.

---

**Exercise 1  Diasporas in cities**

Where do you hear heritage languages spoken in cities? Restaurants? Train stations in particular suburbs? Do people of all ages speak the language? If an old person speaks to a young person, in what language do they reply? How would you approach this community to do a project? Is the city a 'field site' in this case (go back to our definition of what constitutes fieldwork – §1.2.3).

---

Language shift can be mapped across a generational cline. While older speakers often speak a conservative variety of the language, innovations are present in the speech of younger members of the community. Differences between the speech of generations are often described as mistakes or errors, and linguists generally reflect this sentiment labelling younger speakers as partial or semi-speakers. Some languages which have been examined in detail are East Sutherland Gaelic spoken in Scotland (Dorian, 1978), Pennsylvania and Texas German spoken in the US (Boas, 2009), Oberwart Hungarian spoken in Austria (Gal, 1979) and Dyirbal spoken in north Queensland (Australia) (Schmidt, 1985).

Innovations in language shift varieties are often characterised by allomorphic reduction, the simplification of grammatical systems, syncretism in inflectional paradigms (case, gender, verb conjugations etc.) and synthetic systems becoming analytic (e.g. case being replaced by prepositions). These innovations can be the result of internal changes which may be accelerated in obsolescence situations or language contact with a socially dominant language. More recently, this approach to characterising language shift has been challenged with a variety of complexification processes identified as being responsible for the development of these varieties.

## 10.3 SPECIAL CONSIDERATIONS

The usual fieldwork protocols around the roles and responsibilities of fieldworkers within a speech community and workflow considerations such as equipment and software choice, and archiving also apply to contact languages. You can read about these issues in Chapters 2–4. But there are also specific considerations for documenting contact languages in the field which we discuss here.

### 10.3.1 How much to document?

Apart from the lack of prestige of contact languages in the linguistics community, writing an entire grammatical description of a contact language, particularly a newly developed one, can be a tall order! A developing grammar contains a lot of variation as it begins to stabilise, and it may only stabilise within a generation, particularly in cases of language shift (see §10.3.3). Instead, it may make more sense to focus on individual linguistic structures. For example, there is no (published) grammar of Gurindji Kriol, but there are many papers on aspects of the grammar, such as case-marking, serial verb constructions, spatial relations and phonological contrasts. All of these papers make reference to equivalent structures in the source languages, Gurindji and Kriol, to gain a deeper understanding of how they developed. In many cases, this has meant also undertaking primary documentation of these structures in Gurindji and Kriol themselves.

### 10.3.2 Existing documentation of source languages

Contact languages can be documented in isolation from their source languages, where the contact language is treated as a system where all of the parts are considered "synchronically interdependent" (cf. Saussure, 1916, p. 86). After all, linguists use this methodology all the time with more established languages such as English – you can write a grammar of English as a standalone entity – you don't need to write about the large French component of English with reference to Norman French! Nonetheless the existence of descriptions of the source languages of new varieties does help you get a deeper understanding of the structure of the new language. In some cases, grammars or thorough descriptions of the source languages may exist, but in many other cases they may not. Even where descriptive materials are available, they might not have enough detail about particular phenomena. It may be necessary to also use particular elicitation materials (see §10.4) on the source languages to elicit equivalent structures. In the case of Thrace Romani, good descriptive grammars of Romani and Turkish already existed which gave Adamou a head start in understanding the contact situation. Gurindji and Kriol both lack descriptive grammars, although reasonable grammatical notes on both languages existed. These notes didn't have detailed discussions of some structures of interest, including case-marking (for Gurindji) or preposition and word order (for Kriol), so further investigation of these structures in the source languages was required before the contact situation could be understood.

### 10.3.3 Linguistic variation

Many contact languages are recent developments and, by nature, new languages contain high levels of variation as the linguistic systems take shape. Variation can create an extra layer of complication for the field linguist because speakers may have multiple ways of expressing the same concept. Even well-established languages show variation, as sociolinguists such as William Labov (1994b, 1994a) have pointed out extensively! For example, the comparative in English can be expressed using the suffix *-er* or the adverb *more*, but also by double marking e.g. *more happier*. The choice depends on a combination of phonology (the number of syllables in the stem) and social status (double-marking is associated with lower socio-economic classes and younger people). To truly capture the language, variation and what drives the variation (social, discourse-level or grammatical factors) need to be documented.

---

**Exercise 2  Dealing with variation**

How do you know whether you are dealing with one construction which shows variation or two different constructions? If you have a variable construction, but you want to overview the language without getting bogged down in detail or you don't have statistics training, how would you write up the variation you find?

---

Variation in contact languages, particularly in language shift scenarios, has been treated differently from languages with strong speaker bases such as English. Languages undergoing obsolescence are often characterised as displaying high levels of variation and optionality in comparison with conservative varieties of the language. These characteristics are assumed to be symptomatic of a lack of systematicity on the part of speakers. Elsewhere in linguistic theory, variation does not represent grammatical fragmentation; instead, it is a crucial component of language evolution (Croft, 2000; Labov, 1994a; Mufwene, 2001).

A more nuanced view of variation in situations of contact and shift involves recasting it as a part of a principled reorganisation of grammar. Indeed this view was expressed by Dorian in the introduction of her 1989 edited volume, but has had little uptake.

> The earlier view that a contracting [obsolescencing] language was unworthy of study because 'corrupt', 'broken down', 'deviant' (all from the point of view of former norms or from that of standard-language norms) has now almost been stood on its head. The very deviance which was off-putting at one time is what we look to now for clues to organisational principles in language and cognition generally. The 'errors' of imperfect speakers may also be indications of an active and innovative language processing capacity.
>
> (Dorian, 1989, pp. 2–3)

In the end, if language shift is not treated differently from other types of language change (not driven by loss), then similar patterns and processes of change should be expected. For further discussions of documenting variation in the field, see Meyerhoff et al. (2012).

### 10.3.4 Language pride

Language ability may be the source of some pride in communities and the inability to speak a heritage language may demarcate different groups or generations within a community. Communities may be embarrassed about language loss or the changing nature of their heritage language and may not want you to describe it. The act of documentation puts the contact language in the public domain and can undermine the self-presentation of the community. For example, Gurindji Kriol has a low social prestige status in Kalkaringi compared with Gurindji. Older people generally describe it in terms of the loss of Gurindji, rather than the creation of a new language, or the maintenance of Gurindji in a mixed form. Older people complain that the younger generations do not speak Gurindji correctly, rather than thinking of Gurindji Kriol as a separate language. For example Biddy Wavehill is critical of the use of Gurindji Kriol allative suffix *-ngkirri* rather than the 'correct' Gurindji allomorph *-ngkurra* or *-kurra*.

> *Ngurnayinangkulu kurru karrinyana karu yu nou kula-lu marnana jutup. Ngulu marnani 'Nyawa-**ngkirri**'. Nyawa**ngkirri**-ma, nyampayila ngulu marnana 'Murlangkurra'. 'Kawayi murlangkurra,' kuya yu nou. An 'Pinka-**kirri**,' jei tok rong jarran. 'Pinka-**kurra**,' kuya. 'Pinka-**kurra** kanyjurra'. 'Nyawa**ngkirri**,' dat not rait word jaru. Ngurnayinangkulu kurru karrinyana kuya laik ngurnayinangkulu jutuk kuya-rnangku jarrakap brobli-wei.*

> We listen to the kids, you know, and they don't talk properly. For example, they are always saying 'nyawa**ngkirri**' for 'that way'. They always say 'nyawa**ngkirri**' not 'murla**ngkurra**' which is wrong. You should say 'murla**ngkurra**'. And they also say 'pinka-**kirri**' for 'to the river' which is wrong. They should say 'pinka-**kurra**'. 'Nyawa**ngkirri**' is not proper Gurindji. We listen to the kids and they don't talk as well as I am talking to you.
> 
> (Meakins, 2010, p. 230)

Younger people, who are the main speakers of Gurindji Kriol, were initially reticent to discuss their speech style, aware that they did not speak Gurindji in a traditional manner. Even so Gurindji Kriol has a lot of covert prestige among its speakers and they did want it documented. The solution was to split the documentation of Gurindji and Gurindji Kriol between the two Gurindji communities. The documentation of Gurindji was focused at Kalkaringi because the majority of speakers lived here, and Gurindji Kriol work occurred 8 kilometres away at Daguragu, which has a younger age profile. It meant that the young people at Daguragu were able to work on their language without facing criticism from their community leaders.

### 10.3.5 Gender of researchers

Depending on your gender, it may be inappropriate for you to work with either men or women. These problems are common to newly developed contact languages where they are spoken only by younger generations. It is not generally unusual for fe/male linguists to work with people of the opposite gender in documentation projects, particularly endangerment situations where speakers are much older and respected for their language abilities. Working with younger people of the opposite gender whose language skills are not considered noteworthy by the community because the new variety has little status in the community can be both socially inappropriate and linguistically inexplicable from a community perspective. Related problems occur in language acquisition for male researchers (see §9.3.5).

---

**Exercise 3 Dealing with gender sensitivities in the field**

If you think that gender is relevant for variation you are noticing in a contact language and think you need to make recordings with members of the opposite gender, but sense this would be met with raised eyebrows by the community, how would you go about this?

---

This was an issue for both the Greek Thrace project and Gurindji Kriol project. In the Greek Thrace project, Adamou mainly worked with female speakers and was under constant supervision when working with male speakers of her own age. In the case of Gurindji Kriol, no adult male speakers are represented in the data, only boys under the age of 14, a result of the fact that it was culturally inappropriate for Meakins, a (then) young woman, to work alone with young men. Working with young men would have been disapproved of because it is unusual for a woman to spend much time alone in a group of men.

## 10.3.6 Speaking a contact language as an 'outsider' linguist

Learning to speak a contact language as an 'outsider' linguist is less straightforward than learning other languages. On the one hand, they are often the main language in a community, which gives you more language learning opportunities. On the other hand, learning them may be actively discouraged by older members of the community for reasons of prestige, and may be discouraged by younger members of the community because they are in-group languages. This is the case with Gurindji Kriol. The Gurindji community will encourage outsider language enthusiasts to learn Gurindji, rather than Gurindji Kriol, despite the fact that Gurindji Kriol is more widespread in the community. Attempts by outsiders to use Gurindji Kriol are often interpreted as acts of mockery or condescension. As with all in-group languages, Gurindji Kriol comes with quite subtle rules about who can speak it and who cannot, in particular the appropriateness of the use of Gurindji Kriol by non-Aboriginal people. Similar observations were made by Mari Rhydwen in a reflective piece about fieldwork in Barunga, a largely Kriol-speaking Aboriginal community in northern Australia.

> I spent my first few months of fieldwork, several years ago, learning to speak Kriol. However, I learned fairly quickly that it was unacceptable for me to assume that I could address someone in Kriol simply on the basis of knowing that he or she was a Kriol speaker.
>
> (Rhydwen, 1995, pp. 114–115)

Rhydwen (1995, p. 117) goes on to suggest that the status of Kriol is similar to the status of other ethnolects of English, such as Black American English, which are in-group languages that express minority identities.

### 10.3.7 Naming a contact language

Salikoko Mufwene (2000, p. 67) is critical of the naming practices around contact languages, suggesting that some linguists believe that they have a "self-license" to go around "baptising" these languages. Indeed it should be recognised that 'outsider' linguists naming contact languages can be a hegemonic practice which perpetuates colonial power. Nonetheless, having a name for a contact language in a speech community is useful for documentation activities, and often the community's own labels for the language, called an 'endonym', reflects the low esteem in which the language is held and is not an appropriate label for the public domain. (Note that naming languages has political and social consequences in all languages).

Gurindji Kriol had no name until recently. The community usually calls it 'Gurindji'. If a distinction between Gurindji and Gurindji Kriol is required, Gurindji is often referred to as 'hard Gurindji', 'rough Gurindji' or 'proper Gurindji', and Gurindji Kriol as 'Gurindji'. The term 'Gurindji' is a relative term used to signify the main language used by Gurindji people rather than a particular language form. Older, more prescriptive members of the Gurindji community refer to Gurindji Kriol as 'Mix'em up' (in reference to its mixed nature) or 'Rubbish Talk', which reveals their estimation of the language. Nonetheless the young Gurindji people who created the term 'Gurindji Kriol' have found it useful within official settings, for example professional development programs for teachers (Meakins, 2012).

## 10.4 METHODS FOR DOCUMENTING CONTACT LANGUAGES

The elicitation methods standard to grammar writing projects (§6.5) are problematic for characterising contact languages for a number of reasons discussed in §10.4.1. Instead the well-worn path of corpus development (§10.4.2) followed by targeted (semi-)experimental elicitation and comprehension tasks (§10.4.5) is beginning to become standard in field-based language contact projects. This path was taken by both the Greek Thrace and Gurindji Kriol projects. It was pioneered by language acquisition (see §9.4.2) and has become common in other areas such as semantic typology.

### 10.4.1 Problems with formal elicitation methods

As with all language documentation, recordings of contact languages should attempt to capture language used in a range of registers (narrative, conversation, song) in a broad range of contexts (at home, fishing, talking to children, in ceremony) (§1.2.4). Nonetheless, often more formal elicitation is required to fully investigate particular structures which may be rare in conversation, and which may involve high levels of variation.

Traditionally, linguistic elicitation involves a dyadic relationship between a linguist and speaker where a linguist questions a speaker on aspects of their language (§6.1). This style of elicitation is generally unsuccessful in the case of contact languages. Often a speaker will target one of the source languages, or a more prestigious variety. Another pitfall is the language of elicitation. If you are interested in the effects of French on Cree in Quebec, using French as the language of elicitation may induce the speaker to accommodate to the linguist, causing problems in teasing out accommodation effects from actual entrenched contact effects. These issues are also relevant when considering how to conduct elicitation in other modalities (see Chapter 8).

---

**Exercise 4 Questionnaire data**

Questionnaires used to be a common way of eliciting variation and contact features. Think of some problems with this method (i.e. what the language of the questionnaire might be and whether it might have some contact patterns).

---

Another problem with the more traditional language description techniques, such as those described in Chapter 6, is that they require languages to be clearly delineated. For a linguist eliciting Gurindji, this is relatively unproblematic. In the case of Gurindji Kriol, the level of variation which is present in the mixed language and the fact that much of this variation is based on Gurindji and Kriol alternates is problematic. Part of a description of Gurindji Kriol involves mapping emergent patterns, and the factors which contribute to these patterns. This type of documentation requires large amounts of data from large numbers of speakers of varying ages within varying communication contexts. A simple linguist-speaker dyad would not begin to capture the dynamism of Gurindji Kriol.

### 10.4.2 Corpus development

Shana Poplack has set benchmarks for the development of language contact corpora since the early 1980s. Poplack (2015, p. 921) maintains that the "gold standard remains the (standard sociolinguistic-style) ... corpus". This corpus is developed through a number of principles including:

- recordings of actual spontaneous productions
    - Don't use individual overheard utterances. They have similar problems to the diary studies of language acquisition in potential inaccurate recall on the part of the linguist (§9.4.1). They also may represent a low frequency construction in the corpus and may receive a disproportionate amount of attention.
    - Don't use questionnaire-style translation equivalents (see §10.4.1 for problems).

- systematically and randomly sampled speakers
    - Don't use social network approaches which involve asking friends-of-friends to participate in a study. This approach may not be representative of a speech community where not everyone knows each other.
- recordings made by locally trained research assistants who are members of the 'in-group' in the speech community
    - As opposed to a linguist who may be fluent in the language(s) but also may induce unwanted accommodation effects (as an L2 learner, an L1 speaker of a different dialect or sociolect, a speaker of the regionally dominant language etc.).

The aim of producing corpora using these principles is to avoid the 'cherry picking' approach which dominates much of the theoretical literature on language contact. For example, various theories make generalisations about restrictions on transferring inflectional morphology from one language to another (Gardani, 2008; Matras & Sakel, 2007; Moravcsik, 1978; Myers-Scotton, 2002; Thomason & Kaufman, 1988). These statements are usually probabilistic rather than categorical (i.e. "it is rare to find X"). These statements are also relative to other transferred elements both within a corpus (i.e. "inflectional morphology is less likely to transfer than nouns") and across corpora (i.e. "inflectional morphology is less likely to transfer than nouns across X corpora"). Yet single examples of transferred inflectional morphology, i.e. 'cherry-picked', utterances are still offered as counter-examples to these probabilistic generalisations and are usually accompanied by claims that the 'rule' has been disproved. But probabilistic statements are not rules (or categorical statements) and in fact predict counter-examples exactly because they are not rules! Poplack (2015) provides an extensive discussion of this problem.

Poplack and her team have created a number of Canadian French and English corpora of varying sizes based on these principles. The largest is the Ottawa-Hull Corpus which consists of 3.5 million words of informal speech data collected from a representative sample of 120 native speakers of Ottawa-Hull French, stratified according to age, sex and minority/majority status of French in their neighbourhood in the National Capital Region.[3] This corpus is enormous and beyond the capabilities of a single linguist in a small language community.

Fieldworkers should not despair though! Depending on the research questions, smaller corpora can yield robust results. For example, the Thrace Romani-Turkish-Greek corpus consists of 5,816 words from 21 speakers, which is small, but sufficient to discuss the use of the Turkish verb in a Romani sentence, a combination that is unusual cross-linguistically. The Gurindji Kriol corpus is larger because the initial research question about optional nominative case-marking required recording a sufficient number of grammatically non-obligatory nouns. Just 6,550 tokens of full nominal subjects were extracted from an 80-hour (57,179-clause) subcorpus of 103 speakers (Meakins & Wilmoth, 2018)! This section offers suggestions for corpus development in the field that follow Poplack's principles, but also shows where compromises can be made.

### 10.4.3 Peer elicitation

The method developed during the Gurindji Kriol project is called 'peer elicitation'. It supplements Poplack's gold standard of naturally occurring speech with semi-formal elicitation to ensure sufficient data for quantitative analyses. Without a team of local research assistants to record, transcribe and annotate data, a corpus of spontaneous speech large enough to undertake quantitative analysis is virtually impossible. Peer elicitation also makes compromises on randomised speaker selection which is not possible in small communities where everyone knows each other.

Peer elicitation also advocates the use of local research assistants (see also §2.4). If you are an 'insider' linguist, this might not be necessary because the language is your unmarked instrument of communication with your friends and family. But if you are an 'outsider' linguist, it is imperative to use local research assistants. Even if you speak the language, you will have an 'accent', at the very least, which marks you out as an outsider and speakers will adjust their language accordingly. The answer to this problem is for the 'outsider' linguist to remove themself as an interlocutor. In peer elicitation, the local research assistant trains the participants in the tasks and therefore 'sets' the language of the task. Participants are then only talking to each other and the research assistant and not the linguist.

Peer elicitation involves semi-experimental tasks, which can be created as a series of games, designed to lead speakers to address the target utterance to a member of their peer group. Where possible, tasks should be based on games that are a part of everyday life for the participants, or are perhaps played at school. This ensures that participants are familiar with the paradigm. Elicitation tasks should also be picture-based or use real-life objects rather than written tasks because most contact languages are either unwritten or use the orthography of regionally dominant languages which may influence the speech of participants. Note that games are not always appropriate. Adamou found that they did not work well for older males in the Romani communities because they found them childish.

> **Exercise 5  Making appropriate tasks or games**
>
> How do you go about designing and implementing tasks for older members of a speech community who have few literacy or computer skills?

Peer elicitation tasks also have the advantage of allowing the language team to design tasks which target particular linguistic structures and can be performed with a large number of people to account for variation. To go back to the example of optional nominative case-marking in Gurindji Kriol. Nominative marking attaches to nouns which are optional. Conversation and narrative data alone did not provide sufficient numbers of nouns to map the parameters of variation of nominative marking within Gurindji Kriol, and to conduct statistical tests of significance. Therefore peer elicitation tasks were used to supplement the data set.

### 10.4.4 (Semi-)experimental methods

This section provides some suggestions for peer elicitation tasks developed for research questions about Gurindji Kriol phonology and morpho-syntax. Many of the tasks are inspired by field manuals developed by the Language and Cognition group at the Max Planck Institute for Psycholinguistics in Nijmegen (the Netherlands) (see also §7.3).[4] Note that the tasks described below are not designed as experiments. For example, the order of presentation of elicitation materials was not randomised or counter-balanced, and some speakers had seen the materials before from observing previous recording sessions.

#### 10.4.4.1 Director-matcher tasks

A number of director-matcher tasks were created that targeted a variety of constructions in Gurindji Kriol, leading the speaker to use a particular construction or sentence constituent. The 'director' and 'matcher' should be peers i.e. similar social status (gender, age, socio-economic status, clan group etc.). See §7.3 for a discussion of the director-matcher paradigm and Figure 10.1 for an example of a picture board used in the Gurindji Kriol study. In this example, you can see Regina Crowson Nangari holding a piece of board to ensure the Quitayah Frith Namija (matcher) can't see Jamieisha Barry Nangala's (director) pictures. This ensures that Jamiesha describes each picture in detail and can't use demonstratives or pointing. Cassandra Algy Nimarra records the tasks using both a video camera and a separate audio recorder in case one device fails to record. Jamieisha wears two lapel

Figure 10.1
Cassandra Algy Nimarra and Felicity Meakins record director-matcher tasks with Jamieisha Barry Nangala, Regina Crowson Nangari and Quitayah Frith Namija (Photo: Jennifer Green 2017)

microphones linked to the two devices. A wireless lapel mic links to the camera to ensure good recording levels from shy participants. Felicity notes down the number of each picture in turn. This annotation is included in the transcript which is done using CLAN.

> **Exercise 6  Making games that elicit clusivity variability**
>
> The community you work in marks clusivity variably in their pronouns (§6.7.4). How would you design a director-matcher task to discover the patterns in the variation?

### 10.4.4.2 Card games

Different types of card games were designed with the Gurindji participants in mind. One card game was played with three or four people as a game of 'Go Fish!'. In one version, a set of cards was used to elicit possessive constructions and specifically dative allomorphy (which showed some variation). Each of the cards consisted of a picture of half of an animal, either a head or a tail, chosen specifically for the phonology of the noun stem. One participant asked the player beside her "Have you got the X's tail/head?" If the player had the right card, she passed it on. If not, she said 'Go Fish!' and the speaker got a new card from a pile of spare cards. The aim of the game for the participants was to get as many pairs of heads and tails as possible.

Bingo is another card game familiar to the Gurindji community. This paradigm was used to elicit ergative suffixes. It was designed to elicit full agent nominals, again often lacking in conversation. The bingo cards consist of a series of pictures where the agents differ only in terms of gender. Speakers were therefore required to say the agent in order to differentiate the pictures. This game operated according to the usual rules of bingo. A speaker was given the pile of shuffled cards. Three to four other participants had one of five bingo sheets in front of them. The bingo sheets contained 12 randomly selected pictures from a possible 32. Participants crossed the pictures out as they heard them said. The first person to cross off all pictures called out "Bingo!" Participants took it in turns to be the 'caller'.

### 10.4.4.3 Picture-prompt books

For more extended texts, picture-prompt books are a useful elicitation tool. They address a number of anxieties speakers may have using their vernacular. For example, in the Australian Indigenous context, it is inappropriate for younger members of a land-holding group to publicly tell stories associated with a place while a more senior member of that group is still alive. Second, being asked to tell spontaneous narratives, for example Labov's 'Danger-of-Death' stories, may create more anxiety for a speaker of a vernacular language who is not normally a spontaneous narrator.

Finally, like director-matcher tasks and card games, picture-prompt books produce comparative data necessary in situations where variation is common.

The most successful books contain only pictures (no words!) to avoid stilted translations, literacy concerns or indeed spontaneous language contact influence from a regionally dominant language. Participants who have been to school are often more comfortable with these books than small children or older speakers who tended to skip backwards and forwards between pages and generally did not associate pictures in a clear linear fashion. Like other peer elicitation activities, picture-prompt books work well with an audience of peers.

A number of picture-prompt books were used to elicit Gurindji Kriol narratives. These books included the Monster book series created by Carmel O'Shannessy (2004) for her work on Light Warlpiri (§9.4.2). Other books are also useful for studying specific structures. *Frog, where are you?* (Mayer, 1994) has been used in numerous studies of information structure and spatial relations such as motion constructions. Using Frog stories provides not only a comparative dataset within the Gurindji Kriol speaking community, but also can be applied more broadly. Despite not being a Gurindji-focused story, adults and children alike enjoyed using the Frog stories immensely. A variation on picture-prompt books is the use of short word-less videos such as Wallace Chafe's *Pear Story* video.[5]

### 10.4.5 Experimental methods

Experimental methods are also useful for probing data from the corpus further. Different types of paradigms such as reaction-time, eye-tracking and picture-match tasks are common in psycholinguistics and will not be overviewed here. Some of these tasks have been used for contact languages, for example Lipski (2016) performed acceptability judgement and language-identification tasks and concurrent memory-loaded repetition with speakers of Media Lengua (Ecuador)), which is a mixed language (§10.2.3). Some adjustments might need to be made for the field, such as using auditory stimuli instead of written stimuli in places where vernacular literacy is not common. For example, Adamou & Shen (2018) used a reaction-time task to determine whether mixed Romani-Turkish sentences have higher processing costs than unilingual L2-Turkish sentences. The experimental methods needed to use auditory stimuli to adapt to a population with no formal education in Romani and Turkish (the participants in this study only had access to the Greek schools, mainly primary). Other difficulties are particular to language contact situations, in particular getting enough participants and assessing bilingual proficiency.

#### 10.4.5.1 Getting enough participants

How many speakers is enough? There is no single answer to this question. This depends on your research question and your methods. If you are a typologist interested in characterising what parts of a language can be borrowed or what sorts of substrate influences are still present in a creole variety, two or three speakers may be sufficient for your study. If you are a local linguist trying to characterise your variety to provide teachers with professional development about the community language situation, it might be sufficient to run a small study with a few people. If you are planning to write a school curriculum in your language, broader grammatical description is required and, with it, larger numbers of speakers.

If there is a lot of variation present, you will be faced with needing large numbers of speakers. The number of speakers may depend on the complexity of the linguistic feature you are interested in. How many different ways can it be expressed and how many different factors drive the choice between variables? For example, in the case of optional nominative marking in Gurindji Kriol, the choice to use or not use the nominative marker depends on word order, whether the speaker has used the marker before, whether an event has occurred or not, whether a co-referential pronoun is also present, among other factors. This study used 6,550 tokens from 103 speakers to model the variation (Meakins & Wilmoth, 2018). Meyerhoff et al. (2012) have a good description of how to calculate how many speakers you need for a study on variation.

For experimental work, see §10.4.5, usually 12 people per category is considered reasonable (i.e. 12 male, 12 female; or 12 adults, 12 children etc.), and at least 30 tokens of each variant per factor. The Romani study of reaction time and language switching which aimed to determine whether mixed Romani-Turkish sentences have higher processing costs than unilingual L2-Turkish sentences used 49 participants in one experiment and 37 in the other. Ten had attended at most primary school, 27 had attended secondary school and above; 23 participants were female and 14 male (Adamou & Shen, 2018). See also §9.4.2.1 for a discussion of numbers of participants and deliberate over-recruiting in studies of language acquisition.

### 10.4.5.2 Assessing language proficiency in bilingual situations

Contact languages such as community-level code-switching and mixed languages are often spoken in situations of language shift where speakers may have varying levels of skills in the source languages. Proficiency in a language may play a role in linguistic variation or contact outcomes and is often a factor which is quantified by psycholinguistic and variationist studies. For example, many psycholinguists perform a raft of language proficiency assessments on participants to gauge whether proficiency affects the linguistic feature under study. Nonetheless these sorts of tests may be inappropriate in particular speech communities. For example, language proficiency is a sensitive topic in language shift communities where a person's self-presentation may be threatened by poor results on proficiency tests. Testing itself may be viewed negatively in communities where education is associated with colonial powers.

In Adamou and Shen's reaction-time tasks to determine whether mixed Romani-Turkish sentences in Greek Thrace have higher processing costs than unilingual L2-Turkish sentences, they relied on participants' self-reported proficiency levels i.e. all 37 declared that they acquired Romani-Turkish and Turkish before the age of three and 27 participants declared Romani to be their primary language of communication. Another approach has been used in experimental work on Gurindji Kriol speakers. In Meakins, Jones & Algy's (2016) study on spatial relations (which involved 105 participants) and Stewart et al's (2018) study of voicing contrasts in stops (which had 103 participants), attained education level was used as a proxy for English proficiency in place of testing.

## 10.5 SUMMARY

Contact languages are a difficult category of language to document. In cases of language endangerment, most speech communities prioritise the spoken heritage language. Nonetheless many contact languages are likely to be classified as 'endangered' in the future as regional languages increase in dominance. Their value will no doubt increase accordingly. For example, Michif, a mixed language spoken in Canada, is now the focus of revitalisation attempts and previous documentation of this language is providing a basis for revitalisation. So if contact languages interest you, they can be a great focus for a documentation project. In this chapter, we outlined four different types of contact languages, and the social dimensions to doing fieldwork which are particular to contact languages. We also discussed the difficulties of collecting naturalistic data and outlined methods for eliciting data.

## 10.6 FURTHER READING

Garrett (2009) has a good discussion about why it is important to document contact languages. Winford (2003), Poplack (2015) and Meakins (2016) have good overviews of pidgin and creole languages, code-switching and mixed languages respectively. Meyerhoff et al. (2012) provide good guidelines for dealing with variation in fieldwork.

## NOTES

1. The *sega* is both music and dance and is at the core of the folklore of Mauritius. It originates from Africa and was introduced in Mauritius in the eighteenth century.
2. http://elar.soas.ac.uk/deposit/0273 Accessed 31 August 2017.
3. www.sociolinguistics.uottawa.ca/holdings/canadian-fe.html Accessed 31 August 2017.
4. http://fieldmanuals.mpi.nl/ Accessed 31 August 2017.
5. http://pearstories.org Accessed 31 August 2017.

## REFERENCES

Adamou, E., & Granqvist, K. (2015). Unevenly mixed Romani languages. *International Journal of Bilingualism*, 19(5), 525–547.

Adamou, E., & Shen, R. (2018). There are no language switching costs when codeswitching is frequent. *International Journal of Bilingualism*.

Bakker, P. (2001). Romani in Europe. In G. Extra & D. Gorder (Eds.), *The other languages of Europe: Demographic, sociolinguistic and educational perspectives* (pp. 293–313). Cleveland, OH: Multilingual Matters.
Boas, H. (2009). *The life and death of Texas German*. Durham, NC: Duke University Press.
Croft, W. (2000). *Explaining language change: An evolutionary approach*. Harlow, England: Longman.
Dorian, N. (1978). The fate of morphological complexity in language death: Evidence from East Sutherland Gaelic. *Language*, 54(3), 590–609.
Dorian, N. (1989). *Investigating obsolescence: Studies in language contraction and death*. Cambridge: Cambridge University Press.
Gal, S. (1979). *Language shift: Social determinants of linguistic change in bilingual Austria*. San Francisco, CA: Academic Press.
Gardani, F. (2008). *Borrowing of inflectional morphemes in language contact*. Frankfurt: Peter Lang.
Garrett, P. (2009). Contact languages as "endangered languages": What is there to lose? *Journal of Pidgin and Creole Languages*, 21(1), 175–190.
Guillemin, D. (2011). *The syntax and semantics of a determiner system: A case study of Mauritian creole*. Amsterdam: John Benjamins.
Labov, W. (1994a). *Principles of linguistic change: Internal factors*. Oxford: Blackwell.
Labov, W. (1994b). *Principles of linguistic change: Social factors*. Oxford: Blackwell.
Lipski, J. (2016). Language switching constraints: More than syntax? Data from Media Lengua. *Bilingualism: Language and Cognition*, 20(4), 722–746.
Matras, Y. (2002). *Romani: A linguistic introduction*. Cambridge: Cambridge University Press.
Matras, Y., & Sakel, J. (Eds.). (2007). *Grammatical borrowing in cross-linguistic perspective*. Berlin: Mouton de Gruyter.
Mayer, M. (1994). *Frog, where are you?* China: Puffin.
Meakins, F. (2010). The importance of understanding language ecologies for revitalisation. In J. Hobson, K. Lowe, S. Poetsch, & M. Walsh (Eds.), *Re-awakening languages: Theory and practice in the revitalisation of Australia's Indigenous languages* (pp. 225–239). Sydney: Sydney University Press.
Meakins, F. (2012). Which mix? Code-switching or a mixed language – Gurindji Kriol. *Journal of Pidgin and Creole Languages*, 27(1), 105–140.
Meakins, F. (2013). Gurindji Kriol. In S. Michaelis, P. Maurer, M. Haspelmath, & M. Huber (Eds.), *The survey of pidgin and creole languages* (Vol. 3, pp. 131–139). Oxford: Oxford University Press.
Meakins, F. (2018). Mixed languages. In M. Aronoff (Ed.), *Oxford research encyclopedia of linguistics*. Oxford: Oxford University Press.
Meakins, F., Jones, C., & Algy, C. (2016). Bilingualism, language shift and the corresponding expansion of spatial cognitive systems. *Language Sciences*, 54, 1–13.
Meakins, F., & Wilmoth, S. (2018). Complex cell-mates: Morphological overabundance resulting from language contact. In P. Arkadiev & F. Gardani (Eds.), *Morphological Complexity*. Oxford: Oxford University Press.
Meyerhoff, M., Adachi, C., Nanvakhsh, G., & Strycharz, A. (2012). Sociolinguistic fieldwork. In N. Thieberger (Ed.), *The Oxford handbook of linguistic fieldwork* (pp. 121–146). Oxford: Oxford University Press.
Moravcsik, E. (1978). Universals of language contact. In J. Greenberg (Ed.), *Universals of human language*, Vol. 1: *Method and theory* (pp. 95–122). Stanford, CA: Stanford University Press.

Mufwene, S. (2000). Creolization is a social, not a structural, process. In I. Neumann-Holzschuh & E. Schneider (Eds.), *Degrees of restructuring in creole languages* (pp. 65–83). Amsterdam: John Benjamins.

Mufwene, S. (2001). *The ecology of language evolution.* Cambridge: Cambridge University Press.

Myers-Scotton, C. (2002). *Contact linguistics: Bilingual encounters and grammatical outcomes.* Oxford and New York, NY: Oxford University Press.

O'Shannessy, C. (2004). *The monster stories: Picture stimulii to elicit lexical subject NPs.* Nijmegen: Max Planck Institute for Psycholinguistics.

Poplack, S. (2015). Code-switching (linguistic). In J. Wright (Ed.), *International encyclopedia of the social and behavioral sciences* (pp. 918–925). Boston, MA: Elsevier.

Rhydwen, M. (1995). Kriol is the colour of Thursday. *International Journal of the Sociology of Language,* 113, 113–119.

Saussure, F. de. (1916). *Course in general linguistics.* London: Duckworth.

Schmidt, A. (1985). *Young people's Dyirbal: An example of language death from Australia.* Cambridge: Cambridge University Press.

Stewart, J., Meakins, F., Algy, C., & Joshua, A. (2018). The development of phonological stratification: Evidence from stop voicing perception in Gurindji Kriol and Roper Kriol. *Journal of Language Contact,* 11(1), 71–112. doi:10.1163/19552629-01101003

Thomason, S. G., & Kaufman, T. (1988). *Language contact, creolization, and genetic linguistics.* Berkeley, CA: University of California Press.

Torres Cacoullos, R., & Travis, C. (2016). Two languages, one effect: Structural priming in code-switching. *Bilingualism: Language and Cognition,* 19(4), 733–753.

Treffers-Daller, J. (1994). *Mixing two languages: French-Dutch contact in a comparative perspective* (Vol. 9). Berlin: Mouton de Gruyter.

Winford, D. (2003). *An introduction to contact linguistics* (Vol. 33). Malden, MA: Blackwell.

# 11

# Verbal art

## 11.1 INTRODUCTION

A great thing about fieldwork is the variety of language use you are exposed to in the speech community. One of the most beautiful of these uses is song. All cultures have some form of poetry or song that may be performed musically or recited in a variety of ways. These tend to be stored in people's memory, even in literate cultures, and often in very large quantities. Poetry and song are examples of what are called verbal art, oral literature or the temporal arts (Barwick, 2012). Other types of verbal art include litany, children's rhyming games, sung tales, poems, ritual speech events, advertising jingles, incantations, charms and spells. In many cultures, the distinction between poetry and song does not exist. As such, musicologists tend to regard poetry and song as points on a continuum rather than as discrete categories.

Verbal art can be thought of as intensively structured use of language. By intensively structured we mean it is subject to structures that are not typical of everyday speech. The occurrence of particular sounds, grammatical structures or meanings can all be regulated in verbal art. Typically, these elements are arranged with respect to a line, e.g. line-final rhyme. In contrast, units of speech can be of any length and need not even be made up of lines. By drawing on the concept of a line, verbal art can make use of other poetic features such as alliteration (the occurrence of the same sound in the same position of a word or line) and parallelism (repetition with minimal variation). Parallelism is exemplified in the following two lines from the verbal art form called *tom yaya* of the Papua New Guinea Highlands (Rumsey, 2011, p. 252):

| *olu*-ma *ngil nyirim* e | The *flies* began to *buzz*. |
| *lupal*-ma *tom turum* e | The *mosquitoes* began to *drone*. |

These two lines show parallelism: repetition with variation occurring in the same position of the line (variation is in italics). The variation here occurs within the same semantic domains. The example also shows another feature of much verbal art: the use of ideophones such as 'buzz' and 'drone'. In these ways, verbal art draws attention to its own form, what Jakobson (1960) calls the "poetic function" of language. This contrasts with everyday speech which gives priority to the communicative function of language. Artistic structures such as rhyme and parallelism can also turn up in speech play or daily conversation where it may invoke the context of formal oratory; however, this chapter limits the discussion to verbal arts, which are often named categories or genres in a speech community.

In this chapter, we discuss how to do fieldwork on verbal arts by taking song as an exemplar. Songs are often the property of whole communities, although some people may be recognised as song experts. In some cultures there are types of verbal art composed by gifted individuals that may be appreciated by some, but not all, members of the community. Other types are composed by ordinary people, and transmitted orally among the population, as is the case with folk songs. In the early 1900s folklorist Cecil Sharp (1973) visited Appalachia to record folk songs and found that there, unlike in England, everyone sang folk songs, young and old. Across cultures we find that songs play a role in imparting the values of society. Some are shared, traded or performed for profit; others are a part of religious, healing or shamanic practices and some are simply performed for entertainment. In many cultures, verbal arts incorporate dance, ritual action and the visual arts. In this context, it is more accurate to talk about 'performance arts' rather than just 'verbal arts'. A multi-disciplinary team of researchers is very useful when working on such performance arts. In this chapter we present the musicologist's wish list to ensure that the linguist's recordings are also useful for musical analysis (Barwick, 2006, 2012).

## 11.2 WHY DOCUMENT SONG AND OTHER VERBAL ARTS?

There are many reasons why verbal art should be included in your linguistic fieldwork:

1. Song is an instance of both language and music that depends on shared human capacities. To understand the human capacity for language, we must also understand the human capacity for music.
2. As with music, the performance of verbal art is often a very pleasurable experience.
3. Verbal art forms are often seen as the pinnacle of a culture's linguistic and musical achievements and so the community may wish to showcase these to outsiders (Evans, 2009).
4. The benefits and uses of recordings of verbal arts may be much more readily apparent to the speech community than recordings of speech. The opportunity to record songs can thus be a great way to build relationships and give back to the community something of great worth.
5. Songs may be the sole means of transmitting important social, cultural and historical information and reproducing the knowledge and norms of society. They can be a mirror of community concerns and values, and can codify emotional responses to objects and events. Just think of the Portuguese concept of *saudade*, a deep longing for an absent something or someone, which permeates the Portuguese song genre *fado*.

6. Songs may contain vocabulary rarely encountered in everyday speech, especially ideophones and emotional vocabulary. They may also reveal taxonomies and links between the natural, social, metaphysical and mythical landscapes, encoded via metaphor and parallelism (Epps & Ramos, 2017; Epps, Webster, & Woodbury, 2017).
7. In cultures where singing is a group activity, performance of songs can be a spectacular arena of language use. Performers and audience may negotiate, praise, criticise and express expectations, thus providing rich data on both language use and the lexicon, much of which would be difficult to obtain from direct elicitation.
8. Song can provide particular perspectives into key aspects of language and culture, and the relationship between them. For example, in Central Australia many verses in Aboriginal music also refer to places, and so singing the verses of a song provides an acoustic interface between the physical and spiritual landscape.
9. In contexts where the language is highly endangered or no longer spoken, song may be all that is remembered. Songs and their templates can play a vital role in language revitalisation (Bracknell, 2017). While these initiatives cannot always reverse the tide of cultural change, song revival can play an important role in cultural identity. The opportunity to learn from archival recordings can also inspire new genres and songs.
10. Verbal art can also shed light on phonology. Like speech, people have intuitions about what forms of verbal art sound good and bad. The ways words are put to music (text-setting) and how verse is formed (poetic meter) are influenced by aspects of phonology (see §5.1). For example, we find that languages with contrastive stress such as English favour aligning stressed syllables with musical beats, whereas languages with fixed stress prioritise matching other aspects of their phonology to a musical template, such as the number of syllables with the number of beats. In languages where heavy and light syllables are contrasted, it is often the mora rather than the syllable that is counted when setting language to a rhythmic structure (Dell & Elmedlaoui, 2008; Deo, 2006; Hayes, 2009). The ways in which lexical tone is matched to melody is another important question in phonology (Morey & Schöpf, 2011).

## 11.3 PREPARING FOR FIELDWORK ON VERBAL ART

Before going into the field, find out if there is any prior documentation of the verbal arts in the community or language region. Remember that anthropologists, folklorists, musicologists, as well as linguists, may have recorded or described verbal art. Watch or listen to any past recordings from the region. Keep in mind, however, that the songs of today may be different to those of the past, as innovation and creativity typically drive musical change. It is not uncommon for the songs of younger and older generations to differ, with each group preferring their own songs or versions as a marker of identity, especially in context of rapid cultural change. Be aware that claims of incorrectness amongst the community may actually be a reflection of changing song styles.

Many types of songs relate to social categories, and to concepts of health, history, philosophy or religion. Read up on as much anthropology and history as possible. If the verbal art in the community involves art and music, explore avenues for possible collaboration in the field with an ethnomusicologist and/or anthropologist. There are some social contexts in which song frequently occurs across human societies. One is in caregiver/infant interactions, e.g. lullabies. Other contexts include entertainment, courtship and religious or ritual expression. Working in these different contexts can require different sensibilities. Children's songs, which are often associated with games and are usually in the public domain, can be a good place to start (see Marsh, 2008; Burling, 1966).

Recording songs associated with religious practices may require great care. In many colonised societies, these may have been suppressed and hidden from outsiders, especially if they have been devalued by the dominant culture. On the other hand, communities may wish to forget songs associated with particular cultural practices they have decided to abandon, such as human sacrifice. Working on such songs may be politically charged. However, there are many Indigenous communities who are actively engaged in teaching, recording and documenting their religious and ritual practices, many in collaboration with linguists (Diamond, 2013). Research on such culturally important forms of expression requires clear community control.

Before going into the field, identify potential research topics such as the following (see also Barwick, 2012, p. 174):

- How are songs classified?
- Are there old and new traditions?
- What linguistic structures are manipulated for artistic effect (e.g. words, syllables, phonemes; is there fixed line length, or rhyme)?
- How does language differ from speech?
- What folk definitions of the song, music and performance genres exist (do they include dance?) (cf. the Kalam definition in §7.6.3)?
- What terms are used for aspects of song (e.g. parts of a song, rhythm, melody, vocal quality, tempo, pitch)?

As part of your metadata, it is a good idea to record information about origins, ownership, rights and interests in songs as early as possible in your fieldwork. This will help to manage recordings and plan any publications. We discuss this further in §11.12.

You should aim to make the best possible field recordings (§3.3.3), as it may be that the songs you record will never be performed again. Take that extra step to ensure that the event can take place in the quietest environment possible, with the least chance of disturbances. The community may later wish to promote their songs on radio, TV or other forms of mass media, and the difference between an amateur or more professional sound recording may make or break whether this is a possibility or not. We discuss this further in §11.12 when we discuss publishing songs.

## 11.4 METHODS FOR DOCUMENTATION

Fieldwork on verbal art involves participant observation, where recordings, notes, film and stills are taken, as well as more structured interviews. In addition to recording performances, it is a good idea to seek information to help you understand the verbal art forms. Fieldwork may thus include audio and visual recording of the following types of events:

- performances of verbal art
- lessons or teaching of verbal art
- exegeses, explanations, translations and retranslations of verbal art
- performer biographies, repertories and song styles
- accounts of song origins and creation (in many cultures songs are created via dreams or some other super-natural processes), when and why they are performed
- commentaries on previously recorded performances of verbal art.

Once you are in the field, try to find out as much as possible about what is going to be performed and by whom. It may be necessary to just listen and observe to get answers. Bear in mind that not all community members may know the answers. Prepare as much as possible, but remember that part of being in the field is not knowing exactly what is going to happen. For these reasons, it is a good idea to participate in a performance in the community before setting out to record one. Participating can occur in a variety of ways, such as being an active listener, watching, dancing, singing or making cups of tea. Take note of the various ways different community members are involved in a performance. There may be many ways that community members participate without actually singing (Ingram, 2013), including by dancing, giving gifts and simply being present and listening. In some cultures, joining in is a sign of equitable and harmonious social relations with the community (Russell & Ingram, 2013, p. 2), so spending the whole time behind a camera with headphones on may be frowned upon. This may not be the case in other cultures where joining in is by invitation only.

Listen and observe how people compliment and complain about songs and their performance. Cecil Sharp (1965) observes that in English and American folk traditions, when someone sings you a folk song, you say, "That was a pretty good song", not "You sang that really nicely". In Central Australia, Aboriginal people value the antiquity of a song, compliment unison voices and measure good dancing by the height of the ensuing dust caused by dancing feet. In many societies singing is something everyone does, and so asking if there are any singers may be met with a quizzical look. When it comes to songs, pay particular attention to older people, as they are often excellent at recalling songs and their meanings, even when their short-term memory is waning.

## 266 Verbal art

In some cultures, fees or gifts are paid to the performers or copyright holders for recording songs. If this is the case, talk to someone in the community about what the appropriate fee or gift might be and who should be remunerated. It may be that only the composer or certain people in the society can perform, talk about, or give permission for songs to be recorded or written about. Listen to the advice of community members as to who you should or shouldn't record. It is much better to have other community members present when recording verbal art. The exchanges between performer and community members often lead to a much richer event. Community members can also be helpful intermediaries between you and the performer, paving the way for a smooth and enjoyable event. Additionally, community members will be better placed to work on transcriptions and translations, having participated in the recording event themselves. If possible, work with a community member to assist in negotiating the appropriate payments or gifts (if required), ensuring permissions are in place, and running and recording the performance event.

## 11.5 RECORDING PERFORMANCES

It is a good idea to film as well as audio-record performances. This is clearly important if the songs are accompanied by dance, ritual action, regular work activities, games and musical instruments. But even in the unlikely event that there is almost no action accompanying the singing, songs can be highly emotive, and this can be seen in the faces and gestures of the performers. An audio recording alone will not capture the tears and smiles of a singer. In group singing, there may be gestural communication and cues that enable the singers to perform in synchrony, although the singers themselves may not be consciously aware of this.

Try to find out in advance whether there will be dancing or preparation of masks and ritual objects, and whether this will occur at night or in daylight. Answers to these questions will help you plan what equipment you need (e.g. lights, types of microphones, number of video cameras) and where to place them. Some songs are intimately linked to a particular ritual action, so it is not ideal if you have filmed a close-up of the singer but missed the accompanying action performed by someone else! The spatial relationships, both within the performance space and between performers and objects, may all be structurally significant and convey meaning. Some other types of sounds may also be considered part of the performance, for example birds, exclamations or what seems to be an argument. For these reasons, it can be a good idea to have someone in the community with you who can draw your attention to the important actions and pivotal points in the performance before they occur. Nevertheless, despite your best efforts it is still possible that the singers might do something completely different from what you expect. Be ready for anything!

Songs should be recorded in the best format possible (ideally 32bit/48khz) (§3.2.1) and with a good microphone, preferably one with a frequency response over the range of 20hz–20,000kHz (§3.2.2). For performances involving more than one person, a stereo microphone should be used. If many people are singing different parts, it is ideal to use multiple single point semi-directional (cardioid) microphones, which will enable you to cut out extraneous sound (§3.2.2). A recording device with multiple channels is great for this (§3.2.1). In a group performance the microphone should be placed within half a metre of the singer to capture the vocals as well as the texture of the group performance. It can be useful to have a range of microphones with different directional characteristics or a microphone that enables you to switch between several patterns (see §3.2.2). If you need to move the microphone during a performance, make sure you do this when there is a break in the singing and not during. If one of the performers is likely to talk as well, an additional wireless lapel microphone on this person is a good idea (§3.2.2).

Musical performances have a large, dynamic range and this must be monitored carefully to avoid clipping (§3.3.2). Never use the automatic volume control on the recording device, as this can change the levels midway through a song as different instruments enter. Always adjust levels in between songs and never during. Tinkering during songs will render them unsuitable for quality publications, broadcast media or for use in a professional soundtrack. A pre-record setting is also particularly useful when recording songs. Pre-record lets you record for a few seconds before switching on the record button. This is useful when you don't know when singing is going to begin, or when you have been instructed to turn off the recorder, but not informed when you should turn it on again! If the singer starts performing before you are ready, you will need to decide if it is appropriate to ask them to start again, or whether this might be considered rude. Once the community sees or hears the recording minus the beginning, it may be that greater care is taken next time to ensure the linguist is ready to start recording when they begin the performance.

If using a separate audio-recorder and camera, it is important to synchronise your devices right at the beginning and leave both devices running for the entire duration of the performance event (cf. §3.3.3). It may be considered rude if you have to clap to synchronise devices again mid-performance. If there is movement and dance it is a good idea to make a sketch or take photos of the whole performance space, including audience. The performance may have important macro-spatial arrangements and movement that cannot be captured if the video is focused on a single group within the whole performance space.

## 11.6 PLAYING BACK RECORDINGS

If possible, play back your recording of the song soon after the performance has finished. Not only do singers often ask to hear the recording straight away, but this is an excellent opportunity to get an explanation of what the song means as well as commentary, corrections, additions or reflections on the performance. Of course, if the performance involves lots of people and takes days to perform, then it is not going to be possible to play the whole recording.

Take a pair of high quality external speakers for this purpose. It is much better to play the sound through these than through the inbuilt speakers of your recording device. If possible, transfer the recording to a hard drive first (this is not always possible). That way there is no risk of accidentally deleting the only copy of the recording as you play it back on your recording device. Furthermore, if you can play transferred files on another device it means that you can record the explanation and discussion of the songs as well. Alternatively you may have a second recording device that you can use to record the explanation and discussion.

As the performance is underway, you should keep notes on the number of songs and try to identify any words or structures, such as lines. This will help you to play back the songs to the singer and find particular songs they may wish to comment on. When playing back the recording or reading your notes, go through one line at a time, or use some other natural division of the song, to clarify form and meaning. If the practice is to repeat a song or line multiple times (but possibly in different musical styles), it may annoy the singer to be asked "What does that mean" when it is actually the same line that they have just explained! Listen carefully and take notes while recording, as this will help you distinguish repetition from new lyrics.

## 11.7 TRANSCRIBING VERBAL ART

The task of transcribing and translating songs can be very rewarding due to their stimulating intellectual content, and their linguistic and musical artistry. Keep in mind, however, that in some cultures the right to translate and work on songs may be dependent on a person's role in society or their relationship to specific songs.

In addition to any social restrictions on who can work on songs, in some cases the style in which verbal art is delivered makes transcription difficult. For example, in soft chanting or non-unison group singing it can be very difficult – if not impossible – to determine the linguistic content. In addition, the gap between lexical content of individual words and the meaning conveyed by these words put together in a song can be vast. Remember that in verbal arts the referential message may be downplayed in favour of formal or aesthetic dimensions, which may be in the style or emotional force of the delivery. Obtaining a spoken explanation or a 'spoken language' version of the songs at the time of performance will greatly assist in the task of transcription and translation.

At the early stages of linguistic transcription, it is a good idea to distinguish the units of the performance, such as a song or poem, from the method of its delivery, such as singing, chanting or speaking. It is possible that people may at times speak the song and sing speech, and thus your transcript should be able to distinguish song lyrics from an everyday word or phrase, and distinguish singing or intoning from speaking. A transcription of a Kaytetye text illustrating the difference between sung and spoken song is shown in Figure 11.1 (Green & Turpin, 2013, pp. 384, 385). This excerpt ends in a portion of singing, labelled '(singing)' consisting of a song text with two lines (LINE 1 and LINE 2). Before this, each of the two lines is spoken, where they are used to refer to the devil character in the story. Without paying

**Figure 11.1**
A text illustrating the difference between sung and spoken song texts
Source: Green & Turpin, 2013, pp. 384, 385

---

Selections from a transcript of a text by Kaytetye man Tommy Thompson showing the difference between song and speech, and between sung and spoken delivery.

\t 119.767
\k  Nyarte  re   two time     '*Angkwerey-angkwereye*'=ye,      nyarte.
\g  this    3sg  twice        Elder.sister-RED(LINE 1)=EMPH    this
\e  It went around twice (singing) '*Big sister, big sister*' (LINE 1).

...

\t 184.243
\k  Him stand up here    aylengke      are-yayne.
\g  stand up here        1duSMSG       see-PST:CNT
\e  'It stopped here and looked at us two!'

\t 184.243
\k  Kwere=lke    ampile-yayne,    '*Artwarlatyawerlewe*'.
\g  3sgDAT=now   follow-PST:CNT   'devil=REL-1SG-hear-PST(LINE 2)
\e  They followed the tracks (of) '*I heard a devil* (LINE 2)'.

(sung whilst travelling in a spiralling motion)

\t 199.396
\k (singing): '*Angkwereye angkwereye,    Artwarlatyawerlewe*'.
\g             LINE 1                    LINE 2
\e           '*Big sister, big sister, I heard a devil*'

---

attention to the difference between song texts and speech words it would be difficult to understand the meaning of the spoken text.

At this early stage in transcription, it is a good idea to label songs sequentially rather than by name, unless you already know what distinguishes one song from another. For example, you may think you have two different songs when in fact it is the same song simply commencing at a different place (think how some people may begin a folk song with the chorus while others with the verse). Keep an open mind about what distinguishes one song from another within the culture; it may not be in features of the text, but rather the music, meter or performance context. Be careful when attributing songs to a single genre (e.g. wedding song, funeral song). In some cases a song, as a musical-linguistic form, may not belong uniquely to a single genre. In one context it may be a wedding song, but in another context a healing song.

Verbal arts are often delivered in a way that differs from speech (e.g. sung, whispered, chanted) and so it is a good idea to keep the transcription of the performed song separate from the transcription of how people explain or 'speak' it. It is not uncommon for these two versions to differ, as vowels may need to be modified for the sung voice to carry at certain pitches and syllables may need to be substituted, added or deleted to adhere to rhyme or other types of poetic form. In some cultures, the text is rarely uttered outside the ritual context, and so it may be edited, contracted or modified in various ways in exegeses. Patterns unique to song, such as line structure, repetition and sound patterning may only be apparent in the sung form. To summarise, when working on song you will be working on two forms: the sung form and the explanation or spoken version, both of which may have multiple versions and both of which should be transcribed and translated.

### 11.7.1 Texts and variation

When it comes to identifying the text and music in a song, there may be different opinions amongst the community as to what these are. This is frequently the case with two or more instances of what is regarded as the same song. In some cultures, multiple perceptions of the texts (and their translations) are a feature of song, whether this is formally recognised or not. There may be different versions of a song (with different words) yet speakers regard these as essentially the same 'song'. In many cases there is no single 'correct' or 'original' form – all variants are of equal status. Morey (2012, p. 119) suggests that in the ritual songs of north-east India, it is perhaps not intended for the forms to be preserved unaltered. Orally transmitted song is often the cumulative result of multiple singers adding their own creative stamp with some forms being selected and others forgotten over time. An understanding of oral transmission is at the heart of comments such as "Ah, you sing it this way but I sing it that way", without implying one as right or wrong. Differences may be the hallmark of individual singers, regions and times. In some cultures people may recognise that some people perform a song better than others, whereas in others it is the singer's own status within the community that determines whether their version of a song is better than someone else's. Variation in orally transmitted songs can be seen in Western school playgrounds in the songs performed by children today (Marsh, 2008, p. 3).

Should there exist an early written form or recording of a song, you might be tempted to consider the more recent version as a variant of that 'original' form; yet even this may be problematic, as there is no guarantee that an earlier documentation of a song is closer to the 'original' than a later documentation. Songs are created from a person's total song experience and memory, and so any version may draw upon the musical and textual formulae of all other songs held in memory by the person who sings it, whether consciously or not. This of course raises questions of how to attribute authorship of songs, which we discuss further in §11.12.1.

Even if an original form can be unambiguously identified, the question remains as to whether this should be regarded as the 'correct' or 'best' form. Sharp (1965, p. 17) cites Beethoven as an example, as Beethoven frequently improved upon his earlier versions of a piece of music. Sharp argues that those "who argue that folk song variants are corruptions of some mysterious original, must ... regard the first draft of a Beethoven melody as the original and all subsequent developments as corruptions, including of course, the melody in its final and published state".

### 11.7.2 Notation systems and software

Transcribing the music of a song has its own complexities and it is best to involve a musicologist in this task. However, if you are familiar with modern musical notation (often called 'staff notation') you may wish to use this as it is widely known, making it easier to convey musical concepts. It may be, however, that staff notation is not the best way to represent the musical contrasts in the culture. As with spoken language, it's a good idea to start with a narrow transcription and then move to a broad transcription once you get more familiar with the musical conventions of the culture. The proprietary software applications Sibelius or Finale are commonly used for Western musical notation, although there is lesser-known free software available such as MuseScore.[1]

If you just want to notate rhythm but not pitch, the 'rhythms' font developed by Matthew Hindson is useful for this.[2] Another way to notate musical rhythm is to use a metrical grid. Although originally developed to represent rhythm in speech (Hayes, 1995; Liberman & Prince, 1977) it can also be used to represent musical rhythm. Figure 11.2 shows a transcription of a line of song in standard modern western music notation and then the same material represented by a metrical grid. If you wish to address questions relating to language and dance, then you may want to use the various dance notation systems, such as Benesh Movement Notation and Labanotation (see Chapter 8 for a discussion of some other ways of annotating movement).[3]

When considering transcription tools for verbal arts, it is particularly useful to be able to see the wave form (note that some software will only display a wave form accurately if sampled at certain rates, usually 16/32 bit). In the field, you may choose to work with a compressed version such as MP3 if you have a large corpus of songs with you. For analysis of songs, the software Transcribe! is useful for marking up points in the audio (and video), making notes, changing tempo and suggesting musical pitch and computing tempo.[4]

Figure 11.2
A transcription of a line of song in modern western music notation of rhythm alone, and the same material represented by a metrical grid
Source: Hayes & Kaun, 1996

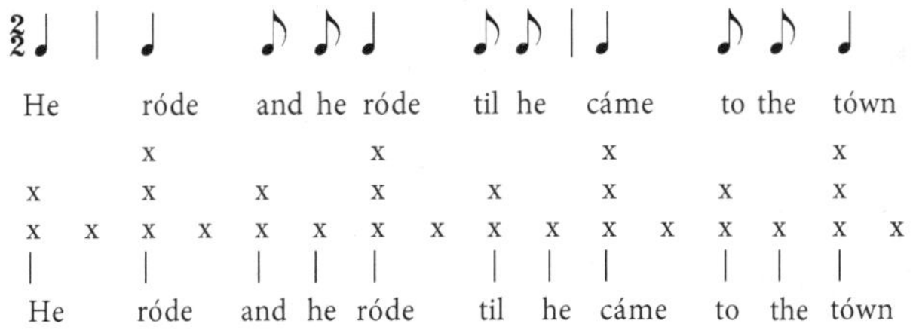

|  | He | róde | and he róde | til he cáme | to the tówn |
|---|----|------|-------------|-------------|-------------|
|  |    |      | x           | x           | x           | x |
|  | x  | x    | x    x      | x    x      | x    x      |
|  | x  x | x  x | x  x  x    | x  x  x    | x  x  x    |
|  | \|  | \|   | \|  \|      | \|  \|      | \|  \|      |
|  | He | róde | and he róde | til he cáme | to the tówn |

## 11.8 FORM IN VERBAL ART

Analysis of songs requires looking for salient patterns, which may be pervasive and obligatory, or occasional and incidental (Epps, Webster, & Woodbury, 2018). Patterns – whether of sound, grammar or meaning – are often organised around the line. Hymes (2003, p. 11) states that "presentation in terms of lines and verses makes visible the shaping artistry of narrators", noting that such presentation makes it far more possible to perceive repetition, parallelism, alliteration and meter (the rhythmic properties of song). For example, lines in English folk songs often have a set number of beats, with beats most often filled by a stressed syllable. This is illustrated in the four 4-beat lines of 'Mary had a little lamb' below, where the beat is filled by a stressed syllable (for example in line 1: *MA-ry HAD a LI-ttle LAMB*). Note that the dash represents an empty beat:

|     | B          | B          | B          | B    |
|-----|------------|------------|------------|------|
|     | Mary       | had a      | little     | lamb |
|     | B          | B          | B          | B    |
| Its | fleece was | white as   | snow       | –    |
|     | B          | B          | B          | B    |
| And | Every      | where that | Mary       | went |
|     | B          | B          | B          | B    |
| The | lamb was   | sure to    | go         | –    |

There may also be rules about where a word boundary must occur. For example, in the French Alexandrine meter this occurs after the sixth syllable in the 12-syllable line. Other poetic traditions constrain not so much the number but the ways in which syllables or stress etc. are positioned in the line. In Tohono O'odham songs (a Native American language and people of the Sonoran Desert) adjacent or line-final stress is not permitted and so the songs systematically manipulate the morphology to avoid this (Fitzgerald, 1998). Songs can also be analysed for their meaning; although the communicative function of language is often downplayed in song. It is common for songs to have multiple meanings, and to be semantically ambiguous. We discuss this further in the next section.

---

**Exercise 1 Scanning a limerick**

Scan the following poem into four lines of equal duration using a metrical grid and include any empty beats. Is the rhythm duple or triple? How many instances of rhyme are there and where must these occur? How would you account for the difference in the number of lines in the metrical and orthographic representation of this genre?

> There once was a linguist that's sweet,
> Who could place London speech within feet

> This philologist told
> Of Germanic of old,
> But left us before he could tweet.
> – Brenda Boerger, SIL; The 2012 Ultimate
> LINGUIST Limerick Champion[5]

## 11.9 TRANSLATING VERBAL ART

After transcribing a performance, further explanations are usually required in order to understand the songs and translate them. As well as paying close attention to the sung form when transcribing, it is a good idea to try to sing or chant the song back to the orator in another recording session to ensure you have grasped the sung form. This way you will soon know whether you are making a mistake. It is usually the case that you will need to ask the singer or someone else appropriate to provide an explanation, translation or exegesis of the songs. This is also a good time to interview the performer about their history and who they learnt the songs from. Prepare a list of questions beforehand and run these by someone else in the community first. Be as informed as you can about the person before you interview them.

Translating songs is notoriously difficult for many reasons. One is that the meanings people derive from songs may be associated with their music and the context they are performed in rather than their lexical content. Another reason is that the words themselves may be perceived differently by different people. In §11.7, we saw how the form of a song may vary from instance to instance, with no one form being the 'correct' or 'original'. But even for the one instance of a song there may be differing perceptions of what the text is, leading to the common phenomenon of misheard lyrics known as 'mondegreens' (based on a mishearing of an English couplet 'and *laid him on the green*', which was later reinterpreted as '… and *Lady Mondegreen*'). Similarly, the meanings of songs also vary from context to context. This is the case in both literate and oral traditions (Morey, 2012; Turpin & Stebbins, 2010). Even if the interpreter of a song regards their interpretation as the right one, there may well be other people with a different view. We recommend you keep track of the source of the differing views on the words and meanings of a song in your metadata.

It is important to document community views about the authoritative source of verbal art and their meanings. In Aboriginal Australia, it is common that only the person with hereditary rights to a song can interpret it. Explanations of songs are often framed in phrases such as "My grandfather said it meant X". If an interpreter (or singer) of a song points out their lineage, or regional affiliation or some other social affiliation, it may reflect that the meanings of songs are socially or regionally ascribed. Epps, Webster, & Woodbury (2018) recount a similar example in

Navajo culture, where the researcher found that asking a Navajo speaker what they thought the poet intended was often met with silence. The researcher "soon realized that, for Navajos, direct speculation about what was going on in other people's minds was highly culturally inappropriate, and was in fact associated with 'witchcraft'".

Another common feature in songs is the use of words or phrases with multiple or deliberately broad meanings. Many forms of verbal art also have broader meanings and significances that are not derived from their linguistic content. In such cases, a glossed and translated text may remain opaque unless additional exegeses or explanations of the cultural knowledge or logic behind such texts are included.

A further issue is how to bring out the aesthetic qualities of the texts and present them to a wider audience. For example, how might you translate vocables or euphonics, such as "lalala" (often glossed VOC), archaic or special song words; and changes in linguistic variety or register, which may represent particular characters or places? You might also consider how poetic structures such as metaphor, rhyme, alliteration, parallelism and puns might be represented. For songs that are viewed as enacting particular events, such as making rain, healing the sick or other types of performatives (think of the pronouncement of marriage), you might also consider how these functions are to be communicated. Representing such poetic features in the language of another culture can require creative thinking, so an explanation of how the translator arrived at their translations can be highly insightful. If it is possible to collect multiple translations of a single song this can be highly revealing (Mitchell & Webster, 2011). The three translations of the Navajo poem by Rex Lee Jim are from Webster (2017, p. 178); and they demonstrate the sonic and semantic resonances of words and poetry and the insights gained from multiple translations (Epps, Webster, & Woodbury, 2018):

| éh | (1) Wow | (2) Oh | (3) Oh |
|---|---|---|---|
| tsidił ga' | the stick game | these stick dice | Bang |
| da'dildił | are stomping | rebounding, rebounding | bang, bang |
| yiits'a' | I hear | it sounds | it sounds |

## 11.10 MANAGING RECORDINGS

In this section we discuss ways to manage and compare a corpus of verbal art, drawing on the methodology described by Turpin & Henderson (2015) and Barwick (2006). In terms of the recordings, it is useful to mark up each song in a performance. This can be done with a separate tier in ELAN (§4.3.2) or in a sound editing program and exported as individual song files and assembled in an iTunes database. The latter has the advantage of enabling songs to be easily retrieved, played and

#### Figure 11.3

File hierarchy of the archival recording JS01_153.wav transcribed and segmented into sequential song items (JS01_153-01.mp3 etc.). The original audio file is JS01_153.wav and the transcription of this audio is in various formats – .eaf, .trs, .pfsx and .txt (Illustration: Maxine Addinsall)

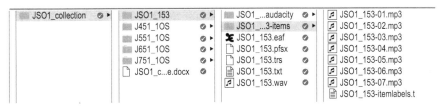

Note: The extension .trs is a Transcriber file.
Source: cf. Turpin & Henderson, 2015

exported to return to the community and it is unlikely to become obsolete in the near future.

We recommend using the sound editing software Audacity,[6] which has a number of advantages over other software such as Sound Studio (not the least of which is that Sound Studio erases markers after a certain number of saves). Figure 11.3 shows a resulting folder and file structure for working on recordings of songs.

> **Exercise 2 File naming**
>
> How does the file naming system above compare to those discussed in §4.2.1? How would you ensure that the metadata for the whole recording is carried through to every exported song file?

Putting extracted songs into your local iTunes database is a useful way of managing recordings on your computer. This widely used software keeps songs and their metadata together through the iTunes Library.it file, which iTunes uses to organise the songs in your library and the metadata that you've created. As the song is being played, information provided by tradition bearers can be entered directly into the iTunes database. The iTunes metadata can also be exported as a catalogue by selecting all the songs and copying and pasting into a blank Excel spreadsheet. It is also important to back up the metadata in a spreadsheet regularly in the advent of an iTunes database malfunction.

You can create an iTunes playlist for playback in the field for analysis of the songs, and as a prompt for discussion. Playlists can be loaded onto a portable music player connected to high quality portable speakers via a 1/8-inch cable. Make sure to record the playback of the songs as well as the speaker's explanation of the songs to ensure the song and the explanation stay together.

When preparing a playlist of songs for fieldwork, it is a good idea to exclude exemplars of songs that have interruptions or any other sorts of noise or talk that could detract from the task of explaining and translating the songs. Make sure you test the playlist before heading into the field to check all songs play correctly, as some playback devices cannot play recordings sampled at any other rate than 16bit/32khz or MP3.

When playing back archival recordings to people in the community, it is a good idea to find someone in the community who you can quietly check with first about the appropriateness of playing the songs publicly. This is especially important when working on legacy recordings, where the context and content of the recordings may be unknown and the metadata limited. Furthermore, the community's views on the songs themselves may have changed over time due to social or political events (e.g. the death of someone in the community, changes in land tenure or the adoption of a new religion). You want to prepare the community as much as possible, as you want to avoid playing publicly any songs that could cause offence or grief.

## 11.11 COPIES FOR THE COMMUNITY

Performers and other community members no doubt will want copies of a performance or collections of songs, such as all the songs sung by person X, or all the songs of repertoire X. There are multiple ways of returning recordings to the community. You may provide physical copies on CD, DVD or USB sticks, or if the community has internet access and approves, media can be uploaded to Facebook or YouTube for broader access. In iTunes, playlists can be created which can be burnt to CD, transferred to a USB stick or uploaded onto the internet.

Stephen Morey works on endangered languages on the India-Myanmar border and has recorded many songs performed by native speakers in numerous languages. When one of the major speakers passes away, he puts one of their songs or stories on Facebook as a tribute. Family members express their appreciation for the public recognition of these people and their skills.

Making copies of videos for the community takes more time than audio, but of course the reward is so much more for the users. It may not be possible to do this whilst in the field. In general, leave copies of new audio recordings with the relevant community members before leaving the field, and on subsequent fieldtrips bring back edited video. A summary of the software useful for working on verbal arts is listed below.

- For transcribing: ELAN and/or Transcriber (see §4.3.2) software
- For segmenting: Audacity free software (or Sound Studio), LAME MP3 codec[7]
- For analysis: Transcribe![8]
- For managing files and export: iTunes.

## 11.12 PUBLISHING VERBAL ART

The community may want to publish recordings of their songs or other verbal art. This can help the community promote their songs, develop a public profile for performers and provide an opportunity to acknowledge and protect the rights of both the creators and performers. Having the audio and/or video of songs available also adds value to any text publications of songs you compile. Few published ethnographic field recordings make money, so it would be unwise to present this as an economic opportunity. In this section we discuss the issues and steps involved in publishing songs.

If the community and you wish to make a quality multimedia package, you will need to work with a sound engineer and/or producer and designer. You will also need to ensure appropriate legal and financial arrangements are in place to protect copyright and other intellectual property rights (§2.4.4). For wide distribution, both physical and digital publishing (e.g. iTunes, Spotify) options are important. For all these reasons, it is a good idea to engage a record label, especially one that specialises in ethnographic or Indigenous music (for example, Smithsonian Folkways in the US and Skinnyfish Music or CAAMA Music in Australia). Ethnomusicologist Steven Feld's album of Kaluli songs is one such example, where he teamed up with musician Mickey Hart and the Rykodisc record label. Talk to the record label as early as possible in the project; they may even collaborate with you to seek funds to produce a quality recording.

> **Feld in the field**
>
> When I went to Papua New Guinea in 1975 with that stereo Nagra, anthropologists – certainly anthropology doctoral students – were writing ethnographic monographs as a principal standard for representation. Recording for radio broadcast or LP production was understood to be totally secondary or superfluous in terms of serious ethnographic representation. I wanted to buck that trend. My first New Guinea publication was also the inaugural LP in the Institute of New Guinea Studies series. I wanted to accomplish two things: to herald in sound the publication of my ethnographic monograph, *Sound and Sentiment*, which came out the next year, and to honor a commitment to helping Papua New Guinea's newly independent government and research institute start an LP record series to encourage researchers to make field-recordings into circulatable representations of cultural history.
>
> (Steven Feld interviewed by Angus Carlyle – Lane & Carlyle, 2013)
>
> *Voices of the Rainforest* is a recorded soundscape of a day in the life of the Kaluli people of Papua New Guinea. As the day progresses, one hears birds, water, insects and other ambient voices of the rainforest

> interspersed with Kaluli songs and instrumental sounds of work, leisure and ritual. Proceeds from the sale of these go to the non-profit Bosavi Peoples Fund, supporting educational, medical, social and environmental initiatives.

For academic publishing of songs there are a number of options for including audio or video with the analysis of songs:

- CD/DVDs with detailed sleeve notes or web delivery (e.g. iTunes)
- uploading audio/video files to a website to accompany a publication
- embedding audio/video into a digital pdf publication (e.g. Adobe Acrobat)
- embedding audio into a hardcopy publication using QR codes or Soundprinting.

New possibilities will continue to emerge as technology changes. No matter which format is chosen, it is crucial to obtain permissions from the copyright holders of songs to reproduce their songs; and evidence. Evidence of this is usually required by the publisher. Unlike speech, songs are often considered creative works and are often owned by individuals or groups of individuals. Under international copyright law, songs, poetry, music and dances are defined as 'works' and so researchers have a responsibility "to acknowledge the moral and legal rights of musicians and performers under traditional and international law" (Barwick, 2012, p. 172). In addition to the intellectual property rights discussed in §2.4.4, many countries also have specific creative arts laws that aim to protect singers and other artists.[9] Local views of song ownership, which may or may not be formalised, may be quite different. It is a good idea to include this in publications of songs, such as the following from the book *Jardiwanpa yawulyu: Warlpiri women's songs from Yuendumu* (Gallagher et al., 2014, p. 2):

> The songs, stories and images in this book contain traditional knowledge of the Warlpiri people, and have been presented and published with the consent of the knowledge custodians. Dealing with any part of the knowledge for any purpose that has not been authorised may breach the customary laws of the Warlpiri people, and may also breach copyright and moral rights under the Copyright Act 1968 (Australian Commonwealth). Please contact the publisher for further details.

Commercial release of albums can be a good idea for wide access; however, there is always the potential for third parties to use commercial releases in ways that violate the performer's legal and moral rights, or represent the performers and their community in ways that the community and performers do not like, and no doubt many other ways yet to be imagined. The community and researcher can remain powerless against large commercial companies who wish to use recordings in such ways (Feld, 2000; Seeger, 2004).

Some tradition bearers may feel it inappropriate to sell recordings of verbal art and decide against royalties (even though royalties are usually small). In the

Kaytetye women's songs project in Central Australia, which produced a recording of women's songs from the land-holding group of Arnerre, the community decided that the album would only be available to libraries and community organisations and distributed via the local language and culture centre. Other groups in Central Australia have decided to sell their books, but with the profits of sales going to support future publications.

### 11.12.1 Copyright and authorship

While the rapidly changing face of technology brings exciting possibilities for accessing songs, it also poses challenges for controlling the use of recordings. It may be the case that the songs you have recorded and studied are also known outside their place of origin, so if possible try to find out who else sings the songs or where they are from. You don't want to attribute intellectual and artistic creation to someone only to find out that they are widely known and owned.

Copyright of verbal art forms can be complex (see also §2.4.4 for a broader discussion of copyright). We mentioned that in many cultures songs are created via dreams or some other supernatural processes and are communal or traditional, which is not covered under copyright laws. This is also the case with many English folk songs, which were orally transmitted and altered by many people, over many years, in many places. The early folklorist Cecil Sharp (1965, p. 13) describes authorship in this situation as "belong[ing] equally to all those who have taken part in the transmission". Whilst in the past authorship has often been sidestepped by attributing songs as 'Traditional' or 'Anonymous', better practice is to attribute authorship to the language community as a whole, or some other appropriate group of individuals. For example, "Song X, as sung by person/people X" or "The song repertory of person/people X".

In addition to the assigning of authorship, it is important to acknowledge all people involved in the documentation process and the roles they have played, as discussed in §2.6. In some instances, the owners of verbal art forms may not be the performers and so it is a good idea to state that permission has been granted by the custodians or copyright holders in any publications (e.g. "We kindly thank the copyright holders of the songs, The Jones family, who have given us permission to reproduce their songs here").

## 11.13 ARCHIVING AND ACCESS

Here we further the discussion of archiving (§4.4) by considering archiving in relation to songs. This chapter has pointed out that in a living singing tradition a song is continually evolving. A recording captures just one way that a song can be realised, that is, by a particular group of people at a particular time in a particular place. Archiving privileges those forms that are recorded and Morey (2012, p. 120) raises the question of whether these may "potentially change the way in which that tradition is viewed and passed on". In highly endangered contexts, the recordings might only constitute portions of a song, and so the implications of having only partial records are even greater. In some cases, archiving is at odds with traditional transmission processes, as you can read in the Tai Ahom case study.

> ### Tai Ahom (India) tradition of manuscripts copying
>
> In the endangered Tai Ahom cultures of north-east India, there is a tradition of copying manuscripts of ritual song texts and destroying the previous version. In the process, these manuscripts are sometimes consciously altered. It seems that neither the manuscript nor the text inscribed in it is intended to be a fixed form persisting into the future. The ritual songs themselves long predate the practice of writing, which was first done on bark and silk but is now done on paper. From the point of view of the linguist and archivist, the practice of destroying the previous version of the manuscript is problematic because of information that is lost in the process. While the tradition there is to include the name, date and location of the copyist, information of greater historical depth, as well as the fine drawings that some older manuscripts have, are all lost in this process. By preserving photographs of these older manuscripts while allowing the new one to be preserved as well, a new tradition of the transfer of the contents of the manuscript across time and place is created. The archive is preserving aspects of a living tradition that were not preserved in the past. Thus the archived forms are in a sense creating something new, which is not a traditional practice, but is the result of the relationship between the archive, linguist and the community. The alternative of not archiving at all may well mean the loss of the tradition altogether, which is not ideal either. Nevertheless, it is important to be aware that what is being preserved is not the tradition of the manuscripts and their transmission, but a snapshot of that tradition collected on the dates that the manuscript was photographed (For further information see Morey, 2012).

As songs are often regarded as having cultural and symbolic capital and metaphysical power, custodians may choose to restrict access to song recordings whereas they might not want to do so for speech. There may be concerns over potential unintended usage of song recordings, including the possibility of causing physical damage in the world where songs have metaphysical power. Morey (pers. comm.) recalls that after the Wihu festival in 2008 in northern India, the couple who performed a traditional welcome to their house came to see him the next morning quite worried that he might have suffered ill effects of the songs which have real power. A lack of understanding about the archive and how access conditions are adhered to might also lead custodians to err on the side of caution, with more restrictive access conditions.

Recordings can be used as a resource for learning; while this is seen as a good thing if in the hands of the right people, the community may not feel they can control this. It is very easy, for example, for a USB to be lost, copied or stolen, and if the recordings are online, one cannot control who else may be sitting beside a person who has legitimate access. In some cultures learning songs is not a right, but rather something one must prove oneself worthy of, and it is difficult to reflect these conditions in the access instructions for records in the archives. This is currently not a practicality that the archive can support. As a researcher, however, by facilitating a more direct link between the archives and the community, issues of community access and use may be improved over time.

> ### Arrernte women's song project
>
> Ceremonial song-poetry of Central Australia is held in high esteem and seen as the pinnacle of cultural proficiency. In the Arrernte Women's songs project, many Arrernte people have teamed up with researchers to make recordings of their verbal art for posterity and to assist their descendants in learning songs. Nevertheless, they also want strict control of their distribution. Community members who work in archiving and technology express the view that recordings of songs hold metaphysical power, capital and responsibility and that they must be treated with great care by both researchers and community members. To impress upon people the responsibility of cultural learning, some Arrernte women decided to award people deemed responsible enough to have a recording with a USB stick on a lanyard with a statement from the community elder about the responsibility this comes with, thus creating a new ritual for the modern era (Perkins, 2016).

## 11.14 PERFORMANCES AND INTERCULTURAL EXCHANGES

Fieldwork on songs opens up a number of other ways to disseminate and promote a community's verbal arts that can benefit the community and research. Intercultural performances, exhibitions, ethnographic field recordings and films are exciting opportunities for both the researcher and the community to promote their verbal arts to a new audience. This can provide educational and development opportunities for the community. Visits to archives and universities can also lead to better understandings of research, collaboration and better archiving practices, as well as promoting your projects and the language and culture of the people with whom you work. We encourage researchers to build into their research plan opportunities for community members to participate in intercultural exchanges of performances, workshops and exhibitions of their verbal arts and related cultural practices.

> ### Exercise 3  Recording verbal art traditions in your own culture
>
> In this exercise you will investigate the verbal arts of your grandparents' generations in your own culture. Explain to a grandparent or friend from an older generation that you are doing a task for your university subject and that you

would like to record them (if they don't want to be recorded just use a pen and paper). Ask if they can recall any songs or poetry from their childhood. Did they sing any nursery rhymes, lullabies, church songs or love songs? You should have a few exemplars up your sleeve to try to trigger their memory. Try to write them down, noting any explanations they give. Ask about any meanings or associations they have. Do they remind them of a place, people and times? How did they learn the songs, did they pass them on? If recording, ask if they would like you to play the recording back to them. Does this elicit any further comments? Note any unclear words or meanings. How different are the songs to speech? Transcribe the song/poem(s) text. You might like to try the rhythm in either a metrical grid or musical notation too. What is the relationship between the stressed syllables and the strong positions of the meter? What is the relationship between word boundaries (prosodic, lexical, morphological) and boundaries of the poetic form, e.g. line, verse, half-line (also called 'hemistich')?

## 11.15 SUMMARY

In this chapter we aimed to encourage field linguists to pay attention to verbal arts, such as poetry and song. We outlined the benefits of this and suggested a methodology for working on verbal arts, managing recordings and disseminating them in the community. We discussed differences between the form and function of verbal arts and speech, and considered how verbal art can be considered as having multiple layers of translations. We also discussed issues to consider when publishing and archiving songs and suggested intercultural exchanges as an exciting context for disseminating and promoting fieldwork that benefits the community.

## 11.16 FURTHER READING

For a discussion of the importance of verbal art to linguistic fieldwork see Epps, Webster & Woodbury (2018), and for tools and techniques for recording verbal arts see Barwick (2012). For a particularly African focus on fieldwork on song from a musicological perspective see Wasamba (2015). For an introduction to the formal properties of verbal arts see Fabb (1997).

## NOTES

1. https://musescore.org/en Accessed 27 August 2017.
2. www.music-notation.info/en/fonts/Rhythms.html Accessed 27 August 2017.
3. www.rad.org.uk/study/Benesh and http://dancenotation.org/lnbasics/frame0.html Accessed 27 August 2017.
4. www.seventhstring.com/xscribe/download.html Accessed 27 August 2017.

5   https://linguistlist.org/fund-drive/2012/limericks.cfm.
6   www.audacityteam.org/.
7   http://lame.sourceforge.net Accessed 27 August 2017.
8   www.seventhstring.com Accessed 27 August 2017.
9   Despite this, there are instances of laws being broken and communities not having the power or money to afford legal action to assert their right (Feld, 2000).

# REFERENCES

Barwick, L. (2006). A musicologist's wishlist: Some issues, practices and practicalities in musical aspects of language documentation. *Language Documentation & Conservation*, (3), 53–62.

Barwick, L. (2012). Including music and the temporal arts in language documentation. In N. Thieberger (Ed.), *The Oxford handbook of linguistic fieldwork* (pp. 166–179). Oxford: Oxford University Press.

Bracknell, C. (2017). Maaya waab (play with sound): Song language and spoken language in the south-west of Western Australia. In J. Wafer & M. Turpin, (Eds.), *Recirculating songs: Revitalising the singing practices of Indigenous Australia* (pp. 45–57). Canberra: Pacific Linguistics.

Burling, R. (1966). The metrics of children's verse: A cross-linguistic study. *American Anthropologist*, 68(6), 1418–1441.

Dell, F., & Elmedlaoui, M. (2008). *Poetic meter and musical form in Tashlhiyt Berber songs*. Cologne: Köppe.

Deo, A. (2006). *Diachronic change and synchronic typology: Tense and aspect in Modern Indo-Aryan languages*. Palo Alto, CA: Stanford University.

Diamond, B. (2013). Metaphors, mood, medium, and modelling: Indigenous music workshops and citizenship. In I. Russell & C. Ingram (Eds.), *Taking part in music* (pp. 69–82). Aberdeen: Aberdeen University Press.

Epps, P., & Ramos, D. P. (2017). Enactive aesthetics: The ethnopoetics of incantation. Presented at the Rethinking Native American Discourse: Rhetoric and Poetics 30.

Epps, P., Webster, A. K., & Woodbury, A. C. (2017). A holistic humanities of speaking: Franz Boas and the continuing centrality of texts 1. *International Journal of American Linguistics*, 83(1), 41–78.

Epps, P., Webster, A. K., & Woodbury, A. (2018). Documenting speech play and verbal art: A tutorial. In P. Jenks & L. Michaels (Eds.), *Language Documentation & Conservation: A volume of tutorials in documentary linguistics*, 12.

Evans, N. (2009). Two plus one makes thirteen: Senary numerals in the Morehead-Maro region. *Linguistic Typology*, 13(2), 321–335.

Fabb, N. (1997). *Linguistics and literature: Language in the verbal arts of the world*. London: Blackwell Wiley.

Feld, S. (2000). A sweet lullaby for world music. *Public Culture*, 12(1), 145–171.

Fitzgerald, C. (1998). The meter of Tohono O'odham songs. *International Journal of American Linguistics*, 64, 1–36. https://doi.org/DOI: 10.1086/466345

Gallagher, C., Brown, P., Curran, G., & Martin, B. (2014). *Jardiwanpa Yawulyu. Warlpiri women's songs from Yuendumu*. Darwin: Batchelor Press.

Green, J., & Turpin, M. (2013). If you go down to the soak today: Symbolism and structure in an Arandic children's story. *Anthropological Linguistics*, 55(4), 358–394.

Hayes, B. (1995). *Metrical stress theory*. Chicago, IL: University of Chicago Press.

Hayes, B. (2009). Textsetting as constraint conflict. In J.-L. Aroui & A. Arleo (Eds.), *Towards a typology of poetic forms: From language to metrics and beyond* (pp. 43–61). Amsterdam: John Benjamins.

Hayes, B., & Kaun, A. (1996). The role of phonological phrasing in sung and chanted verse. *Linguistic Review*, 13, 243–303.

Hymes, D. (2003). *Now I know only that far: Essays in ethnopoetics*. Lincoln, NE: University of Nebraska Press.

Ingram, C. (2013). Understanding musical participation: "Listening" participants and big song singers in Kam villages, southwestern China. In C. Ingram & I. Russell (Eds.), *Taking part in music: Case studies in ethnomusicology* (pp. 53–68). Aberdeen: Aberdeen University Press.

Jakobson, R. (1960). Closing statement: Linguistics and poetics. In T. A. Sebeok (Ed.), *Style in language* (pp. 350–377). Cambridge, MA: MIT Press.

Lane, C., & Carlyle, A. (2013). *In the field: The art of field recording*. London: Uniform Books.

Liberman, M., & Prince, A. (1977). On stress and linguistic rhythm. *Linguistics Inquiry*, 8, 249–336.

Marsh, K. (2008). *The musical playground: Global tradition and change in children's songs and games*. New York, NY: Oxford University Press.

Mitchell, B., & Webster, A. K. (2011). "We don't know what we become": Navajo ethnopoetics and an expressive feature in a poem by Rex Lee Jim. *Anthropological Linguistics*, 53(3), 259–286.

Morey, S. (2012). Documentation of traditional songs and ritual texts: Issues for archiving. In N. Thieberger, L. Barwick, R. Billington, & J. Vaughan (Eds.), *Sustainable data from digital research* (pp. 119–136). Melbourne: University of Melbourne.

Morey, S., & Schöpf, J. (2011). Tone in speech and singing: A field experiment to research their relation in endangered languages of north east India. *Language Documentation and Description*, 10, 37–60.

Perkins, R. (2016). Songs to live by. *The Monthly*, 124, 30–35.

Rumsey, A. (2011). Style, plot, and character in Tom Yaya Tales from Ku Waru. In A. Rumsey & D. Niles (Eds.), *Sung tales from the Papua New Guinea highlands studies in form, meaning, and sociocultural context*. Canberra: Australian National University ePress.

Russell, I., & Ingram, C. (2013). *Taking part in music: Case studies in ethnomusicology*. Aberdeen: Aberdeen University Press.

Seeger, A. (2004). New technology requires new collaborations: Changing ourselves to better shape the future. *Musicology Australia*, 27(1), 94–110.

Sharp, C. (1965). *English folk song: Some conclusions*. Belmont, CA: Wadsworth.

Sharp, C. (1973). *English folk songs from the Southern Appalachians*. London: Oxford University Press.

Turpin, M., & Henderson, L. (2015). Tools for analyzing verbal art in the field. *Language Documentation and Description*, 9, 89–109.

Turpin, M., & Stebbins, T. (2010). The language of song: Some recent approaches in description and analysis. *Australian Journal of Linguistics*, 30(1), 1–17.

Wasamba, P. (2015). *Contemporary oral literature fieldwork: A researcher's guide*. Nairobi: University of Nairobi Press.

Webster, A. K. (2017). "So it's got three meanings dil dil": Seductive ideophony and the sounds of Navajo poetry. *Canadian Journal of Linguistics*, 62(2), 173–195.

# 12

# A final word

Nicholas Evans, a linguist who has worked extensively with speakers of endangered languages in northern Australia and Papua New Guinea, describes the urgency and importance of the task of field linguists.

> (In) 2003, I attended the funeral of Charlie Wardaga, my teacher, friend, and classificatory elder brother … The book and volume of his brain had been the last to hold several languages of the region: Ilgar, which is the language of his own Mangalara clan, but also Garig, Manangkardi and Marrku … Although we had managed to transfer a small fraction of this knowledge into a more durable form before he died, as recordings and fieldnotes, our work had begun too late … For his children and other clan members, the loss of such a knowledgeable senior relative took away their last chance of learning their own language and the full tribal knowledge that it communicated…
> 
> (Evans, 2011, p. xvii)

Many of us who work in the field are familiar with these heart-wrenching stories, whether they concern our own families, or those of whom we have come to respect and admire in the processes of documenting other people's languages from an 'outsider', yet potentially honorary 'insider' perspective. We hope that this book equips all researchers with the necessary skills, and also a solid grounding in the ethical dimensions of following the fieldwork path, which at times can be a challenging track to pursue. We also hope that we have reflected some of the enthusiasm and excitement that can come from learning new languages, meeting new people and in the end making some contribution to counter the catastrophic loss of language diversity the world is facing. And maybe discovering new words, previously unattested phonological phenomena, grammatical structures and new signs for things along the way!

Across the globe there are many people wanting to learn and engage with their heritage languages in meaningful ways. What this loss of language diversity means to language communities is ultimately not for linguists to determine, but solid research practices and transferring research materials to "durable form" can mean that the doors are not shut before people who speak endangered languages have had a chance to form their own opinions and determine their own strategies for protecting their cultural heritage.

In spite of loss, the diversity of the world's languages is truly breath-taking. The case studies discussed in this textbook are just a sample of the many hundreds of projects currently underway across the globe. There is no shortage of projects yet to be undertaken, languages to document, and research questions to be answered about the uniquely human capacity for language. Capturing the breadth and complexity of the world's languages often means undertaking field research in remote regions and adopting the highest standards in data collection and curation. Although field research also takes place in urban settings, the aim of this book has been to ensure that students undertaking research on endangered languages in remote areas or in countries which have undergone European expansion are well prepared for the challenges of fieldwork in these complex settings.

This book has been designed to train prospective field linguists in methods to record, annotate and archive quality linguistic data in an ethical and responsible manner. This data is crucial for the development of audio-visual language corpora which form the basis of many outputs standard to documentation projects, such as grammars, dictionaries and text collections, as well as being a crucial contribution to community efforts to maintain or revive their languages. They consist of examples of language-in-use across a range of communicative contexts and genres, including narratives, elicitation sequences, procedural texts and conversation.

As well as corpus development, different subfields of linguistics, e.g. phonology, morpho-syntax and semantics, all require different types of data for answering research questions specific to these subfields. We discuss specific elicitation techniques including (semi-)experimental tasks that are required to delve deeper into these subfields, and the equipment set-ups and annotation standards required to elicit this data. Other subfields require even more specialised methods and ethical considerations, for example gesture and sign language, language acquisition, contact languages and the verbal arts. Suggestions for how to get started in designing field projects are detailed in these chapters, and in doing so, this textbook takes the students beyond the fundamentals of documentation and into more sophisticated tools and methods for these advanced topics.

We have presented a broad view of language which extends beyond speech into the multimodal, performative and aesthetic dimensions of communication. We have encouraged students to adopt a community-orientated approach which aims to build collaborative language teams. In addition to the more standard linguistic methods, we hope to have encouraged students to reach out to other disciplines – anthropology, musicology, history and scientific subfields such as biology – to provide depth to their documentation projects. Of course not all of this can be achieved in the short time-span of a PhD or small documentation grant, but we hope to have inspired students to imagine their practice as field linguists as involving long-term collaborative relationships with speech communities. For the fieldworker who does not aspire to a long-term relationship with a given speech community, we press upon you the importance of making your research data accessible through appropriate archiving and by working towards community publications as part of your responsibilities to the communities you work with and for.

Like the resilient shoots of the bush potato, a plant that thrives on disturbed ground and engenders new plants that flourish on the surface, working on endangered languages provides an opportunity for renewal that can be immensely rewarding both for the people you work with and for you, the field linguist.

## REFERENCE

Evans, N. (2011). *Dying words: Endangered languages and what they have to tell us*. Malden, MA: John Wiley & Sons.

# Appendices

# Appendix 1: Map of major languages referred to in this book

**Map 1**
Map of locations of major languages referred to in this book (Map: Brenda Thornley)

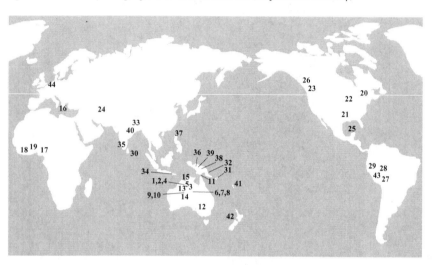

1. Gurindji (Australia)
2. Bilinarra (Australia)
3. Jingulu (Australia)
4. Gurindji Kriol (Australia)
5. Kriol (Australia)
6. Alyawarr (Australia)
7. Kaytetye (Australia)
8. Anmatyerr (Australia)
9. Light Warlpiri (Australia)
10. Warlpiri (Australia)
11. Kalaw Kawaw Ya (Australia)
12. Auslan (Australia)
13. Central Australian alternate sign languages
14. Ngaatjatjarra (Australia)
15. Murrinhpatha (Australia)
16. Thrace Romani (Greece)
17. Ikaan (Nigeria)
18. Adamorobe Sign Language (AdaSL) (Ghana)
19. Avatime (Ghana)
20. Mohawk (Quebec, Canada)
21. Choctaw (Mississippi/Oklahoma, US)
22. Lakota (North and South Dakota, US)
23. Tlingit (British Columbia, Canada)
24. Archi (Dagestan)
25. Yucatec Maya Sign Language (YMSL) (Mexico)
26. Koyukon (Alaska, US)
27. Jarawara (Brazil)
28. Tariana (Brazil)
29. Shiwiar (Ecuador)
30. Tamil (Sri Lanka)
31. Yélî Dnye (Rossel Island, PNG)
32. Nen (Western Province, PNG)
33. Mueshaungx (Tibet)
34. Kata Kolok Sign Language (Bali, Indonesia)
35. Indian Sign Language (ISL)
36. Awiakay (East Sepik Province, PNG)
37. Bikol, (Southern Luzon, Philippines)
38. Kalam (Madang Province, PNG)
39. Kaluli (Southern Highlands Province, PNG)
40. Chintang (Eastern Nepal)
41. Bislama (Vanuatu)
42. New Zealand Sign Language (NZSL)
43. Iquito (Peru)
44. Sign Language of the Netherlands (NGT)

# Appendix 2: Answers to exercises

**Chapter 1** Introduction

Exercise 1 Discuss why you think the following are or aren't examples of fieldwork?

- You speak an undescribed, endangered language. You are writing a grammar of your language and you decide which sentences are grammatical and ungrammatical yourself.

*This is not fieldwork because it doesn't involve engaging with a speech community.*

- You are working with a refugee group in the city where you live, documenting their language.

*This is urban fieldwork. You need to be aware that there might be contact influences between the refugee language and the language of the city. Try to work with first generation refugees, not their children (unless it is a contact language study). You also need to make sure that you gather previously published works on the language (family) to help understand the dynamics of the language in the new language ecology.*

- You and some other students are a field methods class at your university working with a speaker of a small language spoken elsewhere in your country.

*This is not fieldwork. It is examining a language in isolation from its speech community and context of usage. Nonetheless it is a good way of practising methodologies and honing your skills before hitting the reality of fieldwork (i.e. multiple speakers, messy data, ethical concerns, noisy recording environments with bad light etc.). You also have the teacher mediating between yourself (the student) and the language speaker. Many tasks that the fieldworker would have to do themselves in the field have also been undertaken by the teacher (e.g. choice of language, structure of fieldwork sessions, payments and logistics involving the language speaker).*

- You work on your own language in the field which you call home.

*This is fieldwork because it involves documenting a language in its community of users. It may feel odd for you and somewhat clinical to call this fieldwork, however.*

- You live in Kuala Lumpur and record yourself outside pronouncing words to figure out the vowel space of your English variety and are infected with malaria in the process.

*Just because you contract an exotic tropical disease doesn't mean you are conducting fieldwork!*

- You are a phonetician and accompany another linguist to the field and spend a week making enough recordings for your thesis.

*This is considered fieldwork because it is recording language in its speech community. Bear in mind though that you may not gain much knowledge of the language and its community in such a short trip and follow the more seasoned field linguist's lead in the field in terms of behaviour and protocols.*

- You hear that speakers of an endangered language from western China are visiting the anthropology department and you conduct a number of psycholinguistic tasks in the lab while they are there.

*This is not typical fieldwork because it is recording language outside the place where it is spoken on a day-to-day basis; and because you are working and living in your usual location. It would also be unlikely that approval for such work could be organised in a short time, which is not to say that such work might not be valuable.*

### Exercise 2 Being conscience of your presence

It is well known in ethnography that your presence changes the way people behave. This is called the 'observer's paradox'. Imagine you work in a community where only the oldest people speak the language under study and most of the community has shifted to the regionally dominant language which you also speak. How might people change the way they speak in your presence. How can you minimise the influence of your presence?

*If you are a speaker of a regionally dominant language, such as English, and you are only just beginning to learn the local language, community members might adjust their own language to accommodate to you. For example they may code-switch into English or calque their semantics or grammatical structures on English expressions or grammatical patterns. You can minimise this influence by engaging local assistants, training them in research methods and how to use recording equipment. You can also try taking a back-seat role in elicitation sessions.*

### Exercise 3 Who is a speaker?

You work in a Stage 8 community where children are no longer learning the language and it is only spoken by older generations. What types of speakers will you encounter in terms of their spoken, comprehension and literacy skills in the heritage language and the regionally dominant language? How do you put together a language team to document the language?

*The children may be speakers of the regionally dominant language which you speak. They will probably be learning literacy in this language. Their parents will have a similar skill set, but may also understand or speak a little of their heritage language. They will make excellent members of a local research team, for example helping with transcription and translation, and also interpreting. The grandparents will form the core of the team as speakers of the language. It is quite possible that they do not speak the regionally dominant language and will be unlikely to be literate in either language. This combination of language skills across the generations will form a solid team for documenting the language.*

**Chapter 2** Planning for fieldwork

Exercise 1  Your motivations for undertaking fieldwork

Discuss whether you see yourself doing linguistic fieldwork. What would your motivations for undertaking fieldwork be (e.g. do you speak an under-described language, do you have a burning theoretical question)? What sort of field linguist would you be? What skills do you already have and which skills would you want to develop further?

*Some motivations for undertaking fieldwork include a desire to learn your heritage language, to get a deeper understanding of the structures of your language, to experience the world through another language, to help empower a minority group, or to test a particular linguistic theory. You might like to have a long-term relationship with a community and get to know their language well; or you may prefer to work in a community for just a short time to answer specific linguistic questions and then go to another community. You may enjoy being in unfamiliar settings and enjoy intellectual challenges. Some good skills to have in the field include patience, humour and perseverance.*

Exercise 2  How should your work be credited?

- You are a younger speaker of a language who has teamed up with your linguist to write dictionary definitions based on recordings you have both made with older speakers. The linguist names you as a co-author but the local council says that community elders are the 'holders' of the language and therefore should be the authors. What should you do?

*One solution would be to do as the council instructs (which may be to put everyone down as an author, or no-one) and state in the front matter of the dictionary the different contributions people made. For example 'dictionary definitions provided by [older fluent speaker]', 'dictionary definitions written by [younger literate person]', 'dictionary compiled by [linguist]', 'biological information provided by [collaborating scientist]'. By clearly delineating roles, you can often include all contributions.*

- You enjoy organising people but are less interested in actual linguistic analysis. You have assisted your linguist in arranging for 50 people to participate in a study on morpho-syntactic variation. You have interpreted the information sheets, arranged for consent forms to be signed, and conducted the tasks. You haven't participated in the analysis or write-up. Should you be an author or acknowledged in a footnote?

*It might be appropriate to attribute authorship to the logistical organiser. For example, if the study involved experimental tasks, it is common to have many co-authors and list everyone who was involved in the work. You can also explain the exact contributions in a footnote. This is something to negotiate of course. In the end, you might not agree with the interpretation of the findings and want your contribution acknowledged, but not to be named as an author.*

## Chapter 3  Equipment and recording

### Exercise 1  What microphone for what purpose?

The location for recording a two-person conversation is going to be a tin shed. This is less than ideal as the sound bounces off the tin, making it difficult to hear. The tin can also interfere with radio microphones. What microphones and sound absorption methods could you use? Where would be the ideal place for the language speakers to sit and microphones to be placed?

*It would be best to use wired microphones to reduce the risk of interference. The consultants would ideally sit with their backs to a corner of the shed and the microphone facing them, in to the corner. Blankets or other material padding could be placed on the walls behind the speakers to absorb sound. This will cushion the effect of sound waves bouncing off the tin shed.*

### Exercise 2  Light in your recording

The recording shown in Figure 3.3 took place in early morning light. What direction is the narrator facing? What is the benefit of early morning light for this type of recording?

*We know that the narrator is facing south because his shadow is being cast westwards by the sun rising in the east. This early morning light means that a shadow isn't being cast on the narrator's face, which happens when the sun is higher. He also doesn't have his back to the sun which would cause back lighting with the effect of darkening his face on the film recording. In addition, the space in front of the narrator where he will draw will not be over-shadowed. Facing directly into the sun can be uncomfortable for speakers, so early morning or late afternoon light is best.*

### Exercise 3  Peak clipping in video

What do you think the visual equivalent of clipping an audio signal is? How would you set up a camera to avoid this?

*Clipping occurs in video when parts of the action cannot be seen on film because of poor framing techniques. In gesture and sign language research this might occur if an action involves a large sign or gesture space. To avoid this, have the participant extend their arms and adjust the video framing before you start recording. Clipping also happens if you are making recordings about procedural activities and the speaker reaches out of the frame for a crucial ingredient, object etc. To avoid this, you might be able to ask the person to explain what they are planning before commencing the recording to give you an idea of what is important in the context. If a close-up of the speaker is important, use two cameras, one as a close-up and another as a long shot,*

Appendix 2: Answers to exercises 295

which captures the context. Another common context where clipping of video images occurs is in child language research where children walk in and out of the frame. This is inevitable, so just make sure the child is wearing a radio microphone so that at least their utterances are captured with consistent levels of audio.

**Chapter 4** Data management, annotation and archiving

Exercise 1 Deciphering metadata

Look at the image of an old analogue tape in Figure 4.1. What metadata can you extract from what you can see? What other questions would you like to ask about this recording? What could go wrong if the label falls off?

*Things you can tell from the label:*

- *The recording was made on 27/11/97 (although this might be an assumption!).*
- *Someone called Myf, who may also be MT, was involved in the recording. Perhaps they were the transcriber, as indicated by the abbreviation 'tr'.*
- *The recording was made at a place called Barrow Creek.*
- *The tape label or identity (equivalent of recording name) is IAD No 763.*
- *The tape has a sticker on it labelling it MASTER – this probably means that it is the original recording and not a copy.*

*Questions you might have about the recording:*

- *Who, what or where is Thangkenharenge?*
- *What does the second date (23/5/02) on the tape refer to?*
- *What does "megafiles 'K'" refer to?*
- *What has been crossed out?*
- *Is there any catalogue that answers these questions and has it been archived?*

*If the label falls off the tape, it still might be the case that some metadata was recorded on the tape itself. If this isn't the case, it's a disaster and it would be very hard to know who the speakers and linguist are (if MT in fact refers to a person) and what the language on the tape is.*

Exercise 2 Making a corpus accessible to the speech community

You work in a community which does not have electricity or access to the internet. The community wants to make use of your work in the school. How do you ensure that a corpus is useful in a community that does not have access to the online corpus?

*After the first field trip, you will have produced a lot of transcriptions and recordings. Before you return to the community for another trip, print out as much as you can. If you have time, format the transcripts in a readable manner e.g. paragraph chunks of language text followed by a translation (or whatever is appropriate in the community). Think about being even more creative! In the first field trip, play the recordings back to the school children or community artists so they can draw pictures to accompany the story. They will feel more connection to the produced book and it will be more likely to be used as a result. Again, before you return to the community, turn the pictures and texts into nicely formatted story books (easily done in Word or PowerPoint). Make sure you laminate the pages and bind them with wire (not plastic) so they survive weather and enthusiastic small children. Make class sets, not just individual copies of books. Do not just print out ELAN or CLAN files as the formats are not useful or aesthetically compelling to non-technical users. Put the recordings onto portable MP3 players and bring plenty of spare batteries (or rechargeable batteries and a solar set up which you can leave at the school).*

## Chapter 5 Phonetics and phonology

### Exercise 1 Word elicitation

After dividing up the Swadesh wordlist and eliciting words from a speaker of a different language, you may have found that for some words the speaker had to think hard for an equivalent in their language. Some reasons for this might be because the word in the elicitation language has multiple different senses (cf. 'fly' which is both a noun and verb in English), or the word is not very common in either of the languages, or that the concept itself does not translate easily between the languages.

### Exercise 2 Minimal pairs that do the most work

The data shows four lots of minimal pairs. The first pair *gadaj* and *gardaj* are the best minimal pair as they are both of the same part of speech (verbs).

| 1 | gadaj | coverb | 'cut' |
|---|---|---|---|
|   | gardaj | coverb | 'strangle' |
| 2 | garu | noun | 'child' |
|   | garru | verb | 'will' |
| 3 | bad | coverb | 'feel about' |
|   | dad | noun | 'on top' |
| 4 | ngaja | conjunction | 'admonitive' |
|   | ngaba | noun | 'big brother' |

### Exercise 3 Stops exercise

1.

| p | b | t | d | ʈ | ɽ | k | g |
|---|---|---|---|---|---|---|---|
| ['paɽaɽa] 3 | ['kɛbi] 1 | ['tubu] 6 | [ndi] 5 | ['tæːʈi] 4 | ['paɽaɽa] 3 | [kaː] 7 | ['ŋgaːŋgaː] 2 |
| [po] 12 | ['tubu] 6 | [tiː] 13 | [ndɛː] 29 | [tɛː] 11 | [tæːʈi] 4 | [kĩː] 10 | [ŋgaː] 9 |
| [pɔɽu] 14 | ['mbala] 8 | ['tiɽə] 19 | | [tɔ̃ː] 18 | ['pɔɽu] 14 | [kéʈikaː] 16 | ['kugu] 27 |
| ['pəbə] 23 | [mbu] 15 | [taː] 22 | | [taː] 25 | [kéʈikaː] 16 | [kaː] 21 | ['ŋgəŋgə] 28 |
| ['pəːɽɯ] 24 | ['neːbi] 20 | ['taːgɯ] 32 | | ['tæːtɯː] 17 | ['tiɽə] 19 | ['kugu] 27 | ['ŋgɛːɽɛ] 30 |
| ['pibi] 26 | ['pibi] 26 | | | | ['pəːɽɯ] 24 | | ['taːgɯ] 32 |
| ['pæːpæː] 31 | ['pəbə] 23 | | | | | | |

*Appendix 2: Answers to exercises*

2.

| p | b | t | d | ʈ | ɽ | k | g |
|---|---|---|---|---|---|---|---|
| #__a 3 | ɛ__i 1 | #__u 6 | n__i 5 | #__æː 4 | a__a 3 | #__aː 7 | ŋ__a: 2, 9 |
| #__o 12 | u__u 6 | #__iː 13 | n__ɛ: 29 | #__ɛː 11 | æː__i 4 | #__ɪ̃: 10 | u__u 27 |
| #__ɔ 14 | m__a 8 | #__i 19 |  | #__ɔ̃: 18 | ɔ__u 14 | #__é_ 16 | ŋ__ə 28 |
| #__ə 23 | m__u 15 | #__ɑ: 22, 32 |  | #__a: 25 | é__i 16 | i__a: 16 | ŋ__ɛ: 30 |
| #__ə: 24 | e:__i 20 |  |  | #__æː 17 | i__ə 19 | #__a: 21 | a:__ɯ 32 |
| #__i 26 | i__i 26 |  |  | æː__ɯ: 17 | ɔː__ɯ 24 | #__u 27 |  |
| æː__æː 31 | ə__ə 23 |  |  |  | ɛː__ɛ 30 |  |  |

3. The data shows the following complementary distribution:

[p] /#__         [t] /#__,        [ʈ] /#__         [k] /#__
    V__V:            V__V:            V__V:            V__V:
[b] /N__, /      [d] /N__,        [ɽ] /V__V(short) [g] / N__,
    V__V(short)                                       /V__V(short)

a) The non-retroflex voiceless stops [p, t, k] are in complementary distribution with their voiced counterparts [b, d, g].
b) The voiceless retroflex stop [ʈ] is in complementary distribution to the retroflex tap [ɽ].

4. Allophony Rules:

   1. Post-nasal voicing rule: Stops (/p/, /t/, and /k/) are voiced following a nasal.
   2. Intervocalic voicing rule: Peripheral stops (/p/ and /k/) become voiced intervocalically when preceding a short vowel.
   3. Intervocalic tap rule: /ʈ/ -> /ɽ/ when preceding a short vowel.

5. The unvoiced stop series can be regarded as the phoneme because it is a condition that holds for all stops words initially and following a long vowel. Furthermore, voicing following a nasal is phonetically motivated. The voiced stop only occurs preceding a short vowel.

## Exercise 4  Voiceless stops in English

An example of target words that can be used to determine the following conditions for aspiration:

   1. stress / unstressed e.g. key / lucky; pee / hippy; decant / descant; open / oppose
   2. simple / complex onset e.g.: Pam / spam, pin / spin, til / still, pill / spill, kill / skill; can / scan; pan / span

*Appendix 2: Answers to exercises*

3. intervening glide or liquid between stop and vowel, e.g. pop vs plop, prop; coop, cub vs cube; test, taste vs twist
4. complex coda e.g. cold / scold; tilt / stilt.

Exercise 5  Dealing with multiple spelling systems.

1. Chart the different letters for each word as follows:

| word | EM | NM | NS | Difference |
|---|---|---|---|---|
| 1 | al<u>d</u>ola | al<u>t</u>urla | al<u>t</u>urle | d (EM), t (N)* |
|  | ald<u>o</u>la | alt<u>u</u>rla | alt<u>u</u>rle | o (EM), u (N) |
|  | aldo<u>l</u>a | altur<u>l</u>a | altur<u>l</u>e | l (EM), rl (N) |
|  | aldol<u>a</u> | alturl<u>a</u> | alturl<u>e</u> | e# (NS), a# (M) |
| 2 | <u>J</u>abalpa | <u>Y</u>aparlpa | <u>Y</u>aperlpe | #j (EM), #y (N) |
|  | Ja<u>b</u>alpa | Ya<u>p</u>arlpa | Ya<u>p</u>erlpe | b (EM), p (N) |
|  | Jab<u>a</u>lpa | Yap<u>a</u>rlpa | Yap<u>e</u>rlpe | e (NS), a (M) [second syllable] |
|  | Jaba<u>l</u>pa | Ypa<u>rl</u>pa | Yape<u>rl</u>pe | l (EM), rl (N) |
|  | Jabalp<u>a</u> | Yaparlp<u>a</u> | Yaperlp<u>e</u> | e# (NS), a# (M) |
| 3 | kw<u>a</u>ra | kw<u>aa</u>rra | kw<u>a</u>rre | aa (NM), a (EM, NS) [first syllable] |
|  | kwa<u>r</u>a | kwaa<u>rr</u>a | kwa<u>rr</u>e | r (EM), rr (N) |
|  | kwar<u>a</u> | kwaarr<u>a</u> | kwarr<u>e</u> | e# (NS), a# (M) |
| 4 | kw<u>a</u>ta | kw<u>aa</u>rta | kw<u>a</u>rte | aa (NM), a (EM, NS) [first syllable] |
|  | kwa<u>t</u>a | kwaa<u>rt</u>a | kwa<u>rt</u>e | t (EM), rt (N) |
|  | kwat<u>a</u> | kwaart<u>a</u> | kwart<u>e</u> | e# (NS), a# (M) |
| 5 | k<u>n</u>ulja | k<u>ng</u>ulya | k<u>ng</u>welye | n (EM), ng (N) |
|  | kn<u>u</u>lja | kn<u>gu</u>lya | kn<u>gwe</u>lye | we (NS), u (M) [between consonants] |
|  | knul<u>j</u>a | kngul<u>y</u>a | kngwel<u>y</u>e | j (EM), y (N) |
|  | knulj<u>a</u> | kngulyf<u>a</u> | kngwely<u>e</u> | e# (NS), a# (M) |
| 6 | ma<u>n</u>kama | m<u>aa</u>ngkama | m<u>a</u>ngkeme | aa (NM), a (EM, NS) [first syllable] |
|  | ma<u>n</u>kama | maa<u>ng</u>kama | ma<u>ng</u>keme | n (EM), ng (N) |
|  | mank<u>a</u>ma | maangk<u>a</u>ma | mangk<u>e</u>me | e (NS), a (M) [second syllable] |
|  | mankam<u>a</u> | maangkam<u>a</u> | mangkem<u>e</u> | e# (NS), a# (M) |

* We use (N) as shorthand for New Missionary and New Secular orthographies; and (M) for Early Missionary and New Missionary orthographies

*Appendix 2: Answers to exercises* 299

2. Compare the orthographies and make a numbered list of (a) the differences in consonants (b) the differences in vowels.

| (a) Consonants | EM | NM | NS | word |
|---|---|---|---|---|
| d (EM), t (N) | al<u>d</u>ola | al<u>t</u>urla | al<u>t</u>urle | 1 |
| t (EM), rt (N) | kwa<u>t</u>a | kwaa<u>rt</u>a | kwa<u>rt</u>e | 4 |
| b (EM), p (N) | Ja<u>b</u>alpa | Ya<u>p</u>arlpa | Ya<u>p</u>erlpe | 2 |
| n (EM), ng (N) [C_] | k<u>n</u>ulja | k<u>ng</u>ulya | k<u>ng</u>welye | 5 |
| "   [_C] | ma<u>n</u>kama | maa<u>ng</u>kama | ma<u>ng</u>keme | 6 |
| l (EM), rl (N) [_C] | Jaba<u>l</u>pa | Ypa<u>rl</u>pa | Ype<u>rl</u>pe | 2 |
| " | aldo<u>l</u>a | altu<u>rl</u>a | altu<u>rl</u>e | 1 |
| r (EM), rr (N) | kwa<u>r</u>a | kwaa<u>rr</u>a | kwa<u>rr</u>e | 3 |
| j (EM), y (N) [C_] | knul<u>j</u>a | kngul<u>y</u>a | kngwel<u>y</u>e | 5 |
| [#_] | <u>J</u>abalpa | <u>Y</u>aparlpa | <u>Y</u>aperlpe | 2 |

| (b) Vowels | EM | NM | NS | word |
|---|---|---|---|---|
| aa (NM), a (EM, NS) [1st syllable] | kw<u>a</u>ra | kw<u>aa</u>rra | kw<u>a</u>rre | 3 |
| " | kw<u>a</u>ta | kw<u>aa</u>rta | kw<u>a</u>rte | 4 |
| " | m<u>a</u>nkama | m<u>aa</u>ngkama | m<u>a</u>ngkeme | 6 |
| e (NS), a (M) [2nd syllable] | Jab<u>a</u>lpa | Yap<u>a</u>rlpa | Yap<u>e</u>rlpe | 2 |
| " | mank<u>a</u>ma | maangk<u>a</u>ma | mangk<u>e</u>me | 6 |
| e# (NS), a# (M) (all six words) | aldol<u>a</u> | alturl<u>a</u> | alturl<u>e</u> | 1 |
| o (EM), u (N) | ald<u>o</u>la | alt<u>u</u>rla | alt<u>u</u>rle | 1 |
| we (NS), u (M) | kn<u>u</u>lja | kn<u>gu</u>lya | kn<u>gwe</u>lye | 5 |

3. What are the differences between the orthographies, considering first (a) consonants and then (b) vowels. Suggest reasons for these differences, including whether some pairs of letters might be digraphs.

   (a) Consonants

   (i) The EM orthography uses voiced and unvoiced stops (d, t, b, p) where N write only unvoiced (t, p). In EM, the voiced counterpart (d, b) only occurs following 'l' and thus d/t and p/b may reflect allophonic variation. The latter orthographies may have taken this allophony into account by using the unvoiced consonant throughout.

   (ii) The EM orthography writes 't' and 'l' where (N) writes 'rt' and 'rl'. These may be digraphs for retroflex consonants. EM may not have

recognised a retroflex / alveolar contrast that the New orthographies make (cf. the two 'l' and 'rl' in 1. 'west').
- (iii) The EM orthography writes 'n' where (N) writes 'ng'. 'Ng' may be a digraph for a velar nasal.
- (iv) The EM orthography writes 'r' where (N) writes 'rr'. 'Rr' may be a digraph for a tap or trill.
- (v) The EM orthography writes 'j' where (N) writes 'y'. This may reflect different orthographies of the source languages: 'j' in German orthography (which the Early missionaries spoke) and 'y' in English orthography (N) are a palatal glide.

(b) Vowels
- (i) The NM orthography writes 'aa' where EM and NS write 'a'. This only occurs in the first CV position of a word (word 3, 4 and 6), but it does not occur in 2. 'Glen Helen'. This may be because 'a' is preceded by a semivowel, 'y'.
- (ii) The NS writes 'e' where (M) write 'a'. This only occurs in the second CV position of a word (words 2 and 6).
- (iii) The NS writes 'e' where (M) write 'a' word-finally. That all words end this way suggests that the final vowel is not phonemic.
- (iv) The EM writes 'o' where (N) write 'u' (word 1). This occurs in the first CV position of a word.
- (v) The NS writes 'we' (possibly a digraph) where (M) write 'u' (word 5). This occurs in the first CV position of a word. This difference, and that involving 'o' just discussed, suggest that EM and NS distinguish two vowel [phonemes ('o' / 'u' and 'we' / 'u' respectively) while NM uses only one vowel, 'u'.

4. All speakers feel strongly that the orthography they use is the best one. What would you do if you were asked to print a dictionary of the language? Would you use three spelling systems, select one, or print three different dictionaries? Discuss the reasons for your answer. Can you think of a digital solution to this dilemma?

*Three orthographies in the one dictionary would be more practical and cheaper to print than three separate dictionaries. Digital delivery of this lexicon could be set up to enable the user to select their preferred orthography.*

## Chapter 6 Morpho-syntax

Exercise 1 Recording stories as a 'newbie' to the community

Imagine you only have a few more days in a speech community before you have to head home. You have only been able to perform formal elicitation with the speakers. You plan to return but the speakers are elderly and you are worried that the elicitation you have done is not very dynamic. There is also a chance that your recordings may be the final record of the language. How do you create situations where speakers will tell stories?

*You need to find out what is really important to the community and make a concerted effort to record them e.g. sacred texts, historical narratives or procedural descriptions of endangered cultural practices. Speakers might require the right combination of people to be present for recordings, so take direction from them about who to gather together. Often this process requires more time and effort than the standard dyadic set-up (linguist-speaker) but the depth of cultural knowledge and complexity of language will increase markedly. If cultural practices are the focus, again help gather the right people, tools, ingredients etc. (and include this as a part of the documentation process – videos like these are useful to playback and elicit voice overs for). This process might involve enlisting younger, more able-bodied people who can assist the elderly speakers in the activity. Have them instruct the younger ones in the procedure, and make sure you record the entire process.*

### Exercise 2  Elicitation versus conversation

What is the best data to get a grasp of:

- Grammatical relations i.e. subjects and objects?

*Elicitation data. You can elicit clauses by manipulating agents and patients (using translation equivalents or act out sequences), and semantic properties such as the animacy and number of agents and patients.*

- Number marking in pronouns?

*Again elicitation data for the above reasons.*

- Focus markers?

*You will not get a great sense of the function of focus marking from clause-level elicitation (except perhaps question-answer sequences which will help with some aspects of focus). For anything discourse-related, you need extended sequences of narratives and conversation.*

- The anaphoric use of pronouns or demonstratives?

*Mostly conversation data is useful for exploring this area of grammar. But you can prompt speakers on particular topics to target these constructions e.g. for demonstratives, have the speaker sit outside and describe how the community has changed over the years e.g. new buildings, areas which have been cleared for gardens etc. If you are interested in gesture, or have a colleague who is, and speakers consent, turn the video camera on.*

- An inverse system where inanimates > animates?

*Definitely elicitation data is required for this area of grammar. Make up transitive sentences which involve (i) inanimates acting on animates e.g. coconuts dropping on someone's head*, or (ii) animates acting on inanimates e.g. *a man eating a coconut*, or equipollent examples i.e. animate > animate, inanimate > inanimate. Remember that it might be humanness or sentience that is the relevant category so vary the actors you use in elicitation. Try to avoid examples relating to violence, remembering that this is a lasting record of the language.

- Variation in the use of a case-marker?

*Generally conversation data. Variation in subject marking (e.g. optional ergativity) usually has a discourse component and probabilistic rather than categorical statements about use in the grammar will be most appropriate. Variation in object marking (e.g. differential object marking) is often related to definiteness or perfectivity and is also often more categorical so you might have more luck with formal elicitation.*

### Exercise 3  Discovering more categories through elicitation

Thinking about (1), how would you continue the elicitation sequence to see if (i) verbs inflect for number with first and second person pronouns, and if (ii) nouns inflect for grammatical relations (subjects and objects)? Give some examples of sentences you would use.

(i) *Try the following sequence and see of the form of the verb changes:*

- I hug them.           (I=subj+**1sg**, hug=transitive+present tense, them=obj+3pl)
- We hug them.          (I=subj+**1pl**, hug=transitive+present tense, them=obj+3pl)
- You hug them.         (you=subj+**2sg**, hug=transitive+present tense, them=obj+3pl)
- Youse/y'all hug them. (you=subj+**2pl**, hug=transitive+present tense, them=obj+3pl)
- They hug me.          (they=subj+3pl, hug=transitive+present tense, me=obj+**1sg**)
- They hug us.          (they=subj+3pl, hug=transitive+present tense, me=obj+**1pl**)
- They hug you.         (they=subj+3pl, hug=transitive+present tense, me=obj+**2sg**)
- They hug youse/y'all. (they=subj+3pl, hug=transitive+present tense, me=obj+**2pl**).

(ii) *Try the following sequence and see of the form of the noun changes:*

- The girl gave the child to the boy.   (A=girl, DO=child, IO=boy)
- The boy gave the girl to the child.   (A=boy, DO=girl, IO=child)
- The child gave the boy to the girl.   (A=child, DO=boy, IO=girl)
- The child gave the girl to the boy.   (A=child, DO=girl, IO=boy).

## Exercise 4  If English were ergative?

If English pronouns patterned in an **ergative** configuration, which pronouns would be the same and which would be different if speakers were to say these sentences:

(1) HE is dreaming.
(2) HIM is carrying HE.

OR

(3) HIM is dreaming.
(4) HE is carrying HIM.

## Exercise 5  Cardinal directions in the field

You have just discovered that cardinal directions are used prolifically in the language you are eliciting. A speaker wants to tell you a story about the places they hunt for game. What sorts of equipment should you use? What are some things you should take into consideration when you are setting up?

*You should use a video camera to capture any important contextual cues and accompanying gestures. Use a compass and try to orientate the speaker along an axis (north-south or east-west) as much as possible without interfering with the story because it helps in analysis later. You might also take a map, or use a stills camera to make a photograph of any maps created during the session. For example some people might make sketch maps on the ground, and these can be an important component of the utterance.*

## Exercise 6  Eliciting evidentiality

What are the kinds of scenarios you would construct with speakers to figure out how evidentiality is encoded in the language? What sorts of sentences would you use?

- *I saw the dog bite Mary on the leg.*          *(direct evidence)*
- *I heard the dog bite Mary on the leg.*        *(auditory evidence, inferential)*
- *Someone told me that the dog bit Mary on the leg.*   *(second hand information)*
- *I see a wound on Mary's leg, a dog bit her.*  *(visual evidence, inferential)*

## Exercise 7  Linguistic terminology in learners' guides

Below are some examples of terms you might use instead of linguistic jargon. They are based on their major function in the language. A good place to look for layperson's descriptions of glosses is on the SIL Glossary of Linguistic Terms website (www.glossary.sil.org Accessed 31 August 2017):

## 304  Appendix 2: Answers to exercises

| Linguistic term | Potential layperson's term | Potential layperson's gloss |
|---|---|---|
| Ergative | Agent | agent |
| Allative | Goal | to |
| 1st person unit augmented pronoun | Us two (+ one more) | us3 |
| Past tense | Before | before |
| Proprietive | Having | having |
| Dual | Two | two |
| Inchoative | Become | become |
| Visual evidential | Saw | saw |

## Chapter 7  Semantic fieldwork and lexicography

Exercise 1  What is a leg?

Choose five dictionaries of diverse languages and compare their terminology for 'leg' and its different parts.

*Compare the definitions and discuss the differences. Does the definition of 'leg' include the whole leg minus the foot (as in English), or the lower leg + foot, or the upper leg only? Discuss how you might have elicited these different meanings in the field. For example, you might get the speaker to point to the parts of the lower limb included in their definition of 'leg'. You might also give speakers an outline of a body and get them to colour in different parts of the body and label them.*

Exercise 2  Stargazing in Alaska

Consider the names for the constellation *Ursa major* in the Alaskan languages.

- In the field, how would you check that the Alaskan term does refer to this constellation and not some other?

*You might ask consultants to draw the images they see or use a star chart or star wheel, which enables you to set the night sky for the particular time of year and for a particular place.*

- How would you investigate the basis for the names, that is, the basis for the polysemy?

*Some areas to explore in working out the basis for the polysemy might be whether the timing of this star signals a time of year or that certain plants or animals are available. Does the pattern of the stars look like something (as in astrology)? Is there a creation story about the caribou, or sea-otter etc. that the stars remind people of?*

- What information would you put in the dictionaries for this entry?

*As well as the literal meaning of the constellation names, you might include the context that gives rise to the polysemy. Be aware though that some sorts of mythological knowledge are restricted in some cultures, and so you should always check before making this knowledge publicly available.*

### Exercise 3  Odd one out (or in!)

You have developed a stimulus set of plant pictures to get an understanding of ethnobotanical categorisation in the language you are working on. Participants have been asked to group 'like' pictures together. Some people comment that some plants are "strangers" and others are "real". What kind of distinction could these words be referring to?

*The distinction might refer to an endemic vs a non-local species; or prototypical vs peripheral members (e.g. birds that don't fly); or a common vs a rare member of a category.*

### Exercise 4  How many meanings?

Below are three meanings of the one phonological form in Kaytetye. How would you go about working out whether the words are homonyms, whether there is one or more polysemous words or one word with a broad monosemous meaning?

**ampwernarrenke** *v.i.*

1. (of honey) to go hard and lumpy, due to cold weather
2. to be scared, shy or frightened
3. to shiver from cold.

*Explore the semantics of arguments that the verb can take (e.g. people, animates, inanimates). With an animate subject, can a clause have two different meanings? For example, "The boy is shy" or "The boy is cold"? If so, this suggests two related meanings or monosemy. What happens when you combine different subjects, e.g. "The honey and people shivered/went hard". Is there a zeugma effect? If so, this suggests there are two different meanings. (Zeugma is where a word applies to multiple words in the sentence but with a different meaning, e.g. "You are free to <u>execute</u> your <u>laws</u>, and your <u>citizens</u>, as you see fit".)*

### Exercise 5  What folk definitions reveal about a culture

What do you think this very precise way of describing the way to lie down might show about Warlpiri cultural practices? Can you write a folk definition about something special from your own culture?

*The definition suggests that spatial relations using cardinal directions is important in Warlpiri culture and communicative practices. This is what is referred to as an absolute frame of reference, and the definition shows that even descriptions of small-scale* actions (such as lying down) can utilise this frame. The definition also suggests that there may be particular cultural practices associated with domestic spaces, for example sleeping with one's head to the east. Compare your own folk definitions. In your language would you say something like, "Move the computer cursor a little to the north?" or would you use terms like 'left', and 'right' instead?

Exercise 6  Reverse engineering the Nafaanra to English Dictionary

Below are three entries in the SIL *Nafaanra to English Dictionary*, a language spoken in West Africa. These have been exported from a text file that uses MDF fields. What fields have been used in these entries? (You will need to consult the full range of MDF fields at the SIL website).

\lx lexeme
\ps part of speech
\de definition
\xv example sentence (in vernacular language)
\xe example sentence translation (in English)
\sn sense number
\pl plural form

Exercise 7  Making a dictionary entry

Choose around five words from a particular semantic domain and draft dictionary entries for them. Include at least the following fields:

- Definition – ideally you would ask your consultant for his/her definition in the language concerned
- Gloss – simple one word/phrase English or other target language equivalents.
- Grammatical information (e.g. if it is a noun, what classifier is used with it).
- Pragmatic information (e.g. what register it belongs to).
- Encyclopaedic information.
- An illustrative sentence. It is best to use sentences a speaker has uttered (and approved); constructed examples are to be avoided.
- Divisions into senses and sub-entries.
- Semantic domain codes for each of the senses.
- Reversal codes for the headword.

Use MDF codes to mark up your data.

*This exercise will work well if students in the field methods class are working on a language and making primary recordings themselves. It may be a good idea to work in groups. If there is no particular language that the class is working on, another suggestion is for the students to work on this exercise in their own language (although it would be better if they are not simply consulting published dictionaries). The aim is*

*Appendix 2: Answers to exercises*

*to familiarise students with the processes involved in structuring linguistic data for outputs such as dictionaries.*

## Chapter 8 Sign and gesture

Exercise 1 Including gesture in the written grammar of a language

Do you think that the gestures of speakers of a language should be described in a grammar of that language? Are there any particular parts of a grammar that you think might benefit from this approach?

*This is actually a hard question to answer, and if you are having difficulty with it rest assured that it is a question that occupies the minds of experienced researchers who work on gesture! It raises issues about what grammars aim to reflect (are they mainly about the structure of speech or are they also about language-in-use), and whether or not some kinds of actions are grammaticalised, and if so are some more or less grammaticalised than others. It also gets to the heart of what we think 'language' is. We have already seen how certain types of words, such as demonstratives, typically go with gesture. This would be a great place to start if you were considering incorporating something about the role of gesture into your grammar.*

Exercise 2 Eliciting signs for kin

Your research is in a community where there is a shared sign language as well as several spoken languages, and you are trying to find out more about signs for kin terms. The signers are literate in English, but not in the heritage language of the community. The terminology of the kinship systems is very different between all of these languages. What sort of tasks could you design to help determine what signs are used for kin terms and what they mean?

*In this situation one way to get to the meanings of the signs in this domain would be to assemble some visual prompts, such as photos of people in the community, that can be used to generate data about signs for kin terms. This could be a very enjoyable exercise, and a 'visual library of relations' could form the basis of questions such as, "What do you call X?" and "What does X call you?" If they are available, genealogies may also be useful, or they could be made as part of the research project. It is clearly important not to use written prompts (such as the word for 'uncle' written in either the vernacular language or the heritage language of the community) as you do not know what the relationship is between the ways that the spoken languages of the community classify kin, and what the impact of the spoken languages of the community is on the ways that the shared sign language reflects kin categories. A great research project!*

Exercise 3 Time, gesture and orientation

You are not sure how to understand the ways that people gesture about time in the language you are working on. You notice that when people talk about 'morning' they point in one direction, and when they talk about 'afternoon' they point to another. You are not sure whether this action is anchored to the body and thus shows a left/right distinction or whether the speakers/signers are using of an absolute frame of reference (i.e. fixed bearings such as north, south, east, west). How could you test these possibilities further? What else should you look out for if you are working inside a building?

*One way to test whether the sign or gesture is anchored to fixed bearings, such as compass directions, or to the person's body (their left or right side, or even their front or back) is to use the rotation paradigm, a method that has been used extensively to explore different frames of reference in languages. You could try to elicit conversations about times of the day with the participants facing in different directions on repeated occasions. Although it may be possible to record naturalistic data, you would be very lucky if there were enough fortuitous spontaneous examples that helped answer this question (for example conversations about time while sitting in relaxed outdoors locations: on one occasion facing north and on others facing south, or east etc.). The alternative is a semi-experimental method where data is recorded in a fixed location, and yet the spatial orientation of recording set-up is varied, or rotated from one session to the next. If the actions are consistently deployed in the same direction, regardless of the direction in which the participant is facing (for example when someone signs* MORNING *the sign is directed to the east no matter which way they are facing), then this suggests that an absolute frame is being employed. If the action was always directed towards the person's right or left-hand side, no matter which way they are facing, then this suggests that the action is based on the body axis (or relative frame). It is very important that you keep careful account of the direction that people are facing in recordings, and this becomes part of your metadata. If you are working inside a building it would be relevant to note whether a participant was directing an action in absolute space (perhaps to the east) or whether they were actually pointing at a clock on the wall inside the room!*

### Exercise 4  Is it a sign or a gesture?

Look again at Tjawina's example above. Do you think that the expressive action shown is a sign or a gesture? What else would you need to know about the communicative practices of Ngaatjatjarra people in order to answer this question?

*There are several ways to approach this question. One would be to try to find out if Ngaatjatjarra people or their neighbours have an 'alternate' sign language (one that is used instead of speech in some circumstances). It is already clear from this example that the action goes with speech. If the answer is in the affirmative then you would still need to try to find more examples of this particular action, ideally in naturalistic situations such as conversation, in order to establish whether or not it is part of a more conventionalised sign repertoire, or whether it is a one-off action that may not occur in a similar form again. Another thing to look at would be whether this action is found in sequences of actions that form more complex utterances. Another method, discussed in this book, would be to devise a sort of 'action' quiz, and see if this action has shared meanings in the community, and people understand the meaning of the action alone, without supporting speech. Lastly it would be interesting to see if the Ngaatjatjarra have any metalanguage to talk about different types of communicative action – are there any Ngaatjatjarra words for 'signing', 'gesturing' or 'pointing'?*

Exercise 5  Get your multimodal palette together!

It is now time to see if you can go through the steps of making an audio-visual recording right through to a preliminary analysis of a several short utterances. In this task you will:

- make a short video recording
- get the files off the camera, name the files and create a set of basic metadata
- design an ELAN template or choose a simple ready-made one
- annotate the data
- decide how you would represent and cite several examples in a linguistic text.

*The aim of this exercise is to familiarise the students with the steps involved in making an audio-visual recording, transferring the data from the recording devices, and then taking the first steps in data annotation. You may decide to collaborate in the recording part of the task – as a class, or in groups. Choosing a topic that is likely to be gesture-rich will make this task more interesting. Suggestions might be a simple interaction where interlocutors are asked to give directions to a place, or an interaction over a meal (after the main course when people's hands are free!).*

## Chapter 9  Child language acquisition

Exercise 1  Archiving child language corpora

Pick one of the field studies of acquisition mentioned above. Where are the recordings archived? Is the video available? Is the audio available? Are the names anonymised?

*An example answer might be: The Chintang/Puma DoBeS documentation project is housed in The Language Archive: https://corpus1.mpi.nl/ds/asv/;jsessionid=44CB94 615BA6DE54A6565EE273CD0F45?0&openpath=node:337085. None of the audio, video or transcripts are freely available to researchers (because they contain children) but they can be accessed on request.*

Exercise 2  Consent dilemmas

What would you do in the following situation? You have obtained from the archive someone else's corpus of videos which was made 20 years earlier. The consent forms show that the parents gave permission on behalf of their children for other researchers to use these recordings. You return to the community to find the families. One of the focus children, now an adult, wants their videos deleted. Should they have a say in how these recordings are used, archived and accessed?

*Ideally participant consent should be constantly updated. Practically this is generally not possible for a number of reasons – (i) it is a time-consuming task on the part of the* researcher, or the archive, and (ii) metadata in archival deposits may not be detailed enough and 'future-proofed' and so it might be very difficult to interpret the instructions, or find the people who have rights to the materials, (iii) the researcher who made the recordings may have passed away.

Participants may change their minds over time for various reasons. If a participant no longer wants their recordings to be available for research, talk to them about their concerns. It might be something which can be resolved (e.g. they may be happy with anonymised transcripts to continue to be used in research but not the recordings themselves). If the issue can't be resolved, then you should update the consent information, and if possible document the new access instructions.

You should inform the archive of these concerns, and not use this material in your research.

Exercise 3  Between recruitment and recording comes ….

A local research assistant has introduced you to a number of families and you are keen to get started recording. You set up all of your gear and start recording. For the first hour the child sits mutely and the caregivers nervously try to get the child to speak. Before leaping into recording, what sorts of things can you do to make recording a comfortable scenario for everyone involved?

*Making recordings straightaway without getting to know participants can be very confronting, particularly for children if you are not from their culture. Some time is needed to get to know the family. Spend some time with the family without the recording equipment – go fishing together, help in their garden, play with the children (if it is a culture where adults play with children). Introduce the recording equipment slowly – allow the child to 'play' with it (with care of course!). Make a short, silly recording and play it back so they can see themselves. Once the child relaxes around you and the equipment, they will no doubt behave more naturally in recording sessions.*

Exercise 4  Recording sessions and media 'objects'

Read the passage on the Murrinhpatha camera and microphone set-up. How many media objects will result from this session? How many separate video and audio recordings are happening simultaneously? How would you label each of these objects?

*One session will produce two audio-visual recordings. Although there are three sources of audio (one shotgun and two wireless mics), they are being recorded directly into the cameras. These two audio-visual recordings can then be synched in ELAN.*

Exercise 5  Experiments in the field – what's possible and what's not?

Many of the tasks described above require laboratory conditions which are not possible in the field. Think about each of the methods and why they might work or not work in field conditions. Can you think of ways of adjusting some methods so they will work in the field, or what additional equipment you might need to make them work?

*'Act out' and 'Picture-choice tasks' are definitely possible in the field. 'Act out' in particular does not require technology, just props and a quiet place to work to help children attend to the task. Note though that if you can't pre-record the stimulus, it will require a research assistant to say sentences in exactly the same way each time. 'Picture-choice tasks' are best done using computers and again pre-recorded audio stimuli, but again they can be undertaken using laminated cards and spoken renditions of stimuli. Tasks such as 'intermodal preferential looking paradigm' are possible if the community has electricity and a quiet indoor place to work in, and which can be stripped of other distractions.*

## Chapter 10  Contact languages

### Exercise 1  Diasporas in cities

Where do you hear heritage languages spoken in cities? Restaurants? Train stations in particular suburbs? Do people of all ages speak the language? If an old person speaks to a young person, in what language do they reply? How would you approach this community to do a project? Is the city a 'field site' in this case (go back to our definition of what constitutes fieldwork – §1.2.3).

*Heritage languages are often heard in high immigration suburbs, in particular places where diaspora groups gather e.g. community halls, places of worship, restaurants specialising in home cuisines, public transport hubs (immigrants are often poor and therefore high users of public transport). Language vitality among diaspora groups varies, but it is often the case that adults continue to speak their language among themselves, but younger generations shift to fit in with peers at school. Younger generations often start speaking the dominant language among themselves and even addressing their parent using this language. If you are interested in working with diaspora groups, you might try approaching a community organisation or church group. This research setting would be considered 'fieldwork' because it is documenting language in its context of use. You need to be mindful of what it is that you are documenting though – the language as it was spoken in its original context, or a new variety which has changed in its new context. Both are good research projects, but the object of study needs to be clearly defined.*

### Exercise 2  Dealing with variation

How do you know whether you are dealing with one construction which shows variation or two different constructions? If you have a variable construction, but you want to overview the language without getting bogged down in detail or you don't have statistics training, how would you write up the variation you find?

*This is a tricky question! If you have two different constructions, they will usually vary in 'categorical' ways which relate to the grammar of the clause i.e. one construction* is always used when the subject is definite and the other construction is always used when the subject is indefinite. If you are dealing with a single construction which shows variation, the variation will usually be 'probabilistic' i.e. the variant will tend to be used in one context and not in others, and is often driven by sociolinguistic categories e.g. age or gender, or discourse factors, but also grammatical cues! If you have a variable construction, find as many examples of it in the corpus as you can, provide the basic percentage in the grammar and an overtly tentative explanation e.g. "X construction is used 70 per cent (n=15) of the time and seems to be used by younger speakers in past tense clauses".

### Exercise 3  Dealing with gender sensitivities in the field

If you think that gender is relevant for variation you are noticing in a contact language and think you need to make recordings with members of the opposite gender, how would you go about this?

*In this case, try to find someone of the opposite gender whom you can train to collect the data. It will solve two main problems: (i) the issue of working in mixed gender groups, and (ii) the issue of someone of the opposite gender accommodating to you.*

### Exercise 4  Questionnaire data

Questionnaires used to be a common way of eliciting variation and contact features. Think of some problems with this method (i.e. what the language of the questionnaire might be, and whether it might have some contact patterns).

*Questionnaires can be very problematic and are not recommended as a method for eliciting variation and contact features. If questionnaires are written in the regionally dominant language, e.g. English, French or Spanish, the answers provided by participants may be direct translations and therefore somewhat calqued on the English, French or Spanish words and constructions used. Questionnaires also tend to operate on the clause level and the variation may be influenced by discourse features which won't be captured in questionnaires.*

### Exercise 5  Making appropriate tasks or games

How do you go about designing and implementing tasks for older members of a speech community who have few literacy or computer skills?

*Hang out with older people in the community. Are there particular games they play together e.g. card or board games? If it is appropriate to do so, join in the games and figure out the rules and props used. Find out when people speak during the game and what stimulates the speech e.g. the name of a card, requests for board game markers. Design activities around the format and rules of the games – make props e.g. cards or markers which will stimulate utterances containing the constructions that you are interested in.*

## Exercise 6  Making games that elicit clusivity variability

The community you work in marks clusivity variably in their pronouns (§6.7.4). How would you design a director-matcher task to discover the patterns in the variation?

*This is something that you can do once you have recruited participants for the language project. Take photos of each of the participants, singularly and in groups with other participants. Design games or activities which stimulate utterances containing the clusivity. Note that because you are interested in pronouns, you need to create scenarios where you use the pictures to establish the actors in a scenario that are then referred to anaphorically using pronouns.*

## Chapter 11  Verbal art

### Exercise 1  Scanning a limerick

Scan the following poem into four lines of equal duration using a metrical grid and include any empty beats. Is the rhythm duple or triple? How many instances of rhyme are there and where must these occur? How would you account for the difference in the number of lines in the metrical and orthographic representation of this genre?

|          | B            | B                | B            | B   |
|----------|--------------|------------------|--------------|-----|
| There    | once was a   | línguist that's  | Sweet        | Ø   |
|          | B            | B                | B            | B   |
| Who could| place London | speech within    | feet         | Ø   |
|          | B            | B                | B            | B   |
| This phi-| lólogist     | tóld of          | Ger-mánic of | old |
|          | B            | B                | B            | B   |
| But      | left us      | befóre he could  | tweet        | Ø   |

*The poem is a limerick and it has triple rhythm. Lines one, two and four rhyme and have the same line final rhyme. The two hemistiches of line three also have a different final rhyme. While the standard orthographic tradition puts the two hemistiches of line three on separate lines, its meter is four lines of four beats.*

### Exercise 2  File naming

How does the file naming system above compare to those discussed in §4.2.1? How would you ensure that the metadata for the whole recording is carried through to every exported song file?

*This file name is similar to the file naming in §4.2.1 in that it commences with the initials of the recordist; however, following this, instead of the year, it uses the archive collection number (presumably sequential), followed by an underscore and a file number, again presumably sequential. Thus, unlike the file names in §4.2.1, there is no language, date or linguistic type (e.g. sign) in this file name.*

### Exercise 3  Recording verbal art traditions in your own culture

In this exercise you will investigate the verbal arts of your grandparents' generations in your own culture. Explain to a grandparent or friend from an older generation that you are doing a task for your university subject and that you would like to record them (if they don't want to be recorded just use a pen and paper). Ask if they can recall any songs or poetry from their childhood. Did they sing any nursery rhymes, lullabies, church songs or love songs? You should have a few exemplars up your sleeve to try to trigger their memory. Try to write them down, noting any explanations they give. Ask about any meanings or associations they have. Do they remind them of a place, people and times? How did they learn the songs, did they pass them on? If recording, ask if they would like you to play the recording back to them. Does this elicit any further comments? Note any unclear words or meanings. How different are the songs to speech?

*This exercise consists of making a recording of a verbal art piece and transcribing and analysing it. You should reflect on the effect of exemplifying as a means of elicitation, and playback as a means of checking meaning and contextual information.*

# Appendix 3: Glossary

**annotation** – any descriptive or analytic notations applied to raw language data. The data may be audio, video or textual. The added notations may include transcriptions of all sorts (e.g. phonetic features, word class, discourse structures, semantic information and so on).

**auxiliary language** – a language which is not the primary or native language of a community, for example a sign language used by hearing people, an alternate register or liturgical language.

**back translation** – the process of translating a document previously translated into another language back to the original language.

**carrier phrase** – the phrase that the target word occurs in when conducting a linguistic experiment.

**complementary distribution** – the occurrence of speech sounds in mutually exclusive environments.

**consent** – when conducting fieldwork with people you need to ensure that each person understands the project and has agreed to work on it before they start working with you. Documenting this agreement is called 'informed consent'.

**contact language** – a language which arose from contact between two or more languages in the minds of bilingual speakers. Typical examples are pidgins, creoles and mixed languages.

**corpus** – a systematic collection of either written, spoken or signed language that can be used as the data for a linguistic description; often used to mean that it is in a machine readable form.

**Creative Commons (CC) licences** – international legal tools for licensing content in relation to copying, modifying and redistribution for commercial or non-commercial uses.

**creole language** – a native language developed from a mixture of different languages. Unlike a pidgin, a creole language is a complete language, used in a community and acquired by children as their native language.

**deictic centre** – a reference point in relation to which a deictic expression is to be interpreted. The deictic centre is most typically the present time or location of the speaker. Often the deictic centre needs to be made explicit in a text taken out of context.

**director-matcher task** – ways of eliciting language that involve two participants (a director and a matcher). Usually the director chooses a picture (or other form of stimuli) from a set and describes it to the matcher, who, based on this description, selects from her identical set.

**elicitation (formal)** – the act of obtaining language data from another person which involves the use of questionnaires, stimuli or translation equivalents.

**encyclopaedic dictionary** – a dictionary that includes extensive cultural and encyclopaedic information, discussing each headword in depth.

**finder list** – a section at the end of a bilingual dictionary that reverses the direction of the languages. A finder list or 'reversal' assists a user in getting to the right part of the main dictionary where they can find out more about a word and its meanings.

**folk definition** – a native speaker's or popular explanation of the meaning of a word or phrase.

**folk taxonomy** – a popular classification system.

**gatekeeper organisation** – an organisation that has authority over the area or people where you wish to do fieldwork. These organisations protect the people they represent (e.g. against fraudulent activities) and can offer advice, official approvals or endorsement of research.

**grammaticality judgement** – a native speaker's judgement on the well-formedness of an utterance. Grammaticality is a matter of linguistic intuition, and reflects the innate linguistic competence of speakers.

**homophone** – words that sound the same but have different meanings, e.g. *aloud* and *allowed*.

**homonym** – homophones that are spelt the same way, e.g. *bank* (river) and *bank* (financial institution).

**ideophone** – a word that evokes an idea in sound (e.g. *whoosh* in English). Ideophones are found in many of the world's languages, although they are claimed to be relatively uncommon in Western languages.

**'insider' linguist** – someone who is a native speaker of the language they study or is from the community that speaks the language.

**intellectual property rights** – refers to a collection of rights including copyright, patents and trademarks.

**interoperability** – the ability of different types of software to import or export into formats used by other software.

**language acquisition** – the study of how children acquire language(s).

**language description** – a grammar (including phonology), text collection and dictionary (or at least a wordlist).

**language documentation** – a record of the linguistic practices and traditions of a speech community. Language documentation prioritises texts and a variety of different types of speech.

**language vitality** – the extent that a language is used as a means of communication in various social contexts. The most significant indicator of a language's vitality is its daily use in the home. A language with high vitality would be one that is used extensively both inside and outside the home, by all generations, and for most, if not all, topics.

**Leipzig Glossing Rules** – standardised labels for interlinear morphological glosses.

**lexicography** – the craft of compiling, writing and editing dictionaries which involves analysing and describing the semantic, syntagmatic and paradigmatic relationships within the lexicon (of a language).

**lingua franca** – a language that is adopted as a common language between speakers whose native languages are different.

**metadata** – is data about data. Metadata essentially answers the who, what, why, where, when and how questions about a fieldwork 'session' and the audio-visual or other items resulting from the fieldwork.

**meter (poetic)** – the rhythmic structure of a verse or lines in verse. Many verse forms use a specific verse meter, or a set of meters.

**metrical grid** – a way of representing rhythm in speech, poetry and song. Syllables are arranged along the bottom row and 'x' represents prominence; the higher the column of 'x's the higher the prominence.

**minimal pair** – words that are identical except for one feature or sound.

**mixed language** – a language which is the result of extensive community bilingualism and code-switching, often developed as an expression of an altered identity, be it new, or differing significantly from an older identity.

**Multi Dictionary Formatter** – software designed by SIL International which converts a well-structured dictionary database into a formatted dictionary.

**nasal harmony** – a phonological pattern where nasalisation extends over a sequence of segments.

**non-linguistic stimuli** – images, sounds, smells or touch stimuli used to elicit semantic, phonetic or morpho-syntactic contrasts.

**oral literature** – a broad term that covers the verbal arts as well as myths, legends, proverbs, riddles, tongue-twisters, word games, recitations and historical narratives.

**orthography** – a spelling system used to write a language.

**'outsider' linguist** – someone who is not a native speaker of the language they study and comes from a different culture.

**participatory models of linguistic research** – research that values everyone's unique contribution equally; including a community member's unique knowledge in knowing about their community, ways of working etc.

**performance arts** – verbal arts that may include non-linguistic aspects such as dance, visual designs and ritual actions.

**phonemic principle** – a principle used in orthographic design that states there should be a one-to-one correspondence between the orthographic and phonemic representation of a word.

**phonetic transcription** – a transcription of linguistic sounds using the International Phonetic Alphabet which includes phones as well as tone, stress, nasalisation as well as other prosodic and suprasegmental features.

**pidgin language** – a non-native simplified colonial language (e.g. English, French, Arabic) used as a *lingua franca* between a number of groups, which otherwise do not have a shared language.

**poetic function** – the use of language for artistic affect that draws attention to its own form. This contrasts with everyday speech which prioritises the communicative function of language.

**polysemy** – the association of a word with two or more distinct meanings.

**project information statement** – an explanation about what the research project is.

**proprietary** – software which is developed by a commercial company. Typically the source code for proprietary software is not made available for further development by amateur programmers.

**psycholinguistics** – a branch of linguistics that is particularly concerned with cognitive approaches to the study of languages and how they are acquired and used.

**recruitment** – finding language speakers to work with. It is important to recruit people in an ethical manner, e.g. without coercion or misinformation; and by stating clearly your aims, what the work will involve and what people will and won't get out of it.

**register** – a variety of language used for a particular purpose or in a particular social setting e.g. baby talk or mother-in-law language.

**scansion** – analysing a line of verse to determine its metrical properties.

**segmental inventory** – the chart of contrastive discrete sounds in a language, specifically the consonants and vowels.

**semantic domain** – an area of meaning and the words used to discuss it.

**source language** – in lexicography the source language is the language from which the translation is made.

**Swadesh list** – a wordlist of 100 and 200 concepts that exist in most languages and used for basic elicitation and comparison.

**target word** – the word that you would like the speaker to say.

**target language** – 1. the language being researched 2. in lexicography the target language is the language of the translation, used to define lexical units in the source language.

**taxonomy** – a network of superordinate and (generic)-subordinate relations. These can be diagrammed as a tree with the generic represented with a higher node and hypernyms connected to them by lines.

**temporal arts** – verbal arts that may include non-linguistic aspects such as dance, visual designs and ritual actions.

**text-setting** – the way in which an oral or written text is aligned to a musical tune.

**Traditional Knowledge (TK) licences** – can be used separately or in combination with CC licences to add conditions of use and information about how material should be respectfully and ethically treated according to community expectations and obligations, i.e. moral rights.

**transcription** – the systematic representation of language in a written form. The original language might be utterances (speech or sign language) or a pre-existing text in another writing system.

**verbal art** – artistic forms of language including poetry, song, rhyming games, sung tales, poems, ritual speech events, spells, advertising jingles, incantations, charms and spells, children's chants.

**vernacular language** – the native language spoken by a specific population, which can be distinguished from a literary, national or standard variety of the language.

**version control** – Making sure that multiple conflicting versions of a file are not created, e.g. by several people working on it at the same time.

**vocable** – a sequence of speech sounds from a given language which form one or more syllables but does not represent a word of the language.

**wug word** – a made up word that adheres to the sound system of a language and is used to gauge linguistic awareness.

# Appendix 4: Acronyms

**AIATSIS** – Australian Institute of Aboriginal and Torres Strait Islander Studies
**AILLA** – Archive of the Indigenous Languages of Latin America
**ANLA** – Alaska Native Language Archive
**ANVIL** – software used for annotation of sign and gesture
**CHAT** – the statistical software package associated with the annotation software CHAT
**CLAN** – annotation software associated with the statistical package CLAN
**DoBeS** – The Documentation of Endangered Languages programme including the TLA archive of language documentation from around the world funded by the Volkswagen Foundation
**DRIL** – Documenting and Revitalising Indigenous Languages, a training program to support the long-term maintenance of Australian Indigenous languages
**ELAN** – a software developed by the Max Planck Institute for Psycholinguistics in Nijmegen (the Netherlands) to assist with segmenting, transcribing and annotating speech, sign and gesture
**ELAR** – Endangered Language Archive is a digital archive for materials on endangered languages, based at SOAS, the University of London
**ELDP** – Endangered Languages Documentation Program funded by the Hans Rausing Foundation
**IMDI** – ISLE Meta Data Initiative, a metadata schema endorsed and adopted by some documentary linguists, particularly those who worked through the DoBeS program (Documentation of Endangered Languages programme funded by the Volkswagen Foundation)
**LAD** – the Language Acquisition Device is what the generativist tradition argues all humans possess, an innate module in the brain dedicated to language
**OLAC** – Open Languages Archive Community, an international partnership of institutions and individuals who work towards consensus on best practice for the digital archiving of language resources
**PARADISEC** – Pacific and Regional Archive for Digital Sources in Endangered Cultures
**RNLD** – Research Network for Linguistic Diversity
**TLA** – The Language Archive houses materials created by the DoBeS documentation projects and linguistic resources and tools developed by the Max Planck Institute for Psycholinguistics in Nijmegen (the Netherlands)

# Index

ablative 141; *see also* case
absolute 196, 303, 305–306; *see also* frame of reference
access: and archiving 279; of research materials 31–32; platforms 88–89; open 91–92
accommodation effects 124, 251–252
accusative 126, 131–133, 139; *see also* case
acknowledgement *see* authorship
acoustic properties 98–99, 107
active *see* knowledge, voice
actor 233; *see also* agent
Adamorobe Sign Language (AdaSL) 5, 191, 289
adaptors 56, 58, 60
adjectives 124–125, 143
adpositions 140; *see also* prepositions; postpositions
adverbs 125, 134–135, 144, 247
advisor 25, 36, 44, 60; *see also* supervisor
Afrikaans 82
agent 136, 255, 301; *see also* grammatical relations
agentivity 218–219; bias 218–219
agreement marking 125, 138, 143, 146, 149, 174
agreements *see* copyright; research agreements
Ahtna 86, 159
AIATSIS (Australian Institute of Aboriginal and Torres Strait Islander Studies) 87, 155, 315
AILLA (Archive of the Indigenous Languages of Latin America) 86, 315
Akan 191
Aktionsart 133–134; *see also* aspect
Alaskan languages 86, 159, 170, 289, 302, 315
albums 277–279
Algonquian languages 133
alienability *see* possession
allative 139–140, 248, 301; *see also* case
alliteration 97, 261, 272, 274
allophones 100, 102–105, 109, 296–298
alphabet 115; *see also* IPA, orthography; script
Alyawarr 1, 21, 87, 158, 289

American English 6, 97; Black American English 250
American Sign Language (ASL) 156
analogue recordings 49–50, 56, 84, 89
animacy 127, 132–133, 138, 143, 161
ANLA (Alaska Native Language Archive) 86, 315
Anmatyerr 1, 166–169, 173–174, 204, 207–208, 210, 289
annotation 18, 69, 79–83, 92; of sign languages and gesture 191, 193, 199, 211
anonymity 35, 192–193, 205, 223; *see also* consent, ethics
anthropology 8, 71, 264, 286
antipassive *see* voice
ANVIL 199, 315
Appalachia 262
appropriation 32
Arabic 66, 79, 196, 240, 314
Arandic languages 117, 123, 129, 173; *see also* Arrarnta, Arrernte, Anmatyerr, Alyawarr, Kaytetye
Archi 178–179, 289
archiving 83–92
argument disambiguation 231, 233
Arnhem Land 197
Arrarnta 117
Arrernte 117, 185, 281
articles 125, 143
articulation 98, 112–113; of sign and gesture 63, 197–198
aspect 125, 133–135; *see also* Aktionsart
aspiration 96, 98, 106–107, 115, 296
astronomy 159, 180, 182
atelic *see* Aktionsart
Athabaskan languages 133, 170
Audacity 63, 275–276
audio connectors 54; equipment 50–55; recording 61–65; stimuli 161
Auslan 197, 201, 203, 213, 289
Australian Aboriginal 87, 130, 224, 249, 263, 265, 273; *see also* Indigenous peoples
authorship 38–40, 270, 279, 292
auxiliary verbs 146, 244

Avatime 190, 289
avoidance language 162–163; *see also* special registers
Awiakay 163–164, 289

back translation 128
backdrops for filming 197
background noise 52–53, 63–64, 112
Bali 203, 289
Bantu languages 143
batteries 50–51, 55, 57–58, 61, 228
Benesh Movement Notation 271
Berber languages 132
Biao Min 179
Bible 13–16, 28–29
Bikol 167, 289
Bilinarra 40, 101, 135–136, 139–141, 149, 289
bilingual dictionaries 165, 168–169, 173
bilingual education 86, 243
bilingualism 110; and contact languages 238–239; community 243; and language proficiency 256–258
biology 168, 180, 286
Bislama 31, 123, 289
Boasian trilogy 8–9, 122
borrowing 101, 110, 143, 175, 239–240
bound pronouns *see* pronouns
broad transcription 97
Broadcast Wav Format (BWF) 76
British Sign Language (BSL) 56

cables 54–55, 58, 60, 68
calquing 139
cameras *see* video recording
Canadian languages 179, 252, 258
Cantonese 82
cardinal directions 141–142, 176, 185, 196, 300, 303; *see also* absolute
cardioid microphone 52
carrier phrases 110–112, 312
case 124–126, 131–133, 137, 139–141, 146, 174, 231–233, 244, 257
cassette tape 49, 77–78, 294
Catalan 82
CDs 90, 276, 278
ceremonies 42, 57, 163, 186; *see also* special registers
chargers for equipment 58
CHAT 80, 82, 315
CHILDES (Child Language Data Exchange System) 82
children *see* consent; ethics; language acquisition
Chintang 216–220, 224–231, 289

Choctaw 136, 289
citation of linguistic data 40, 92
CLAN 18, 82–83, 124, 315
class *see* conjugation classes; word classes
classification systems 157–158, 313; Linnaean 154; noun 142–143; scientific 158, 168; *see also* taxonomies
clause-level elicitation 126–127
clitics 122–123, 146–147
clusivity 125, 138–139, 255, 310
code-switching 242–244, 257–258
collaborators *see* research assistants
commercial use of languages 32–34, 278, 312; *see also* rights
community leaders 5, 37, 239
complementary distribution 102–105, 296, 312
complex predicates 125, 134, 137; *see also* verbs
condenser microphone 52
conjugation classes 125, 134–136, 174, 295, 245
connectors 54–55
consent 8, 16, 30, 34–38, 70; verbal 241; and children 222, 225; and sign languages 192; *see also* ethics
consonants: phonotactics 99; voicing 104, 106, 109; interdental 112; alveolar 115; and orthography 115–116, 165, 179, 297–298
consonant clusters 99, 109, 110, 116
consultants 25, 44, 60–61, 66, 96, 70, 111; payment to 35, 42–43, 222
contact languages 238–240; and documentation methods 250–258; types of 240–245; *see also* language contact; creole languages; mixed languages; pidgin languages
control of research 30–31
Conversation Analysis 79, 82
copyright 32–33, 39, 45, 147, 277–279; *see also* rights
councils 26, 29–30, 41, 58
Creative Commons (CC) licences 33, 312
credit *see* authorship
Cree 179, 251
creole languages 11, 123, 128, 238, 240–241, 258, 312; *see also* contact languages
cultural knowledge 31–33, 77, 92, 159, 171, 174–175, 262; *see also* knowledge systems
Cushitic languages 132
custodians 34, 278–280; *see also* ownership; intellectual property rights

Daly languages 89, 129
dance and verbal art 171, 262, 266–267, 271, 278, 314–315

data management 73–92, 177
database 77–78, 82, 177–179, 275
dative 137, 139, 141, 255; *see also* case
deaf 5, 8, 186–187, 191, 194, 203, 209, 211; communities, 8, 191–192, 194
decoding tests 196–197
deictic centre 138, 312
deixis 125, 140–141
demonstratives 122, 125, 140–141, 143, 160, 185, 254
derivation *see* morphology
derived words 168, 170
descriptive linguistics 122; *see also* linguistic description
determiners 124, 131
diaries 69, 100, 225, 229, 251
diaspora 6, 244–245, 308–309; *see also* urban fieldwork
dictionaries 164–168; bilingual 165, 168–169, 173; contents of 168–174; digital 165, 177–180; entries 168–169, 175–176, 178–180, 304; *see also* encyclopaedic dictionaries
differential object marking 133
digraphs 115–116
direct-inverse systems 127, 133
director-matcher task 160
discourse types 9, 109
disease 42, 223–224; *see also* health
diversity *see* linguistic diversity
dual *see* number
Dutch 202, 240
DVDs 276, 278
Dyirbal 135, 151, 245, 260

editing 56, 64, 274–275
ejectives 98
electricity 51, 90, 228, 294
electronic equipment 58–59
electropalatography 113
elicitation methods: cards games 255; director-matcher tasks 254–255; list 154; picture-prompt books 233, 255–256
encyclopaedic dictionaries 167, 171–172, 312
English: morpho-syntax 126, 144, 146; phonology 96–98, 101–102, 106, 108; *see also* Indo-European languages
environment *see* phonetic environment; weather
ergativity 126, 131–133, 136, 221–222, 233, 300; optional 133; *see also* case
ethics 34–36, 45, 95, 222–223, 285–286; applications 34–38, 192; committee 8, 34, 36, 222

Ethnologue 10, 28
ethnobiology 1, 20, 158
ethnomusicologists 264, 277
European languages 217, 240
evidentiality 144–145, 301
example sentences 40, 129, 172–173; *see also* illustrative examples
experimental: design 109–112; methods 256–257, 308; studies 230–232

feminine *see* gender
fieldwork *see* remote field sites; urban fieldwork
file naming 73–75
finder lists 165, 173, 312
First Nations 3, 147, 186; *see also* Indigenous peoples; Australian Aboriginal
FLEx 168, 177–178
focus *see* information structure
folk definitions 171–172, 264
folk songs 262, 265, 269, 272, 279
folk taxonomies 157
folklorists 262–263, 279
font 165
formal elicitation 121–122, 124, 129, 142; problems with 250–251
frame of reference 196, 303; *see also* spatial relations
frame rates 65
free variation 102
French 123, 165, 178, 217, 240–242, 251–252
funding 17, 29, 34, 85, 219–220, 239
fuzzy search 165

gatekeeper organisations 30
gavagai problem 127
gender: in nouns, 142–143; in pronouns, 138; of researcher, 223, 248–249
genitive 121, 137, 146; *see also* possession; case
German 131–132, 143
gesture 187–189; annotation 199–203; metadata 193; in publications 204–209; research methods 193–199
glossing 128, 148–149, 180, 202; *see also* Leipzig Glossing Rules; morphological glosses
grammatical analysis 18, 147
grammatical relations 122, 126, 131–133
grammaticality judgements 8, 127, 256, 313
graphemes 115–116
Greek 242–243
Gurindji 16–21, 175–176, 231, 244, 246, 248–257, 289
Gurindji Kriol, 85, 244, 246, 248–254, 256–257, 289

Hamburg Sign Language Notation System (HamNoSys) 204
handshape 197, 202, 204, 209
headphones 50, 56, 58, 63–64, 67, 83, 265
headword, 168–169, 173, 180
health 42, 167, 223–224, 264
hearing: individuals 185–186; problems 110, 224
heritage languages 11–12, 31, 239, 245, 248, 285
Hindi 126, 133
homesign 187
homonyms 105–106, 168–170, 302
homophones 100, 106, 169
Hopi 157
'hub and spokes' model of archiving 89
hypertext grammar 147, 149
hypernym 157
hyponym 157

ideophone, 101, 261, 263, 313
Ikaan 89, 289
illiterate *see* literacy
illustrative examples 172–173, 180, 304 *see also* example sentences
Iltyem-Iltyem sign language project 204, 210
imperative 134–136
imperfective 134–136; *see also* aspect
inanimate *see* animacy
Indigenous peoples 33, 35, 38, 224, 238; *see also* Australian Aboriginal
Indo-European languages 126, 142, 217
Indo-Iranian languages 126
infant 232; *see also* language acquisition
inflection *see* morphology
inflectional paradigms 176, 245
informants 39, 241
information structure 79, 82, 125, 133, 142, 256
innovation: and language shift 245; and musical change 263
insider *see* linguist
instrumental phonetic fieldwork 112–114
intellectual property rights 32–33, 277–278, 313
internet 37, 90–91, 165, 276
interpreters 11, 37, 192–193; *see also* translators
interrogatives 109, 125, 155
intonation 82–83, 108–109, 111
Inuktitut 179, 219
IPA (International Phonetic Alphabet) 79, 96, 99

Iquito 177–178, 289
isolating languages 145
iTunes 274–278

Jahai 156
Jaminjung 139, 141
Japanese 82, 97, 190
Jarawara 144, 289
Jingulu 142–143, 151–152, 205, 289

Kabardian 136–137
Kalam 163, 171, 289
Kalaw Kawaw Ya (KKY) 129–130, 289
Kaluli 277–278, 289
Kata Kolok Sign Language 203, 289
Kaytetye 1, 21, 67, 102–103, 107, 111, 158, 170, 268–269, 279, 289
kinship: kintax 129; relations, 162; systems 129, 157, 167, 173–174, 194–195; terms 154, 195
knowledge systems 16, 158; *see also* cultural knowledge
Koyukon 159, 170, 289
Kriol 36, 128, 231, 240, 244, 246, 249–251, 289
Kuuk Thaayorre 196

Labanotation 271
Lakota 147–148, 178, 289
landing pages 88–89
language: change 12, 239, 247; conservation 23, 46, 93–94, 119–120, 182–183, 283; contact 11, 238; documentation 8–9, 83, 122; endangerment 6, 10–12, 258; loss 10, 130, 238, 285; maintenance 130, 248, 316; obsolescence 245, 247; revitalisation 9, 86, 114, 258, 263; shift 11, 111, 221, 244–245, 247, 257; vitality 10–11, 28, 313
language acquisition 216–219, 307, 313; experimental studies 230–234; of sign and gesture 189–190; *see also* ethics
Language Acquisition Device (LAD) 216, 316
language centres 16, 29, 224
Larike 139
Latin 245
legacy: materials 43, 88, 91; recordings 11, 17, 50, 276
legal *see* rights
Leipzig Glossing Rules 128, 149, 313; *see also* morphological glosses
lens hood 57
lexemes 145, 175–176
lexical database 153
lexicography 164–168, 180, 313

lexicon 157, 160, 175, 238, 244, 263, 313; see also vocabulary
Lexique Pro 175, 177
licences 32–33, 312, 315; Creative Commons (CC) 33, 312; Traditional Knowledge (TK) 33, 315; software 33
Light Warlpiri 221, 226, 229, 231–233, 289
limericks 272–273
*lingua franca* 11, 37, 240–241, 313–314
linguist: 'insider' 2, 4–6, 7, 25, 123, 219, 230, 313; 'outsider' 2, 4–6, 16, 25, 123, 191, 220, 224, 249–250, 253, 314; see also gender
linguistic description 8–9, 251, 313; see also descriptive linguistics
linguistic diversity 2, 10, 21, 89, 130, 187, 220, 285
Linnaean classification 153
list intonation 111
literacy 28, 37, 115–116, 173, 191–193, 195, 253, 256
loan words 101, 242
locative 139–140, 195; see also case
longitudinal: corpus 218, 221, 225–230; studies 216, 219, 225–226
ludlings 97
luggage 42, 61
lullabies 264, 282
Luzon 167, 289
lyrics 268, 273; misheard 273

machine-readable 193, 203, 312
Mandarin 218; fieldwork manuals 44
Māori 209
maps 43, 89, 174, 198, 301; sketch 69, 198, 301
Martha's Vineyard Sign Language 186
masculine see gender
Mauritian Creole 241–242; see also creole languages
Max Planck Institute (MPI) 80, 85, 113, 160, 195, 254
mean length of utterance (MLU) 227, 230
meaning see semantics
media: files 60, 73, 76–77, 82, 210; 'objects' 228
Media Lengua 256; see also mixed languages
melody 263–264, 271
memory cards 51, 57–58
metadata 75–78, 193, 264, 273, 275
metaphors 87, 196, 263, 274
meter in poetry 263, 269, 272, 313
metrical grids 271–272, 314
Michif 258; see also mixed languages
microphones 50–56, 61–64, 112, 228, 266–267; cables 54; types of 52
migrants see urban fieldwork

minimal: pairs 101–106, 126, 168, 314; triplets 101
minority groups 4–5, 222, 224, 238, 250; see also Indigenous peoples
Mirndi languages 141–143
Miromaa Community Dictionary Maker 177
missionaries 13–16, 26, 117, 147
Mississippi 136, 289
mixed languages 231, 242–244, 248, 250–251, 256–258, 314; see also contact languages
modal verbs 146, 211
Mohawk 3–4, 124, 289
mondegreens 273; see also lyrics
monitoring headphones 56
monolingual fieldwork 11, 43, 123, 164
monosemy 170, 303
morae 97, 263
morphemes 97, 128, 145–146, 227
morphological glosses 18, 79, 82, 201, 313
morphology 108, 142, 174, 220, 272; derivational 145–146, 244; inflectional 145–146, 174, 217–218, 242, 252
'mother-in-law' language 162; see also special registers
Motu 14–15
Mudburra 205, 215
Mueshaungx 97, 290
multilingualism 28, 112, 192, 236, 244
multimodal: communication 2, 31, 194, 286; data 190, 205, 208
Mumbai deaf community 194
Murrinhpatha 129, 216, 219–221, 223–231, 289
museums 25, 84
musicology 21, 64, 261–263, 271, 286
mythology 155, 159, 314; see also religion

Nafaanra 176, 303
Nahuatl 179
naming: files 73–75, 275; contact languages 250; see also classification; taxonomies
narratives, 9, 17, 122, 195, 255–256, 253, 314
narrators 39, 67–68, 200, 206, 255, 272
narrow transcription 97
nasalisation 98, 100, 104, 113, 314
nasals 98, 104, 109, 296; nasal harmony 113
native speaker intuitions 12, 97, 105–108, 263
natural world 20, 158–159
naturalistic methods 62, 91, 193, 225, 227
Navajo 168, 184, 274, 284
Nen 13–15, 289
Nepali 217–218, 225, 230, 289
neuter see gender
New Zealand Sign Language (NZSL) 192, 209, 289

Ngaatjatjarra 200–201, 289
Ngarinyman 21
Ngumpin-Yapa languages 139
noise floor 52; *see also* background noise
nomenclature *see* classification; taxonomies
nominals 143, 145, 231, 244; *see also* noun
nominative 126, 132, 139, 143, 252–253, 257; *see also* case
nonce words 110
non-linguistic stimuli 160–162
notation systems 79, 101, 204, 209, 271, 282; *see also* script
notebooks 68–69, 84, 99, 124
noun classes 135, 142–143; *see also* gender
noun phrases (NPs) 124–125, 137, 145
number 122, 139–140, 142, 163, 218

object 126, 131–133, 136, 139, 141, 217–218; *see also* grammatical relations
oblique 139; *see also* case
observer effect 8, 192
Oceanic languages 157
Omotic languages 132
online: access 85, 88, 91; dictionaries 178–179, 197–198, 204, 209–210
oral and nasal airflow masks 113
oral transmission 33, 262, 270, 279; literature 261
orthography 29, 97, 108, 114–119, 165, 253, 297–298, 314; *see also* script; spelling systems
outsider *see* linguist
ownership 31–32, 36, 151, 264, 278; *see also* custodians

Papuan languages 141, 143, 163, 171
parser 177
participants *see* consent; compensation; ethics
particles 125, 155
partitive 149n5; *see also* case
parts of speech 98, 106, 124, 178; *see also* word classes
past *see* tense
patent 32–33, 34, 313
patient 136, 233; *see also* grammatical relations
payment *see* compensation
perfective 126, 133–136, 299; *see also* aspect
permission 30, 37–38, 77, 222, 266, 278–279; *see also* consent
person 138–139; and the animacy hierarchy 133
phonation 107, 113
phonemes 96, 98, 100–102, 104–105, 107, 115, 126, 264, 296

phonemic: analysis 106–107; transcription 106–107
phones 36, 54, 60–61, 100, 102, 165, 179, 188, 193, 314
phonetic: analysis 50; environment 102–105, 109–110; transcription 79, 83, 96–97, 99–100
phonological: analysis 96, 100–105, 116, 118, 194; contrasts 98; inventory 106; transcription 79
phonotactics 108, 118–119
photography 57, 65
picture dictionaries 166
pidgin languages 238, 240, 243–244, 312, 314; *see also* contact languages
Pitjantjatjara 132
Pitta-Pitta 141
planning 25–45
playback 56, 63–64, 275–276, 298, 311
playlist 275–276
plural *see* number
poetry 97, 261, 274, 278
pointing *see* gesture
polysemy 159–160, 169, 170–171, 182, 302
polysynthetic languages 145, 168, 217–218, 220–221, 227, 237
Portuguese 86, 262
possession 121, 137, 140, 149; alienable 137, 141; inalienable 137
possessive 137, 195, 255; *see also* case
postpositions 125
potential 135–136
Praat 80, 83, 99, 106, 199
pragmatics 94, 180, 190
predicates 125, 134, 137, 150
prepositions 125, 146, 245–246
present *see* tense
prestige 114, 238, 241, 246, 248–249; *see also* language pride
proficiency testing 257–258
progressive 134; *see also* aspect
pronouns 122–123, 125–126, 129–133, 137–140, 142, 212
pronunciation guide 174
proprietary 80, 210, 271, 314; *see also* software
prosody 108–109, 142, 185, 242
publishing 38–39, 129, 147; dictionaries 165, 177; songs 277–279
Punjabi 156

QR codes 205, 278
quantitative methods 8, 82, 226, 253
Quechua 3, 119, 251, 289
questionnaires 130, 154, 160, 197, 251, 310

reciprocals 140, 160, 195
recursion 216–217
refugees *see* urban fieldwork
registers 97, 101–102, 162–163, 274, 314; *see also* special registers
relational databases 77–78
religion 15–16, 116–117, 159, 163, 186, 262, 264, 276
remote field sites 2, 6–8, 89, 198, 210, 225, 286
remuneration 35, 42–43, 222
repetition 261, 268, 270, 272
research agreements 16, 35, 41
research assistants 2, 191, 223; local 218, 224, 226, 252–253, 291
respect register 162–163
responsibilities of linguists 2, 5, 29–30, 45, 245, 278, 286
restrictions: on access 37, 91–91, 280; copyright 33; cultural 30, 77, 175
reversals *see* finder lists
rhyme 264, 272, 274, 310–311
rhythm 264, 271–272, 314
riddles 314
rights 30, 32–34, 77, 95, 277–278; *see also* copyright; intellectual property rights
rituals 91, 245, 261–262, 266, 270, 280–281; *see also* special registers
RNLD (Research Network for Linguistic Diversity) 45, 92, 316
Romance languages 143, 157
root 146, 168, 177–178

Samoan 219, 234, 236
sand stories *see* stories
Savosavo 156
scientific: knowledge 20, 157–158, 168; nomenclature 157
script 79, 115, 204; *see also* notation systems; orthography
segmental inventory 106; *see also* phonological
semantic domains 100, 104–105, 153–157, 167, 180, 315
semelfactive 134; *see also* aspect
serial verb constructions (SVCs) 190
Sesotho 219, 234
sex *see* gender
Shiwiar 113–114, 289
sign languages 185–211; types of sign languages 186, 187; metadata 193; filming 197–199; sign dictionaries 209, 210
Sign Writing 204
SIL International 92, 128, 154, 177–178, 209, 211
singular *see* number

Sino-Tibetan languages 97, 217
Siouan languages 147
sociolinguistics 6, 8, 102, 111, 247, 251
socio-political considerations 116
software 80, 271; *see also* licences
song 261–267; publishing 277–279; transcribing 268–271; translating 273–274
source language 169
Spanish 11, 123, 128, 165, 177, 242
spatial relations 140–141
special registers 28, 162–164
spectrogram software 99
speech register 97
spelling systems 97, 115–118; *see also* orthography
static palatography 113
statistical analysis 82, 162, 230–231, 253, 315
stative 134; *see also* Aktionsart
stem 97, 136, 147, 227, 247, 255
stereo: recording 50–52, 77, 228; microphone 51–52, 63, 266
storage 50–51, 57–58, 89, 228
stories 31, 38–39, 121; sand 66–67, 206–208; *see also* elicitation methods
stress 104–106, 108–109, 263, 272, 296, 314
subject 122, 126, 131–133, 136, 139, 217–219, 233; *see also* grammatical relations
subtitles 15, 80–81
superordinate 157
supervisor 25, 36, 44, 49, 60, 220; *see also* advisor
suppletive forms 131, 147
suprasegmental features 108, 115, 314
Swadesh lists 100, 154, 295, 315; *see also* wordlists
Swahili 134
Swati 143
syllable 96–97, 108–110, 136, 263, 272
syncretism 245
syntax 9, 124, 145, 217

taboos 28, 91, 155, 175; *see also* restrictions
Tahitian 178
Tai Ahom 280
Tai Phake 108
TAM (tense aspect mood) 133, 149, 242, 244
Tamil 143, 289
tape *see* cassette tape
target: language 11, 123, 158, 169, 216, 221; word 70, 110
Tariana 144–145, 289
Tasmanian languages 48–49
taxonomies 157–160, 171, 263, 315; *see also* folk taxonomies
technological obsolescence 50, 89

telic 134; *see also* Aktionsart
temporal arts 261, 315
tense 125–126, 133, 135, 145, 283; and language acquisition 217–218
Teop 172
text-setting 263
Thrace Romani 242–243, 246, 252–253, 256–257, 289
TLA (The Language Archive) 85, 220, 315–316
Tlingit 5, 159, 289
Tohono O'odham 171, 272
Tok Pisin 14–15; *see also* creole language
tokens 99
tonal: categories 102, 107–108; contrasts 97, 106–107, 109, 111
tonal languages 107, 118
tone 107–108, 115, 143, 263, 314
Toolbox 117, 175, 177
topic *see* information structure
Torres Strait 87, 129, 237, 315
trademark *see* intellectual property rights
Traditional Knowledge (TK) licences 33, 315
training: cross-cultural 43; linguistic 3, 5, 29–31, 191; literacy 13
Transcriber 82, 276
transcribers 77, 225, 230
transcription 97
transfer 252
transitivity *see* verbs
translation *see* back translation
translators 11, 77, 274; *see also* interpreters
transport 27, 42, 50–51; *see also* vehicles
tripods 56–57, 66–67, 198
Turkish 190, 242–243, 246, 252, 256–257
typology 2, 160, 171, 189, 221
Tzeltal 141, 219, 234

ultrasound 113
unicode fonts 100, 177
universities 29, 34, 84, 281
unique identifier 73
urban fieldwork 6–7, 31, 188, 194, 245, 286, 290
USB sticks 58, 90, 276, 280–281

vaccinations 41–42, 224; *see also* health
variation: and contact languages 246–248, 251, 253, 257; inter-speaker 2, 12, 157, 160; and song 9, 261–282; cultural knowledge 31, 62; recording 63, 66; archiving 84, 86; phonology 97

vehicles 41–42, 50, 59; *see also* transport
verbal arts *see* poetry; song
verb classes *see* conjugation classes
verbs 125, 131, 133–137, 161, 168, 217–218; transitivity 126, 129, 131, 136, 139, 219; *see also* complex predicates
verse 263, 272, 282, 313, 315
video recording 65–68; equipment 55–57; *see also* cameras
Vietnamese 142
visa 41–43
visual prompts *see* non-linguistic stimuli
vocabulary: eliciting 154–160
voice: active 36, 136–137; antipassive 136–137; middle 136; passive 11, 136, 139, 147, 233, 235
voicing 98, 100–102, 104, 106, 109, 258
vowels: phonological analysis 100–105; stress 108–109; in song 269, 296–297
vulnerable populations 8, 35, 222; *see also* Indigenous peoples

Walmajarri 34
Warlpiri 122–124, 139, 172, 219, 229, 231–233, 278, 289; *see also* Light Warlpiri
waveform 63, 80, 199, 271; analysis 98–99
weather: and fieldwork 42, 59–61; and recording 229, 294
welfare policies 222
windshields 53–54, 63
word classes 101, 124–125, 145–146; *see also* parts of speech
word order 112, 124, 131–132, 231–233, 246, 257
word boundaries 99, 102, 272, 282
wordlists 154–155, 167
wug words 110, 230, 315

Xanthi 243
XLR 52, 54–56, 58, 68, 228; *see also* cables

Yélî Dnye 104–105, 141, 153, 156, 161, 289
Yolŋu Matha 179
youth *see* language acquisition
Yucatec Maya 196, 214, 289
Yucatec Maya Sign Language (YMSL) 196, 289
Yuman languages 132

zeugma 303
zooming 66